Mental Disorders, Medications, and Clinical Social Work

Second Edition

Mental Disorders, Medications, and Clinical Social Work

Second Edition

Sonia G. Austrian

COLUMBIA UNIVERSITY PRESS   NEW YORK

Columbia University Press
Publishers Since 1893
New York, Chichester, West Sussex
Copyright © 2000 Columbia University Press
All rights reserved

Library of Congress Cataloging-in-Publication Data

Austrian, Sonia G.
   Mental disorders, medications, and clinical social work / Sonia G. Austrian —
2nd ed.
     p.   cm.
   Includes bibliographical references and index.
   ISBN 0–231–11296–3 (cloth : alk. paper)
     1. Psychiatric social work   2. Psychology, Pathological.   3. Mental
   illness — Chemotherapy.   4. Psychotropic drugs.   I. Title.

HV689.A88 2000
362.2′0425—dc21   00–024069

Casebound editions of Columbia University Press books are printed on permanent
and durable acid-free paper.
Printed in the United States of America
c 10 9 8 7 6 5 4 3 2 1

To the late Carol H. Meyer
teacher, colleague, and friend
with lasting appreciation

Contents

Acknowledgments

I am very grateful for the support and encouragement of many friends and of my family. There are several people whose very substantial contributions must be noted.

Dr. William A. Frosch, professor and vice chairman, Department of Psychiatry, New York Presbyterian Hospital–Weill Medical College of Cornell University, was very kind and generous in reading most of the original manuscript and making invaluable suggestions.

Dr. John Clarkin, director of psychology, Department of Psychiatry, New York Presbyterian Hospital–Weill Medical College of Cornell University, once again gave me his cheerful, enthusiastic support and contributed the chapter on psychological and neuropsychological assessment. This chapter is a shortened version of "Psychological and Neuropsychological Assessment" in R. E. Hales, S. C. Yudofsky, and J. A. Talbott, eds., *Textbook of Psychiatry*, 2d ed. (Washington, D.C.: American Psychiatric Press, 1994). His coauthor Dr. Eric Fertuck made an important contribution in updating the testing and placing its importance in the context of the managed care environment.

Dr. Sharon Hird, clinical assistant professor of psychiatry, NYU Medical School, and director of the Dual Diagnosis Treatment Unit, Bellevue Hospital Center, despite many responsibilities, found the time to research and update the chapter on psychotropic medications and psychiatric consultation. In addition, she has been a source of knowledge, support, and friendship. Dr. Hird also reviewed the chapter on substance-related disorders.

Without the support of Dr. Robert Millman, Saul Steinberg Professor of Public Health and Professor of Psychiatry, New York Presbyterian Hospital–Weill Medical College of Cornell University, completion of the original manuscript would not have been possible. Dr. Millman gave me the time, support, and flexibility to work on this project.

The staffs of the Weill Medical College Library and of the library at the Westchester Division, New York Presbyterian Hospital, were extremely help-ful, good-humored, and considerate, as I consistently had overdue books, needed interlibrary loans, and help in locating sources, and I am most appreciative.

I also thank the staff and students of the Employee Assistance Program Consortium, especially Lori Urov, M.S.W., who toiled in the library prior to the publication of the first edition to keep me accurate; and Jo LeDonne, who never seemed to mind the many times I needed her to do the numerous tasks involved in producing a manuscript. My thanks go also to former stu-dents in my psychopathology classes at the Columbia University School of Social Work, who gave me constructive criticism and good suggestions that helped me to develop this second edition.

John Michel, executive editor, Columbia University Press, has been a wonderful source of support and a good friend.

Finally, I do not know how to fully express my ongoing gratitude to Maxine Greene, whose intelligence, imagination, and friendship have been very important to me.

Preface

      The surgeon general's report released in December 1999 (Pear 1999) stated that one in five Americans experiences a diagnosable mental disorder in any given year. Mental illness is the second leading cause of disability, and treatment costs $69 billion annually. Social workers are by far the largest group of mental health providers in the United States. There are approximately 200,000 clinically trained social workers, more than the combined total number of providers in the three other mental health professions: psychology, psychiatry, and clinical nursing. Even though more clients receive mental health services from social workers than from other professionals, most of the texts on mental disorders and medications used in schools of social work have been written or compiled by psychiatrists and psychologists. This book has been written to provide students and beginning social workers with specific information about an area of clinical social work that intersects psychiatry, assessment, and intervention with people who have mental disorders. Rather than taking a linear, psychiatric approach, this book attempts to adhere to social work norms and uses as its framework the ecosystems perspective, which considers person-in-environment. It uses the social work terms *exploration*, *assessment*, and *intervention* rather than the medical terms *study*, *diagnosis*, and *treatment*. For advanced clinicians who may want to seek literature on specific disorders, a comprehensive list of references and additional readings has been provided.

      Many social workers may work in interdisciplinary settings where they can call upon professionals from other disciplines to confirm their assessments, or with whom they can consult prior to intervention. Clients may

need psychotropic medications, and although social workers cannot prescribe such medications, they are often involved in monitoring them, as well
as in educating the client and family about their effects and possible side
effects. Medications can be prescribed only by a physician with training in
biochemistry and pharmacology; thus a chapter has been included by a
psychiatrist on the role and function of medications, in order to familiarize
the reader with current medications and their effectiveness and possible side
effects. Because the chapter discusses a medical treatment directed toward
symptom relief, it refers to symptoms as presented in the *Diagnostic and
Statistical Manual of Mental Disorders* (*DSM-IV*). Psychological testing and
diagnostic scales are used in some settings as assessment tools or adjuncts to
psychosocial assessments; hence a chapter by psychologists is included to
help the reader understand the purpose of various tests and the range of
information that they may yield.

While the categories of mental disorders are the same as those in *DSM-
IV*, it must be noted that this book (except for chapter 12, on medications)
does not contain specific *DSM-IV* criteria, nor does it attempt to include
all the disorders in the manual or within any specific disorder. The goal
here has been to present these disorders from a social work ecosystems perspective, rather than from a medical perspective, emphasizing the need for
a good psychosocial assessment in order to determine what factors may have
contributed to the disorder as well as those that may be useful in intervention
planning. Because of the bureaucratic demands for classification, social
workers will need to be familiar with *DSM-IV*, and it is hoped that more
agencies and institutions will require use of Axis IV, which specifies the
psychosocial and environmental problems that may be present, and Axis V,
the global assessment of functioning scale. Both of these tools are best completed by people who have social work training.

The book primarily aims to encourage social workers to practice within
the framework and expertise of our profession when helping people with
mental disorders. This second edition features expanded discussion of the
effects of managed care on intervention planning. It includes a new model
of short-term intervention (ISTT) developed by Goldstein and Noonan to
help social workers meet the demands of managed care, and it also expands
on cognitive-behavioral therapy (CBT) and interpersonal therapy (IPT),
models that are currently in greater use.

Mental Disorders, Medications, and Clinical Social Work

Second Edition

1 Introduction

Social work is a profession with its own mission, knowledge base, and repertoire of skills. It serves clients who present a broad spectrum of problems in a range of settings, and its activities include direct service, case management, advocacy, and program planning. Clinical social work has incorrectly been assumed to be synonymous with psychiatric social work. Clinical social work actually refers to direct, "hands-on" interventions with clients, individually, within families, or in groups, and encompasses all fields of practice. It is a mistake to think that social work services to people with mental disorders are rendered exclusively in mental health settings. Social workers in all settings encounter people who are affected by mental disorders. Affected clients include those suffering from mental disorders, their close friends, and their family members.

Contemporary social work training can be differentiated from training of other mental health professionals by its emphasis on assessing the whole person. As a result, the social worker can arrive at an understanding of what factors may have caused or contributed to the development of a mental disorder and what needs to be modified in the person and/or the environment to improve coping and mastery. Adhering to a psychosocial perspective distinguishes social workers from all other mental health disciplines (Meyer 1992). Social workers are not "nonmedical psychiatrists" or "psychotherapists" but members of a profession who can make a unique contribution to helping people with mental disorders, among other problems.

Beginning in the 1970s, in response to the publishing of Harriett Bartlett's seminal book *The Common Base of Social Work Practice*, social work scholars sought to identify common elements in social work practice that could be used as a foundation for a core knowledge base. There was recognition that knowledge of case phenomena and professional skills, rather than adherence to a methodology, should determine intervention. With this came a shift in the orientation of practice from the linear, causal approach, with its emphasis on specific methodology, to the more inclusive ecosystems perspective, with its emphasis on biopsychosocial assessment, which considered each case holistically, leading to a case-indicated choice of method.

Moving from a linear (medical/psychiatric) approach to the broader ecosystems perspective involved a change in terminology. In 1970 Meyer (1995) introduced the semantic and, of even more importance, epistemological change from study, diagnosis, and treatment, which viewed the clinician as the "authority," to exploration, assessment, and intervention, which involved a joint effort on the part of the social worker *and* the client. The ecosystems perspective—a unifying conceptual construction—provides a framework for examining and understanding the complexity of a case, while focusing on the interaction and reciprocity between person and environment. *Eco* refers to the relationship of person to environment; *systems* refers to the interrelatedness, within a systematically defined boundary, of personal and institutional factors impinging on the client. The ecosystems perspective requires thorough assessment, consideration of interrelated phenomena, and intervention based on contextual considerations. The clinician needs to have a broad knowledge base, experience in evaluating interview content, an awareness of a range of possible interventions, an ability to listen, and the presence of a client (with the exception of most of those who are mandated) who can, and wants to, participate in the process. The clinician may also need to accept that the client may have some problems that are not amenable to intervention. This framework is not linked to any methodology; it represents the "what is," not the "how to," of a case (Meyer 1983, 1993).

The ecosystems perspective places primary responsibility for successful case intervention on the complex skill of assessment, which Meyer defines as

> the thinking process that seeks out the meaning of case situations, puts the particular case in some order, and leads to appropriate interventions. . . . Assessment is the intellectual tool for understanding the client's psychosocial situation, and for determining "what is the matter."

(1993:2)

The process of assessment, as outlined by Meyer, uses a rigorous, defined method beginning with (1) *exploration*—listening to the client's unique story and acquiring and organizing case data. Since it is not possible, nor relevant, to obtain a full history of the individual, efforts should be made to obtain salient and relevant information that will enhance understanding of the context and cause of problems in adaptation and coping. After the raw data have been gathered, the process moves to (2) *inferential thinking,* which involves reviewing the data to determine what they mean, whether they are consistent and logical and whether conclusions are derived from worker intuition and/or direct evidence from the data. The clinician makes decisions about how to use the data on the basis of professional knowledge of similar cases or classes of clients, theoretical orientation, and the type of setting and availability of resources. The next step is (3) *evaluation,* which involves assessment of client functioning, given the defined problem areas. This includes evaluating the strengths and weaknesses of the person in the environment. Although steps 2 and 3 primarily involve the worker, step (4) *problem definition* moves the process back to client and worker, for without mutual agreement about how to frame the problem, intervention may be seriously hampered. At this point, the "presenting request" may have been modified to the "presenting problem" by the first three steps. While the client may present many problems, what must be agreed on are the problem(s) and the context that will be the focus of the intervention. In addition, there must be recognition of what is "doable," given the constraints of the case and the setting. We strive to understand the "whole case," yet we act on a part of it, thus we "think globally and act locally." The final step is (5) *intervention planning,* based on the preceding four steps. Here the client and worker contract with respect to modality, time frame, and the need to focus on the defined problem; they also discuss the anticipated outcome. Thus, assessment, while grounded in professional knowledge and skill, is an individualized process that demands recognition of the uniqueness of person and situation. It is an ongoing process, with intervention subject to modification as new data emerge. A knowledge of cultural differences and perceptions of mental disorders is essential to providing a thorough assessment and good intervention planning.

The following chapters will suggest questions that are useful, within the above framework, in assessing the presence of a particular mental disorder. Social workers should be familiar with such tools as the Ego Assessment (Goldstein 1984), which will help guide realistic intervention planning, and the Mental Status Examination (MacKinnon and Yudofsky 1988). Ego Assessment does not follow a prescribed format but is based on knowledge of ego functions. It seeks to evaluate past and present areas of ego strengths and ego deficits. Whether used formally or informally, it should almost always be part of an assessment. The formal Mental Status Examination is rarely used by social workers. Some or all the general areas will, however, be covered in a psychosocial assessment. These include:

1. General description: appearance, motor behavior, speech, and attitude
2. Emotions: mood, affectual range, appropriateness
3. Perceptual disturbances: hallucinations and illusions, depersonalization, and derealization
4. Thought disturbances: process, content, distortions, delusions, capacity for abstract thinking, preoccupations, intelligence
5. Memory: remote, recent, immediate
6. Sensorial: level of consciousness, orientation
7. Impulse control
8. Judgment
9. Insight
10. Reliability

Certain exercises may be employed as part of the Mental Status Examination if there is a need to further assess suspected areas of difficulties including memory, orientation, and judgment.

It is the author's contention that the *Diagnostic and Statistical Manual of Mental Disorders* is antithetical to the social work tradition of valuing the uniqueness of individuals and their situations and to the assessment process that is at the core of the ecosystems perspective. Assessment involves individualizing treatment for a client and recognizing the client's uniqueness, while classification systems such as the *DSM* look for group phenomena and rely on generalizations, highlighting similarities and overlooking differences, and disregarding context. Although *DSM-IV* acknowledges that people with mental disorders are heterogeneous and that no category is "a completely discrete entity with absolute boundaries" (xxii), it still establishes criteria with defining features. The term *diagnosis* implies an initial effort to narrow case data to fit a diagnostic category, while *assessment* recognizes the client's individuality, defines that person's problem within its unique context, and arrives at a personalized intervention. Relying primarily on the *DSM-IV* might actually impede intervention, because the categories provide no clues to what interventions in the environment may be essential, or at the very least, important to enable better adaptation and coping. As psychiatry moves more and more toward a biochemical explanation of many mental disorders, it may further avoid consideration of the environment, and as any social worker knows, lifting a mood or modifying bizarre behavior is important, but the person may still exist in the context of an environment that, without change, may not provide the needed support, resources, and structure to promote better coping and adaptation.

Although psychiatry has moved from referring to a person as "depressive" to describing that individual as "a person with depression," the emphasis is on a list of exclusionary criteria rather than consideration of what in the person's environment is causing or exacerbating the symptoms. Dumont (1987), in his forthright criticism of *DSM-III-R*, emphasizes that by omitting conditions of life and considering only "the qualities of a human being," the person is only an "object." He refers to the theoretical bias as favoring "narrow-minded, white, middle-class parameters of individual pathology" (10), thus making it difficult to be used effectively by professionals serving primarily the poor and minority populations. While *DSM-IV* (American Psychiatric Association 1994) offers a list of psychosocial and environmental problems to be used on Axis IV, it suggests using those present in the past year or those occurring prior to that only if they "clearly contribute to the mental disorder or have become a focus of treatment, for example, combat experiences leading to posttraumatic stress disorder" (29), not fully recognizing the complexity, chronicity, and insidiousness of many environmental problems experienced by social work clients. It should also be noted that use of Axis IV, psychosocial and environmental problems, and Axis V, global assessment of functioning, is optional, although both would be considered essential to a rigorous psychosocial assessment. For example, according to *DSM-IV*, a person could be considered as having dysthymia, a chronically depressed mood for at least two years (349), and intervention planned without the clinician's being aware of stressors, such as a history of unemployment, single parenthood, many losses, or a chronic medical condition. There is little or no attempt to view the person and the symptoms in a context, or to individualize the case, a requirement for good social work practice. *DSM-IV* infers that the problem rests within the person (or *possibly* the environment); it does not acknowledge that the two rarely can be considered separately. It should be added, in fairness, that the lack of individualization of a case also occurs in areas of practice other than mental health, such as the use of DRGs in medical settings and UCRs in child welfare settings. The result of depending on criteria such as *DSM-IV* can be that several clients, with widely differing life circumstances or experiences, could receive the same diagnosis. The development of classifications may facilitate accurate communication across disciplines, but classification can interfere with full understanding of a client's problems, which can be obtained only through exploration of aspects not listed in the criteria. In spite of an increased awareness among the general population of the impact of social factors on mental health, the medical model still prevails, which results in the stereotyping, misdiagnosis, and possible obstruction of intervention.

Though the diagnostic manuals were intended to establish a common language and to enhance capabilities for research, any system of classification can lead to labeling. Labeling and diagnostic jargon are often welcomed, especially by inexperienced clinicians, who may feel an almost magical sense of security by naming a symptom or cluster of symptoms. They may feel they "understand" the client and can control the disorder, even though causation is unknown. Clinicians need to think very carefully about labeling a person, as it can have major, even life-threatening, consequences (Anonymous 1990). Ethical questions arise as insurance companies and behavioral managed care (the mental disorders and substance abuse subset of managed care) organizations promote classification and labeling. The dilemma often involves deliberate misdiagnosis (Kirk and Kutchins 1988). Clinicians, not knowing who may have access to a diagnosis, may choose to give a more benign label than assessment warrants to avoid stigma or even to avoid a negative response from the client. Where disability claims or behavioral managed care are concerned, clinicians may choose to label the clients sicker than they are in order to ensure reimbursement for services. Just as ethics require that the diagnosis should be shared with the client, the clinician may need to acknowledge falsification, even while encouraging the client to trust and be honest in sessions. The clinician may then be seen as presenting a philosophy of "do as I say, not as I do."

Kirk and Kutchins (1992) refer to the expansion of the mental health "industry" in terms of employment, public and private expenditures, and the use of psychiatric diagnosis to manipulate service delivery when assistance with "human problems" can be reimbursed, as well as allowing mental health providers to select their clientele. In reviewing *DSM-III-R* and *DSM-IV*, Kirk and Kutchins (1992, 1997) criticize the reliability studies on the categories as flawed, incompletely reported, and inconsistent, thus raising serious doubts as to their usefulness in planning intervention as well as in designing health policy. As social workers well know, the problems of person-in-environment, the problems of living, often defy classification, because variables including history, personality, culture, support systems, and socioeconomic status may vary significantly from case to case. Kutchins and Kirk (1997) further criticize the *DSM*s for trying to *construct* categories out of everyday behavior, leading to including more behaviors that might not be regarded as abnormal.

Clinicians trying to work within behavioral managed care are finding that *DSM* is used as a management tool rather than a clinical tool, as its categories are the key factor in determining type and length of intervention in the name of cost-effectiveness. The alliance between *DSM-IV*, and behavioral managed care with its emphasis on "medical necessity" has led to a return to a more linear, medical model of assessment and intervention. Thus clients who were formerly seen for marital, family, work, or social relationship problems now *must* be given an Axis I diagnosis, given to clinical disorders or other conditions that may be the focus of clinical attention.

Because obtaining authorization for intervention is frequently based on evaluation of a client's level of impairment (Axis V), social workers who prefer cognitive and behavioral methodologies will probably have less difficulty adhering to the demands of managed care than will those who prefer a psychosocial or psychodynamic approach. Medication and short term–focused intervention are being touted as the preferable methodologies, or as Tucker states (1998): Managed care criteria → "x" intervention and "y" drugs, thus treating the diagnosis rather than the client. This raises the important question of how people with long-standing character pathology will receive case-indicated intervention. Another question, with widespread social and public health implications, is what will be done to help persons with chronic mental disorders or chemical dependency, which if untreated may lead to medical overuse, school problems, domestic violence, lateness, absenteeism, crime, and family problems (Austrian 1998).

Eda Goldstein and Maryellen Noonan (1999), responding to the demands of managed care and noting that there has not been an integrated framework for short-term intervention by social workers, have designed a new model, "Integrative Short-Term Treatment (ISTT)," applicable to the many problems and diverse populations encountered by social workers. They refer to their model as "eclectic," based on concepts derived from ego psychology, crisis intervention, and cognitive-behavioral theory, all based in turn on the ecosystems perspective (Goldstein and Noonan 1999). This model calls for eight to twenty-five sessions, which may initially be weekly and then, later, spaced out to allow for a longer intervention.

Goldstein and Noonan (1999:57–59) list ten "distinguishing character-istics" of ISST:

1. Conscious use of time
2. High level of worker activity
3. Quick engagement
4. Rapid assessment including
   a. Presenting problem and possible underlying problems
   b. Current and past person in situation relevant to presenting problem
   c. What may be interfering with problem identification
   d. What is amenable to change
   e. What are the available internal and external resources
5. Partializing and focusing to establish *clear* goals
6. Flexibility of approach and intervention techniques
7. Differential use of worker-client relationship
8. Emphasis on client strengths and expectations
9. Collaboration, linkage, and advocacy
10. Acceptance of the limitations of treatment

Like cognitive-behavioral therapy (CBT), interpersonal therapy (IPT), and dialectic behavioral therapy (DBT), ISTT is divided into three phases: beginning, middle, and end (Goldstein and Noonan 1999):

1. Beginning
   a. Problem identification
   b. Biopsychosocial assessment
   c. Engagement
   d. Selection of goals and foci
   e. Contracting
2. Middle
   a. Implementing intervention plan
   b. Maintaining focus
   c. Monitoring progress
   d. Dealing with obstacles to change
   e. Managing client-worker relationship
3. End
   a. Addressing termination and implications
   b. Reviewing progress and identifying unresolved issues

    c. Resolving worker-client relationship
    d. Referral and follow-up

Since agencies and hospitals are increasingly requiring the use of *DSM-IV* in order to complete statistical forms and to get reimbursement, a brief discussion of how it is used will follow.

DSM-IV offers sixteen categories of mental disorders, as well as a section on "conditions that may be a focus of clinical attention," which include "psychological factors affecting medical conditions," "parent-child relationship problems," "sibling relationship problems," and "noncompliance with treatment" (675–86). Each disorder has a four-digit numerical code; some have a fifth digit that defines "specifiers," such as subtypes or degree of severity of the disorder.

Axis I lists the clinical disorders or conditions that are the focus of attention. More than one diagnosis is permitted, as long as the presenting disorder is listed first. Axis II is used for personality disorders and mental retardation; again the presenting disorder is listed first. It is assumed that the principal diagnosis is on Axis I, so if the Axis II diagnosis is primary, it must be noted as "principal diagnosis" or "reason for visits." Axis III, based on ICD-9-CM codes, gives information about the person's medical conditions, so it is important that clinicians include a physical examination as part of a complete assessment. Axis IV groups psychosocial and environmental problems, usually experienced within the past year, into the following nine categories and suggests that specific factors are listed under each relevant category:

1. Problems with primary support group
2. Problems related to social environment
3. Educational problems
4. Occupational problems
5. Housing problems
6. Economic problems
7. Problems with respect to health care services
8. Problems related to interaction with the legal system/crime
9. Other

Axis V rates current psychological, social, and occupational functioning on the Global Assessment of Functioning Scale (GAF). The scale can also assess functioning over a given period of time, or track changes during the intervention. The potential for use of a multiaxial assessment as an interdisciplinary tool to make a biopsychosocial assessment (Austrian, Linn, and Miller 1981) has not materialized, although renewed interest in primary care medicine suggests it should be considered.

While *DSMs* and other classification systems will be required to meet bureaucratic requirements for "accountability," it is hoped that social workers will continue to see that rigorous assessment of person-in-environment defines our profession and that the classification systems thus far developed are too narrow to serve as more than an adjunct to this process.

This book is intended to help social workers go beyond classification and place primary importance on assessment and intervention planning. Since a *DSM-IV* diagnosis is increasingly being mandated, a compromise between the effort to go beyond classification and the requirement to determine a *DSM* classification may be defining the diagnosis as part of the assessment. Assessment interview questions will be suggested in each chapter and a range of theories of etiology given to help identify the presence of a particular mental disorder and to suggest intervention possibilities.

We must never permit classification systems to let us lose sight of the uniqueness of our clients and of their environments. Dumont (1987), commenting on the vast amount of information given in *DSM-III-R*, likens the process of choosing a "cubicle" for a client to choosing from an "endless, infernal Chinese menu." He advocates the less time-wasting (and more accurate) process of describing our clients in words, rather than numbers or jargon based on "quick and superficial observation," which is unidimensional and ignores context. Let us listen to Dumont, be true to the purpose of our profession, and resist falling into the classification trap.

2 Anxiety Disorders

A certain amount of anxiety is normal, and it is appropriate in situations that may be new, may involve performance, or may be unpleasant but unavoidable. Anxiety is an anticipatory signal that there is a conscious or unconscious threat to life, emotional stability, or equilibrium. It may be anticipated or it may be experienced without warning. Cause and sources may be known or elusive. In most instances, anxiety may be annoying but is a normal emotion and can be dealt with. Anxiety becomes a disorder when it interferes with the individual's daily living demands and perhaps also with the needs and lives of close family and friends. It is then most often an intrapsychic response to an unrecognized threat, as opposed to fear, which is almost always a response to an external, known threat that is non-conflictual in origin.

Although *phobia* is a Latin word and anxiety states have long been identified in the literature, it was not until the late nineteenth century that panic attacks, agoraphobia, and anxiety neuroses were defined as separate disorders (Taylor and Arnow 1988). In 1980 the authors of *DSM-III* chose to replace the term *neurosis* with *disorder*, basing classification on shared descriptive symptoms of unknown etiology, rather than on presumed common etiology. *DSM-IV* includes the following anxiety disorders: (1) panic disorder, (2) generalized anxiety disorder, (3) obsessive-compulsive disorder, (4) phobias, and (5) posttraumatic stress disorder. *DSM-IV* separates panic disorders into two categories, with or without agoraphobia. Anxiety disorders, like mood disorders, are very common, yet often go untreated unless they severely affect functioning, as in panic disorder or obsessive-compulsive disorder.

Definitions

Anxiety is a response to a threat. It alerts the individual to danger. It differs from fear in that the source is often unknown, although there are circumstances in which a specific identified stressor will result in situational anxiety that recedes when the stressful event is over. Usually, however, anxiety is defined as an unpleasant feeling, directed toward the future, without a recognizable source. There are biological and psychological responses observable in anxiety disorders, and the anxiety may be episodic or it may be omnipresent and not clearly linked to a specific event (free-floating).

Panic disorder is characterized by sudden panic attacks that may take minutes or hours to subside. The attacks may be experienced as shortness of breath, chest pains, trembling, or dizziness accompanied by a sense of impending doom or of sudden, overwhelming terror. The term *panic* is derived from the name of the half-man, half-goat Greek god Pan, who was blamed for causing terror, with or without cause, especially in travelers. People may suffer from panic disorders with or without agoraphobia.

Agoraphobia is a fear of leaving home, of being alone, or of being somewhere where escape may be difficult. It is most often associated with panic disorder. Fear of a panic attack will lead to anticipatory anxiety and ultimately to avoidance of situations associated with the onset of panic attacks. This withdrawal serves as protection against a fear of losing control, harming oneself, or even dying.

Generalized anxiety disorder is characterized by unrealistic or excessive anxiety over two or more life situations, which lasts for at least six months and is accompanied by physical symptoms such as insomnia, sweating, muscle tension, and irritability.

Obsessive-compulsive disorder is characterized by two distinct phenomena: (1) persistent, intrusive, unwanted thoughts, impulses, images, or ideas that the individual feels are out of his or her control (obsessions) and (2) repetitive, ego-alien, ritualistic behaviors (compulsions) in response to the anxiety engendered by the obsessions that cause distress and interfere with the individual's life.

Phobic disorder involves persistent, irrational fears of situations, activities, or objects. Exposure, actual or anticipated, to them induces an immediate anxiety response. Since there is often anticipatory anxiety, individuals with this disorder will try to avoid what is feared.

Posttraumatic stress disorder is observed in people who have suffered from the effects of an event outside the realm of usual experience that would be distressing for almost anyone. Reaction to the event may occur days, weeks, or years after, and is reexperienced intrapsychically by nightmares, flashbacks, recollections, and reminders, such as the anniversary of the event. There may also be intrusive daytime memories, cognitions, and affective responses often triggered unexpectedly. It is often seen not as a disorder but as a maladaptive way of coping.

Epidemiology

Anxiety disorders are the disorders most frequently found in the general population. The National Comorbidity Survey (Kessler et al. 1994) found that anxiety, a universal emotion, has a lifetime prevalence of 24.9 percent (19.2 percent for men and 30.5 percent for women), and a twelve-month prevalence of 17.2 percent (11.8 percent for men and 22.6 percent for women). Anxiety disorders have a twelve-month prevalence significantly greater than that of affective or substance abuse disorders, thus suggesting that they are more chronic. There is no significant difference in prevalence among races. Eighty million prescriptions are written annually for anti-anxiety medications (Taylor and Arnow 1988); the majority of sufferers are, however, seen by internists rather than by mental health professionals.

The Comorbidity Survey found lifetime prevalence of panic disorders with or without agoraphobia to be 3.5 percent (2 percent for men and 5 percent for women) and the twelve-month prevalence 2.3 percent (1.3 percent for men and 3.2 percent for women), with onset usually in the mid- to late twenties and rarely after age forty. Most people who experience panic attacks or panic disorders have some degree of avoidance behavior. When this becomes extreme and restrictive, it is agoraphobia, which was found to have a lifetime prevalence of 5.3 percent (3.5 percent for men and 7.0 percent for women) and a twelve-month prevalence of 2.8 percent (1.7 percent for men and 3.8 percent for women). The mean age of onset is twenty-five, and it occurs more frequently in nonwhite people with a low level of education (Ballenger 1990). Agoraphobia is rarely seen in a pure form; it is most often associated with panic attacks and panic disorder.

Generalized anxiety disorder was found in the Comorbidity Survey to have a lifetime prevalence of 5.1 percent (3.6 percent for men and 6.6 percent for women) and a twelve-month prevalence of 3.1 percent (2.0 percent for men and 4.3 percent for women) with onset most often occurring in the mid-twenties.

The age of onset of phobias depends on the subtype of phobia. Specific phobias (called *simple phobias* in DSM-III-R), such as fear of animals, tend to have the earliest age of onset, often in childhood, followed by social phobias, which often first appear in adolescence, and finally by agoraphobia, with onset usually in adulthood (Kendler et al. 1992). The National Co-morbidity Survey found a 13.3 percent lifetime prevalence (11.1 percent for men and 15.5 percent for women) and a 7.9 percent twelve-month preva-lence (6.6 percent for men and 9.1 percent for women) of social phobia. Social phobia occurs more often in people who are single, less educated, and from lower socioeconomic classes (Kendler et al. 1992). Simple phobia was found to have a lifetime prevalence of 11.3 percent (6.7 percent for men and 15.7 percent for women) and a twelve-month prevalence of 8.8 percent (4.4 percent for men and 13.2 percent for women). The findings on the prevalence of social and simple phobias may be low because few people suffering from these disorders seek treatment, choosing rather to arrange their lives to avoid frightening situations or encounters. Sufferers thus prob-ably do not acknowledge a phobia.

Obsessive-compulsive disorder is believed to affect at least 2.5 percent of the general population, although it is probable that it is present to a larger degree in a milder form. Almost everyone has had some obsessions or com-pulsions for periods of time, and obsessive-compulsive traits are not uncom-mon, particularly in adolescents. This disorder affects men and women about equally, is more common in the unmarried, in higher socioeconomic classes, and in people with a higher I.Q. than average (Rowe 1989). The age of onset is usually in later adolescence or early adulthood.

The National Comorbidity Survey found that posttraumatic stress disor-der has a lifetime prevalence of 7.8 percent. Men who suffer from this dis-order are most frequently Vietnam veterans who were wounded in combat, killed people, or witnessed deaths. Women and children with this disorder have usually suffered from physical or sexual abuse or from seeing someone hurt or killed. There is no mean age of onset, nor does it affect any identi-fiable segment of the population.

Assessment

Diagnosis of anxiety disorders is difficult, because everyone at times ex-periences normal anxiety; in addition, the symptoms of anxiety are associated with several mental and physical disorders. Another problem in diagnosing anxiety is that people do not come to the attention of mental health providers until the symptoms have become debilitating, and thus many suffer needlessly and may lead restricted lives when it is not necessary that they do so.

There is a group of mental disorders in which a prolonged state of anxiety is the predominant symptom, often associated with avoidant behavior. To assess whether a symptom of anxiety is a normal response or an excessive one that represents an anxiety disorder, three components must be examined: (1) physical arousal, (2) cognitive response, and (3) coping strategies (Coryell and Winokur 1991). An abnormal response in at least one of these three components indicates a disorder. An anxiety disorder may be characterized by excessive physical arousal, especially with respect to the autonomic nervous system. Cognitive processes may be distorted, for instead of appraising the environment to determine the extent of possible danger, a person with an anxiety disorder will be affected by internal, perhaps unrealistic, responses and may overestimate potential harm and become excessively fearful. Instead of attempting to avoid danger or at least minimize the effects of a potentially anxiety-provoking situation, people with anxiety disorders have developed maladaptive coping mechanisms that can lead to avoidant behavior rather than to development of skills to master the situation, or if skills are developed, they are inadequate and the anxiety is prolonged. Questions to be addressed in the assessment include:

Is the person experiencing physical symptoms for which there is no apparent organic basis?
Does the person focus on the "internal," personal thoughts, and bodily processes with extreme concern about the possibility of harm?
Is there apparent impairment of the person's ability to reason logically about frightening thoughts?
Are coping strategies maladaptive, with a greater reliance on avoidant behavior?

Usually difficulties are evident in at least one of these three areas. Further questions to narrow down the type of anxiety disorder include:

Is the anxiety acute?
Are there recognizable stressors?
Is the anxiety primary or secondary to another diagnosis (frequently depression)?

To what degree does the individual avoid feared situations or objects?
Are there any obsessive-compulsive behaviors present?
Is there any evidence of social phobia?
Is there a history of trauma?

Assessment of an anxiety disorder must be done in such a way that the client does not feel diminished or criticized, for the presenting symptoms often appear "crazy" to others or even to the client, who, instead of getting sympathy, may have been ridiculed or not taken seriously.

Because the physical symptoms of panic disorder can be frightening, many people will seek out internists or related specialists before turning to mental health professionals for help. Common symptoms that occur suddenly, and unpredictably, may include chest pain, shortness of breath, tachycardia, dizziness, trembling, sweating, headache, diarrhea, or epigastric pain. Following a negative physical examination, while validating the physical symptoms, assessment should include questions about feelings at the time of onset and identification of the person's greatest fear. When assessing for the presence of a panic disorder, it is helpful to the person to ask in detail about physical symptoms and whether they occur in certain situations, spontaneously, or both. Sufferers describe an overwhelming state of terror, unrelated to any identifiable event in their life, that suddenly overcomes them and may be accompanied by a fear of dying, of going crazy, or of being out of control. The degree to which these fears interfere with daily functioning must be assessed; it must also be determined if they have resulted in agoraphobia. The essential factor is the recurrence of the attacks. Episodes may occur repeatedly over an extended period of time or become chronic. Between the onset of the panic attacks, people usually experience nervousness and apprehension in varying degrees. While DSM-III-R and DSM-IV specify a time frame to substantiate the diagnosis, clinicians often use the diagnosis based on symptoms regardless of timing (Gitlin 1990). The self-report Stanford Panic Diary (Taylor and Arnow 1988) can be helpful: the client is asked to note each panic attack, symptoms, what he or she was doing at the time, what were the accompanying thoughts, and how long the attack lasted. It is also important to ask what makes the particular situation better or worse than other occurrences, as well as how the attacks affect others.

Panic disorders appear to occur across a spectrum ranging from infrequent panic attacks to agoraphobia developed because of the debilitating effects of the panic disorder. Assessing the severity of the disorder must be done with caution, for many people who suffer from agoraphobia are ashamed, guilty, and fearful that they will be regarded as "crazy." People with panic disorder who develop chronic anticipatory anxiety may become agoraphobic in an effort to avoid situations and places where they fear they may be alone, may be unable to seek help, or may lose control and embarrass themselves because of their fear that they may have a panic attack. They have a fear of fear. Asking if a person fears experiencing anxiety in situations or places where others usually would not be afraid may be helpful in identifying agoraphobia. Establishing the sequence of events is important, because panic attacks must occur before the onset of agoraphobia in order to warrant a diagnosis of panic attacks with agoraphobia. It can be helpful in assessing the impact of agoraphobia to talk with relatives and friends, particularly if the person seems disinclined to reveal all existing phobias contributing to the agoraphobia. When there is evidence of agoraphobia, a careful history should be obtained of the development of the avoidant behavior, how the person has tried to cope, whether there is any evidence of secondary gain as it affects work or family life, and, if suspected, the identity of the "phobic partner," who may actually support the presence of a phobia or be needed to accompany the person on outings. Because people with panic disorders often fear being alone, in strange circumstances, or needing help, it may be useful to ask about a history of separation anxiety.

Generalized anxiety disorder can be distinguished from common anxiety by its frequency, intensity, persistence, and duration. There is usually excessive, often anticipatory, anxiety over at least two life circumstances for a period of at least six months. Some sufferers cannot point to any specific concern but rather say they are waiting "for something awful to happen" and may appear hypervigilant, distractible, and irritable. The person will report constant worrying, resulting in appraising the possibility of danger as much more likely or greater than can be supported by evidence. In assessing generalized anxiety disorder, it is important to evaluate whether the anxiety is realistic and whether its presence is felt more often than not. Evaluation must also be made of possible stressors. While generalized anxiety disorder is usually chronic, its severity may be intensified by unexpected changes or stresses. When an object of the anxiety is identified, questions must be directed toward obtaining a history of when the anxiety began, whether the degree of anxiety is warranted, and how the person has coped in the past with similar situations. For example, if a client is excessively anxious about making a presentation at a business meeting, it would be useful to explore areas such as familiarity with those who will be present, knowledge about the topic to be presented, and especially the person's past and current work history.

Interviews with people close to the person who is suffering from general anxiety disorder may describe the person as being a "chronic worrier," preoccupied with and ruminating about future illness, unable to cope, overconcerned with finances, and fearful of being embarrassed. These cognitive processes distinguish the disorder from panic, as both disorders have similar physiological symptoms. The Spielberger State-Trait Anxiety Inventory and the Hamilton Anxiety Interview are assessment instruments that are helpful in the diagnosis (Taylor and Arnow 1988).

People who suffer from obsessive-compulsive disorder are aware that their actions are unusual and will seek help if it becomes difficult to hide their odd actions from others. Assessment should include a history of the onset of the behavior (compulsion), what behavior has become ritualistic, what fear (obsession) it is meant to combat, whether the need to perform the behavior has increased, and in what way(s) it may interfere with the person's life. The person often will report, on assessment, excessive preoccupation with fears related to contamination or disease. The sufferer may experience a compulsion to wash or to clean repeatedly, yet never feel clean or safe. Others may report being preoccupied with whether they have done common household tasks, such as turning off the stove or locking the front door, or whether they have done harm to others. These preoccupations necessitate compulsive checking and rechecking several or even hundreds of times a day, depending on the severity. They experience "pathological doubt" (Gitlin 1990). People with this disorder often come to the attention of mental health professionals only after consulting internists or surgeons who they hoped would "confirm" their fears. They have experienced discomfort from the persistent and recurrent thoughts (obsessions) and the accompanying repetitive, ritualistic behaviors (compulsions) that they have come to realize are excessive and purposeless, as well as time-consuming, often to the extent of interfering with their normal routine. Because they are uncomfortable with these symptoms and aware that their fears are unrealistic, they may experience embarrassment, and if they seek help, they may initially focus on other problems or seek treatment for the anxiety that they experience when they cannot suppress the obsessions and compulsions. An initial clue is an obsessive-compulsive aspect to their personality. Only with careful, sensitive, and specific exploration is it possible to comfortably delineate their obsessions and compulsions.

Specific phobias are usually persistent, irrational fears about one class of living beings, such as dogs, snakes, or insects; phobias also may be fear of actions, such as driving over bridges or flying. Regardless of the object of fear, the specific phobia may never come to the attention of mental health professionals, because people will assiduously avoid frightening situations, even to the point of inconveniencing themselves or others. People who suffer from specific phobias usually do not seek help unless they are forced to overcome the fear (for example, a person may be able to keep his or her job requiring travel only if a fear of flying can be overcome) or if they decide they want to overcome the fear (for example, a person who is afraid of heights yet wants badly to learn to ski). An assessment would include identifying the feared living things, object, or situation; duration of the fear; whether others in the family have a similar fear; and method(s) that the person uses to avoid what is feared. A specific phobia is usually associated with specific situations. Assessment would include identifying the situation(s); whether the fear of embarrassment of humiliation has any basis in reality (for example, fears of speaking in public when one has had a stuttering problem); how pervasive the fears are; how the person has tried to cope with the fears; and how much the phobia interferes with daily functioning. A diagnosis of specific phobia excludes fear of being alone or in public places away from home (agoraphobia) and fear of embarrassment in certain social situations (social phobias).

People suffering from social phobias report that they are very sensitive to thoughts of being scrutinized and that they are easily embarrassed or humiliated. They experience physical symptoms such as sweating, trembling, blushing, and "weak knees," and feel certain that others can see their nervousness and embarrassment. Some report feeling "paralyzed" by their anxiety. It is important to assess the pervasiveness of the disorder. Some people with social phobia experience it as a discrete performance anxiety related to public speaking, auditioning, or acting and have chosen to avoid such situations even though doing so might limit their career choices. Others experience a generalized social anxiety that affects their work and personal lives. They will avoid eating in public, using public toilets, meeting new people, attending parties or conferences, and will distance themselves from employers and colleagues. When asked about their fears, they usually report a fear of doing something that would embarrass or in some way call attention to them. People who experience social phobia have excessive anticipatory anxiety, and there is often a secondary diagnosis of depression or alcoholism.

Posttraumatic stress disorder differs from other anxiety disorders because it is related to an actual experience that the sufferer has undergone that almost anyone would consider very upsetting. The experience may have been a natural disaster, a war, an accident, or an assault by another person, including ongoing physical or sexual abuse. It is also possible that the person may have been not the victim but a witness to an assault, accident, or murder. Assessment for the presence of posttraumatic stress disorder may be very complex, for although the diagnosis must include a history of a traumatic event, it is possible that the memory of the event may have been repressed, or that a person who acknowledges the trauma may not associate it with existing feelings and behaviors. It also must be stated that "recovered memories" may be iatrogenic, and thus fallible. The clinician must be careful to listen to the facts as presented and not lead the person to unwarranted conclusions. When there is a known trauma, such as participation in the Vietnam War, being at the scene of a disaster, or abuse, assessment should include focusing on issues related to the trauma and previous attempts to cope. Several types of symptoms, lasting from minutes to days, may be reported:

1. Intrusive memories, nightmares, or flashbacks during which the individual feels as if the trauma has recurred
2. Feelings of anxiety in situations that resemble or recall the trauma
3. Intense distress when exposed to situations resembling the trauma or on the anniversary of the trauma
4. Avoidance of anything or anyone reminiscent of the trauma
5. "Amnesia" about the details of the trauma
6. Reported inability to feel emotions
7. Hypervigilance
8. Problems with memory or concentration
9. Inappropriate outbursts of anger
10. Survivor guilt

People who suffer from posttraumatic stress disorder may not have made the connection between the symptoms and the trauma and more often seek intervention for problems of depression, substance abuse, domestic violence, marital problems, anxiety, sexual problems, low self-esteem, or suicidal ideation. Thus it is important to take a careful history that includes asking specifically about traumatic events, especially those involving victimization. Posttraumatic stress disorder may resemble other anxiety disorders or emotional disorders, but it can be distinguished by the severe stress that has caused the onset of symptoms.

Clinical Course

As noted previously, many people who experience anxiety never come to the attention of mental health professionals. For most, anxiety is transitory and does not interfere appreciably with daily functioning.

Panic disorders usually consist of recurrent episodes of panic attacks that may occur several times a week or even daily, although some people have only one episode followed by total remission. For some, the disorder is chronic. The onset initially is unexpected, and the individual suddenly experiences extreme tension with fears of death or impending catastrophe. Frequently the person has been under the stress of separation or loss within the past six months. After the initial attack has subsided, and between attacks, the individual usually feels somewhat tense and apprehensive about the possibility of further attacks, although some report feeling calm. If the apprehension becomes too great, agoraphobia will develop, which in its most severe form forces the person to become homebound. Seventy percent of those suffering from panic disorder also have, or will have, experienced a major depression (Ballenger 1990). The prognosis is poorer when both disorders are present than when either alone is present.

People who suffer from generalized anxiety disorder are usually excessively worried, but their anxiety causes little impairment in their lives. They are usually able to adapt to their chronic anxiety unless it is accompanied by panic attacks or depression.

Specific phobias often resolve themselves and disappear in time, especially if they began in childhood. If the phobia continues into adulthood, it usually does not interfere with daily functioning. If it does, it can be resolved only with treatment.

Social phobias, ranging from feelings of uneasiness to panic, are usually chronic unless the person seeks treatment. The resulting isolation may put the individual at high risk for developing depression or self-medicating with alcohol or barbiturates. Some studies have shown that people with social phobias have higher rates of suicidal ideation and financial dependency (Kendler et al. 1992).

Obsessive-compulsive disorder is usually experienced as chronic mild symptoms interspersed with acute episodes over a period of months or years.

The onset is usually insidious and lacks any identifiable stressor. The prognosis for improvement with treatment is best if the episodes are transitory and the symptoms relatively circumscribed. Ten percent of those suffering from this disorder have a progressively downhill course, in which the symptoms become all-consuming (Gitlin 1990). As symptoms become more severe or chronic, they are frequently accompanied by symptoms of depression, anxiety, and avoidant behavior, including phobias. Complications may be depression or abuse of alcohol or tranquilizers.

Posttraumatic stress disorder often results in intrusive thoughts or dreams about the trauma, or in feelings of emotional numbness. These experiences are usually episodic, but if they are chronic they may result in withdrawal or alienation from others. The person's life may center, consciously or unconsciously, on the trauma, and may be accompanied by somatic symptoms and chronic anxiety to the extent that normal functioning is impaired. Without treatment, depression, substance abuse, and family problems may complicate the prognosis. In cases where there was a history of physical or sexual abuse that included a violation of trust, the most serious symptom is dissociation.

Etiology

Researchers believe that panic disorders have a neurobiological basis. There is evidence of a genetic predisposition, as 15 to 20 percent of those with this disorder have biological relatives who also suffer from panic disorders. Monozygotic twins are five times more likely to have this disorder than dizygotic twins (Ballenger 1990). It is not clear that there is any genetic predisposition to agoraphobia, and it may be that it is learned behavior in family members who also experience it. There is no clear evidence of a genetic predisposition for generalized anxiety disorder; however, research indicates the probability of a neurobiological base similar to that found for panic disorder. Psychodynamic theory suggests that panic disorders and generalized anxiety disorders have roots in separation anxiety disorders seen in childhood and are triggered in adulthood by separations or loss of social supports. Freud believed anxiety to be a signal that the individual was in danger and that the danger often was related to poor impulse control or to fear of loss of love or of self-esteem. Cognitive-behavioral theorists believe that anxiety is a learned response to parental behavior or classical conditioning (Kaplan and Sadock 1996:195). Panic occurs as a learned reaction to stimuli (Shear 1997:1025).

There is no evidence for a genetic or a neurobiological basis for specific or social phobias. Although it is not definitively known why some objects or situations are feared, social learning theory suggests that family members learn fears from each other, particularly from parents, and that fears can be unlearned. It is also possible that there are cultural factors that determine social phobias and that in some instances of specific phobias the object may be linked to a traumatic experience in childhood. Genetic epidemiologists believe that phobias result from one or more risk factors: individual-specific environment, family environment, and ge netic factors (Kendler 1992).

Twin studies have shown some evidence of genetic and neurobiological vulnerability for obsessive-compulsive disorders. Fifty to 70 percent of those who suffer from obsessive-compulsive disorders have obsessional personalities (Gitlin 1990) and family members with obsessional traits. Psychodynamic theory suggests that obsessive-compulsive disorders are the most complex of the anxiety disorders. The sufferer experiences anxiety caused by the threat of acting on impulses that are not successfully controlled by the defense of repression. The defenses of isolation, reaction formation, undoing, and displacement are then activated and are manifested in obsessions and compulsions. Social learning theory suggests that when a person experiences anxiety related to particular events, he or she employs rituals to lessen the anxiety that, if successful, result in repetitive ritualistic and compulsive behaviors (Waldinger 1990).

Some individuals may have a premorbid personality that predisposes them to developing posttraumatic stress disorder. It also may be that these people lack sufficient support systems when faced with a specific stressor. It is certain that a recognizable stressor existed before the development of this disorder, and the more often the person was subjected to the trauma, the more serious the symptoms. While wars and natural disasters may be the specific trauma, it has been found that many persons who suffer from posttraumatic stress disorder may have been childhood victims of physical or sexual abuse or may have witnessed domestic violence, rape, or murder.

Differential Diagnosis

The presence of anxiety does not necessarily indicate a diagnosis of an anxiety disorder. Anxiety symptoms, like those of depression, can be observed in a range of physical and emotional disorders. Because people with anxiety disorders experience a broad range of somatic symptoms, it is important to include a physical examination as part of the assessment process. Physical disorders that have symptoms similar to those found in anxiety disorders are cardiovascular, respiratory, endocrine, or neurological illnesses, withdrawal from drugs or alcohol, and AIDS or symptoms related to being HIV-positive. The physical symptoms experienced with panic disorder are particularly upsetting, and people may initially seek reassurance from their internists that they are not about to have a heart attack or stroke. Assessment should include questions about use of cocaine, alcohol, amphetamines, and hallucinogens. Nicotine and caffeine also may cause anxiety, as can aspirin, anticholinergics, steroids (Taylor and Arnow 1988), and other medications.

Before a diagnosis of obsessive-compulsive disorder is made, careful assessment is necessary in order to rule out anxiety secondary to a mood disorder, schizophrenia, some personality disorders, a physical disease, or substance abuse. Although the rituals observed in people with obsessive-compulsive disorder may resemble those observed in people with schizophrenia, assessment will indicate that these rituals are ego-dystonic, while in schizophrenia they are ego-syntonic. Concerns with death, failure, and disease may suggest a mood disorder, but assessment should show that the vegetative signs seen with mood disorders are not present and the person's mood does not appear to be depressed.

Since anxiety may be a symptom of other mental disorders, clinicians sometimes overlook the possibility that an anxiety disorder should be the primary diagnosis. Again, a thorough history is necessary to determine the presence or absence of prominent features of an anxiety disorder. such as episodes of panic, phobias, or compulsive behavior; a history of avoiding specific situations or experiences; and a history of ritualistic behavior. Avoidant personality disorders, substance abuse, and depression frequently coexist with anxiety disorders, thus complicating the diagnostic picture, although an accurate history should reveal which disorder came first, making it the primary diagnosis. People with social phobias tend to avoid situations in which they fear they will be embarrassed or humiliated, while those with avoidant personality disorders will avoid most intimate situations. People with generalized anxiety disorder may seem depressed, but usually lack the classic vegetative signs of depression. People with obsessive-compulsive disorder may appear to ruminate, as do some people with depression, but for the former, the thoughts are ego-dystonic.

People suffering from posttraumatic stress disorder may have phobias, panic disorder, generalized anxiety disorder, depression, or dysthymia, but if there is an established history of trauma PTSD is the primary diagnosis.

Intervention

Following assessment, intervention should be based on the type of anxiety disorder identified. Medication, together with therapy, has proved very effective for treating anxiety disorders, with the exception of specific phobias, where there is no evidence of need. The combination of medication and therapy also appears to possess questionable value with posttraumatic stress disorder; thus a psychiatric consultation will be needed in planning intervention.

Medication

Drugs, such as alcohol and opiates, have been used to treat the symptoms of anxiety for centuries. Today, anxiety disorders are treated by specific antianxiety medications and by antidepressants.

People with panic disorders have been effectively treated with tricyclic antidepressants such as desipramine (Norpramine), clomipramine (Anafranil), or imipramine (Tofranil); MAO inhibitors (MAOIs) such as phenelzine (Nardil); and serotonin-specific reuptake inhibitors (SSRIs) such as fluoxetine (Prozac), sertraline (Zoloft), and fluvoxamine (Luvox). Benzodiazepines such as clonazepam (Klonopin), lorazepam (Ativan), or diazepam (Valium) are also used. The tricyclics usually are the treatment of choice because there are no dietary restrictions as there are with the MAO inhibitors and there is less likelihood of dependency than with benzodiazepines; however, those MAOIs most often used are phenelzine (Nardil) and tranylcypromine (Parnate). Some people with panic disorders experience a stimulant response that may exacerbate the feelings of panic, and they will need the addition of a beta-blocker (Inderol) or a benzodiazepine tranquilizer (Gitlin 1990). A major problem, however, with the tricyclics is the delay before the person feels any relief. Tapering off of the medication should wait until symptoms have been in remission for six months to a year, and if they recur the dosage must be raised to an effective level.

Benzodiazepines are usually prescribed for people suffering from generalized anxiety disorder; the prescription may specify that the medication be taken at regular intervals, or on an as-needed basis (p.r.n.). Diazepam (Valium) or clonazepam (Klonopin) are frequently prescribed for more chronic stress, while lorazepam (Ativan) is prescribed p.r.n. or for more acute intervention (Gitlin 1990). Problems resulting from use of benzodiazepines include initial excessive sedating effects, as well as later dependency and problems with withdrawal of the medication. There is a higher risk of dependency with short-acting drugs such as alprazolam and lorazepam. Buspirone (Buspar) is often prescribed and does not have a sedative effect, but it needs to be taken regularly, takes at least two weeks to become effective, and cannot be prescribed to be used p.r.n. Antidepressants such as doxepin (Sinequan) or trazodone (Desyrel) are prescribed when anxiety causes insomnia, and imipramine (Tofranil) has also proved very effective, but it must be taken for six to eight weeks to become fully effective (Brawman-Mintzer and Lydiard 1997). Beta-blockers, such as Inderol, are used when the anxiety symptoms are primarily physiological.

Treatment with medication is usually not indicated for people suffering from specific phobias, although some have been helped by taking benzodiazepines p.r.n. People suffering from social phobias, however, can be helped with medication. Beta-blockers (Inderol or Tenormin) are effective when a person experiences performance anxiety, and either can be taken just before the event. When the social phobias are pervasive, MAO inhibitors, such as phenelzine (Nardil) or tranylcypromine (Parnate), or the benzodiazepine clonazepam (Klonopin) are often prescribed (Staff 1994). The prescribed dosage of medication is usually gradually reduced after the client has been free of symptoms for six to twelve months.

Many people suffering from obsessive-compulsive disorder seek help only when it really interferes with daily functioning. Clomipramine (Anafranil), a medication introduced in 1990, has proved very effective for 60 to 70 percent of those seeking treatment (Gitlin 1990). Other medications used, but considered somewhat less effective, are serotonin reuptake inhibitors fluoxetine (Prozac), fluvoxamine (Luvox), paroxetine (Paxil), sertraline (Zoloft), and the atypical antidepressant trazodone (Desyrel) (March et al. 1997) Medication must be continued until the person is symptom-free for six to twelve months. It is then gradually withdrawn.

If medication is given to people suffering from posttraumatic stress disorder, it is usually to reduce some of the most distressing symptoms, thus making the person more amenable to the necessary psychotherapeutic intervention. Tricyclic antidepressants such as imipramine (Tofranil) or amitriptyline (Elavil); an MAO inhibitor, such as phenelzine (Nardil); the selective serotonin reuptake inhibitors fluoxetine (Prozac), Fluvoxamine (Luvox), sertraline (Zoloft), and paroxetine (Paxil); and the mood stabilizers lithium carbonate and carbamazepine (Tegretol) are used to lessen hypervigilance, depression, and sudden, angry outbursts (Gitlin 1990; Kaplan and Sadock 1996).

Psychotherapy

Most forms of anxiety disorders respond to a combination of medication and psychotherapy. Intervention includes exposure-based procedures, in vivo if possible, or in imagery. This approach has proved especially effective for people suffering from panic disorders, phobias, obsessive-compulsive disorder, and posttraumatic stress disorder, when used in combination with medication to control the anxiety symptoms. The therapy seeks to reduce the intensity and frequency of symptoms so that the client is more comfortable looking at the underlying issues.

A psychodynamic intervention is based on the premise that anxiety is related to early separation anxiety, to a fear of loss of love, and to castration anxiety. Analytically oriented therapy aims at gaining insight into the unconscious conflicts that generate anxiety and cause the symptoms of anxiety disorders. This approach is long-term and is not considered particularly effective. Supportive psychotherapy offering encouragement, reassurance, empathy, advice, and some psychoeducation has proved more effective, especially when used in combination with medication; it thus can be a collaborative intervention between social workers and psychiatrists. The social worker must first recognize with the client that the client is very fearful. At this stage, it is of secondary importance whether the fears have an unrealistic basis. The person may have been criticized or ridiculed for the fear; the worker must convey respect and acceptance while helping the person to look more realistically at the fear. With people suffering from phobias, the worker must consider whether the observed behavior may offer some indirect benefit to the person's personal or professional life. Whether the intervention is analytically oriented or supportive, it is very important that the therapist avoid being too protective. The overprotective therapist runs the risk of encouraging the dependency of the client, which probably already exists in the person's relationships. This is especially likely for those experiencing panic disorders and phobias.

People who have suffered trauma need to be viewed as individuals, and not as members of a subgroup made up of people affected by that type of trauma. Because the client may be aware that others have not been so distressed in the aftermath of the event, he or she may experience shame, guilt, and low self-esteem. If death or major injury was involved, there may also be "survivor guilt." People suffering from posttraumatic stress disorder clearly need to be helped to identify the trauma and find more functional ways to cope with the aftermath. Establishing a trusting relationship can be very difficult, especially with some veterans, who see themselves as victims. They fought in an unpopular war and received negative responses when they returned home; as a result, they exhibit feelings of suspicion and paranoia that may make it difficult to engage them in the assessment process.

Another group of people suffering from posttraumatic stress disorder are victims of sexual or physical abuse or people who as children witnessed physical violence, rape, or murder. In many cases, memories have been repressed, or the person feels too much shame or guilt to disclose the abuse. If symptoms such as shame, guilt, poor self-esteem, and a sense of victimization are presented, suggesting a history of trauma, the social worker should sensitively ask about it. Shame is almost inevitable and may relate to feelings about the perpetrator, but more often results from self-blame: "What did I do to deserve the abuse?" or "Why did I not deserve to be protected?" The feeling of shame can result in a self-image of being inadequate, "bad," deserving of abuse, powerless, and frequently further victimized in other relationships. It is important that, as part of the intervention, the worker elicit the feeling of shame, as it may serve as a defense against acknowledging abuse that has been hidden from the self or others. The clinician must proceed slowly, so as not to enhance feelings of shame but rather to undo feelings of humiliation. In time, to help feelings of shame diminish, there must be validation of the person's rage at having been a victim of abuse. Since these traumas involved a violation of trust, this validation must be done after the worker/client relationship has begun to be established. To establish that relationship, which is dependent on trust, will not be easy, because the trauma may have been viewed as a "secret," even within the family. People who are victims of abuse have a justifiable fear of trusting. In addition, they expect not to be believed, or perhaps even to be blamed, if they discuss the abuse. The success of the intervention depends largely on the worker's ability to help the client separate past from present and to defuse the misperception that abuse is inevitable. Victims of abuse may report inability to remember or to experience emotion about the trauma. When they are able to acknowledge the abuse, they may report experiencing dissociation from themselves, and from the world, as it took place. Assessment must proceed cautiously and in a safe atmosphere, since the victim may never have shared this information with anyone before. The experience that the person has been through must be acknowledged and validated, and "triggers," including high-risk situations, that produce symptoms must be identified. Questions about depression and substance abuse are important, because these are frequently the secondary disorders (comorbid) experienced by people with posttraumatic stress disorder. When a behavioral approach is used with a person suffering from posttraumatic stress disorder, there is less emphasis on the trauma itself, with most of the focus placed on symptom relief and control of behavior. There is no complete "cure" for posttraumatic stress disorder, for memories will remain, but new coping skills can be learned, and often persons can become involved in helping others who have had similar experiences; for example, parents of murdered children have established nationwide self-help groups. Psychoeducation about this disorder is an essential part of the intervention.

Symptom-focused cognitive-behavioral interventions (CBT) are also often used to help people with generalized anxiety disorder, social phobia, panic disorder, phobias, and obsessive-compulsive disorder. This approach usually takes no more than a year, and a response should be seen within ten sessions (Taylor and Arnow 1988). When used for generalized anxiety disorder, the approach is usually a combination of relaxation techniques and biofeedback. Social skills training, including assertiveness training, has been helpful for persons suffering from social phobias. With panic disorder, phobias, and obsessive-compulsive disorder, the usual treatment involves in vivo (or imaging) exposure to the situation or object that causes anxiety and defensive behavior. Depending on the severity of the symptoms, the social worker must determine whether the exposure can best be experienced by the person alone, which is highly unlikely, by the person as part of a group of clients who suffer from the same symptoms, or whether the person needs to be accompanied by the therapist or by a family member. Frequently the person suffering from anxiety has already involved the family, and generally it is not advisable to support this dependency. There are three methods of exposure that need to take place in a supportive, safe environment:

1. *Flooding* involves immediate and intense exposure and causes a high level of anxiety that may result in the person's leaving treatment.
2. *Desensitization* is a slower process, involving gradual exposure coupled with reassurance, thus controlling the level of anxiety.
3. *Return* is going back to the actual situation being avoided if this is possible, or in sessions imagining a return.
   Exposure in imagination often is the only realistic method for people suffering from posttraumatic stress disorder. Actual exposure, when possible, is continued for people suffering from panic or phobias, until the fear is diminished and coping in-

creased. Exposure, though not permitting the practice of rituals, is the behavioral method used for people suffering from obsessive-compulsive disorder. This approach is more effective with compulsions than obsessions, which respond better to medication.

Cognitive-behavioral practitioners feel that the person learns through the family, conditioning, or observation to anticipate danger or harm in certain situations. The person experiences anxiety and inability to cope, and feels inadequate to avert the threat. Avoidant behavior, phobias, or obsessive-compulsive behavior may develop in order to avoid the perceived danger. CBT seeks to help the person look at the anxiety-producing thoughts and identify cognitive distortions and maladaptive behavioral responses. The situation, event, or object is examined by imaging or, preferably, through in vivo exposure, and the person is asked to record the accompanying feelings, to correct distortions, and to restructure thinking. This approach, involving desensitization with symptom alleviation, is thought to be most useful for people suffering from panic disorder with agoraphobia and generalized anxiety disorder (Coryell and Winokur 1991). Relaxation and thought-stopping techniques are often taught to help reduce the anxiety, as well as assertiveness and social skills training and new problem-solving techniques.

Social workers trained in the ecosystems perspective are particularly aware of the impact of the environment, including the family, on individuals. When making an assessment of a person suffering from an anxiety disorder, it is very important to identify the person's specific environmental stressors and to ascertain whether these perceptions are realistic. If the stressors can be identified, part of the intervention will be directed toward alleviating or modifying them to help minimize the anxiety.

It is also very important to include the family of the person in the assessment process, and in many cases as part of the intervention. Because people usually do not seek help unless their behavior is interfering with daily living, it is probable that the behavior is affecting the family. Psychoeducation may help family members understand the nature of anxiety disorders and how the person uses the resultant behavior, which may appear peculiar, to help avoid the anxiety, no matter how unrealistically. When a person suffers from a phobia, especially agoraphobia, a family member may become the "phobic partner" needed to accompany the person to dreaded situations or even to remain home with the person. This family member may need help in recognizing his or her own feelings about this role, in exploring whether the phobia may have secondary gain for either or both partners, and in relinquishing the role without guilt. Conversely, the family member, if not already excessively involved, may be used in the desensitization process, accompanying the person through the stages necessary to overcome the phobia. The social worker must be alert, however, not to foster too great a dependency on this family member. Family members can also help people suffering from compulsions by offering reassurance, thus possibly lessening the responding obsessive behavior. Finally, of course, family or marital treatment is clearly indicated if the assessment revealed that family or marital problems were a major stressor contributing to the anxiety. A study comparing twelve weeks of cognitive-behavioral group therapy with an MAOI for social phobia showed that both were helpful, but the medication was more effective (Heimberg et al. 1998).

Groups have not proved particularly useful in helping people with most anxiety disorders. In some instances, people suffering from panic disorder with agoraphobia have benefited from group support, where members reassure each other that they are not "crazy." In vivo desensitization has also been somewhat effective for groups of people.

As noted before, posttraumatic disorders differ from other anxiety disorders because of the reality basis for the anxiety. Psychoeducation of family members and the public about the traumas of service in Vietnam and the traumas of abuse is a very important task for social workers. Because many Americans opposed the Vietnam War, the veterans of that war often did not receive as much support and caring as veterans of the two world wars did. With regard to abuse, people would rather not know about it, its aftermath, or its prevalence. It is important that family members be educated to understand that maladaptive behavior exhibited by the affected family member may be in direct response to the trauma, even if it occurred many years before. The public needs to understand the concept of posttraumatic stress, as well as the lifelong impact of abuse and the need for preventive programs.

Families can be very supportive if a person seeks to reexperience the trauma by recall, direct exposure, imagination, or hypnosis. The social worker can enlist the family in helping the person to feel safe in confronting the event and linking it emotionally and intellectually to the presenting symptoms. Families need to be helped to see that talking about the trauma is much more helpful than encouraging the person to "forget about it," which may not be possible. In addition, as the person is trying to receive help in overcoming the symptoms that he or she is experiencing, the social worker should help families to provide an environment that is as predictable and stable as possible.

Social workers who work with victims of abuse must assess very carefully whether confrontation of the abuser would be helpful or harmful. Variables to be considered include how long ago the abuse occurred, age of the abuser, current relationship with the abuser, and—most important—what will occur as a result of the confrontation. Groups can be helpful when they are made up of people who all suffered the same type of trauma. Group members have an understanding of what each has been through, find it easier to trust each other, and feel less isolated. They can help each other by offering comfort and sympathy, and through mutual aid attain a greater sense of competency. Self-help groups for people who have experienced abuse are usually short-term, although it is not uncommon for group members to continue to support each other outside of the structured group (Graziano 1992).

Although anxiety disorders are the most prevalent of all mental disorders, they rarely come to the attention of mental health professionals. With the exception of people suffering from posttraumatic stress disorder, there frequently is no clear cause for the disorder, although genetic endowment, family behavior, and environmental stressors may predispose an individual to an anxiety disorder. When an individual asks for help with anxiety, careful assessment is indicated to determine whether the severity of the anxiety is realistic or not and what type of intervention is indicated. Anxiety should always be assessed with relation to the situation, because often anxiety is appropriate and can even motivate the sufferer to action.

3   Mood Disorders

Mood disorders, also referred to as affective disorders, involve episodes of depression or mania or both. We all go through periods of sadness that we may call depression, as well as periods of elation, in which we may even say that we are "on a high." We think of these as moods, and we usually know the cause and can fairly accurately predict the duration.

With mood disorders, the cause may not be clear and duration is related to a variety of biopsychosocial factors. When the mood persists and disrupts an individual's relationships, ability to function at work, and perhaps even physical well-being, it should be considered a disorder. *DSM-IV* includes two types of mood disorders:

1. Bipolar disorders
   a. Bipolar disorders
   b. Cyclothymia
2. Unipolar depressive disorders
   a. Major depressive episode
   b. Dysthymic disorder

Bipolar disorder and major depression represent the extremes, and cyclothymia and dysthymia fall between them. Major depression has a lifetime prevalence of 17 percent and is the most common mental disorder. Although current diagnostic thinking uses duration of episodes as a criterion, it would appear that mood disorders actually exist on a continuum. For example, many people with cyclothymia are vulnerable for episodes of mania and major depression, and many diagnosed with dysthymia experience major depression. Even though major depression is the most common mental dis-order, mood disorders are the most undertreated of all mental disorders.

Depression is second only to coronary heart disease in the number of days people spend in the hospital or disabled at home. It is estimated that the annual cost is $11.7 billion in days lost at work, $12.1 billion in decreased productivity, and $7.5 billion in costs for psychiatric intervention, including medication, psychotherapy, and hospitalization (Greenberg et al. 1993).

Definitions

Bipolar disorder is also known as manic-depressive disorder. This disorder is frequently marked by periods of inconsolable sadness and despair (major depression) alternating or intermixed with periods of extreme cheerfulness, energy, extravagance, and talkativeness that may suddenly turn into rage and hostility (mania). Usually the presence of one of the moods is followed by a period of the opposite mood. *DSM-IV* divides bipolar disorder into bipolar I, which is manifested by major depressive and manic episodes, and bipolar II, which is characterized by major depressive and hypomanic episodes (American Psychiatric Association 1994).

Cyclothymia is a term derived from the Greek meaning "cyclic mood." It is a milder, more chronic form of bipolar disorder; an individual is not free of symptoms for more than two months in a period of at least two years. The mood swings are less extreme: the manic phase is termed *hypomania*, and the depressed phase is less severe than a major depression.

Major depressive disorder (unipolar) is a disorder characterized by at least two weeks of a persistent depressed mood in a person with no history of mania. While in most cases there is remission within six months, an episode can last from several weeks to several months.

Dysthymia (formerly neurotic depression) is a term derived from the Greek meaning "ill humor" or "a bad state of mind." It is a milder, more chronic depressive disorder: an individual is not free of symptoms for more than two months in a period of at least two years. It is insidious, chronic, lingering, and often misunderstood, misdiagnosed, and mistreated.

Epidemiology

The NIMH Epidemiological Catchment Area study estimated that one or more affective disorders were found in 9.5 percent of the population during a year (Regier et al. 1993). The National Comorbidity Survey (Kessler et al. 1994) found a lifetime prevalence of 19.3 percent for any affective disorder (14.7 percent for men and 23.9 percent for women) and a twelve-month prevalence of 11.3 percent (7.5 percent for men and 14.1 percent for women). Additional findings showed white and Hispanic people were more prone to depression than black people were.

It is estimated that less than 1 percent of the population have bipolar disorder, and a somewhat higher percentage, approximately 2 percent, have cyclothymic disorder. The National Comorbidity Survey reported a lifetime prevalence of 1.6 percent for manic episodes (Kessler et al. 1994). Bipolar and cyclothymic disorders are seen to affect men and women equally. The age of onset of these disorders is usually between adolescence and age thirty and rarely over age fifty.

Major depression is the most common of all mental disorders: it is estimated that more than 20 percent of the population will experience some degree of depression at some point in their lives (Waldinger 1990). The National Comorbidity Survey (Kessler et al. 1994) found a lifetime prevalence of 17.1 percent for a major depressive episode (12.7 percent for men and 21.3 percent for women) and a twelve-month prevalence of 10.3 percent (7.7 percent for men and 12.9 percent for women). The same survey found a 6.4 percent lifetime prevalence for dysthymia (4.8 percent for men and 8.0 percent for women) and a twelve-month prevalence of 2.5 percent (2.1 percent for men and 3.0 percent for women). Dysthymia affects 36 percent of people seen in psychiatric clinics (Markowitz, Moran, and Kocsis 1992). Women are twice as likely as men to experience a major depression, and dysthymia also is thought to be more prevalent in women than in men. It is currently believed that the gender discrepancy is not biologically based, although hormonal changes occurring with menstruation, childbirth, and menopause can cause depressive symptoms. Social and cultural risk factors are viewed as more relevant causes. These can include, for women, a higher rate of poverty, unhappy marriages, physical, sexual, and emotional abuse, less opportunity to change one's life pattern, greater cultural acceptance of women's acknowledgment and discussion of depression, and the greater prevalence of women patients seen in psychiatric hospitals and clinics. Though major depressions can occur at any age, the first episode is usually in the twenties. The age of onset of dysthymia is usually in adolescence, young adulthood, or even childhood. Depression occurs in all socioeconomic groups, and there is evidence that it has increased since World War II.

Perry (1994) reported that rates of current depression, ranging from adjustment reaction with depression to major depression, were higher for people who are HIV-positive or have AIDS than for the general population. They may also experience mania for the first time; however, there are no data on prevalence.

Assessment for Bipolar Disorder

Bipolar disorder is one of the simplest mood disorders to assess, because the generally accepted criteria meet standards for both validity and reliability. The cyclical pattern of depression and mania is easily recognizable, there is a genetic predisposition, and a treatment, lithium, is effective in the majority of diagnosed cases. There must be at least one documented manic episode. The usual initial episode, often noticed in adolescence, is depressive in women and manic in men (American Psychiatric Association 1994), followed respectively by at least one episode of mania or depression. In periods when the disorder is not present, there is no evidence of bizarre behavior. Symptoms of a manic phase include grandiosity, extravagance, loud and rapid speech, excessive euphoria, little need for sleep, promiscuity, substance abuse, flight of ideas, lability of mood, and hyperactivity. Furthermore, there often is little or no awareness that the behavior is unusual and that intervention should be sought. The depressed stage has the same symptoms as in unipolar depression.

A person suffering from mania may be unaware of changes in personality and may feel energized and particularly well. In addition, the increased agitation, distractibility, flight of ideas, and pressured speech may add to the difficulty of focusing on the interview. Often it is helpful to interview someone close to the client who can give a history of the onset of mania and how the person now differs from the usual. To help the individual consider what is happening, the worker might ask questions like the following:

Have you been feeling better than usual or euphoric?
Have you felt "speedy" or irritable?

Have you been sleeping less?
Talking more?
More active?
Spending more?
Getting into trouble?
Sexually promiscuous?

Although in some cases the mania may have blocked virtually all reality testing, in less severe situations such questions may cause some awareness that there is a change in behavior. With cyclothymic disorder, the symptoms are not as severe or as disabling, and the disorder is harder to diagnose. The erratic behavior and difficulties with interpersonal relationships may suggest a personality disorder, and thus the assessment should bear out the cyclical change of mood from hypomania to depression.

Assessment for Unipolar Depression

Depression was first described by the ancient Greeks, who referred to melancholia as "black bile," and references to it have appeared in the Bible and in medical literature since ancient days. Assessing major depression or dysthymia is much more complex than assessing bipolar disorders. Because depression may be caused by physical illness or substance abuse, or may follow a psychotic episode, it is essential that a thorough assessment obtain accurate information from the individual and also, if possible, from significant others. Those who suffer from depression often feel so hopeless and worthless that they are unable to give an accurate picture of the onset, or of their premorbid personality.

People who do not seek professional help for their depression may be ashamed of their feelings, responding to others who tell them to "cheer up," thus making it appear that the mood is under their conscious control. Going to a medical clinic or an internist is, for many, more acceptable than going to a mental health professional, for there is less stigma in having a physical problem than there is in having an emotional disorder. As a result, many people with depression are misdiagnosed and do not receive appropriate treatment. Depressed people who see doctors repeatedly for physical illnesses, as well as for vague physical symptoms, account for a large share of the national health costs. Because the majority of people suffering from depression do not seek help, it is important that social workers in all settings consider the possibility of depression when making an assessment. A mother who appears to be neglecting or abusing a child may be suffering from depression, as may be a person who engages in substance abuse, one who commits domestic violence, or one who voices vague psychosomatic complaints. Assessment of people who are HIV-positive or who have AIDS reveals that they are more likely to have an adjustment reaction with depression or a major depression than dysthymia (Perry 1994). Because of the physical problems that are part of the disease, the focus ought to be less on assessment of these symptoms than on mood and on feelings of despair, worthlessness, guilt, isolation, and fears about the disease process and of death.

In assessing for depression, it is important to obtain the following information:

age of onset
number of previous episodes
medical history, preferably including data from a recent physical
    examination
familial history of depression
perception of support systems
substance abuse history
information about any stressful life events, particularly losses, occur-
    ring during the six months before onset

Interviewing a person suffering from depression can be difficult, as the person may feel hopeless and helpless, speech may be retarded, and it may be difficult for the person to remember when times were better. A person suffering from a severe depression may not be able to get to an interview alone. It is useful for the social worker to speak with the accompanying person to get a picture of the onset, possible contributing factors, and pre-morbid functioning. Whether alone or accompanied, the person is frequently pessimistic about the outcome and may be passive; therefore, the interviewer may need to be fairly active in exploring. One must be very careful to avoid false reassurance in an effort to make the client feel better. It is likely that the client has been told by friends and family that the mood will pass, to "snap out of it," while he or she feels that things will never get better and that the depressed mood will be constant. Thus any suggestion to the contrary may affect the worker's credibility in the eyes of the client. The worker can better solidify the working relationship by recognizing how bad the client feels and saying, "I know you may not believe this, but in time you will feel better." To further the process of assessment, the worker might add that knowing more about the client and the client's situation will facilitate the helping process. When exploring, it is useful to ask questions such as "What were things like before you felt depressed?" "Who are the important people in your life?" and "What was your old self like?" These questions may lead to a better understanding of the severity of the depression, the client's self-image before onset, and people who might need to be contacted for assessment or possibly to provide support. There are several standardized tests that can be used to confirm a diagnosis of depression suggested by a biopsychosocial assessment. These include the Beck Depression Inventory, the Hamilton Rating Scale for Depression, the Schizophrenia and Affective Disorders Scale (SADS), the projective Thematic Apperception Test (TAT) and the Minnesota Multiphasic Personality Inventory (MMPI). Symptoms of depression are affective, cognitive, vegetative, physical, and motivational. In addition, there frequently are problems in interpersonal relationships.

Affective Symptoms

The mood of a person with depression may appear as sad, discouraged, or uncaring. Although depression may not be verbalized, one can observe it, as the client may look sad, posture appears weary, speech lacks an expressive tone, and attention to grooming and personal hygiene may have diminished. The individual, or a family member, will refer to *anhedonia*, the inability to experience pleasure from people and activities once enjoyed. There may be a loss of libido and a general feeling of emptiness and loss of interest in life. Some sufferers express feelings of uselessness and may state that others would be better off "if I were dead." Some report that their mood is more depressed in the morning and that there is some improvement during the day. Some people with depression also experience anxiety, uneasiness, fear, or feelings of impending disaster. At times this anxiety is experienced as palpitations, rapid pulse, churning stomach, or problems breathing. A diagnostic problem may arise because the symptoms suggest a diagnosis of anxiety, and thus other signs of depression should have been noted and remain present before the onset of the anxiety. People with depression may also appear angry and speak of being unloved or mistreated. The anger is frequently directed at those the individual hopes will gratify the unmet needs. The anger and demands may make life miserable for those closest to the depressed person.

Cognitive Symptoms

A person with depression may often appear to be preoccupied with himself and his plight. Conversation may be monotonous, with much ruminating about the past, which is frequently falsely perceived as having been a much better time. There are feelings of low self-esteem, hopelessness, helplessness, and worthlessness. The person may experience guilt, especially when there has been a significant loss. In a small number of severely depressed people, the guilt may be recognized in the content of hallucinations or delusions. Because there is so much preoccupation with the self, people with depression often complain about an inability to concentrate and about recent memory loss. Many find it difficult to make decisions.

Vegetative Symptoms

Many people with depression complain of diminished appetite, and a severely depressed person may refuse to eat, to the point of needing hospitalization. A small number will overeat or binge-eat. Sleep disturbance, particularly early awakening with no hope of resuming sleep, is frequently reported, and others report problems falling asleep as they become overwhelmed with thoughts about their lives, past and present. A small group report sleeping too much. Many show symptoms of psychomotor retardation, such as slow, limited speech, limited movement, and loss of energy. Some, often the elderly, display psychomotor agitation, such as pacing, jitters, or hand wringing.

Physical Symptoms

As noted above, there is less stigma attached to physical illness than to emotional illness, and there is a high rate of hypochondriasis among people with depression. Most common concerns are feelings of fatigue, weakness, headaches and backaches, gastrointestinal disorders, and chest pain. Some become concerned that they may have a serious, or even terminal, disease that only they recognize.

Motivational Symptoms

When a person is depressed, usual daily activities often seem burdensome, and performance in the home, at school, or at work deteriorates. Initially some will withdraw, sit alone, and read, but as the depression increases, passively watching television may be all that they can manage. The person may experience guilt when necessary activities are neglected. Suicidal thoughts may be present, but the person is too immobilized and lacks the motivation to plan and execute an attempt.

Symptoms Present in Interpersonal Relationships

Being around a depressed person is often very difficult, and the person often suffers from social isolation. The person may crave love and attention from others but fails to reciprocate or alienates others through clinging, dependent behavior, self-preoccupation, and complaining. Family and friends are often frustrated by attempts to make the person feel better and eventually respond in anger or withdrawal, sometimes also resulting in guilt. People suffering from depression tend not be feel supported by, and do not enjoy, others and may tend to be argumentative and thus lose friends.

Clinical Course

For most people with bipolar disorder (manic-depressive illness), the episode that first leads to diagnosis is manic, although there usually has been an unreported depressive episode earlier. Often the family will complain about the observed manic behavior, although they may have ignored previous depressive withdrawal. Mania may last for weeks or months. It is followed by depression, or by a normal mood period followed by a period of depression. The manic periods may feature a very rapid onset, and they are usually shorter than the contrasting periods of the slower-developing major depression, with mania lasting an average of about four months and depression, six months. Some people may go for periods of years without these mood fluctuations, while others may experience them on a predictable yearly basis. Untreated, episodes may become more frequent and of longer duration. Even so, there will be periods of normal mood.

Subgroups include people who experience the fluctuation on a weekly or even hourly basis, as well as those who may experience both moods concurrently. Functioning during the active periods may be severely impaired. While most people with this disorder have normal periods, some suffer from a chronic form of bipolar disorder.

Cyclothymia is more chronic, though less severe than bipolar disorder. The onset is more insidious, length of mood disturbance shorter but more frequent, and degree of impairment less marked. There is increased vulnerability for episodes of mania or major depression, though what is usually observed is hypomania and milder depression, together with chaotic interpersonal problems and erratic behavior. Often people with this disorder see it as characterological and do not seek help unless there is marked deterioration.

Forty percent of those suffering from major depression suffer only one episode, which comes on rapidly, often following one or more stressful life events, and from which there is complete recovery. Most acute depressions are self-limiting, lasting an average of eight months, and have a good prognosis even without intervention. With medication, the length of the episode can be significantly reduced. For 50 percent of people, the depression will occur slowly and, following recovery, will recur within two years, with the possibility for an average lifetime recurrence of six episodes. A few people may never fully recover, remaining functionally impaired, and some experience psychotic symptoms. People with major depressions, or their families, are more apt to seek help for the disorder than are people with other mood disorders, because of the effects that their impairment has on their day-to-day functioning and interpersonal relationships.

People with dysthymia suffer from low-grade but chronic depression that can last for years and, like cyclothymia, may be mistakenly seen as characterological. These people frequently say they do not remember a time when they were not depressed, yet they may function relatively well outside of interpersonal relationships. The initial onset may be insidious. Without intervention, this milder depression will persist. Dysthymia may precede, and later follow, an episode of major depression, during which it is most likely that intervention will be sought. Dysthymia can be more persistent but less severe than major depression; there is often a poorer level of baseline functioning, and there is a poorer prognosis. If dysthymia and major depression coexist ("double depression"), the prognosis is even poorer (Wells et al. 1992).

Suicide

There are about thirty thousand documented suicides every year in the United States, although the actual number is probably higher. Many suicides are disguised as accidents, overdoses, homicides, or reported as other causes of death to protect survivors. It is the eighth leading cause of death for all people, but the third leading cause for people fifteen to twenty-four years of age. The highest rates are for white men over sixty, especially those over seventy-five. More men than women commit suicide, usually with firearms or by hanging; however, women make three times as many attempts, usually with pills or by slashing their wrists. White people are twice as likely as other ethnic groups to commit suicide, with the exception of Native Americans, who have the highest rate of suicide. The rate is even more dramatic among young men who are members of tribes that are rapidly moving away from their indigenous culture. Suicide is more common for people living alone who never married, those who are separated or divorced, and those who are widowed, than for those married with children. Suicide rates are higher for Protestants than for Jews or Catholics, whose religions regard it as a sin.

No one really knows why people choose to end their lives. The reasons are complex, and there are a multitude of predisposing and immediate risk factors that may be psychosocial, biological, or psychiatric. One of the most difficult problems facing health care professionals is the ability to predict and prevent suicide. Many people who commit suicide have seen a physician within a week or a month of their death.

It is estimated that 90 percent of people who commit suicide are suffering from an emotional disorder, most often depression. The cause of death of 15 percent of people with mood disorders, and of 25 percent of those with bipolar disorder, is suicide (Grinspoon and Bakalar 1990a). Other diagnoses that are correlated with high suicide rates are schizophrenia, alcoholism, dementia, and panic disorders. People under thirty who commit suicide frequently are substance abusers or people with antisocial personality disorders. People between thirty and sixty who commit suicide usually have mood disorders, and those over sixty most frequently have organic mental disorders or depression secondary to chronic physical illness. Such personality traits as hostility, impulsivity, depression, and excessive feelings of guilt and shame are associated with increased risk of suicide. There appear to be biological factors that increase vulnerability. It has been found that among adolescents there is a greater risk for those with I.Q.'s of over 130; researchers speculate that they are cognitively better able to develop and carry out a plan. For the elderly, there is increased risk as they lose their mobility, their sight, and their general physical health. Diminished cognitive functioning, due to medical illness, depression, dementia, or awareness of the onset of Alzheimer's disease may also lead to suicide. Twin and adoption studies have indicated a genetic vulnerability.

Assessments reveal that suicidal ideation is common in people who are HIV-positive, and thus this is a population at significant risk. It is important when assessing these people to ask about this and inquire if they have a plan to commit suicide. Often people will report thinking about the possibility of suicide, but are not actually suicidal (Winiarski 1991).

A study of homosexual and bisexual men with AIDS, who are most often young adults, showed the risk of suicide to be thirty-six times greater than for men in general between twenty and fifty-nine, and sixty-six times greater than for the general public (Marzuk et al. 1988). Often depression and cognitive impairment are the first signs that AIDS may have invaded the brain. If a person develops HIV-related dementia (which afflicts about 50 percent of those who are HIV-infected), there is progressive cognitive and motor impairment. People with AIDS may experience feelings of humiliation, guilt, and hopelessness that, combined with extreme debilitation and loss of social and financial supports, may result in suicide. The study cited above showed that most people with AIDS who commit suicide do it within nine months of diagnosis, not in the advanced stage. When a person with AIDS also develops Kaposi's sarcoma, there is a higher rate of suicide than when any other opportunistic disease develops (Breitbart 1988). Ethical issues concerning the right to commit suicide when facing a debilitating disease are often raised with regard to people with AIDS. A clinician working with this population needs to be very self-aware and to have thought through his or her own feelings and issues related to this possibility.

Psychosocial stressors very often are related to loss. It is believed that people who suffered early losses are more predisposed to suicide, especially if the loss was through parental suicide. Other losses include physical health, jobs, financial security, previous roles, and, most important, loss of partners, friends, and caretakers who make up one's social network. For the elderly these losses can be compounded by declining years and ill health.

Assessment of suicidal potential is very difficult and involves skilled, effective interviewing that depends greatly on establishing an empathic and supportive relationship that will allow the person to feel accepted while telling his or her story. The interviewer should be nonjudgmental and objective, and should indicate concern and a degree of urgency. It is important to be aware of one's own feelings about suicide and to know if they will adversely affect the assessment and intervention. A person who is feeling suicidal will pick up on any anxiety being experienced by the interviewer, as well as any negative or moralistic feelings. In addition to noting what is being said, it is important to observe body language and to realize what is not being said. Open-ended questions, such as "How are things going?" and "Tell me about your sadness," are initially helpful in establishing the relationship, before direct questions about a plan should be asked. Assessment of defense mechanisms is important, for those who use defenses such as denial, projection, and splitting probably are less able to cope with stress than those who use humor and sublimation. While expediency of the assessment may be indicated, it is useful to include a mental status that should reveal the presence of delusions and of command hallucinations, each of which heightens the risk.

Assessments should focus initially on current and recent life events that are having an impact on the individual. Expressions of frustration and hopelessness should be viewed as verbal clues and taken seriously. For example, the worker should be acutely aware of statements like "I can't take it anymore" and "I might as well give up." One should also note behavior such as abruptly making a will, giving things away, or taking a sudden interest in buying a cemetery plot. Attention also should be paid to a sudden interest in guns or an increase in accidents.

Generally the assessment will follow the format for depression, but it is essential to get a psychiatric history, especially of depression, for often suicide occurs as a severe depression lifts and the person is better able to develop and implement a plan. A history of past suicide attempts is needed, for if they have occurred, they are a strong indicator of risk: 40 percent of people who commit suicide have made at least one earlier attempt. A family history of suicidal behavior also is important, for the risk is four times greater if a close relative has committed suicide.

If, as the relationship develops, the interviewer feels the person is suicidal, questions should be more focused: "Do you ever think you would be better off dead?" "How close have you come to killing yourself? What stopped you? Did anyone know?" These questions are designed to determine if there is a plan, the degree of lethality, the ease with which the person can implement the plan, and the likelihood of rescue.

Social workers can neither prescribe medication nor admit a person to a hospital; thus, if the assessment indicates high risk for suicide, an immediate psychiatric consultation is indicated. If a psychiatrist is not available, the person should be escorted to a psychiatric emergency room. The person may accept the need to be admitted voluntarily, or may need to be involuntarily committed by two physicians, one of whom must be a psychiatrist. If the person is not admitted, a friend or relative should be alerted to stay with the person, an appointment should be made for the next day, and the person given an emergency telephone number to contact in the interim. An important thing to remember is that people who talk about suicide also commit suicide. Eighty percent of those who kill themselves have given some warning of intent. Intervention planning should assume intent and err in the direction of caution.

Etiology

Despite much research, the etiologies of bipolar and unipolar mood disorders are not known. As with other emotional disorders, there appear to be variants in symptomatology that suggest that many factors are involved in the development of mood disorders and that no single cause likely will be found.

The genetic roots of bipolar disorder have undergone extensive study. Twin, adoption, and family studies offer strong evidence of family transmission. While bipolar disorder affects 1 percent of the population, studies have shown that a child with one parent who has bipolar disorder has a 30 percent chance of developing a mood disorder and those with two parents who have bipolar disorder have a 75 percent chance. At least 50 percent of people with bipolar disorder have at least one relative with a mood disorder. Classical twin studies comparing monozygotic twins to dizygotic twins show that if one monozygotic twin suffers from mania, there is a 80 percent chance that the other twin will also, and that nearly all people with a monozygotic twin who has bipolar disorder will suffer from some mood disorder. This high concordance rate strongly suggests genetic vulnerability. Dizygotic twins are no more likely to get bipolar disorder than are any two siblings (Grinspoon and Bakalar 1990a).

Adoption studies show that children who have a biological parent with bipolar disorder are three times more likely to develop the disorder than if only an adoptive parent has it. People who are genetically vulnerable to bipolar disorder are also vulnerable to unipolar depression, but the reverse is not true. This suggests a greater genetic predisposition to bipolar disorder (Grinspoon and Bakalar 1990a). It is not yet clear whether one or more genes are involved.

The data supporting heredity as a predisposing factor for depression are not as dramatic. While there is evidence that 25 percent of people with major depression have first-degree relatives with some mood disorder, and that people with any type of depression frequently have close relatives who also suffered from depression, it is not clear whether depression is transmitted through genes or through learned behavior. Some studies have shown that there is a 65 percent concordance rate for depression in monozygotic twins and only a 16 percent rate for dizygotic twins, suggesting a genetic predisposition (Waldinger 1990).

Researchers have looked at neurotransmitters as causes of depression. They possibly provide the way by which the gene exerts its effect. Most believe that norepinephrine and serotonin are tied to depression and that depression occurs when the regulatory function of the neuroreceptors breaks down. Antidepressant medications appear to help adjust the pathways and receptor sites, and thus allow the neurotransmitters to travel more smoothly and evenly. Urine tests can give indications of the breakdown of norepinephrine and serotonin. Because neurotransmitters and the endocrine system are closely interdependent, some disorders of the endocrine system also cause depression. Cushing's disease and Addison's disease (both disorders of the adrenal glands), as well as hypothyroidism, have been shown to cause depression. Researchers have also looked at the relationship between sleep patterns and depression. Especially close attention was paid to the increased amount of REM sleep experienced by people with depression.

Social workers have a particular interest in the psychosocial factors that may predispose a person to depression. These areas are more difficult to research, as memory may not be accurate and cultural expectations may have an effect. Studies have, however, shown that people who suffered early losses, rejection or unavailability of parents, or who were raised in chaotic or unaffectionate households are more prone to depression. Many theorists suggest that loss often causes depression. Feelings about early unresolved losses and separations may resurface with later separations and losses. Anniversaries of deaths may cause sadness. Holidays may revive feelings of earlier deprivation and impoverishment. Losses may also involve threats to self-confidence and self-esteem that might result in losing the respect, approval, or love of significant others. Such losses may include unemployment, failure in school, a major illness, a disrupted relationship, or a traumatic injury. Paradoxically, depression may also result from success. A promotion at work into a position of increased responsibility and status may evoke a person's fear of exposure as a fraud and failure.

There is a relationship between depression and lack of support systems, but it is not always clear which is the cause and which is the effect. Depression appears to have been on the increase since World War II. This increase may be attributable to the mobility of the population, which removes people from familial support systems and hinders them from establishing long-term close friendships. The increase also may be caused by the demands of the workplace or the greater complexity of the postwar world. In the past decade, increasing unemployment, the continued breakdown of the nuclear family, and the faltering economy have likely been contributing factors. It is also true that depression may impair relationships with friends and family, who become frustrated and withdraw.

The original psychodynamic formulation, described by Freud in *Mourning and Melancholia* (1917), saw depression as an unconscious reaction to the loss of a loved one, whereby the individual directs feelings of anger and blame onto the self. More recent theorists see depression as caused by the early loss of people on whom the individual depended for approval and self-esteem.

Proponents of interpersonal therapy (IPT) believe that depression results from losses caused by role disruptions, isolation, life transitions, or deficits in social skills that preclude establishing relationships. Problems with interpersonal relationships are felt to cause depression because they lead to difficulties in all areas of psychosocial functioning.

Cognitive theorists (Beck 1967) view the etiology of depression as resulting from the person's pervasively negative view of his or her self, life, the world, and the future. A sense of learned helplessness may contribute to feelings that one is unable to alter anything of significance in the environment. The individual who is suffering from depression also is likely to assume responsibility for everything that has gone wrong.

Depression is a biopsychosocial disorder caused by factors that may be genetic, physiological, chemical, environmental, familial, cultural, or social. In most cases, depression probably results from combinations of these factors, which together increase individual vulnerability. No single cause is likely, and the course and symptoms of mood disorders may vary considerably.

Differential Diagnosis

It is particularly difficult to establish a diagnosis of depression when it is accompanied by physical illness, for a side effect of the illness may be depression because of the severity of the illness, the degree of disability, or the possibility of loss of finances, support systems, and established roles (*secondary depression*). Diseases such as AIDS, cancer, diabetes, rheumatoid arthritis, endocrine disorders, infections, strokes, and neurological disorders may have symptoms also seen in depression, such as loss of energy, fatigue, insomnia, loss of libido, social withdrawal, and possibly suicidal ideation.

Physicians, because of limitations in their training, fear of the patient's negative reaction, or uncertainty about management, may be reluctant to suggest that, in addition to the physical illness, the patient may be experiencing depression. Social workers, who emphasize assessing the psychosocial factors that may impinge on the individual, should work with physicians to explore whether a diagnosis of depression is also indicated. Careful assessment is required to know whether physical illness and depression coexist (*compound depression*) or whether one illness is masking the other, possibly resulting in inadequate intervention. Assessment of whether depression predated the physical illness or results from it will have implications for intervention planning and possibly for assessing the probability that the person, especially if an elderly person, will follow recommendations. In addition to physical diseases that may cause depression, other organic causes can be reactions to some medications, such as steroids (which may also cause mania) and oral contraceptives, or to chronic substance abuse. Symptoms of dementia, such as problems in concentration, confusion, and memory loss, may also resemble severe depression, so careful assessment is imperative. The depression may arise in response to recognition of deterioration in cognitive functioning.

Depressive symptoms, ranging from adjustment disorder with depression to major depression, are the psychiatric problems most frequently observed in people who test positive for HIV. Assessment may be complicated, since some physical symptoms of the early stages of AIDS are the same as those for major depression, and thus emphasis should be on affective, rather than physical, symptoms. Mania is sometimes observed in people with AIDS who had no previous psychiatric history; this situation is of particular concern, as the person may indulge in increased sexual activity (Winiarski 1991).

Depression often accompanies schizophrenia, and usually follows acute schizophrenic episodes. If the depression occurs before or concomitantly, then there is greater likelihood that depression is the primary diagnosis. When the symptoms of depression and schizophrenia are mixed, the diagnosis may be schizoaffective disorder.

Because people with anxiety often experience depression, it is sometimes difficult to establish the primary diagnosis. Many of the symptoms are similar, and only careful assessment can determine which disorder came first. People with both disorders are usually severely ill and hard to treat.

Assessment is needed to distinguish between personality disorders and mood disorders, or to establish that both are present. Symptoms of dysthymia may look characterological, and as dysthymia may be long-lasting, it is hard to separate the two. Major depression is easier to identify, as its episodic nature is inconsistent with the long-lasting presence of personality disorders. Some of the erratic behavior of people with personality disorders may be misdiagnosed as bipolar or cyclothymic disorder, and thus it is important to inquire about family history and response to medication. Taking a developmental history is crucial, as identification of early personality factors may suggest a personality disorder as primary and a mood disorder as secondary. In addition, treatment-resistant bipolar disorder suggests misdiagnosis (Bolton and Gunderson 1996).

Finally the normal emotional response to loss (reactive depression), particularly to the death of a loved one, may appear to be a major depression. Grief is not a mental disorder. Most people who experience reactive depression do not come from a family with a history of mental disorders, and symptoms usually begin within weeks, or no more than two to three months after the loss. In addition, the person who experiences grief focuses on the loss and on the effect of the loss rather than on his or her own feelings, to the exclusion of thoughts about the deceased. Grieving usually lasts between six months and a year, with a decrease in intensity followed by a return to normal. If the grief is unresolved, as indicated by a continued longing for the deceased, unresolved feelings of ambivalence or anger, or preoccupation with the deceased, then the social worker should assess the possibility that the client had undergone other unresolved significant losses. The clinician also should assess the presence or absence of support systems and the possibility that a major depression is present.

Grief does not follow a prescribed pattern, however; common phases are shock, even if the death was anticipated; numbness, which changes to a feeling of emptiness; and disbelief, even to the extent of denying the death. The initial period is usually followed by a period of sadness, which may be accompanied by guilt about aspects of the relationship or about—even if unrealistic—not having prevented the death. Grieving people may go through a period of reliving the events surrounding the death until they can accept it emotionally. Eventually it becomes possible to remember the deceased without excessive sadness, and there are other signs of recovery as well, including reaching out to friends and thinking about the future. Intervention is directed, in part, to the survivor's establishment of an identity without the deceased. Grief reactions respond to encouragement to express feelings, connection to support systems, and the passage of time.

Cultural factors, as well as the individual's behavior before the loss, may affect the length of grief and mourning and must be explored in assessment.

Some cultures have what may seem to be unusual customs relating to the mourning process, and such cultural norms must be considered before judging the individual's reaction. Although grieving may last beyond a year, this is not cause for concern unless a person's functioning remains seriously impaired. In that case, consideration must be given to whether bereavement has caused the onset of a major depression.

Intervention

As has been indicated, assessment of a primary mood disorder, especially depression, is difficult and involves exploration of many factors, since the mood disorder may be masked by physical problems and other mental disorders. Social workers are trained to look at all of the factors that are impinging on the individual, but they must be aware that interviewing a person in a manic or a depressed state presents specific difficulties.

Following assessment, a plan for intervention must be made. Various interventions for mood disorders, and particularly for depression, are possible. The choice will depend not only on the assessment but also on the training of the mental health professional, the cost, and the acceptability of the intervention to the client. Certain interventions, such as cognitive-behavioral therapy (CBT) and interpersonal therapy (IPT), have been designed specifically for people suffering from depression.

Medication

Lithium, although recognized earlier, became widely accepted as the drug of choice for people suffering from acute mania in the 1970s. It is the mainstay of treatment for bipolar disorders, although it has been less successful in preventing bipolar depression than in treating mania, in which there is a 70 percent success rate (Gitlin 1990; Waldinger 1990). Although it may take several weeks to get the full effect, the normalization of mood usually begins to be apparent in seven to ten days. The dosage of lithium is regulated by assessing the amount of lithium present in the blood; thus people taking this medication must be aware of the need for regular blood tests, initially weekly and eventually about every three to four months. People who take lithium may have to continue taking it for years or perhaps a lifetime, depending on the severity and frequency of episodes. Because of side effects, if the client appears to be doing well, dosages are lowered or the medication is stopped to determine if it is still needed. The most common side effects are increased urination, thirst, nausea, irritability, and weight gain. Some people experience cognitive side effects, such as loss of concentration and memory problems, and some complain of diminishing creativity, which is a particular problem, since the disorder disproportionately affects those in the arts, television, and advertising. The most serious side effect is lithium toxicity, which, if not recognized, can cause neurological damage. Some people may require an antidepressant or an anticonvulsant medication in addition to the lithium. The antidepressant, however, may trigger a bout of mania and thus must be closely monitored. Since 20 to 40 percent of persons treated with lithium do not experience symptom relief, three anticonvulsant drugs—carbamazepine (Tegretol), sodium valproate (Depakene or Depakote), and verapamil (Calan)—have been used and found effective for maintenance (Solomon et al. 1995).

In treating depression, tricyclic antidepressants, first discovered in the late 1950s, or the newer heterocyclic antidepressants discovered in the last decade, are used most frequently; they report 70 percent effectiveness. The choice of medication depends partly on current effectiveness, the client's previous successes with antidepressants, and the side effects. Among the more commonly used tricyclics are imipramine (Tofranil), amitriptyline (Elavil), clomipramine (Anafranil), desipramine (Norpramine), doxepin (Sinequan), and nortriptyline (Pamelor). The most common side effects with tricyclics include dry mouth, constipation, sedation, sexual difficulties, weight gain, and cardiac side effects. Some of these will subside with continued use, but in some cases they are severe enough that the client discontinues the medication. These medications take from two to three weeks to act effectively and usually are continued for several months after the depression is no longer present.

Monoamine oxidase (MAO) inhibitors were discovered at the same time as the tricyclics, and they also act on the neurotransmitters, including norepinephrine and serotonin. Among the best-known are tranylcypromine (Parnate), isocarboxazid (Marplan), and phenelzine (Nardil). A major problem with prescribing MAO inhibitors is the necessity for dietary restrictions. People taking these medications cannot eat most cheeses, yogurt, chocolate, liver, fermented meats, and smoked fish and may not drink many alcoholic beverages, especially red wine. Some over-the-counter and some prescribed medications, especially those that contain stimulants, also produce adverse side effects. MAO inhibitors also have side effects similar to the tricyclics, except that the sexual problems are even more frequent.

Fluoxetine (Prozac), sertraline (Zoloft), paroxetine (Paxil), and fluvoxamine (Luvox) are among the newer group of antidepressants, selective serotonin reuptake inhibitors (SSRIs). They are believed to have fewer side effects, have less potential to be lethal, and act in a shorter period of time. They are easier to administer and have proved effective for some patients who do not respond to tricyclics. The mildness of side effects makes them especially preferable for the elderly and for moderately depressed people.

Three atypical antidepressants frequently used are trazodone (Desyrel) and amoxapine (Asendin), often prescribed for insomnia, and bupropion (Wellbutrin), whose use is limited, as there is an increased risk of seizures. Finally, there are some new antidepressants—nefazadone (Serzone) and mirtazapine (Remeron), serotonin transport blockers and antagonists, and venlafaxine (Effexor), a serotonin-norepinephrine reuptake inhibitor—both of which look promising, since there appear to be few side effects. On July 17, 1998, the Food and Drug Administration (FDA) gave approval to a new SSRI, citalopram hydrobromide (Celexa), which has shown good results in Europe and has fewer sexual side effects (NAMI-FACTS 1998).

Hospitalization

People suffering from acute, highly disruptive mania may require hospitalization and treatment with antipsychotic medication in addition to lithium, which does not take effect immediately. Their behavior may be so bizarre and out of control that hospitalization is necessary for their survival. Seclusion rooms, limit-setting, and sometimes restraints are necessary to control people suffering from mania until medication takes effect.

People suffering from severe depression, accompanied by hallucinations and delusions, or with acute suicidal ideation may also require hospitalization and antipsychotic medication. Some severely depressed people do not, or cannot, take care of their daily needs and thus require hospitalization.

Electroconvulsive Therapy (ECT)

ECT ("shock treatment"), a controversial form of intervention, involves electric current being passed through the brain to produce seizures. It is the seizure, not the shock, that produces the healing. ECT was used extensively before the development of the new medications and is currently used when people do not respond to medication. The intervention involves giving the person a muscle relaxant and a mild barbiturate, then attaching electrodes to the temples, through which the current is passed. It is believed to be effective for 75 to 85 percent of those treated (Foderaro 1993). ECT is primarily used for the treatment of severe mood disorders, and the treatment regimen is usually six to twelve treatments given over a period of two to four weeks. It is more often used for severe depression, especially with psychotic or suicidal ideation, than for mania. It is highly effective and is now a medically safe procedure that can be conducted on an outpatient basis. Hospitalization should be considered, however, because of the major side effect, memory loss. Recent memory is most affected, but most people will regain their memory within six months, although some never do remember the hospitalization nor fully regain their memory. ECT is safer than drugs for elderly people who may have physical illnesses requiring complex medication protocols.

Psychotherapy

Although medication has proved very effective for mood disorders, psychotherapy is usually also indicated, and most people treated successfully for depression receive medication plus some form of psychotherapy. In addition to education about the disorders, people may also need help with their feelings and with reestablishing their lives and the relationships that have often been disrupted. Although social workers cannot prescribe or distribute medication, they can be helpful in providing education and support to people and their families in order to ensure that medication is taken for as long as medically indicated. There are several types of supportive psychotherapy that social workers, depending on their orientation, use to help people suffering from depression; these are related to what is believed to be the etiology. Until the depression lifts, people should be discouraged from making any major life changes. Attainable goals should be established, and the person should be encouraged to resume, or initiate, activities and contact with others. The clinician should be available for crises and should be alert to the emergence of destructive impulses.

With people suffering from mania, the most helpful supportive treatment is trying to help them repair some of the consequences of their disruptive behavior while in a manic state. People suffering from depression need to enhance defensive functioning in order to help protect themselves from the emotional pain and dilute the feelings of blame, guilt, and self-condemnation. It is important to help the person learn to ask others for help and to identify areas of adaptive functioning that are intact. The worker should try to avoid anything that might sound critical, give advice very sparingly in spite of the client's apparent dependency needs, and urge the client to put off decisions until the depressed feelings have lifted.

Psychodynamic therapy is a form of treatment that is not specifically for depression. Its focus is on object relationships and the individual's intrapsychic wishes and conflicts. Its basis, with respect to depression, is in Freud's assumption that depression stems from loss of a parent through death or rejection. The resulting effects on the person include feelings of low self-esteem, rejection of the self, and punitive, possibly self-destructive, behavior. The intervention involves looking at childhood experiences, recognizing and confronting the defenses used, and analyzing transferential feelings, thoughts, and behaviors toward the parents, the clinician, and others. This usually long-term approach has been modified to look more at the relationship of present to past, and proponents such as Malan and Davenloo have developed a shorter-term psychodynamic approach.

Behavioral therapists feel that depression results from learned helplessness and lack of positive reinforcement. Frequently a twelve-session approach is used for depression, focusing on recognition of pleasurable events that provide positive reinforcement and avoidance of unpleasurable events that result in negative reinforcement and depression. The person suffering from depression is helped, through assertiveness training and the enhancement of social skills, to change his or her environment. The client may even be advised to find new friends and new activities. To overcome feelings of helplessness, there is an emphasis on self-monitoring, self-evaluation, and self-reward.

Cognitive-behavioral therapy (CBT), developed by Beck specifically for depression, is a brief, twelve- to sixteen-session treatment, sometimes followed by monthly maintenance sessions. It is based on the assumption that depression results from a cognitive deficit, whereby the people tend to see themselves and their future in negative and self-defeating terms. The intervention seeks to correct these perceptions, offer a new way of thinking, and thus alleviate the depression. Sessions are very structured and rely on an agenda, assigned homework, and a detailed journal recording the week's activities and related feelings, which the person must bring to each session. There is an emphasis on psychoeducation, improving communication and social skills, and assertiveness training. Families may act as objective reporters, and couple therapy is indicated if the distorted cognitions involve the relationship.

Interpersonal therapy (IPT) was designed in the 1970s, initially in the form of a treatment manual developed primarily for research specifically on persons suffering from acute major depression (Klerman et al. 1984; Markowitz 1998a). Since then it has been extended to treatment of other forms of mood disorders as well as other disorders.

IPT is closely related to psychodynamic therapy and also to the works of Bowlby and Sullivan. While the psychodynamic approach focuses on the intrapsychic, on unconscious mental processes, and on object relations, IPT focuses on interpersonal interactions and social role expectations, past and present. It is a short-term (often as few as twelve to sixteen sessions, but sometime extended for as long as a year) approach that focuses on current interpersonal relationships, the here and now, while also exploring genetic, developmental, and personality factors that might cause vulnerability to depression.

While it may appear to be somewhat like behavioral and cognitive interventions, in practice IPT, though structured, is less confining (Markowitz 1998b). The intervention strives to link mood and current interpersonal experiences in four areas: grief, role dispute, role transition, and interpersonal deficits. There are three phases: (1) developing an understanding of what depression is, based on social, biological, and medical data, with a distinction made between normal sadness and clinical depression; identifying symptoms; determining the problem focus and setting a framework and contract for the intervention, (2) focusing on current interpersonal problem area(s) identified through assessment of early family relationships, previous significant relationships, and friendship patterns and on alleviating symptoms, and (3) termination, during which feelings are discussed, progress is evaluated, and although the individual has usually improved, an outline is made of work that remains to be done without the therapist. If there is reason to believe that further intervention is necessary, IPT suggests following the initial outline, including termination, and then negotiating a new time frame defining frequency of sessions and new goals (Markowitz 1998b) with a goal of maintaining recovery. This maintenance plan (IPT-M) is more important for persons with dysthymia than for those suffering from major depression. In this era of managed care, there has been increased interest in its applicability to other Axis I disorders, and research is being conducted with persons suffering from anxiety disorders, bulimia, and even the Axis II diagnosis of borderline personality disorder.

Markowitz et al. (1998c) modified IPT as an intervention for persons who are HIV-positive, focusing on illness, grief, role transitions, and death. In a recent study comparing IPT, CBT, supportive intervention, and imipramine plus support, depressed and HIV-positive persons who received IPT alone or imipramine plus supportive counseling showed significant improvement in depressive symptoms over those receiving CBT or supportive counseling alone (Markowitz et al. 1998c; Swartz and Markowitz 1998). It is believed that the success with IPT was due to the category for intervention of "interpersonal deficits," as persons who are HIV-positive often need help with mourning life upheavals resulting from bereavements and role disruptions and also need intervention to encourage adjustment and new life goals.

The National Institute of Mental Health (NIMH) conducted a sixteen-session study of 239 severely depressed people to evaluate the relative effectiveness of IPT, cognitive-behavioral therapy (CBT), imipramine, and a placebo. Those receiving imipramine or the placebo were seen weekly, but only for medication management. All four groups of randomly assigned people showed improvement, with only small differences. Imipramine worked best and fastest; as would be expected, the placebo was least effective. IPT was somewhat more effective than CBT for severely disturbed people, but not as effective as imipramine. For the less severely depressed, there was no significant difference between IPT and CBT, or between imipramine and placebo plus supportive medication management. A follow-up study of the four interventions (Shea et al. 1992) indicated that sixteen weeks was not sufficient for full recovery and lasting remission. An NIMH study currently in progress compares (1) IPT, (2) a form of supportive psychotherapy, and (3) sertraline (Zoloft), a serotonin reuptake inhibiting antidepressant (Markowitz 1998b).

Group intervention has value for some people suffering from depression but is not the proper modality for others and should be suggested only after careful assessment. For some, it lessens the isolation, is less anxiety-provoking than individual intervention, and is helpful in recognizing that the person is not alone in feeling hopeless, helpless, and worthless. Psychoeducation groups have been helpful for people with depression or bipolar disorder. There is a sharing of experiences about the effect the symptoms have had on themselves and on their families. These groups also give a sense of optimism about the likely effects of psychotherapy and medication. Self-help groups, such as Widow to Widow, groups for parents whose children have been murdered or committed suicide, and groups for people suffering loss because of a chronic, debilitating illness have proved very helpful.

Groups are contraindicated for very withdrawn, severely depressed people, at least initially. Such people are often too withdrawn, their speech is retarded, their self-image is very poor, and they are not likely to participate for fear of rejection or because of intense feelings of guilt and shame. A supportive, reassuring individual intervention is more helpful at this stage.

Social workers traditionally work with families, and because living with a person who is suffering from depression can be very difficult, anger-provoking, demanding, and at times overwhelming, there is a great need for intervention with the family. Depression may lead to self-involvement, lack of interest in the family and in its social functioning, lack of attention to family daily needs, inability to express positive or affectionate feelings, fatigue, and inability to make or act on decisions. Communication is usually disrupted, irritability and anger may be misinterpreted, and efforts by family members to help are rejected, misunderstood, or responded to with anger. A major depression experienced by a family member has a substantial impact on the whole family.

Since it is not always clear whether family problems cause depression or depression causes family problems, family assessment is very important. The assessment should include how the family functioned before onset of the depression, the developmental stage of the family, patterns of communication, including level of expressed emotion, family alliances, strengths, stressors, history of depression, support systems, physical health, and finances.

Consideration should also be given to how individual family members are handling the effects of the depression and to identification of their concerns, worries, expectations, and fears. Being with a depressed person may result in a sense of aloneness that may lead to sexual problems, increased substance abuse, disruption of a marriage, and feelings of guilt. It is important to assure young children that they did not cause the depression and to see that others try to meet the needs of the children that the depressed person may not be able to meet at this time. Children may also become depressed or have social difficulties, and they may need to be evaluated for possible intervention. Marital or family treatment may be indicated after the acute phase has passed. Studies have shown a strong correlation between family problems and the onset, course, and outcome of a depressive episode, and intervention may involve considering separation or divorce as an option.

Family intervention needs to include education about the disorder. While most psychoeducation has been directed toward families with a member who has schizophrenia, it is also used with family members of people suffering from depression. Families are helped to understand that depression is an illness and not a willful act, a personality trait, or within the person's conscious control. Recent and ongoing stressors need to be explored, problem-solving techniques identified, aftercare planned if the person has been hospitalized, and education provided about the need for medication. Identifying family needs and considering what modifications of family functioning must take place during the acute phase, and also to ensure remission, is another component. The goal is to improve the functioning of the entire family and to enhance individuals' and the family's sense of self-worth.

Psychoeducation workshops disseminate information to a group of families and thus lessen the isolation and sense of shame. Individual vulnerability to stress is discussed in terms of genetic, biochemical, and life-events factors, thus decreasing personal responsibility and blame for depression. How depression manifests itself is also discussed, in terms of both the individual's behavior and the possible responses from the family. Treatment options are defined. Families are urged to try to avoid expressions of criticism, anger, and false reassurance, as well as taking over too many of the person's responsibilities in an effort to help. Families are also urged to attend to their own needs without guilt and to accept the fact that at times they may have negative feelings toward the depressed person. Finally, they are helped to identify symptoms that might indicate exacerbation of the depression, learn how to handle suicidal ideation and threats, and move toward acceptance that hospitalization may be necessary. Workshop models may either include the family member who is suffering from depression or be for families alone. Both approaches have the goals of modifying the interaction between family members, focusing on individual and family strengths, pointing out options and choices, and emphasizing that there is hope for change.

There is no setting in which social workers are employed where they will not encounter depression, whether reactive or of long standing. There is no one cause of mood disorders and no one way to treat them. Genetics, life experiences, stressors, and individual personality are factors that may predispose an individual to these disorders. Depression may cover the spectrum, from a transient sad mood to an incapacitating major depression. Thus it would appear that mood disorders must be looked at as a range of syndromes that, in each case, need careful assessment followed by case-indicated intervention.

Social workers assessing individuals from the ecosystems perspective should proceed with research that might help to classify causes of depression, population groups that might have greater vulnerability, and possibly relationships to life events, in order to suggest paths to prevention. Although it is known that there is a relationship between stress and depression and that depression is more likely to occur after stressful life events, particularly those involving loss ("exit events"), further research is needed to explore why some individuals are more vulnerable to depression than are others who experience the same stressors.

4   Somatoform and Factitious Disorders

All of us are aware of the close relationship of mind and body. We have all experienced "aches and pains" that have no apparent organic cause, and many of us have experienced physical symptoms while also being aware of feelings of anxiety or depression. In a given week, 80 percent of *healthy* people are believed to experience somatic symptoms (Kellner 1991a). Somatic symptoms range from common, transient symptoms, such as mild headaches, fatigue, or back pain, to chronic, incapacitating, and extremely distressing symptoms. It has been estimated that up to 30 percent of visits to internists or primary care physicians are responses to symptoms caused by a mental disorder rather than a physical disease. It is still more acceptable to many people to acknowledge a physical disorder than a mental disorder, and doctors frequently pursue the medical route while ignoring the possibility of an emotional cause.

As early as 1900 B.C. ancient Egyptians described what would today be classified as somatoform disorders. "Hysteria" was believed to be caused by upward dislocation of the uterus, which then displaced other organs, resulting in the development of multiple physical symptoms. The treatment goal was to return the uterus to its rightful place (Smith 1990). Early Greek medicine attributed the etiology of many illnesses to the relationship between the individual's four *humors* (juices) and *pneuma* (spirit/soul). Other variables influencing illness included hygiene, climate, diet, and exercise. The Greeks recognized disorders termed *hysteria* and *hypochondriasis* that involved physical and behavioral symptoms. Their diagnoses can be considered forerunners to what are now regarded as somatization disorders. Belief in the "wandering uterus" continued and was seen as the cause of hysterical symptoms. Until the seventeenth century, when a physician, Thomas Sydenham, discounted this theory and identified an emotional origin, the womb was seen as an important factor in the etiology of hysteria (Smith 1990).

The pejorative distinction between physical and mental disorders is a rather recent development in medical history. In earlier societies, if stigma was attached to illness, it was based on etiology and social interpretation, such as whether the illness was caused by witchcraft or by punishment from, most often, the deceased (Fabrega 1991). The idea of nervous energy or nervous "forces" playing a part in the etiology of illness began in the seventeenth century. William Cullen, in the eighteenth century, coined the term *neurosis* to refer to this energy, or force, which caused a range of "nervous diseases" that might be medical, neurological, or psychiatric (Fabrega 1991). As psychiatry became more differentiated, so did disorders such as hypochondriasis, hysteria, and neurasthenia, which were then regarded as psychological rather than organic. In 1859 a French physician, Briquet, studied a group of patients who experienced chronic, multiple physical symptoms without the presence of a medical disease. This phenomenon, later termed Briquet's syndrome, is now known as somatization disorder. As discussed in the chapter on dissociative disorders, both Janet and Freud studied the disorder known as "hysteria." In addition, Freud used the term *conversion* to define what he believed was the transformation of repressed nervous energy, associated with unexpressed emotion, into physical symptoms (Kirmayer and Robbins 1991c). A series of studies in the 1950s and 1960s ended the traditional association between dissociative hysteria and conversion, but it was not until the publication of *DSM-III* that psychiatry officially recognized the existence of a disorder, somatoform, that, while manifested in physical symptoms, actually has psychosocial origins. *DSM-III* discontinued the category of *hysterical neurosis* used in *DSM-II*, choosing to divide manifestations of this disorder into two new categories of disorders with hysterical neurosis, *conversion type*, falling under somatoform disorders, while hysterical neurosis, *dissociative type*, falling under dissociative disorders. Some view this separation as questionable. *DSM-IV*, which does not use the term *neurosis*, continues this separation, labeling the somatoform disorder as *conversion disorder*.

Somatoform disorders present problems for the person who suffers from them and who is frequently stigmatized and viewed as a malingerer. The family often is impatient with chronic physical complaints, the employer may resent frequent absenteeism, and the physician may feel frustrated and ineffectual in treating people with these disorders. Somatization disorders represent a serious public health problem, because they are a major cause of overutilization of inpatient and outpatient medical services, as well as a leading cause of absenteeism, limits on job activity, and disability claims.

Social workers, who are accustomed to biopsychosocial assessment, can play an important role in helping to identify and provide services for people with these disorders. As a result of their training, social workers may be more sensitive than physicians and nurse practitioners—whose training emphasizes physical symptomatology—to stresses in the environment as well as to the symptoms of depression and anxiety. A study of social workers in a primary care setting showed that a routine, thorough assessment of patients in the setting, coming for an annual checkup or presenting with physical symptoms, resulted in social service intervention in 50 percent of the cases. Eleven percent were then seen for concrete services, 62 percent for supportive intervention, and 27 percent for a combination of concrete and supportive services (Miller et al. 1984). Additional data indicated that social service intervention led to less frequent visits to medical care providers, thus freeing up their time to treat patients with documented medical problems (Miller and Austrian 1980).

Definitions

Somatization is the process, usually unconscious, through which emotional stress, psychiatric or psychosocial, is experienced and communicated as physical distress. It represents an idiosyncratic abnormal pattern of illness behavior and implies that in the absence of organic disease, there is some underlying emotional process that is being somatized. The body or bodily symptoms are used for psychological purposes or personal gain (Folks, Ford, and Houck 1998).

Somatoform disorders are defined as those disorders in which a person experiences physical symptoms, suggesting medical disease, in the absence of any organic disease. Symptoms cause distress or impairment in major areas of functioning. These unexplained symptoms are related to underlying psychiatric or psychosocial problems, with emotional problems presenting in the form of somatic illnesses. With the exception of somatization disorder, somatoform disorders can be viewed as patterns of reaction symptoms resulting from some underlying pathology that needs exploration (Kirmayer and Robbins 1991c). The person feels no control over the presence of the symptoms. Somatoform disorders can occur concomitantly with medical disorders. They are often chronic and debilitating.

Functional symptoms are physical symptoms that have no accepted organic explanation. They represent a disturbance of physiological function rather than of anatomical structure (Kirmayer and Robbins 1991c). Psychosocial stress and psychological conflicts are presumed to cause or to exacerbate these symptoms. These symptoms are experienced as just as real as those of organic origin.

Somatization disorder is a chronic psychiatric disorder with multiple, recurrent, unexplained medical symptoms or a situation in which complaints about, or impairment from, the symptoms far exceed what would be expected. DSM-IV requires at least four pain symptoms, two gastrointestinal symptoms, one sexual symptom, and one pseudoneurological symptom to establish this diagnosis (American Psychiatric Association 1994). It is regarded as the most serious of the somatoform disorders.

Conversion disorder is defined as the involuntary loss or change in sensory and motor functions so that the symptom(s) appear to be those of a physical or neurological disorder such as deafness, blindness, loss of consciousness, seizures, paralysis, or loss of sensation, but is caused by unconscious psychiatric or psychosocial stressors, not by physical disease. This is the classic disorder that fascinated Freud, who referred to it as *hysterical neurosis* (Waldinger 1990), the prototype neurosis.

Body dysmorphic disorder is a perception of, or excessive preoccupation with, an imagined physical defect or an exaggerated distortion of a minimal or minor defect in a person who appears normal to others.

Pain disorder involves a preoccupation with pain in the absence of physical disease, or, if there is an organic cause, the pain is experienced in excess of what would be expected. The pain is sufficiently severe as to significantly impair social and vocational functioning.

Pain is neither a purely physiological nor a purely psychological state (Mufson 1999) and requires a multidisciplinary assessment.

Hypochondriasis as a disorder ranges from excessive concern about possibly contracting a physical disease to the firm conviction that one has the disease. It results from unrealistic or inaccurate interpretation of physical symptoms or sensations. There may be an acute, transient symptom or a chronic sensitivity to bodily symptoms resulting in impaired functioning. It is not as intense a preoccupation as is a delusion.

Factitious illness is the conscious presentation of physical symptoms when the person is aware of no organic cause. The person misrepresents history and symptoms, and apparently derives satisfaction from being considered ill and intentionally misleads the medical care providers. There is often a compulsive quality to this disorder (Frances, Clarkin, and Perry 1984). Factitious illness is not real, genuine, or natural.

Munchausen syndrome is the prototype of factitious disorders, named after an eighteenth-century German soldier who was a notorious fabricator. People with this disorder go from hospital to hospital, often in different cities, giving lengthy untrue medical histories. They are frequently admitted to hospitals and undergo unnecessary surgical procedures. This syndrome is the most extreme factitious disorder, characterized by pathological lying, simulation of disease, and wandering (Folks, Ford, and Houck 1998:368)

A variant is *Munchausen syndrome by proxy*, in which a parent makes up a false medical history for a child and subjects the child to many medical tests and hospitalization. The variant is a form of child abuse and must be reported to child welfare authorities (Iezzi and Adams 1993).

Malingering is also a intentional presentation of physical or psychological symptoms for which there is no organic cause, or an exaggeration of symptoms or disabilities. The purpose is usually to use illness to avoid some task, legal action, or commitment, or to obtain disability or other insurance benefits, and often this intent can be inferred by the observer.

Epidemiology

Statistics show that women are nine times more likely than men to experience somatoform disorders. This may be because women are generally believed to be more attuned to their bodies and less reluctant to recognize and report symptoms. Only hypochondriasis is found equally in men and women. Studies have also shown that people of lower socioeconomic status and with less education are more likely to perceive distress in terms of physical rather than emotional symptoms. This is particularly true for the Hispanic population, where there is great stigma associated with mental disorders, which are perceived as an indication of weakness. Nonmarried people, especially those who live alone, also have a greater prevalence of somatoform disorders than do married people (Robbins and Kirmayer 1991).

A study at six sites indicated that somatization disorder had an average prevalence of 0.1 percent (Escobar et al. 1991). Hypochondriasis is much more common, affecting 8 percent of the general population (Robbins and Kirmayer 1991). The lifetime incidence of isolated conversion symptoms may be as high as 25 to 33 percent; however, the incidence of conversion disorders seen by psychiatrists is as low as 0.01–0.02 percent (Barsky 1989). Pain, especially lower back pain, is one of the most frequent medical complaints, and its origin is often difficult to detect, thus making it hard to determine the prevalence of somatoform pain disorder.

Munchausen syndrome is twice as common in men as in women. Mothers are more often involved in Munchausen by proxy than are fathers (Iezzi and Adams 1993).

Assessment

It must be noted that people who have somatoform disorders are really experiencing the reported symptoms and are in physical distress. While assessment may strongly suggest that the cause is psychiatric or psychosocial, it is also important that the person have a thorough physical examination and that the person making the psychosocial assessment work closely with those making the medical assessment. Most often, the psychogenic etiology of the symptoms is determined through inference, rather than through direct statements from the person with the disorder, but assessment must be careful and thorough, so as to avoid arriving at unwarranted conclusions. It may be hard to distinguish whether psychosocial factors cause, coexist with, or are the consequences of somatic symptoms. Since there is no question that stress exacerbates physical symptoms, assessment must carefully evaluate current stressors in the person's environment. Studies have shown that psychosocial stress may decrease immune competency and thus predispose a person to infection, as well as induce somatization (Kellner 1991a). Somatoform disorders are very difficult to distinguish from medical disorders and often from each other, and there is a danger that a person, without a very careful biopsychosocial assessment, will be caught in limbo between health and mental health services. Illness, for some, may be a means to find a solution to their personal, work, or financial problems.

People with somatoform disorders usually present in one of three ways: (1) with exclusively physical symptoms in spite of demonstrable mental or psychosocial problems; (2) convinced of the presence of a physical illness, or excessively worried about contracting a disease, with no evidence of a disease nor valid cause for concern; or (3) seeking confirmation of disability for financial or personal gain. Studies have shown that negative *affectivity*, defined as the presence of negative mood and self-concept, pessimism, dissatisfaction, and trait anxiety, is highly correlated with hypervigilance about

the body and with reporting of physical sensations and symptoms of unknown origin (Pennebaker and Watson 1991). It is also useful to get a history
of the family of origin's response to illness: sickness may have offered the
only way to get positive, nurturing attention. It is important to determine
how illness is regarded by those in the person's immediate environment.

Conversion disorder has usually been found to occur when the individual
is under considerable stress, often from interpersonal conflict. It is experienced as ego-alien, with the person perceiving the symptom as involuntary;
"something is happening to me." It is difficult to make an accurate assessment of a conversion disorder, as conversion symptoms may occur as an
unexplained medical symptom or a symptom of somatization disorder, rather
than an isolated acute symptom. It is rare that there is only one episode of
conversion disorder, and there also often is a history of unexplained somatic
symptoms. Assessment should include exploration for possible secondary
gain.

Assessment of a somatization disorder should reveal a history of unexplained medical symptoms that usually begins in adolescence with the onset
of menarche. The symptoms usually are gastrointestinal, menstrual or sexual, cardiopulmonary, musculoskeletal pain, or neurological. The person
will give a history of outpatient "doctor shopping," inpatient stays, past sur-
geries, medication use, impairment of social and vocational functioning,
seeking disability benefits, or suspected iatrogenic disease. Perceived poor
health usually began in adolescence and has often impaired all aspects of
the person's social, physical, emotional, and vocational life. What may suggest that persons are suffering from somatization disorder is self-reporting
indicating that they see themselves as sicker than they appear and mention
of more signs and symptoms than usually described by people with chronic
diseases such as rheumatoid arthritis, diabetes, hypertension, or cardiopulmonary problems. People with this disorder see themselves as among the
sickest in the general population and as disabled. Depression and anxiety
are often present, and the sufferers frequently abuse alcohol, possibly as a
way of self-medicating. A person with somatization disorder focuses on symptoms rather than on disease.

People suffering from hypochondriasis will express fear of having, or of
possibly contracting, a serious disease. They are hypervigilant about signs or
bodily sensations and will interpret them to be symptomatic of a particular
disease or group of diseases. The concern expressed is usually not so much
about the symptoms themselves but rather about the implications of the
symptoms, i.e., what disease is indicated. Although many physicians suspect

this diagnosis, because of its pejorative nature this is rarely the primary diagnosis (Noyes et al. 1993).

People with somatoform pain disorder are usually preoccupied with their bodies, and pain will be the focus of their attention. The experience of pain often causes depression or anxiety, which then may further exacerbate the symptom.

A very important area to explore is to what degree the person suffering from a somatoform disorder *wants* to get better, what giving up the physical symptoms will involve, and what may be the "secondary gain." People with somatization disorders may use their symptoms to control and manipulate others, to hold on to a relationship, or to divert attention from other problematic aspects of their lives. Asking how illness was handled in childhood may help the social worker to understand how the client expects others to respond to physical complaints. Some clients may experience *alexithymia*, a deficit in articulating needs or in experiencing and expressing emotions except through physical symptoms, which may be vague and poorly described (Taylor 1989).

Assessment to identify factitious disorder or malingering would reveal that the person is *conscious* of deliberately deluding the medical provider. There is usually an overreporting of symptoms, especially of those that are rare or particularly severe. Questions should be directed toward determining why the sick role is preferred, as well as toward the secondary gain of choosing the particular symptoms. History may show that people with this disorder often do not cooperate with the process of medical evaluation or with prescribed treatment. It is helpful to get information from family members about the person's activities and behavior when not in a medical setting or when unaware of being observed for validation of the assessment. Persons with Munchausen syndrome are more concerned with seeking medical services than with the possibility of "cure." They appear to want the identity of a patient. When a child is a victim of Munchausen by proxy, it is difficult not to be struck by the lack of concern shown by the parent(s) about symptoms and the emphasis on the medical procedures being sought.

Clinical Course

People suffering from somatoform disorders rarely make a connection between their somatic complaints and their psychiatric or psychosocial problems, and if their medical provider is not attuned to looking for the latter problems, they may go unnoticed. This oversight can lead to an increased use of medical examinations, tests, and even surgery.

It is estimated that approximately 50 percent of people suffering from somatization disorder are medically hospitalized in a given year and that their health care utilization is nine times greater than that of the general population (Smith 1990). This overutilization of medical resources would be avoided if a proper diagnosis had been made. If not properly assessed and if there is no mental health intervention, the prognosis is poor, because somatization disorder, when untreated, is chronic and prone to relapse. Onset is usually in middle to late adolescence, a typical episode lasts six to nine months, and remission is usually between nine and twelve months in duration.

People with hypochondriasis are more apt to respond to reassurance from physicians, and thus are less likely to overuse medical services than are people with other somatoform disorders (Robbins and Kirmayer 1991). However, if a person has a combination of somatoform disorders involving a history of multiple, unexplained somatic symptoms and a belief in a vulnerability to contracting illness, then the prognosis for successful intervention is poor, and use of medical services is greatly increased.

The presence of a somatoform disorder can cause secondary problems for the individual. Studies have shown that a person suffering from this disorder will probably experience greater physical suffering when he or she actually *does* contract a physical disease. In addition, somatoform disorders are often accompanied by secondary depression or anxiety.

Differential Diagnosis

Studies have shown that 20 to 30 percent of medical patients have psychiatric symptoms and diagnoses, most often depression or anxiety (Simon 1991). There is a positive correlation between depression and somatic symptoms: people who suffer from somatoform disorders tend to be more depressed than do people with documented physical disorders. There is also a correlation between anxiety disorders, particularly generalized anxiety and panic disorders, and somatic symptoms (Kellner 1991a). For people with somatoform disorders, assessment often will indicate that, rather than suffering only from symptoms that may be classified with either/or diagnoses, the person may be suffering "parallel" disorders. That is, in addition to suffering the somatoform disorder, they may also be suffering an anxiety or mood disorder, or a "real" medical illness. People with a primary diagnosis of an anxiety or mood disorder usually do not have a lengthy history of, or multiple, unexplained somatic symptoms.

People who appear to have body dysmorphic disorder in a mild degree of severity may actually be experiencing social anxiety or problems with self-esteem. If the symptoms are unusually intense, consideration should be given to assessing for a major depression, schizophrenia, paranoid disorder, or organic brain syndrome.

Depression may, in a small number of people, result in pain that may be misdiagnosed as somatoform pain disorder. If the person is given antidepressant medication, the pain should diminish if the primary diagnosis is depression. Antidepressants have also been found to be effective in reducing physical pain with a defined organic base.

Some somatic syndromes seen in medical settings do not have identifiable organic causes and suggest an emotional component either coexisting with, or causing, the disorder. Among these are fibromyalgia, irritable bowel syndrome, and chronic fatigue syndrome. Fibromyalgia involves chronic musculoskeletal pain and stiffness, similar to rheumatoid arthritis, but people with this disorder generally seek out more medical attention and present with a broader range of symptoms. Irritable bowel syndrome is characterized by abdominal pain and distention, and change in bowel habits. Studies have shown a high rate of major psychosocial problems and stressful life events, especially marital, financial, and vocational, in people with irritable bowel syndrome. People with this syndrome also frequently suffer symptoms of depression and anxiety. It is not clear what causes chronic fatigue syndrome. Although more credence is being given to the presence of an acute viral infection as the cause, depression, anxiety, stressful lifestyle, and alcoholism have also been cited as causes. Inadequate knowledge may result in such syndromes' being considered functional, and clearly more research is needed before identifying these functional somatic syndromes as falling within the category of somatization disorder (Kirmayer and Robbins 1991b). Since the etiology of these syndromes is so unclear, people suffering from them may also experience self-doubt, worry, and even lack of support from close friends or family because of the ambiguity of the illness. The intervention plan must address both the physiological dysfunction and the emotional distress.

There are several additional diseases, including multiple sclerosis, lupus erythematosus, and hyperparathyroidism, that present complex symptomatolgy and may be misdiagnosed as a somatization disorder because the symptoms alternate between remission and presence. Care must be given to the particular combination of symptoms that are signs of the disease before making a diagnosis (Smith 1990). Laboratory tests are also indicated.

Etiology

There are varied theories about the etiology of somatoform disorders, which remains very unclear. What is clear, however, is that there is a relationship between mind and body and that distress in one often affects the other.

Physically, some people may be more sensitive to sensory stimuli and have a low tolerance for pain. A person who has had a serious, documented physical illness in the past, accompanied by anxiety or depression, may become hypervigilant to physical symptoms and perhaps more vulnerable to suffering from hypochondriasis.

It is possible that overconcern with physical symptoms may be, in part, learned behavior. People suffering from somatoform disorders may have been raised by family members who also had a history of chronic, unexplained physical symptoms, or they may have learned that certain needs were met only when a person articulated the presence of physical symptoms. Such people may then develop a hypervigilance and sensitivity to bodily sensations, as well as a greater tendency to call attention to the symptoms.

Cognitive theory suggests that people who suffer from somatoform disorders may actually experience more intense body awareness, preoccupation with, and attention to, sensations and symptoms, and also have a greater tendency to worry. In addition, studies have shown a high correlation between negative affectivity and hypochondriasis (Robbins and Kirmayer 1991).

The original psychoanalytic explanation of somatoform disorders was that the physical symptoms permitted expression of distress while keeping unacceptable thoughts, feelings, and impulses out of conscious awareness. More recent psychodynamic thinking still views the symptoms as largely ineffective defenses against depression and anxiety. Some studies have suggested that unexpressed hostility and anger may make a person more vulnerable to developing somatic symptoms of unknown physical origin. Developing somatic symptoms may be felt to be the only way to get attention, and people with somatoform disorders may use their illness to manipulate others. Finally, people who were childhood trauma victims have been found to have more adult physical symptoms if they have tended to hide their experiences. Pelvic pain and abdominal functional symptoms are more common in women who have a history of sexual abuse than in the general population (Kellner 1991a).

Family studies found somatization disorders in 10 to 20 percent of first-degree female relatives of women who also suffer from this disorder, which may be attributable to social, economic, and cultural factors (Barsky 1989).

Intervention

People with somatoform disorders are usually very reluctant to seek intervention by mental health professionals, clearly preferring to recognize physical rather than emotional causes of their distress, and, if they are experiencing anxiety or depression, they see that as a consequence of the physical. Others may seek intervention in order to get support for their disability and to obtain benefits. Many respond to the suggestion of intervention with annoyance, frustration, or skepticism, and may seek other medical opinions, feeling that they have been misunderstood.

Before referral for mental health services, the person will need to be helped to understand that the referral is not a rejection and that the physical symptoms are accepted as real and not "all in your head." This is a process that will take time and persistence, and it can be effective only if a trusting relationship has been established between the physician or social worker and the person with the disorder. Recognition and acceptance must be given to the suffering caused by the symptoms, as well as the reassurance that mental health services are an adjunct to continued medical visits. The person should be assured that the medical and mental health professionals will communicate regularly to better help him or her. Reassurance is the primary technique used in working with people with somatoform disorders, and they need to understand that the mental health professional will try to help with the emotional consequences of unpleasant physical symptoms.

Management of a chronic condition must be a fundamental goal of intervention. If it is assessed that the presented physical symptoms seen in a person with a somatoform disorder are "masking" an anxiety disorder or an affective disorder, then intervention should be geared toward alleviating the depression or anxiety through psychotherapy and medication, as indicated.

If the depression or anxiety is the primary diagnosis, it is expected that, with intervention, the physical symptoms will abate or at least diminish in intensity.

Cognitive and behavioral techniques can be used with people suffering from somatoform disorders. These techniques focus on giving support, providing education about symptoms, learning relaxation and distraction techniques to lessen attention to symptoms, and developing better skills to handle life stresses.

Assessment of the family's attitude toward illness is important when intervening with people suffering from somatoform disorders. The family may resent and be angered by the somatization or may actually reinforce it. Intervention should be directed toward helping the family to understand the disorder, to tolerate aspects of the person's behavior, and to learn to respond appropriately, without guilt, to excessive demands to listen to or care for the person. Studies have shown that hypochondriasis tends to be more prevalent in people who frequently speak to family members about their health and who engender concern about the possibility of a serious illness, thus perhaps resulting in secondary gain.

Groups with a supportive, rather than insight, orientation have been helpful for some people suffering from somatoform disorders. The social support of the group can lead to decrease in utilization of medical services. Social workers can be helpful in educating group members about services that may be available to them and in facilitating discussion to focus on ways of coping with symptoms rather than on complaints.

Medication is useful when assessment indicates the presence of anxiety or depression that may be exacerbating physical symptoms or compounding the distress. If medication is given, it is important to educate the person about the coexistence of physical and emotional disorders and to note that attention is needed for both. People need to be informed about possible side effects of the medication, but the nature of somatoform disorders requires very careful monitoring. The possibility that "knowledge" could cause additional functional symptoms means that medication should be used sparingly.

Because factitious disorders and malingering are consciously induced, the prognosis for intervention is very poor.

Assessment of and intervention planning for people with somatoform disorders is clearly difficult and involves close communication between providers of physical and mental health care. Diagnosed physical illness and somatization can coexist, as can somatoform disorders and mood or anxiety disorders. Interaction of emotional and physical symptoms is complex, and at times it is unclear what is cause and what is effect. It would appear that a vicious cycle is not uncommon where a mood or anxiety disorder intensifies awareness of somatic symptoms that may cause intensification of the emotional symptoms.

In this era of concern about health and mental health costs, it is clear that social workers who have been trained to make biopsychosocial assessments can play a prominent role. The interaction of psyche (mind) and soma (body) is strong, and distress in one area affects the other, as clearly shown in people suffering from somatoform disorders. Inclusion of social workers on primary health care teams would help in early identification of psychosocial stressors and lead to the most appropriate use of medical services.

5　Dissociative Disorders

We all experience moments of dissociation. We ask ourselves how we "got there so fast," speak of "spacing out" or "feeling like I was watching myself as I gave my presentation," or find ourselves daydreaming when we should have been listening. There are a range of dissociative experiences, from those experienced by everyone to severe dissociative identity disorder (previously known as multiple personality disorder). Dissociative identity disorder is one of the most controversial mental disorders and is subject to intense skepticism. The literature ranges from passionate discourses recognizing it as a *real* psychiatric disorder to equally passionate claims that it does not exist.

While dissociative identity disorder is very rarely encountered in clinical practice, as more attention is paid to the prevalence of sexual abuse of children—the core trauma believed to be the etiology of dissociative identity disorder—clinicians need to consider this as a *possible* diagnosis. A word of caution, however, is indicated. Childhood sexual abuse is often hard to document, as it usually is reported when the person is an adult, memories may be vague or inaccurate, and there is often little opportunity to get information from others in the family of origin, so accurate assessment must be handled by skilled, experienced, unbiased clinicians. Another concern may be the bias of the clinician, who may be overzealous in looking for evidence of sexual abuse and may inadvertently lead the client, especially one who may be highly suggestible or eager to please, to "remember" incidents that did not occur. Clinicians must be knowledgeable about the processes of memory and repression and must also recognize their potential power to direct client thinking. Since "recovered" memories may not always be accurate, it is important to obtain some supporting evidence from outside sources; while sexual abuse certainly occurs, so do false accusations that can lead to serious family disruption and even litigation. We all have different capacities for remembering and forgetting, and memories may include truth, partial truth, and distortion. Clinicians and clients ought to acknowledge this and not draw conclusions about abuse just from a set of symptoms.

The debate about recovered memory continues, with political overtones. Defenders say that opponents encourage a backlash against the rights of abused women, and feminism in general, choosing to view women as gullible, passive, and able to be manipulated by their therapists, and by denying the validity of recovered memories promote the regressive "blaming the victim." Opponents accuse proponents of providing false explanations for vague and ambiguous symptoms and allowing the client to assume a victim stance, blaming shortcomings and problems on others. They are concerned that as a result of what they refer to as "false memory syndrome," families have been destroyed and actual experiences of child abuse are discredited (*Harvard Mental Health Letter* 1999:August). The controversy extends also to whether the focus of the intervention should be on investigating childhood with the accompanying reconstruction of the past or on the client's present and future. The limitations that managed care places on number of sessions, of course, encourages intervention that is more present-oriented.

Myths, legends, religion, and literature all refer to transformation of identity in order to have power, be invulnerable, and to have the tools to cope better. Children, exposed to comics, television, and movies, as well as through their own imagination, often believe in their "ability" to change identity for brief periods of time. Images of shamans, changed into animals or embodying spirits, may be found in Paleolithic cave paintings and contemporary Eskimo art (Putnam 1989). The shaman, trained to be a master of self-hypnosis, displays many of the features of dissociative identity disorder, yet is not considered to have a mental disorder. Demon possession was a maladaptive form of identity transformation common among Christians from the Middle Ages into the mid-nineteenth century. A usually polite, devout person would suddenly be "possessed" by a demon personality who would be insulting and blasphemous. The "cure" for possession was exorcism, involving theological debate, threats, and commands between the exorcists and the demon. At the end of the process, there was a culturally sanctioned, religious integration ritual. By the middle of the nineteenth century cases were noted in which the person was possessed not by a demon but by a dead relative or neighbor and help was sought from physicians rather than clergy (Ross 1989).

Psychiatric literature includes descriptions of two cases, one seen in 1789 and one in 1815 (Greaves 1993), which would be diagnosed today as dissociative identity disorder. This disorder did not generate real interest among mental health professionals until the late nineteenth century. In France, Charcot and Janet studied hypnosis and hysteria, a common diagnosis used for women. Janet studied patients with amnesia, fugue states, and what he referred to as "successive existences" that were capable of independent lives, although there is some question about whether these "existences" may have been iatrogenic. He thought that trauma caused the symptoms, that treatment would involve bringing split-off memories into consciousness (Ross 1989), and that the splitting of mental functions was the basis of hysteria. In America, William James and Morton Prince recognized, and supported investigation of, the phenomenon of plurality of selves. Prince, who has been described as the "father of multiple personality syndrome" saw it as similar to hysteria (North et al. 1993). In 1895 Freud and Bleuler published *Studies on Hysteria*, describing cases of women with dissociative disorders (which they referred to as hysteria) whom they felt had been victims of childhood sexual abuse. Within a couple of years, however, Freud repudiated his seduction hypothesis in favor of his theory that amnesia and hysterical symptoms resulted from repression of intolerable affects or drives. Patients exhibiting dissociative disorders were believed to have unresolved incestuous fantasies—another example of "blaming the victim." Freud also repudiated his early belief in the usefulness of hypnosis and broke with Jung over Jung's interests in parapsychology and dissociation. Freud's theories, which tended to blame the mother and ignore the father and viewed masochism as a core female trait, were to have a major influence on the study and treatment of women.

Freud's work, leading to the psychoanalytic model with its emphasis on repression, together with Bleuler's work on "the schizophrenias," taken from a Greek word meaning "splitting of the mind," led to a long period during which little attention was paid to the concept of dissociative disorders as a separate clinical entity. People who today might be diagnosed as having dissociative identity disorder were probably misdiagnosed as suffering from schizophrenia.

In the twentieth century, multiple personality disorder was viewed as extremely rare, almost nonexistent. Over the past twenty-five years, there has been renewed interest in dissociative disorders, springing from a renewed interest in hypnosis as a therapeutic tool, the increased awareness of post-traumatic stress, and the efforts of the women's movement, which forced greater recognition of the frequency and impact of abuse of children and women. Identification of sexual abuse by the victim, although its prevalence is not accurately known, occurs more frequently and openly as women recognize that there is no reason to feel shame, to protect the abuser, or to expect not to be believed.

As more women report and seek help for physical and sexual abuse, abuse has become recognized as a major public health problem (Waites 1993). Past or continuing abuse may influence all aspects of a person's life, as it was often perpetrated in childhood by people whom the child would have expected to be responsible for his or her safety and well-being. Thus the ability to form relationships, including those in the workplace, may be severely impaired. A small group of clinicians have concentrated their research on dissociative disorders, and in 1980 these disorders were given a category separate from schizophrenia or hysteria in *DSM-III*. In 1984 the first major conference on dissociative disorders was held, and in 1988 the journal *Dissociation* was introduced. Because of its unusual and dramatic characteristics, dissociative identity disorder has grabbed the attention of the media. Books such as *Sybil* and *The Three Faces of Eve*, based on case histories, have become best-sellers, and people claiming to have dissociative identity disorder may be seen on popular TV talk shows.

Clinicians and researchers working with people who suffer from dissociative disorders did not agree with some of the criteria in *DSM-III* and *DSM-III-R*, and several changes appear in *DSM-IV*'s categorical definitions. It is anticipated that criteria will be further refined as greater recognition and acceptance of these disorders take place.

Definitions

Dissociation is an experience, or a discernible process, in which consciousness is disrupted so that what might usually seem to be consistent, continuous, connected, and integrated is compartmentalized into autonomous groups of feelings, memories, and perceptions that may be remembered in a dreamlike, unreal, or vague state or that are repressed and out of conscious awareness. This way of coping defensively with unbearable anxiety related to traumatic events may be a normal, adaptive technique. Dissociation is a psychobiological mechanism that allows the mind to "flee" what the body is experiencing (Waites 1993); it is not attributable to a physical disorder or accident or to substance abuse; it is a self-defense against trauma. Exiled memories may reappear as intrusive images, physical symptoms, nightmares, or reexperiencing the trauma.

Dissociative disorders first appeared as a category in *DSM-III* replacing dissociative hysteria, which was traditionally linked with conversion hysteria and then became a separate, unrelated category (see chapter 4, on somatoform disorders). Dissociative disorders involve disturbances in identity, consciousness, and memory (Nemiah 1993). Disturbances may be gradual, transient, or chronic.

Pathological dissociation occurs when dissociation becomes too intense or frequent and occurs in inappropriate contexts. A person then undergoes a dissociative reaction resulting in an alternating identity, or set of identities, and an accompanying distance from, or loss of, memory for events occurring during the dissociation.

Dissociative defenses allow a person to compartmentalize memories and perceptions in order to separate from a trauma as it occurs and maintain a sense of control in what is actually a situation in which the person is helpless. These defenses are maladaptive in that they delay working through the trauma and putting it in perspective. In addition, while removing the trauma from conscious awareness, the symptoms produced by these defenses are very present. These symptoms serve as defenses against fear, pain, helplessness, and panic (Spiegel 1993b), and while they may have been adaptive when the person was a child, they become maladaptive when adult social and vocational roles demand continuity of memory, behavior, and sense of self.

Dissociative amnesia involves complete amnesia for self-referential information, such as age, name, marital status, occupation, or personal life history. This information may relate to a traumatic or stressful event, or the onset may follow a trauma or a period of depersonalization. The person's general fund of knowledge remains intact, and there may be awareness of an inability to recall information at the time or in retrospect. Such episodes are usually experienced as brief and self-limiting, and there is spontaneous recovery.

Dissociative fugue usually involves sudden, unexpected, and purposeful travel from one's usual environment, accompanied by loss of self-referential information and the assumption of a new identity. Acute trauma is often a precipitant, and the incidence increases in war or following a natural disaster (Putnam 1989). When recovery of the primary identity occurs, there is reciprocal loss of memory for what occurred during the fugue state. The onset is usually sudden, and a single episode is not uncommon, with spontaneous remission.

Dissociative identity disorder (formerly *multiple personality disorder*) is a chronic dissociative disorder whose cause is most often a traumatic event, usually abuse (Kaplan and Sadock 1996). It involves a series of at least two alternating identities, each of which claims to be autonomous and determines behavior, appearance, and attitudes when it is the "dominant" personality. These "alters" may be unaware of the traumatic experience, or they may remember it. A person with this disorder will experience "absences" of varying lengths of time, which routinely correspond to episodes of distinct, organized behavior that others report differs from usual behavior. This disorder is the most dramatic and most serious of all dissociative disorders and involves difficulty in integrating aspects of identity, memory, and consciousness.

Depersonalization is a persistent or recurrent alteration in one's perception of oneself to the extent that one's reality is temporarily lost. There are feelings of unreality, detachment, or estrangement from oneself or one's body. It is ego-dystonic and has been found to occur in life-threatening circumstances, such as during an accident or when one is subjected to prolonged intolerable conditions, such as a concentration camp. The person feels unreal, like an automaton, dead, or like he or she is in a dream. When emerging from this state a person may not recall events, or may state that he or she recalls them as if in a dream.

Depersonalization disorder is identified when episodes of depersonalization impair functioning or cause the person emotional distress. Impairment may range from slight to severe. The person may report perceived changes in body; feeling that some physical or mental functions occur with a "mind of their own"; watching himself or herself from a distance; having memories of events as if they happened to someone else; or an inability to be sure whether a memory represents something that did or did not occur. There are few feelings except those of strangeness or unreality with respect to the self. Onset can be abrupt and recovery gradual.

Derealization may occur together with, or independently from, depersonalization and is experienced as a feeling of being detached from the environment or of feeling unreal.

Out-of-body experiences are not uncommon and frequently are experienced when a person suffers from depersonalization or dissociative identity disorder. They can also occur if a person is unusually physically relaxed and mentally calm. The person experiences the mind, or sense of awareness, as separated from or outside of the body, but in the same location and with some desire to unite. It can also be experienced as the mind detached from the body.

Near-death experiences have been reported in which a person has a transcendental experience when consciousness reportedly enters another dimension or region (Putnam 1989).

Possession states are common in many cultures and have religious or magical undertones. They may take one of two forms: (1) the person loses all awareness of self and speaks for an intruder or (2) the person is aware of self but feels invaded and not in control of speech or behavior.

Alter personalities are not separate people but persistent senses of self with characteristic affects, values, behaviors, and history. They often react to the same stimuli in dramatically different ways. They may be of different ages and gender and refer to different kinds of relationships with different family members, work associates, and friends. The personalities arise as a defense against overwhelming trauma.

The *host personality* is usually the one who is in control most of a given time period and is almost always the personality that is identified at the onset of intervention. While usually one personality, what sometimes emerges in the course of intervention is that it is made up of several "alters" who cooperate.

Trauma is a psychological wound caused by an event or experience, often a threat to survival, that is outside the norm of human experience and coping abilities and would be upsetting to almost anyone. It is usually dangerous, painful, or life-threatening, such as a natural disaster, war, or a physical assault. The person experiencing the trauma feels a loss of control over environment, body, and any sense of invulnerability (Spiegel 1993b).

Abreaction is the emotional release following the recall of an intolerable, painful event that has been wholly or partially repressed. The process can be extremely painful for both client and clinician. It involves first the disclosure of material about the experience on an informational level, followed by a reliving of the memory of the event in the presence of the clinician. This is not an exact replay of the experience but rather a dissociative memory and should convince the clinician that this event did occur. Abreactions by multiple alters cannot be faked (Ross 1989, 1997).

Epidemiology

Psychogenic amnesia is believed to be fairly common, while psychogenic fugue is rare. There have been no large-scale studies of the prevalence of dissociative identity disorder, but it is felt that although rare, it is probably more prevalent than previously thought and often is improperly diagnosed. While dissociative disorders usually come to the attention of mental health professionals when the person is an adult, the process begins when the trauma occurred, often in childhood. Many people suffering from this disorder are not properly diagnosed until they are in their middle to late twenties. Dissociative identity disorder has been found nine times as often in women as in men, but that ratio is declining as assessment skills improve. There may also be a sampling bias, since women, in addition to being more likely to seek clinical intervention, experience more ongoing physical and sexual abuse and are more likely to self-mutilate or attempt suicide; thus they are more likely to come to the attention of the mental health system. Men who suffer from dissociative identity disorder often turn their violence outward and come to the attention of the criminal justice system. Studies by Ross (N 236) and Putnam (N 100) were reported by Ross (1989). Ross found that the mean age at which people were diagnosed with MPD was 30.8 years, that the diagnosis was identified after 6.7 years of involvement with the mental health system, and that an average of 2.7 other diagnoses had previously been used. In this sample, 84.3 percent of the females had a mean of 15.7 personalities, 79.2 percent of the sample had been sexually abused, and 74.9 percent suffered other forms of physical abuse. Putnam's sample showed people to have a mean age of 35.8 when diagnosed with MPD after 6.8 years of involvement with the mental health system and an average of 3.6 previous other diagnoses. This sample was 86.7 percent female, the women had a mean of 13.3 personalities, 83 percent of the sample had been sexually abused, and 75 percent suffered other forms of physical abuse.

Assessment

It must be kept in mind that dissociative disorders, in the absence of an organic problem or a reaction to substance abuse, are most often acute, time-limited reactions that resulted from trauma, usually in childhood. An NIMH survey in the mid-1980s (Putnam et al. 1986) showed that people who suffer from multiple personality disorders may also have the transient, self-limiting dissociative experiences of amnesia (98 percent), fugue experiences (55 percent), and feelings of depersonalization (53 percent). This section will refer to assessing dissociative identity disorder, a serious, chronic disorder that will not be resolved without treatment.

The difficulty in assessing dissociative identity disorder can be complicated by the fact that people who may suspect the presence of this disorder are very fearful of being regarded as "crazy." Those who suffer from this disorder often experience a range of physiological, neurological, and medical symptoms and may have received several psychiatric diagnoses for which intervention, often with medication, has proved ineffectual. Thus a history, upon assessment, of inability to alleviate symptoms following intervention should lead the mental health professional to consider a diagnosis of dissociative identity disorder. People with this disorder often seek intervention with presenting problems of psychosomatic symptoms, depression, mood swings, or awareness of fairly frequent changes in the way they behave, which may have been brought to their attention by others. Even though they may be capable of holding high-level jobs, they may often have a history of frequent, sudden job changes. Suicide gestures, or attempts, are not infrequent, nor is a history of insomnia or nightmares. A history of victimization as an adult should lead to exploration of possible childhood abuse.

A proper diagnosis can be made only when the clinician determines that the person experiences alter personalities who can be identified and elicited. The clinician must "meet" at least one alter who is relatively enduring, recognized as unique in behavior, and assumes control from time to time. This process usually takes time, and the revelation may come not in the actual session with the clinician but in a telephone call by "a friend" or in a letter.

Because of the nature of the disorder, it may be very difficult to obtain a history. The clinician must proceed with patience and be prepared for inconsistencies; amnesia, perhaps for events over several years, especially in childhood; and contradiction in chronology, if the history is divided among the alters. History is usually provided initially by the host personality, who may sprinkle the account of the history with "I have a terrible memory" or "I can't tell exactly when that happened." The host may present as depressed, anxious, guilty, compulsively good, and suffering from psychophysiological symptoms as well as from loss or distortion of time (Kluft 1993). The interviewer must listen carefully and be alert to the possibility that the person may confabulate or try to change the subject rather than acknowledge amnesia for people or events. After a relationship has been established and the clinician's probing of the host's memory yields no information, questions need to be asked about gaps in history that appear to represent time loss. The person may give a history of performing erratically in school and being told about missing exams, failing to do homework, or suddenly failing a test when previous tests had received high marks. Flashbacks, intrusive memories, memories of events that the person isn't sure occurred, and nightmares all suggest the possibility of dissociative identity disorder. People may report being called liars as others tell them about observed behavior of which they are unaware. As the alters emerge in the sessions, there may be changes in behavior and appearance, including dress, posture, facial expressions, and mannerisms. Changes in tone of voice, manner of speech, or use of vocabulary may occur. Interview content may change, with amnesia for statements that were previously made, unclear associations, and illogical conclusions. Rather than speaking of the self in the first person singular, the person may refer to "we," "he," or "she."

People suffering from dissociative identity disorder often show a fragile sense of identity and can be asked if they have ever felt like more than one person, if they say or do things that they feel are out of character, or if they ever feel as if they are not alone or are watching themselves in action.

Additional questions that can be helpful in establishing the diagnosis of dissociative identity disorder include:

Have you ever found things in your possession and not known how you happen to have them?
Have you ever found that things you own are missing and you have no idea why?
Do people seem to know you whom you do not seem to know?
Does your handwriting ever seem very different from your usual handwriting?
Do you fail to remember significant periods of time?
Do you ever find yourself somewhere and have no idea how you got there?
Are there large parts of your early life that you do not remember?
Do you hear voices inside your head?

When a relationship of deep trust has been established, questions can be directed toward the alters:

Do you feel that there are other people inside of you who control
   you at times?
Do these people have names?
Do you ever feel that one of these people is dominant in any partic-
   ular circumstance?
Do any of these people have behaviors, occupations, or social rela-
   tionships that the other people do not?
Are all the people the same age and gender?
How often do you think these personalities change?

Clinical Course

Little is known about the life course of persons with dissociative disorders,
as the data have been very spotty and the numbers small. It appears, however,
that dissociative identity disorder diminishes in intensity with age, possibly
because of some reconciliation of the personalities (Putnam 1989) or because of the person's adjustment to, and acceptance of, the emotional
turmoil.

A person seeking intervention often appears overwhelmed, depressed,
anxious, and powerless. Alters may be denied, and a crucial point in the intervention occurs when the person is confronted with the diagnosis and existence of alters. At the time of assessment, usually two to four alters are evident, but in the course of intervention an average of thirteen to fifteen alters
may emerge; the mode is three and the median eight to ten (Kluft 1993). As
the alters emerge, the person may elect not to continue with the intervention. The emergence of the alters may also precipitate self-destructive behavior: the NIMH survey revealed that at least 75 percent of people with the diagnosis of MPD had made one or more suicide attempts and 33 percent
suffered from self-mutilation. Studies have shown a mean of thirteen alters
(Putnam 1989) and that they may be layered, so that new alters emerge as
intervention progresses. The NIMH survey suggested that the greater the
trauma, the larger the number of alters, and that people with large numbers
of alters are highly prone to sociopathic or self-destructive behavior.

If the person continues with the intervention, the initial work should
attempt to stabilize the person and establish communication and cooperation between alters. *Fusion of the alters* refers to the process of the alters'
giving up their separateness, which may occur in steps as groups of alters
fuse. Relapse often occurs at this stage. Integration occurs during fusion and

is complete only when a single personality is identified by the person and the clinician. The core work that follows will identify and work through the trauma(s). When this occurs, the person may, for the first time, have to recognize the pain and suffering that he or she has endured, and a reactive depression to this and to the loss of the alters may occur. Finally, there may be a period of mourning for the alters, as well as a struggle to develop and establish more-adaptive coping skills.

Differential Diagnosis

People suffering from dissociative identity disorder are often misdiagnosed as having an affective disorder, partly because they may be reluctant to discuss the symptoms of the disorder and thus may present with feelings of depression, which is felt to be more acceptable. Careful assessment will show that if the correct diagnosis is dissociative identity disorder, the person usually does not feel depressed for any length of time, and mood swings occur frequently and are of short duration. Furthermore, the vegetative symptoms of depression are absent or, if present, are short-lived. Presenting symptoms may suggest an anxiety disorder, but assessment reveals that these symptoms do not last long, suggesting that they are related to the emergence or switching of alter personalities.

As noted above, interest in schizophrenia as a diagnosis sparked an era when people with dissociative identity disorder frequently were inaccurately diagnosed as suffering from schizophrenia or schizoaffective disorder. People with dissociative identity disorder often experience visual and auditory hallucinations. The voices may command, berate, belittle, support, or advise. They may sound adult or talk and cry like a small child. While people suffering from schizophrenia experience the voices as coming from outside of them, people suffering from dissociative identity disorder hear the voices as coming from within and even report discussions among their personalities. Visual hallucinations may involve body distortion or experiences of watching oneself from above or outside, or they may portray violent, bloody scenes that are trauma-related. If delusions are detected, they tend to relate to a belief that the alters are autonomous people and that harming one will not affect another. This is important to note, as it can lead to suicidal gestures or attempts unless the clinician is able to convince the alters that they are not separate but are part of the whole and that what happens to one happens to all. What may appear to be a thought disorder is usually the result of switching from one personality to another. Rather than appearing as a fairly constant symptom, as in schizophrenia, it is usually transient and related to the cycling of personalities as they vie for control over behavior and affect.

Many people suffering from fugue, depersonalization, or dissociative identity disorder experience severe headaches. What distinguishes these headaches from those with an organic base is a limited response or lack of response to standard headache medications. As with all chronic physical complaints, a physical examination is indicated to rule out organic cause. Other physical complaints that indicate the need for a neurological examination are seizures, sudden blindness or paralysis, and numbness or tingling in arms and legs. Physical diseases that may need to be ruled out are Alzheimer's disease, Huntington's chorea, tumors, or head injuries, in which symptoms of dementia may resemble those of dissociative disorders.

Etiology

Current theory about the etiology of dissociative identity disorder is that it results from repeated, severe, sometimes sadistic, childhood trauma that enhances the individual's normal dissociative capacities to the degree that it provides the foundation for the creation and entrenchment of alter personality states developed over a period of time. An NIMH survey of one hundred people suffering from multiple personality disorder showed that 97 percent of those surveyed had experienced severe childhood trauma involving sexual, physical, or emotional abuse. Sixty-eight percent were incest victims, and most reported multiple traumas. Sexual abuse can range along a continuum from exhibitionism to penetration (Graziano 1992). It must be cautioned that this was retrospective information and that little data have been obtained from children who are being traumatized and are experiencing dissociative identity disorder. Some victims may not have been abused themselves but witnessed repeated physical or sexual abuse of siblings or a parent. The NIMH survey found that a surprisingly large number of those surveyed had witnessed the violent death of a close friend or relative, including instances of one parent murdering the other parent (Putnam 1989).

In a recent study (Mulder et al. 1998) of 1,028 randomly selected adults who were given a face-to-face interview, many reported occasional dissociative symptoms; 6.3 percent reported three or more frequently occurring dissociative symptoms. When the data related to the latter were analyzed and compared with the rest of the sample, sexual abuse was found to be 2.5 times more prevalent, physical abuse was 5 times more prevalent, and current psychiatric disorder 4 times greater in this group than in the rest of the sample. This study raises questions about the relationship of sexual abuse and dissociative identity disorder, thus suggesting the need for further research.

Developmental theory teaches that the individual passes through a series of stages leading to the integration of a sense of self. If a child experiences sustained trauma during the early stages of development, the child who may develop dissociative identity disorder will find it adaptive to compartmentalize affective states and memories associated with the trauma and put them out of conscious awareness. This compartmentalization enables the child to escape from the reality of the trauma and the physical pain that often accompanies it. Unfortunately, it also results in a sense of detachment from the self, which in extreme form enables the development of alter personalities. Kluft (1993) suggests that people who develop dissociative identity disorder did not have adequate soothing and restorative experiences with significant others and thus have inadequate stimulus barriers. The dissociative process may be adaptive and even lifesaving for a child but maladaptive for an adult in establishing a sense of self and dealing with inevitable stress. A child who has been abused cannot form an inner representation of a trusted, available, competent caretaker, and thus does not learn self-soothing and emotional self-regulation. Chronic childhood abuse impedes integration of memory, knowledge, emotions, and bodily experiences, and leads to fragmentation of the personality (Herman 1992). Clearly, abuse disturbs parent–child relationships. Often communication has been faulty, intergenerational ego boundaries are weak, parent–child relationships have been too distant or too intrusive, and frequently there is a history of parental alcoholism.

Feminist theory emphasizes the impact of the patriarchal social structure that sanctioned the subordination of women as the property of men, thus intensifying the potential for abuse (Waites 1993). Acceptance of male authority had the potential for misuse of that authority, resulting in abuse of women and children. In addition, women face added risk for abuse because of their smaller physical stature, society's tendency to scapegoat and demean women, and the sexual exploitation of women in films, television, advertising, and fraternity/locker room "jokes."

Intervention

A person who has been repeatedly abused has a history of low self-esteem, depression, problems with intimacy, feelings of powerlessness, self-blame, and feelings of shame. This scenario is especially likely when the abuse occurred during childhood. Since the abuse has probably been shrouded in secrecy, the person is more often apt to seek intervention for depression, marital problems, substance abuse, poor self-image, somatic complaints, interpersonal problems, or anxiety. The clinician needs to be empathic, honest, and actively interested in listening to whatever the person feels able to discuss. He or she must also resist the temptation to try to hasten the process. These people are highly vulnerable, and it is believed that the diagnosis of dissociative identity disorder may in many cases be iatrogenic, because of overzealous practitioners who may jump to conclusions and also, unfortunately, because of the media's current fascination with this diagnosis. Clinicians should be cautious about accepting this diagnosis; they should have the client evaluated by an expert, and while doing the initial assessment they should be especially careful not to direct the client toward considering the possibility of the existence of alters. If the diagnosis is confirmed, intervention must proceed with the clinician accepting the diagnosis but viewing it with some degree of skepticism.

As is true for all interventions, the first step is to engage the client and form an alliance with the goal of developing better coping skills. Because trauma is usually experienced during childhood and at home, the person has limited ability to trust. It will take time to overcome the client's emotional barriers. The clinician should be available, reliable, and empathic when the person feels in crisis and should demonstrate an ability to listen when painful memories and feelings emerge. As the alters emerge in the course of the intervention, the clinician may find it necessary to establish separate, respectful alliances with each. A contract is helpful in establishing the clinician as predictable; it should include information about scheduling of sessions, what to do in crisis, and the possible consequences of self-destructive behavior. Since the disorder resulted from situations in which the person had no real control but could control only by dissociation, it is especially important that during intervention the person have a real sense of arriving at a mutually-agreed-to contract. Crises may be frequent, but they can also be anticipated once the person is known to the clinician and it is possible to identify events or people that will lead to emergence of alters as defenses against remembering the trauma. Crises thus can be prevented, or at least diminished in intensity. The intervention contract should include a plan to follow if the person feels suicidal and an agreement not to abruptly terminate the intervention.

Studies have shown that at the time that people present for intervention, 80 percent indicate no awareness of alternate personalities (Putnam 1989).

A technique that has been helpful in identifying alters when dissociative identity disorder is suspected has been to extend initial sessions three to eight hours, so that as history is given, the alters emerge. Another technique used in the early stages of intervention is to ask the person to write about activities, thoughts, and behaviors in thirty-minute intervals to identify personality shifts and periods of amnesia. The host may be the most resistant personality to recognizing the presence of alters and, therefore, to accepting the diagnosis of dissociative identity disorder.

After a relationship of trust has been established and the clinician senses that the person is aware of a fragile, variable sense of identity, he or she may ask permission to talk with the "other part of you." The host personality may see this as a threat or be competitive and not permit it. If the clinician begins to learn about an alter, but the alter has not emerged directly, it will be necessary to ask for the alter in terms of behavior, such as, "Can I speak to the part of you that likes to go to bars to meet people?" With persistence on the clinician's part, the host's denial of an alter will yield to discomfort and ultimately to introduction to the alter. Some alters may have a great investment in their autonomy and separateness; others may change function in the course of the intervention.

Almost all alter systems include at least one child alter, who retains the memories and feelings of early traumatic experiences. Child alters often have long periods of continuous awareness and may claim to know the other alters (Kluft 1993). While the child alter is often frightened and apparently suffering from the abuse, other child alters can be love-seeking and speak of the abuser in idealized terms. The child alter often resists integration until the trauma has been disclosed and the role of the alter identified.

Two other common alters are the protector and the persecutor, and they may emerge during sessions or outside of them. The protector serves a defensive function, while the persecutor may induce suicide attempts or self-mutilation. A helper alter may be present and serve as an adviser to the clinician. Interviewing the alters will reveal varying levels of awareness of each other, as well as alliances, relationships, and conflicts. Integration is enhanced by how much information one alter has about another. Alters usually have names that may relate to their function or their primary affect or may be a derivative of the person's original name.

Integration of the personalities is developed through stimulating communication between alters, trying to establish common goals and an acceptable way to achieve them through a recognized decision process, and recognition of how, why, and when switching occurs, so that there can be less competition for time. Cooperative functioning also will diminish periods of amnesia. The clinician may have to function as go-between for the alters until they are able to communicate directly and, if so, must be very careful that these communications are accurate and neutral. Patient, slow work with each alter at each level will eventually lead to a coherent, chronological picture of the traumas.

The core work of intervention is understanding the original trauma and the adaptive role of dissociation in mitigating it. Much of the intervention is concerned with control. The alters vie for control, and in the course of the intervention there is a struggle between the person and the clinician over the continued repression or the emergence of the trauma. Intervention involves uncovering secrets that the person kept in order to survive, and thus it requires that the clinician *not* be secretive, but as open and truthful as possible with respect to intervention. The secrets have often involved loose boundaries within families, so the intervention must also include the establishment of rules and boundaries. Secrets emerging during the intervention should not be kept from any of the alters and whatever the clinician interprets, suggests, or comments on should be addressed to all of them. In this way, the clinician is continuously moving the alters toward integration. Since the dissociative identity disorder developed as a survival mechanism, the person's personality system may try to keep from certain alters information that is perceived as intolerable; the clinician's practice of always addressing all of the alters will make this more difficult. Getting in touch with, and revealing, the secrets will be very difficult, and the person may test the clinician to see if his or her knowledge of the secrets can be tolerated or if it will result in abandonment of the person. The clinician must not rush the process of bringing the traumatic experiences and the associated feelings into conscious awareness and must be alert to the fact that the events may be experienced physically as well as emotionally. In any case, the revelation is very difficult for the person suffering from dissociative identity disorder and for the clinician; it will not really be possible without the development of sufficient stability and integration to overcome the defensive function of the alters. Some people never achieve complete integration but settle for communication and cooperation between the alters. In these cases, the extent and effect of the trauma have not been entirely worked through. Some clinicians have chosen not to strive for integration but rather to enhance cooperation and communication between alters, using family intervention techniques to work with the "family" of alters. Integration must include the realization that the fate of any alter is inextricably linked to that of all the others. Finally, intervention must identify and establish new, adaptive ways of coping and of conflict resolution.

Medication is not used to treat dissociative identity disorder, but it may be necessary to treat secondary symptoms such as anxiety or depression. A problem can occur if an alter opposes taking medication or has some idiosyncratic response.

Group work is usually contraindicated, particularly if it is a heterogeneous group that may not be able to adjust to shifts in personalities. Data on homogeneous groups are sparse. Some report that such groups are helpful in accepting the diagnosis, while others report competition over number of alters and control of the group. Group members also may inadvertently elicit the emergence of additional alters within the session and may not be able to handle more than one abreaction at a time.

Members of the family of origin are usually involved in the trauma, and their actions may have resulted in the development of dissociative identity disorder. The family, with its sanctioned right to privacy, has kept the abuse a "secret" and may have even viewed it as a normal part of family life, reinforcing parental, primarily paternal, authority. Usually it is not helpful to initiate family intervention, especially not until there is some integration, as the family is equated with the traumatic experience. Rather than helping with integration, involving the family may actually reinforce the dissociation and fragmentation. Alters may seek to blame and punish, or want to reconcile and be loved. In either case, disappointment is the usual result. Some people seek out siblings or other relatives to validate their memories of the abuse, but this too can prove disappointing. The family may sabotage the efforts to make the person recognize that the victim is not responsible for the abuse and that the abuser may even have committed criminal acts.

Working with the significant people in the person's current life is an essential adjunct to the person's individual work. The focus needs to be on the present, in order to monitor change that results from the move toward integration and later to help the partner/family understand and handle the results of abreaction. Assessment of the partner is important, in order to determine if there is any secondary gain: for example, one of the person's alters may do things that the partner wishes to do but that the other alters (or the integrated personality) will not do. Education about the disorder and the goals and stages of intervention is also important. It is important to help the children of a person with dissociative identity disorder understand that the disorder probably caused the parent to appear inconsistent and unpredictable. It is also necessary to investigate the possibility that one of the alters may have abused the children.

There is some disagreement about whether dissociative identity disorder is a viable diagnosis; similar controversy surrounds contention about the prevalence of the sexual abuse of children. Critics feel that *both* ersatz dissociative identity disorder and recovered memories of sexual abuse can be prompted by overzealous clinician suggestions. In addition, dissociative identity disorder could possibly afford a defendant an insanity defense. Very good assessment skills are necessary, and initial intervention planning must be based primarily on facts, not intuition. It must be cautioned that there has been a proliferation of "recovery specialists," who may not have specialized training and who elicit "memories" through techniques, including hypnosis and suggestion, that at times result in false charges of sexual abuse. Initial assessment must be confirmed by a clinician who has training in assessing dissociative identity disorder; only after that confirmation should a plan for intervention be determined.

If careful assessment results in a diagnosis of a dissociative disorder, the clinician involved must remember that these disorders, especially dissociative identity disorder, are not diseases. They are maladaptive attempts to cope with overwhelming trauma. People seeking intervention for dissociative identity disorder go through tremendous pain, and some are unable to progress beyond the point at which alters are able to communicate and cooperate with each other. If the alters achieve this level of communication, the clinician's next step is to attempt fusion, which involves removing the dissociative barriers that have separated the alters. Successful completion of this step is followed by integration of the personality. Finally, the person, having given up dissociation, must establish more varied, flexible, and adaptive coping mechanisms. Both the person and the clinician must be strongly committed to the often painful process of reconstruction. The commitment may be rewarding, however, since the disorder has a good prognosis if the patient can tolerate identification and exploration of the core trauma(s).

6   Schizophrenia

Schizophrenia has been called the "cancer of mental illness," because we do not know what causes it or how to prevent it. In the 1990s there have been some developments supporting the existence of a solid biological basis for schizophrenia. Among them were advances in brain imaging and neuropathological techniques that have suggested that the limbic system is central to the pathophysiology of schizophrenia and new medications that are very effective in reducing negative symptoms of schizophrenia with fewer adverse neurological effects. Nevertheless, it remains a chronic illness that is very costly, both emotionally and financially, to patient and family. There is now increased interest in the psychosocial factors that may affect onset, intervention, and relapse prevention (Kaplan and Sadock 1996). Schizophrenia is increasingly viewed as a neurodevelopmental disease.

The syndrome has been recognized for more than 3,500 years and has carried a variety of labels. The Greeks termed it *dementia*, and in the nineteenth century several psychoses were identified and labeled *demence precoce, hebephrenia, paranoia*, and *catatonia*. In 1896 a German psychiatrist, Emil Kraepelin, identified symptoms common to these disorders and postulated that there was only one disorder, *dementia praecox*, which afflicted a variety of patients with poor prognoses. Eugene Bleuler published a monograph in 1911 titled *Dementia Praecox or the Group of Schizophrenias*, which disagreed with Kraepelin's belief that the illness was a form of dementia, that it always had an early onset, and that it always led to significant deterioration. Bleuler felt that there was not one illness, dementia praecox, but rather a spectrum of syndromes, the schizophrenias, taken from a Greek word meaning "splitting of the mind." The most prominent feature was a tearing apart (splitting) of psychic functions, especially evident in the loosening of associations between ideas, inappropriate behavior, and disorganization of thought, affect, and actions.

Current thinking supports the idea of a spectrum of disorders, and *DSM-IV* recognizes five forms of schizophrenia. Debate continues, however, over whether it is a single disorder, a group of related diseases, or a set of symptoms stemming from causes unique to each case.

Definitions

Schizophrenia is difficult to describe, because the symptoms vary from one person to another and may also vary at different stages of the illness. Given the lack of evidence that can be reliably measured, the symptoms of schizophrenia define the illness.

Schizophrenia is considered a syndrome with a broad array of symptoms ranging from aimless agitation to total immobility, and from apathy and social withdrawal to bizarre delusions, hallucinations, and incoherent thinking. None of these symptoms appear in all people diagnosed with schizophrenia, and many appear as part of other mental disorders. Symptoms may appear or disappear unpredictably.

DSM-IV recognizes five subtypes of schizophrenia, based on the clinical picture; each subtype offers its own prognostic and treatment implications. People with schizophrenia do not always fit into a subcategory, and thus one may legitimately question the usefulness of these categorizations.

Catatonic type schizophrenia is characterized by marked psychomotor disturbance, sometimes accompanied by alternation between psychomotor excitement and stupor, and often requires medical attention. In the acute phase it is seen as catatonic stupor, mutism, negativism, rigidity, excitement, or bizarre physical posturing. The person may remain in the same physical position for weeks at a time. Echolalia and echopraxia are not uncommon. This disorder is rare in the United States. Onset is usually sudden, and prognosis is good for recovery from the episode, but is guarded for the future. Catatonia is sometimes observed in recent immigrants from primitive cultures and may not have organic causes. Rather, it may be part of religious rituals.

Disorganized type schizophrenia (formerly *hebephreic schizophrenia*) is characterized by thought disturbance, flat or inappropriate affect, grossly disorganized behavior and speech, social impairment, and odd mannerisms. There may be fragmented, poorly defined hallucinations or delusions. People suffering from this type of the disorder usually have early onset and a poor prognosis with a chronic course; few have significant remission. There is often marked regression to primitive, disinhibited, and unorganized behavior.

Paranoid type schizophrenia is characterized by preoccupation with persecutory or grandiose delusions, or with frequent auditory hallucinations related to one theme. These individuals often do not show any impairment in functioning of the sort seen in people suffering from catatonic type or disorganized type schizophrenia, unless the situation interacts with their paranoia. Neither disorganized speech and behavior nor flat or inappropriate affect is present to any significant degree. Unfocused anxiety and anger with argumentative and violent behavior may be observed. Onset is later in life, symptoms are more stable, and possibilities for work and independent functioning are better than for the other categories.

Undifferentiated type schizophrenia (formerly *simple schizophrenia*) is the category used for people who are schizophrenic but whose symptoms do not meet the criteria for the other types, or fall into more than one category. Symptoms include delusions, hallucinations, incoherence, or disorganized behavior.

Residual type schizophrenia is the category used when there has been at least one past episode of schizophrenia, but no current positive symptoms. Signs of the illness include such negative symptoms as blunting, withdrawal, eccentric behavior, thought disorder, or even persistent delusions or hallucinations without strong affect. This disorder is considered chronic or subchronic.

Epidemiology

It is estimated that 1.3 percent of people aged eighteen to fifty-four in the United States suffer from schizophrenia (Pear 1999). One hundred thousand to 150,000 new cases are diagnosed annually (Waldinger 1990). Approximately 25 percent of *all* hospital beds are occupied by people with schizophrenia (Gitlin 1990) and 50 percent of all psychiatric beds (Karno and Norquist 1989). It is estimated that this illness accounts for 75 percent of all expenditures for mental health (Staff 1995:1). The disorder affects equal numbers of men and women, and the age of onset of the initial schizo-

phrenic episode is usually between fifteen and twenty-five for men and between twenty-five and thirty-five for women (Karno and Norquist 1989),
although it can occur later in life. Men tend generally to have a worse
prognosis. There appears to be a higher incidence of schizophrenia in urban
ghettos; according to one theory, the higher incidence may result from the
stress of severe socioeconomic pressures, whereas another theory holds that
people who have schizophrenia drift into these communities because of their
inability to function in middle-class society.

Assessment

Making an assessment of the presence of schizophrenia involves a careful
review of the specific symptoms experienced or observed and of the person's
history. Information should be obtained from the person, and if possible,
from his or her family and friends. Observation and the results of a mental
status examination will confirm the assessment. There must be evidence of
chronic disordered thinking that alters the sense of inner and outer reality
and can be observed in disturbance of thought, speech, perception, affect,
psychomotor activity, interpersonal functioning, and volition.

Thought

Thought disorders affect both the content and the form of mental processes. The major disturbance in content is *delusions*: false beliefs held by
the person despite incontrovertible proof or evidence to the contrary and
not ordinarily accepted by others of similar cultural background. Clinicians
routinely see patients whose thought disorders may include the following:
delusions of persecution; thought broadcasting; thoughts being put into or
taken out of one's head; ideas of reference, in which events or people are
given personal significance (for example, the patient may think that a prominent person on TV is secretly sending a personal message to him or her);
and, though less frequent, somatic or grandiose delusions. There may be
preoccupation with fantasies, which, when combined with an inability to
know where they end, can lead to delusions. For example, a fantasy of being
uniquely important can lead to religious delusions in which the patient
receives messages from God. Thought content may also be vague, concrete,
repetitive, and yield little information.

Disturbances in form of thought can be seen when the person has problems organizing thoughts according to generally accepted rules of logic and reality. Thoughts may be out of sequence, tangential, circumstantial, irrelevant, or incoherent. There may be loosening of associations, so that the person shifts easily between unrelated or marginally connected topics. The person may be preoccupied with minute details, such as bus or train schedules, or may obsess about global or personal issues about which he or she can do nothing. Words may have special meanings, often related to unconscious impulses: for example, the word *leg* may have sexual significance. The clinician may also observe thought blocking, in which there is a sudden interruption in thought.

Speech

As noted above, the speech of the person with schizophrenia may include loose associations, may be incoherent or concrete (marked by an inability to abstract or generalize), or may even seem incomprehensible. Some people with schizophrenia mimic the speech of those around them, in tone or by repeating overheard words or fragments of conversations (echolalia). Though less common, other examples of speech disturbance include condensing or making up new words (neologism); repeating the same word or sentence in a range of circumstances (perseveration); or using rhyming or punning rather than meaning or logic (clanging). Conversation may be vague, stereotyped, or very abstract.

Perception

Hallucinations—internal stimuli perceived as external and real—are the major disturbance in perception. The most common are auditory hallucinations, but the sufferer may experience tactile, somatic, visual, gustatory, or olfactory hallucinations, although these are most often associated with organic mental disorders.

Auditory hallucinations involve perception of voices speaking to the person, often insulting and commenting on behavior. There may be one voice or many, and often they are the voices of familiar people. The person may hear a dialogue between the voices or receive commands from them. During an interview, the person may appear to drift away and may be hearing the voices. A person can be asked if he hears voices that others do not hear.

Hallucinations that are commands must be taken seriously, for they may order homicide or suicide. In assessing hallucinations, questions should involve identification of the voices, the content of the hallucinations, and the circumstances under which the voices are perceived, in order to understand the person's fears, wishes, and the possible implications.

Affect

For many people with schizophrenia, there is disturbance in the regulation and expression of affect, and emotions may be diminished, flat, or blunted. The person may feel disconnected from surrounding events, as if playing a role, and is often lonely and unhappy. Inner conflicts often preclude experiencing pleasure, and any expression of tender feelings will be directed toward a nonthreatening object, such as an animal or a stranger. Affect may be inappropriate and may be related to an inner experience rather than to outer reality; for example, the person may laugh while telling a sad story, or there may be a sudden, unpredictable expression of rage.

Psychomotor Activity

The person may have odd mannerisms, assume bizarre postures, or grimace frequently. In the active phase (see Clinical Course section below), a person with schizophrenia may look strange to even a casual observer, or may seem like an automaton engaged in repetitive, bizarre mannerisms. There is a broad spectrum of disturbance, ranging from catatonia, with a sharp decrease in activity, to very excited, purposeless agitation. The person may appear to be unaware of or unresponsive to his environment.

Interpersonal Functioning

People with schizophrenia are lonely, isolated, often suspicious or irritable, and ambivalent toward others. Thus they appear to be erratic and inconsistent. They have major problems in relating to others and use poor judgment in interpersonal contact. They may show strong dependency and cling too closely to familiar people, or they may be intrusive to strangers. They frequently avoid eye contact. The content of their delusions and hallucinations often directs their relationships and may frighten or alienate others. Real friendships rarely exist, and many schizophrenics choose to associate with other social outcasts. Negativism and doing the opposite of what is requested are seen as an effort to exercise control.

Volition

Following the active phase of schizophrenia, role functioning remains impaired, although the impairment may be inconsistent. For example, a person may function fairly well at work but have severely impaired interpersonal functioning. Many have difficulties with self-initiated, goal-directed activities, lack initiative and motivation, and are highly ambivalent when facing choices. Some are paralyzed by negativism and irrational fears. They also may appear disorganized or act inappropriately, or they may be excessively controlled and rigid.

Positive and Negative Symptoms

Recent research has attempted to classify symptoms as positive or negative. There is some disagreement, however, about which symptoms fall into each category. Another problem is that a person may exhibit both positive and negative symptoms at different stages of the illness.

Positive symptoms include excessive or distorted mental activity with cognitive difficulty, and are experienced as delusions, hallucinations, thought disorders, increased speech, and bizarre behavior. Negative symptoms are more persistent, harder to define, and can be confused with depression or normal characterological behavior. These are flattened affect, social withdrawal and limited social skills, lack of motivation, poor grooming, anhedonia, cognitive and attention deficits, and limited verbal skills. Most research suggests that those with predominantly positive symptoms have better prognoses.

Clinical Course

For a diagnosis of schizophrenia, there is always an *active* phase in which psychotic symptoms, such as hallucinations, delusions, thought disorder, and bizarre behavior, are observed. It is felt that the onset is often exacerbated by a psychosocial stressor. For some, there is a sudden psychotic break, and this active phase is the first sign of the illness.

Before the active phase there is usually a *prodromal* phase, although if the active phase lasts longer than six months it is not necessary to identify this phase. In the prodromal phase the person may exhibit impairment of role functioning, social withdrawal, odd behavior, loss of interests, poor personal care, some communication disturbances, bizarre ideation, and perception disturbance. Prognosis is poor if this phase is insidious and takes many years to develop.

After the active phase there is a *residual* phase, which may look like the prodromal phase. Delusions or hallucinations may be present, coupled with blunted affect and impaired role functioning. The individual does not return to his premorbid level of functioning and usually continues to have chronic symptoms.

Schizophrenia is the most severe of all psychiatric disorders. For many people, schizophrenia is a chronic illness with frequent hospitalizations. The course of the illness varies, however, and a small number of people who suffer from the disorder recover with no residual deficits or stabilize at a lower level of functioning than that at onset.

Though prognosis is guarded, some symptoms suggest a better outcome when present than others; they include acute onset, midlife onset, defined precipitating factors, previously good functioning in work and relationships, no premorbid personality disorder, confusion at onset, and ability to follow a treatment plan. Signs suggesting a poor prognosis are early and insidious onset, history of previous episodes, no definable precipitating factors, withdrawal, inappropriate or shallow affect, schizoid or schizotypal personality disorder, family history of schizophrenia, and problems in following a treatment regimen.

DSM-IV classified the possible clinical course as

1. Continuous when there has been no remission of symptoms during the period of observation
2. Episodic with progressive development of negative symptoms between psychotic episodes
3. Episodic with persistent negative symptoms
4. Episodic with remissions between episodes
5. Partial remission after a single episode
6. Full remission

Depression is common among people with schizophrenia and often follows the disorder's acute phase. Approximately 2 percent of people with schizophrenia will commit suicide, and another 20 percent will make an attempt (Waldinger 1990), usually in the less active phase or during the onset of the first psychotic episode. In the acute phase, attention must be paid to reports of command hallucinations that call for suicide or homicide. People suffering from catatonic or paranoid types of schizophrenia are more prone to homicide than are those with other types of the illness.

Etiology

While much research has been done on the etiology of schizophrenia, much still remains unknown. The search is complicated by the fact that there appears to be a spectrum of the disease and a range of prognoses, possibly suggesting different etiologies for different types.

Much research has been done on the genetic roots of schizophrenia through twin, adoption, and family studies, and clearly it is an inherited disorder. While schizophrenia is found in approximately 1 percent of the population, there is a marked increase in prevalence among first-degree relatives. Classical twin studies compare monozygotic twins to dizygotic twins. If a pair of twins are schizophrenic, they are concordant for the disease; if only one develops schizophrenia, they are discordant. Studies confirmed the hypothesis that genes play a role in predisposition or vulnerability to schizophrenia: concordance rates were significantly different between monozygotic and dizygotic pairs. For monozygotic twins, if one is schizophrenic, there is a 50 to 60 percent probability that both are, while for dizygotic twins, the probability is only 10 to 15 percent, the same as it would be for all siblings (Grinspoon and Bakalar 1990b). Although there are few monozygotic twins raised apart who have schizophrenia, the rate of concordance is the same as for those raised together.

Researchers at NIMH reported in 1990 that they found differences between the brain anatomy of discordant identical twins (Goleman 1990). The twin with schizophrenia was found to have smaller brain volume than the healthy twin, especially in areas involved in thinking, concentration, memory, and perception. Schizophrenia is thus seen as a brain disease involving more than genetic vulnerability. The most striking difference was that the twin with schizophrenia had larger ventricles in the brain, which were filled with the same fluid as found in the spinal cord, implying that missing brain tissue had been replaced by cerebrospinal fluid. Researchers also found wide spaces in the folding at the surface of the brain's cortex, suggesting a failure of brain cells to develop. There was reduction in the size of the left temporal lobe and the front part of a ridge along each lateral ventricle of the brain, areas crucial to decision making, memory, attention, and emotion.

Adoption and family studies support the hypothesis of hereditary vulnerability, finding high correlation between schizophrenia in adopted children and their biological families and none between adoptees and their adoptive families. If one parent had schizophrenia, there was a 16 percent chance that a child would also develop it. If both parents had schizophrenia, the risk for their children was 40 percent (Rowe 1989). Studies have shown a higher rate of schizophrenia in the relatives of women who have the disorder. It is not known what is inherited, or how, or whether the disorder is caused by a structural brain defect, a chemical imbalance, or a personality trait.

Since most antipsychotic medications block the effect of the neurotransmitter dopamine, there has been much interest in the "dopamine hypothesis" (Gitlin 1990), which is predicated on the assumption that there are two types of schizophrenia, each based on a different balance of positive and negative symptoms. Dopamine is one of the neurotransmitters involved in the regulation of cognitive and sensory processes and in regulation of mood. The brain is made up of billions of neurons, with messages received from the presynaptic neuron across a gap, the synapse, to the receptor, postsynaptic neuron. Messages in the brain are transmitted electrically and chemically. An electrical message begins the process, releasing the chemical messenger, the neurotransmitter, across a synapse, to the postsynaptic receptor. The neurotransmitter is then deactivated by returning to its original location and being absorbed back into the presynaptic receptor. Antipsychotic medications block the postsynaptic dopamine receptors and thus the effect of dopamine. Failure to regulate dopamine normally is thought to play a role in schizophrenia, but it is not clear whether this malfunction is the cause of the disorder or a phenomenon resulting from dysregulation elsewhere in the brain.

The range of diagnoses of schizophrenia is not mutually exclusive, and a person may, at different times, experience both positive and negative symptoms. There are, however, two basic types of schizophrenia. Type I schizophrenia has mostly positive symptoms, a fair prognosis, and responds well to antipsychotic medication. The brain structure of people with Type I schizophrenia appears normal on a CAT scan, and there is evidence of excessive dopamine activity, indicating an excessive number of dopamine receptor sites. People with Type II schizophrenia have poor premorbid functioning, persistent and mainly negative symptoms, a poor prognosis, and poor response to medication. These people have abnormal CAT scans, showing enlarged ventricles in the brain, and have normal or decreased dopamine activity. It is known that dopamine levels are higher in adolescence than in later life; thus it may be no coincidence that this is frequently the age of onset of schizophrenia (Grinspoon and Bakalar 1990b; Gitlin 1990).

Many researchers believe that schizophrenia is a disorder of the brain, although to date no abnormality in brain structure or function has been isolated that is common to all people with schizophrenia and to no one else. Again, this finding may be due to the spectrum of the disorder. In addition to the larger ventricles in the brain that have been mentioned, new technology has shown the following: (1) there is low metabolic activity in the prefrontal area of the cerebral cortex, which is the area that determines abstract thinking, planning, emotions, and social functioning; (2) the brains of people with schizophrenia appear to process information abnormally, which may cause hallucinations and delusions; and (3) the frontal lobes of people with schizophrenia are smaller than average. It is still early to state any definitive conclusions about the relation of brain structure to schizophrenia; there is clearly a need to replicate these studies. The major areas of the brain believed to be involved in schizophrenia are (1) the limbic structure, (2) the frontal lobes, and (3) the basal ganglia (Kaplan and Sadock 1997:460).

Environmental factors continue to be explored as influences in the development of schizophrenia. Many suggest that it is caused by a genetic predisposition compounded by environmental stresses. No cluster of environmental factors has been identified that cause schizophrenia. Some research studies have shown a significantly greater percentage of crises and life changes in the three weeks immediately preceding an acute schizophrenic episode than at other times. Thus environmental factors may exacerbate schizophrenia, and assessment must include questions about what, if any, unusual events have taken place in the person's life during recent months.

Differential Diagnosis

Organic mental disorders often have symptoms resembling schizophrenia, such as hallucinations, delusions, and incoherence. Therefore, during assessment it is essential to rule out organic factors that might be responsible for the symptoms. Although the person may experience confusion at the beginning of the active phase, the ongoing disorientation and memory loss seen in organic mental disorders or drug-induced psychosis are not present in schizophrenia.

As previously noted, depression frequently accompanies schizophrenia, and thus it may be difficult to distinguish schizophrenia from psychotic forms of mood disorders and schizoaffective disorder. If periods of depression or mania are brief in relation to schizophrenia, the diagnosis of schizophrenia can be made. If they are lengthy, mood disorder or schizoaffective disorder should be considered as the diagnosis. Usually depression will begin after the onset of schizophrenia, where the latter is the primary diagnosis; if depression is identified before the onset or if there is concomitant onset, then a mood disorder should be suspected. When a person experiences symptoms of a mood disorder followed by hallucinations or delusions without mood symptoms, the diagnosis is schizoaffective disorder. Family history may show the presence of both schizophrenia and mood disorders, and the prognosis for schizoaffective disorder is better than that for schizophrenia, but worse than that for mood disorders.

People with schizotypal, borderline, schizoid, and paranoid personality disorders may experience transient psychotic symptoms that will diminish, allowing a return to the usual level of functioning within hours or days. These transient psychotic symptoms frequently result from psychosocial stressors. It is important to evaluate the content of paranoid ideation to see if there is a delusional quality serious enough to warrant the diagnosis of schizophrenia.

A disorder with psychotic symptoms lasting less than six months, but with prodromal, active, and residual phases, is a schizophreniform disorder. The prognosis for this type of disorder is more hopeful than that for schizophrenia.

Intervention

As previously noted, there is no cure for schizophrenia. Because most cases show residual impairment and a risk of relapse, most interventions are geared to symptom management, social and vocational rehabilitation, and family education. Social workers have many roles in the treatment of schizophrenia, a biopsychosocial disorder.

Medication

The introduction of chlorpromazine (Thorazine), the first of the antipsy-chotic medications (also known as neuroleptics), in 1952 revolutionized the treatment of schizophrenia. Since then, these medications have become the mainstay of treatment for people with schizophrenia. Before these medica-tions were discovered, many who suffered from this illness spent most of their lives in hospitals, experiencing active psychotic symptoms. In 1955 state hospitals in the United States had 552,000 patients; in 1990 they had 119,000. With antipsychotic medication, there are decreases in agitation and in psychotic thinking (hallucinations and delusions), and while impaired functioning remains, many people are able to leave hospitals and function in a range of settings with perhaps intermittent, short hospitalizations. Thus medication is vital in the active stage of schizophrenia as well as for main-tenance. The medication helps with feelings of disintegration and of being overwhelmed. These medications are not without liabilities, however; there are serious, sometimes unpleasant side effects. Because of the side effects, there is growing awareness of the need to keep the dosage as low as possible and to give people "vacations" from medication in order to evaluate ongoing need. Although social workers cannot prescribe medication, they are fre-quently the professionals most in contact with people who have schizophre-nia, and they may be aware of side effects that they can bring to the attention of the prescribing psychiatrist. The social worker can possibly affect the adjustment of the dosage, based on the person's social and vocational func-tioning as assessed by the social worker and relayed to the psychiatrist. It must be cautioned that although medication has helped the majority of people with schizophrenia, some do not respond, and some symptoms are not ameliorated.

Until 1990, when clozapine (Clozaril) was introduced, none of the an-tipsychotic medications developed after chlorpromazine had proved to be more effective. Decisions on which to prescribe are based on the person's reported tolerance, past history with the medication, and, often, on the pro-vider's preference. There are at least two dozen antipsychotic medications, often classified as high-potency (therapeutic effects require relatively small doses) or low-potency drugs (therapeutic effects require larger doses). The low-potency drugs are more sedating, cause dry mouth, constipation, and dizziness but have fewer neurological side effects. Chlorpromazine (Thor-azine), thioridazine (Mellaril), and mesoridazine (Serentil) are low-potency drugs; fluphenazine (Prolixin) and haloperidol (Haldol) are high-potency drugs. Mid-potency medications include perphenazine (Trilafon), trifluoperazine (Stelazine), thiothixene (Navane), chlorprothixene (Taractan), molindone (Moban), and trifluopromazine (Vesprin). Most medications are administered in pill form, but some are given as liquids. Liquid forms of medication are frequently used in hospitals, because it is easier to administer them to noncompliant patients. When outpatients cannot be relied on to follow their medication regime, fluphenazine and haloperidol may be administered by intramuscular injection, because their effects last from two weeks to a month.

Medications begun in the acute phase of schizophrenia may not reach full effectiveness for about six weeks, although some response should be evidenced in three to four weeks. If there is no improvement, a different drug should be tried. Once there is a response, the dosage is lowered to a maintenance level that will control the return of symptoms.

Clozapine (Clozaril), approved by the FDA in 1989 and considered an atypical antipsychotic, has proved highly effective for people who do not respond to other antipsychotic medications, and it appears not to cause neurological side effects. It is believed to affect the neurotransmitters serotonin and norepinephrine more than dopamine. It does, however, have one serious nonneurological side effect: it may cause bone marrow to stop making white blood cells. These cells are important for warding off infections; thus frequent blood tests are indicated, adding to patient inconvenience and treatment expense. Like most neuroleptic drugs, it affects positive symptoms but also relieves negative symptoms.

A newer drug, risperidone (Risperdal), affects dopamine and serotonin and appears to be safer than clozapine. It works faster and affects both positive and negative symptoms. Other new and promising medications that affect both positive and negative symptoms (Staff 1998) are olanzapine (Zyprexa) with fewer extrapyramidal effects, but with the side effects of sedation and weight gain; quetiapine (Seroquel), which has side effects similar to those of olanzapine; sertindole (Serlect), which has a fairly long half-life and thus is useful for uncompliant persons; and ziprasidone (Zeldox), which is helpful not only with symptoms of schizophrenia but also with affective and anxiety symptoms (Kaplan and Sadock 1998).

The presence of side effects often causes people to stop taking medication. Most of them—drowsiness, dizziness, dry mouth, constipation, blurred vision, and sexual dysfunction, especially in males—are temporary or will eventually diminish in severity. Weight gain also presents a problem, especially for women. The most distressing side effects are the neurological symptoms resembling Parkinsonian symptoms. These symptoms can sometimes be relieved by lowering the dosage, as long as psychotic symptoms do not reappear, or by adding anti-Parkinsonian medications such as trihexyphenidyl (Artane) or benztropine (Cogentin).

Tardive dyskinesia is the most persistent side effect, with symptoms appearing months or years after medication is started. Twenty to thirty percent of people in long-term medication treatment for schizophrenia will develop its symptoms, ranging from mild to severe, beginning with involuntary facial tics, jaw movements, lip smacking, tongue thrusting, sucking, eye blinking; over time, the person develops spasmodic and writhing hand, arm, leg, and neck movements. Tardive dyskinesia is more common in women than men and more often seen in older people. Since these symptoms will disappear for many when the antipsychotic medication is discontinued, although for some they are irreversible, it is recommended that the dosage be stopped when symptoms appear. Should psychotic symptoms reappear, the person and family must be helped to accept tardive dyskinesia as a side effect of needed treatment.

Other side effects are similar to those of Parkinson's disease and may be hard to recognize. Akinesia is a state of reduced voluntary, spontaneous movement, such as arm swinging or crossing one's legs. There are few spontaneous facial expressions, and walking may appear rigid. Other symptoms are similar to the negative symptoms of schizophrenia and depression, and the best way to determine if the person is suffering from this side effect is to add anti-Parkinsonian medication in high doses. Akathisia, in contrast, is a state of motor restlessness. The sufferer moves constantly, shifting around when seated, crossing or uncrossing legs, shifting from foot to foot, and has a stated inability to relax, which may be confused with anxiety. Although anti-Parkinsonian medication may be given, it has been found that the beta-blocker propranolol is also useful.

Finally, the least common but most serious side effect is neuroleptic malignant syndrome, whose symptoms are fever, high blood pressure, muscular rigidity, confusion, and stupor. It most frequently occurs after antipsychotic medications are begun or after raising the dosage. The person must be hospitalized medically and the medication discontinued. Though most recover in days or weeks, this side effect is potentially fatal.

Clearly, people need to be observed for signs of side effects, yet also helped to understand the need for medication. A large number of those suffering from schizophrenia relapse because they do not follow their drug regimen after discharge from a hospital. Since remaining on antipsychotic medications for long periods of time is so problematic, however, trials on lower doses or periods without medication should be undertaken if they can be monitored.

Since depression may follow the acute phase of schizophrenia, there are times when adding an antidepressant is indicated. Lithium is sometimes prescribed for people with schizophrenia, but it is not clear why it is effective. It also may be prescribed because of an inaccurate diagnosis. Electroconvulsive therapy (ECT) is sometimes used when catatonic or affective symptoms are present or when the person fails to respond to high doses of medication. Acute, rather than chronic, schizophrenia appears to respond better to ECT.

Milieu (Inpatient) Therapy

People with schizophrenia occupy half of the psychiatric beds in U.S. hospitals, although few now need (or can afford) long-term care. Following the introduction of antipsychotic medications, a program of deinstitutionalization began, which advocated short hospitalizations and early return to the community. Provisions were not made for adequate aftercare, however, especially in large urban areas, resulting in a "revolving door" situation, in which some people never received outpatient medication and therefore required additional hospitalizations.

Up to 70 percent of psychiatric inpatient admissions are readmissions. Indications for admission are as follows: (1) the person has experienced the onset of a psychotic episode with psychotic symptoms and is unable to physically care for himself or herself; (2) an inpatient diagnostic workup is indicated to arrive at a treatment plan and begin medication; (3) the person presents a danger to self and to others, perhaps as a result of command hallucinations; and (4) life events or loss of supports have caused the person to decompensate, with marked decrease in functioning or presence of psychotic symptoms.

On admission of the person, careful monitoring will be necessary, along with a calming, reassuring environment, and limit-setting to help control behavior. Seclusion rooms may be necessary while medication begins to take effect. In the hospital setting, most people, until they receive some supportive individual psychotherapy after they are no longer floridly psychotic, spend much of their time in structured activities, such as occupational and activities therapies, and in groups also attended by the staff of the therapeutic community. The goals of hospitalization are to move the person out of the active phase, to regulate medication, and to bring self-care, social functioning, and, if possible, vocational functioning to levels at which the person can exist outside of the hospital.

Before discharge, a viable treatment plan involving the person and support networks should be created. Unfortunately, such a plan is not always put in place, and the person does not always receive proper aftercare. Treatment planning should address social and vocational needs. Some people are able to return to live with families, but for many, this is not possible or appropriate. Some need supervised living and go to halfway houses, community residences, foster homes, or cooperative-care apartments. Some people may be able to return to a job, but many need to go into prevocational programs, sheltered workshops, or, for those with marked impairment, day hospital programs, where most activities are in groups focusing on social skills, activities of daily living, and vocational planning. Identifying, coordinating, and providing the necessary services for people with schizophrenia are frequently functions of a case manager who often is a social worker.

Psychosocial Rehabilitation

All people with schizophrenia experience impairment in social and vocational functioning. Their world is complex, frightening, and overwhelming, and they are uncertain about functioning competitively and with strangers. They often panic about their future and fear the intensity of their own thoughts and feelings.

A program model that has proved effective is the *Clubhouse Model*, developed by Fountain House in New York City. In 1998 there were more than 150 Clubhouses spread over thirty states and the District of Columbia. Programs also exist in fifteen other countries, including South Korea and Albania. There is no charge for lifetime membership in the Clubhouse. Fountain House has a membership of approximately 15,500, 850 of whom come at least once a month. Average daily attendance is 600. Other programs that are modifications of the Fountain House model have emerged.

Based on the ecosystems perspective that is central to social work practice, the Clubhouse Model focuses on the interaction between person and environment. The setting is a "club," and participants, all of whom are severely disabled psychiatrically, are "members," thus moving them away from the stigma of being labeled "patient." Work is central to the model, with staff and members working side by side in all activities that make the Clubhouse run. The Clubhouse is a community, and work evolves from the daily needs of that community. The focus is on members' strengths, talents, and abilities, in order to help them regain self-worth, a sense of purpose, and confidence, rather than on any specific job training, although the program is considered a prevocational job program. The Clubhouse is a "normalized" environment where members can work and socialize together and develop interpersonal skills. Although case management is done by staff to facilitate obtaining housing, needed services, and entitlements, members are encouraged to seek psychotherapy privately or in clinics.

A work-ordered day provides a stable focus, and it gives external structure to direct and organize the days. Activities in the Clubhouse give a sense of belonging, of being valued and needed. The program serves as a vehicle for helping an estranged and fragmented person to become reengaged with daily living. Clubhouses are open at least five days a week (Fountain House is open 365 days a year), and the work-ordered day parallels normal working hours.

Following successful participation in the day program, some members want, and are capable of, employment outside of the Clubhouse, but lack confidence and job references. Furthermore, employment interviewers may look with disfavor on candidates who have a history of psychiatric hospitalizations. Thus the Clubhouse model provides first an Enclave Program, in which small groups of members tag merchandise, sort proxies, and stuff envelopes. More advanced is the Transitional Employment Program, in which members are placed, usually at entry level, in normal places of business at prevailing wages paid by the employer. Most jobs are part-time, usually twenty hours a week, with one full-time job shared by two members, and they last for a duration of six months, although there is some flexibility in hours and duration. All job training is done by Clubhouse staff. Members may have as many placements as necessary in order to feel comfortable in the world of work. Job failure is seen as a right, not a disaster. Fountain House has approximately 150 members in Transitional Employment at any given time, and there are more than thirty-five employers, including a large law firm, media companies, banks, the Bronx Zoo, a nursing home, and local stores.

The final phase in the work-related program is the Full-Time Employment Program. The Clubhouse provides job placement services, counseling in résumé writing and interviewing techniques, and ongoing support and encouragement as the member encounters stresses and difficulties on the job. Evening support groups, as well as regular meetings, offer suggestions and a sense of security. Each year about one hundred members of Fountain House obtain full-time employment.

Evening, weekend, and holiday programs enable members who are employed, as well as other members, to maintain long-term contact with the Clubhouse and meet their need for companionship and socialization. There is a range of recreational activities within the Clubhouse and organized excursions to outside events. If a member has been absent for a period of time, staff and members participate in outreach activities, not necessarily to urge his or her return, but to show interest and concern.

Close to 40 percent of the members of Fountain House were homeless when they came. A goal of the Housing Program is to help members make the transition to independent living. Shelter is provided for more than two hundred members citywide, in housing ranging from supervised residences to shared and individual apartments. Fountain House staff also help members find apartments and provide up to $1,500 to purchase home furnishings.

Clubhouses are funded with city, state, and federal money, as well as with contributions from individuals and foundations. Most of the staff are trained social workers.

Psychotherapy

As stated above, medication is essential in the treatment of schizophrenia. Psychotherapy without medication and environmental intervention has proved ineffective, and some studies have indicated no benefit from psychotherapy. An ongoing, supportive relationship, however, may help people comply with a medication regimen, and social workers often run groups in medication clinics to monitor the patients and allow them to talk about their feelings and concerns about medication.

Analytically oriented psychotherapy encouraging introspection and self-awareness is considered inappropriate for people with schizophrenia. Such a model might overwhelm the individual with anger, anxiety, or other feelings, resulting in decompensation, with loss of the person's already tenuous hold on reality. Supportive therapy offering advice, consistency, reassurance, and a secure setting has proved most helpful. The focus should be on the reality of the "here and now," with specific, realistic goals. The counselor is active and positive. Attention must be given to symptoms and responses to medication. Structure, which these people often cannot provide for themselves and which they need in order to defuse the inner chaos they may be experiencing, can be achieved by setting a regular time and day for appointments, seeing the person in the same room each time, and making consistent contact with the same provider. Because people with schizophrenia often have difficulty with closeness and intimacy, the counselor must keep some distance, while still being sympathetic and supportive. Counselors will find that forming a relationship is slow. The length of sessions needs to be flexible also, for an agitated person may find that the traditional fifty-minute session is too long and provokes too much anxiety.

Homogeneous groups can be supportive and can help develop social skills and problem-solving techniques. People can share feelings about their illness and about how they can cope. Again, the focus is on coping in the here and now, and group members exchange ideas about tasks of daily living, vocational plans and problems, and establishing and maintaining interpersonal relationships. In the groups people can practice talking and listening, and often there is some assertiveness training with specific tasks. Groups help to reduce isolation and avoidant behavior.

Intervention with Families

More than one-third of those who have chronic schizophrenia live with their families, and many others live nearby, so work with families is essential. Families need to be educated about medications and side effects, how to respond to psychotic behavior, and how to recognize signs of deterioration. They worry about who will take care of the person when they die, and they must find a balance between being overprotective and requiring a greater degree of independence than can be realistically expected.

The family that has a member with schizophrenia faces heavy financial and emotional burdens. Parents may feel ashamed, guilty, disappointed, isolated, and conflicted about how much they do for the person at the expense of other family members or themselves. Family members need a chance to vent these feelings and to be supported by social workers who can empathize with them and help identify strengths both within the family and in the community.

Many families feel the stigma associated with having a relative who is mentally ill. In a study of 156 parents and spouses of persons having a first admission to a psychiatric inpatient service (Phelan, Bromet, and Link 1998), it was found that 50 percent concealed the hospitalization from friends and family, particularly if the person did not live with the family, was female, or had what were considered less severe positive symptoms.

While the concept of the "schizophrenogenic mother" who propelled her child into schizophrenia has long since been given up, schizophrenic disorders are still often associated with emotional conflict and poor communication within families. Parents may be overprotective, indifferent, or create "double binds" by giving mixed messages. It is, however, not clear whether or not these behaviors by the parents may be in response to the insidious onset of the disease or to the cognitive and perceptive deficits of the person with schizophrenia. Generally family life and the person's upbringing are not thought to be the primary causes of schizophrenia.

Families need an understanding of the genetic and biological aspects of the illness. They need training in identifying and solving problems between the person with the disorder and the family. Hospitalizing a person with schizophrenia for the first time can be a frightening and guilt-provoking experience, and it is helpful if social workers can conduct an orientation group for families of new admissions, providing information about the hospital and aftercare, answering questions, and allowing a period of time for families to share their experiences and feelings, possibly lessening guilt, fear, and isolation. Following the hospitalization, some families meet in mutual-aid groups established through the National Alliance for the Mentally Ill, which has chapters in all fifty states and more than 140,000 individual members. The alliance not only facilitates the formation of groups but encourages public education and lobbies for the mentally ill. Most ongoing work with the families is educational, and such terms as *psychoeducation, behavioral family management, supportive family counseling, family crisis management,* and *multiple family groups* are used instead of the term *family therapy.*

For approximately fifteen years, there has been concern with families' index of expressed emotion (EE) as researchers found that people with schizophrenia who came from homes with a high level of EE had a relapse rate four to five times higher if they stopped taking medication or had face-to-face contact with their family. *EE* refers to critical comments, hostility, overinvolvement, overconcern, and intrusiveness. The comments and intrusiveness produce a stimulus overload that, because of the perceptual and cognitive deficits, lead the person with schizophrenia to decompensation. *Communication deviance (CD)* results in double-bind messages, where the emotional content may be missing or overemotional. A major problem is denial of the disorder and insistence that the person act normally, followed by expressions of disappointment when he or she cannot comply. Although EE is a predictor of relapse, it has not been ascertained that it is a cause.

Psychoeducation

Psychoeducation aims at reducing the level of EE and improving communication skills in order to lessen the chance of relapse. The goal is to increase the predictability and stability of the home environment, to set realistic goals, to increase compliance with the medication regimen, and to provide support for the person and family. Since there is no cure for schizophrenia, management of the disorder appears to be the best alternative.

Psychoeducation is rendered in a range of formats. The person with schizophrenia can be included, or families can be worked with separately from the client. Research has indicated that highly successful work can be accomplished in groups of families. This tends to diminish the stigma through identification with others. The emphasis is on education, not blame, and families see themselves as part of the team. The process may consist of meetings in the hospital, survivors' workshops, or bimonthly meetings that may go on for months or years. Ongoing groups usually have ninety-minute sessions focusing on problems and issues raised by the families. If a family has an idiosyncratic problem, a session is arranged for the family with appropriate staff.

Psychoeducation teaches about the illness, medication, and ways in which families can assist in the recovery process. Recuperation is described as long and slow, and at times the person may be incorrectly perceived as lazy or resistant. Families learn to reduce expectations and to view lethargy or restlessness as aspects of the disorder. They are helped to understand the importance of creating barriers to overstimulation through diminishing intensity of affect or of conflict within the family. Communication must be clear, supportive, and simple. Families are urged to minimize negative actions or words, rejections, and conflicts as well as overconcern, overencouragement, and overenthusiasm. Neutral responses are the least stimulating. Families often have become socially isolated and focused on the person with schizophrenia, and through psychoeducation they learn to expand their social networks to meet their own needs and divert some of the attention from the person with the disorder. Respite care is encouraged. Finally, families learn the signs of decompensation and the importance of seeking help as soon as possible. Sharing information and ways of coping are core to the success of psychoeducation.

Psychoeducation helps families to help the person with schizophrenia and it also helps to reduce feelings of stigma and guilt. When the person is included, it often enhances self-esteem, as he or she becomes a participant in understanding the illness and planning for intervention.

Because noncompliance with intervention planning has often led to repeated relapses, approximately thirty-seven states have begun pilot programs to allow for involuntary commitment to outpatient programs for at least 180 days. These programs have often involved amendments to the judiciary and mental health laws. Services include medication, individual and group therapy, intensive case management, supervised housing and day, or partial-day, programs (American Psychiatric Association 1998:1). Although this is a new, and expensive, concept, and thus its future is uncertain, it clearly is worth trying and evaluating over a significant period of time.

Schizophrenia is a diagnostic label applied to a mixed collection of disorders with varying etiology, pathology, dynamics, and clinical course. Social stress, social class, and gender affect incidence and recovery rates. There is genetic vulnerability as well as an indication of deficits in brain structure. Thus it is a disorder that frequently results from the effect of environmental stressors on a person who is genetically vulnerable. Diagnosis may be difficult, as similar symptoms can be found in other mental or physical disorders; thus a thorough assessment is essential. This complex picture has led some to think that schizophrenia would be better labeled "prolonged psychiatric illness."

People with schizophrenia—and their families—need to be connected to a broad range of programs and resources. Social workers, trained in an ecosystems perspective, are best equipped to serve as case managers to assist in meeting these needs, although cutbacks in funding make this role a difficult task.

7   Substance-Related Disorders

Substance abuse is a major social and public health problem that affects millions of Americans and their families. It occurs in all social classes, at all professional levels, and in most cultural and ethnic groups, and it can be comorbid with a variety of mental disorders. Social problems that occur as a result of substance use include family breakup, domestic violence, school and vocational difficulties, poverty, physical disease, and homelessness. The 1999 surgeon general's report (Pear 1999) states that $12.6 billion was spent on treatment for drug and alcohol abuse in 1996. It is impossible to gauge the cost to industry of the increases in accidents, breakage, and decreased productivity that are concomitant with the abuse of, primarily, alcohol, marijuana, and cocaine. The creation of employee assistance programs has been one response of industry to the problem. Substance abuse presents a challenge to public health in terms of primary, secondary, and tertiary prevention. In addition, the AIDS epidemic and the increase in the prevalence of sexually transmitted diseases are clearly linked to the drug problem. Substance abuse also imposes tremendous economic burdens. Entire families are known to suffer from AIDS; in others, children will lose one or both parents. Many infants exposed to drugs and alcohol in utero subsequently may need neonatal intensive care; special medical, psychological, psychiatric, and educational services; and foster care. Pregnant women at risk for substance abuse or involved with partners who are abusing substances need to be identified and provided with prenatal care, special substance abuse treatment programs, and follow-up after delivery.

Substance abuse prevention and intervention are complicated by the fact that tobacco, caffeine, and alcohol are legal, while such substances as marijuana, cocaine, and heroin are illegal. Addictive behavior may also be looked at as destructive (alcoholism, tobacco use, chemical dependency), socially unacceptable (eating disorders, addictive relationships), or socially permissible (workaholism, excessive exercising, excessive spending). Cultural factors must be considered in determining whether the use of substances is viewed as excessive or within normal limits. Finally, the orientation of the person making the assessment will affect intervention. People trained in the mental health professions may have had little training about, or experience with, people who abuse substances, and those trained to work with people who are chemically dependent may know little about symptoms of emotional disorders; thus, approaches to intervention may differ widely. In order for mental health professionals to deliver proper services, the "turf war" must be curtailed and training made broader.

DSM-I and *DSM-II* classified drug and alcohol addiction as a personality disturbance or as a symptom of a personality disorder. *DSM-III-R* established two classifications for substance abuse disorders: *Psychoactive Substance Use Disorders*, which included symptoms of behavior caused by abuse and dependence on nine classes of substances, and *Psychoactive Substance-Induced Organic Mental Disorders*, a subcategory of *Organic Mental Syndromes and Disorders*, which referred to the direct effects of these nine substances, as well as nicotine and caffeine, on the central nervous system. *DSM-IV* combines these two classifications into one, *Substance Related Disorders*, which refers to the eleven substances.

Definitions

Abuse refers to a pattern of misuse of a substance when the person knows that it will exacerbate existing problems or may cause a hazardous situation. Use may be relatively recent in origin, or may be episodic, and does not meet the criteria for dependence. It is a maladaptive pattern that can lead to significant psychosocial, medical, or legal consequences. Although tolerance may result, physiological withdrawal symptoms are uncommon.

Dependence refers to loss of control over the use of a substance, and it is often associated with increased tolerance and the presence of physiological and psychological symptoms when the person is not under the influence of the substance. It may have different degrees of severity from one individual to another. Dependence is often associated with a compulsion or craving—a habit that is abnormally strong and hard to alter. People who are dependent often have to weigh the *negative* consequences against what they perceive to be the *positive* consequences. They often are aware that they are using too much of the substance and may make repeated, unsuccessful attempts to cut down. Dependence usually develops in stages: mild, controllable use; more frequent but still controllable use; and finally, loss of control that interferes with the person's life.

Pathological substance use is continued use with observed impairment in relationships, ability to perform one's work, physical and emotional health, judgment, and frustration tolerance. It is a habitual maladaptive coping process that may involve constant thinking about the substance, being under its influence, or recovering from the effects. People suffering from pathological use also often experience serious financial or legal problems.

Tolerance occurs when the body has adapted to a new chemical environment as a result of the substance use, and there is a need to increase the amount of the substance in order to achieve the results previously obtained at lower doses. Almost all addictive substances eventually produce some level of tolerance, and if a person develops tolerance to one substance there will be tolerance to others in the same class. Degree of tolerance will vary with the drug and the circumstances under which the drug is used. Psychedelic drugs produce a profound tolerance almost immediately, tolerance to amphetamines and opioids develops rapidly as well, and tolerance to alcohol, cocaine, marijuana, and nicotine is usually lower and more idiosyncratic. Some people become less sensitive to the disruptive effects of the drugs and are able to increase the dosage and still function until they finally arrive at a dose that has so many toxic effects that functioning becomes impaired.

Addict refers to a person with a complex set of needs, desires, and habits. The term is derived from the Latin describing a person given to a creditor as a slave because of nonpayment of debts. There are many causes for this disability, and they can vary greatly from person to person and from one addiction to another. Dependence on a substance is marked by overwhelming involvement with the use of the substance and often associated with withdrawal symptoms. A person who is addicted to a substance may make the possession and use of the substance the focus of his or her life, neglecting family, friends, work, and other responsibilities. There is no evidence of a pattern to describe a "typical" person addicted to alcohol or drugs, or subject to any other addiction.

Addiction is difficult to identify and to define, and the definition varies depending on perspective. Addiction appears to mean different things in different situations, but most people agree that the addict's behavior is marked by an all-consuming preoccupation with the acquisition and use of the substance. There is craving, compulsive use, and relapse following withdrawal. It is often not clear when a *habit* becomes an *addiction*. Careful assessment is essential to determine patterns and frequency of use, as well as stressors that may precipitate use. Researchers generally agree that the process of addiction affects a region in the brain that activates a reward response. Knowing that drug dependence has a neurochemical basis does not, however, explain why some people use drugs regularly and heavily, while others use drugs under certain circumstances, or why different people prefer different drugs. Behavioral theorists regard drug addiction as a form of operant conditioning, in which drug use is repeated because of the reinforcement of activation of the brain's reward system through which the user experiences, depending on the drug, pleasure, or relief from discomfort. The pattern of addictive use depends on the chosen drug, the necessary dosage, cultural factors, and the degree of difficulty in obtaining the drug.

Withdrawal is a distinct syndrome that the chemically dependent individual experiences upon reduction or removal of the substance. The syndrome is related to the class of substance use (for example, opiate, alcohol, cocaine) and is accompanied by psychological and physical symptoms. These symptoms often mimic affective, anxiety, and psychotic disorders and can become life-threatening.

Craving is the powerful desire to use a drug. It is experienced by people who are addicted, either when they are trying to obtain a drug that may be unavailable to them or when they are trying to resist taking a drug that is available.

Relapse refers to the behavior of a person who has been abstinent for a period of time and then returns to substance use. It may occur in response to cues that remind the addict of the experience of the desired effects of the substance. These cues may be a familiar bar, the sight of drug paraphernalia, a neighborhood where the substance had been obtained, a group of people with whom the individual used the substance, or even the return of a mood related to drug use.

Codependency is a poorly defined term and may refer to a process of depending on a person who is addicted to a substance or constructing a life that revolves around a person who is abusing the substance.

History

Use and abuse of alcohol and drugs have occurred for millennia. Extraction of pure chemicals from plant material began about two centuries ago, and the development of synthetic drugs in the twentieth century has led to the creation of more powerful and dangerous addictive substances. The invention of the hypodermic needle in the mid-nineteenth century allowed people to take drugs without experiencing the unpleasant taste and also allowed for quicker absorption, thus making them more attractive and effective.

Before the reforms of the Progressive Era (1898–1917), laws to control substance abuse were weak and varied from one state to another. There were no federal laws requiring the labeling of over-the-counter medications, which often contained high doses of alcohol or cocaine until the passage of the Pure Food and Drug Act in 1906. This law required labeling and led to the lowering of amounts of these substances in the medications. In 1908 legislation was passed against the smoking of opium, and in 1915 the Harrison Narcotics Act went into effect, imposing severe restrictions and requiring strict record keeping on the importation, manufacture, and prescription of all opiates and cocaine. Implementation, however, was inconsistent (Musto 1992). Following World War I, increased concern about narcotic abuse led to debate about whether to give addicts maintenance doses of opiates. In 1919 the Narcotics Division of the Internal Revenue Bureau was established, maintenance dosages were not permitted, and policy began to focus on law enforcement to curb drug importation, manufacture, and use. That year also saw the adoption of the Eighteenth Amendment to the U.S. Constitution, which prohibited the sale and use of alcohol. Every state except Connecticut and Rhode Island ratified the amendment, which was enforced until it was repealed in 1933.

Following World War II the fear arose that illicit drug trade and use would increase, and an intensification of punitive measures followed, including providing judges with the right to impose a death sentence when a person was convicted of selling heroin. The advent of the community mental health movement in the 1960s, with a whole range of services available to people who suffered from emotional and substance abuse disorders, together with the increased availability of methadone, moved the country from a punitive to a more biopsychosocial approach to controlling substance abuse. This new approach included the establishment of methadone maintenance and other treatment programs. Fears of a cocaine and, later, a crack epidemic led Reagan-era politicians to start the "War on Drugs," a highly publicized campaign of media manipulation, strong financial support for selective law enforcement, and funding cuts for treatment programs.

In recent years the public has changed its perception of alcohol use, from viewing it as an acceptable accompaniment to social occasions to viewing it as a potentially dangerous substance. The legal drinking age has been federally mandated as twenty-one, and since 1989 the surgeon general has required that alcoholic beverages contain labels warning about use during pregnancy, potential of danger if one drives or operates machinery, and the possibility of physical problems developing as a result of continued alcohol abuse.

Etiology

There is no single cause for substance abuse. People with substance abuse disorders have been regarded as suffering from a disease, experiencing a behavioral problem, being immoral, and having no "willpower." There are many other stereotypes of the alcoholic and the drug addict. The United States Supreme Court in 1988 viewed alcoholism as "willful misconduct." Clinicians who are knowledgeable about the misuse of substances believe that people with substance abuse disorders usually use alcohol and drugs initially for pleasure, or to relieve the pain of anxiety, depression, or the general circumstances of their lives that may cause feelings of inadequacy. Social conditions in which an individual is encouraged to try a substance or continue its use are also a factor. For some, the use with friends is recreational; for others the use with companions may relieve a sense of isolation and hopelessness. In both instances there is the potential for developing a habit that evolves into an addiction, as obtaining and using the substance becomes more and more central to the person's life. Drug use is more likely in an emotionally impoverished environment where the person experiences little satisfaction and feels competent only when under the influence of the substance. People who are reasonably happy with their lives are less inclined to become addicted, and, if they do, they have a better chance of recovery. Thus a person with a family, education, and a job may be more motivated to abstain than is a person who is isolated, unemployed, and faces limited opportunities.

Cultural and social factors must also be considered. Some ethnic groups, including Native Americans and persons of Irish descent, are more susceptible to alcoholism than others, possibly as the result of learned behavior passed from one generation to another. Some cultures, such as Mormon and Muslim, prohibit alcohol use, and others try to limit its use to wine at meals. Social attitudes also play a role in the choice of substance. Addiction to cigarettes has diminished as the public has increasingly come to view smoking as unhealthy and socially unacceptable. A breakdown of social controls can also lead to epidemic addiction, such as the high rates of alcoholism among Native Americans, who were suddenly introduced to alcohol and were unprepared to cope with its effects.

The strongest evidence for a genetic cause of substance abuse is found among alcoholics. The majority of twin and adoption studies support the observation that alcoholism is, in part, genetically determined. Studies show that first-degree relatives are at five times greater risk for alcohol abuse than the general public, and the risk for adopted children is four times greater if a biological parent suffered from alcohol abuse (L'Abate, Farrar, and Serritella 1992). Family studies, however, should be viewed with caution, because family members also share social, cultural, and developmental influences (Anthenelli and Schuckit 1992). The role of hereditary vulnerability has not been clearly shown for other forms of drug dependence, partly because the drug most often misused varies over the years, and thus it is very difficult to get the kind of multigenerational data that are more available on alcohol abuse.

The cognitive-behavioral paradigm of addiction suggests that it develops out of desire for immediate gratification followed by delayed negative consequences. The substance abuse is maintained by the consequences of the use: the pleasurable effects (positive reinforcement) or the ability of the substance to temporarily alleviate a distressing situation or set of feelings (negative reinforcement).

Epidemiology

Statistics on the prevalence of substance abuse are hard to obtain and probably underestimate the problem, as people deny, or are reluctant to discuss, the extent of their use. It is estimated that at least 25 percent of the U.S. population engages in some type of addictive behavior (L'Abate, Farrar, and Serritella 1992). Most alarming has been the rise in substance abuse among children and adolescents. The National Comorbidity Survey (Kessler et al. 1994) estimated a lifetime prevalence of 14.1 percent for alcohol dependence disorder (20.1 percent for men and 8.2 percent for women) and 7.5 percent for drug dependence disorder (9.2 percent for men and 5.9 percent for women). Lifetime prevalence for any substance abuse/dependence was estimated as 26.6 percent (35.4 percent for men and 17.9 percent for women).

There appears to be a disproportionally high rate of substance abuse among people who are black, Hispanic, or Native American. Based on the results of surveys, however, it is probable that the rates are underreported for people who are white, especially in higher economic groups, who hide, or are helped to hide, their addiction better.

With respect to the legal substances that can become addictive, it is estimated that ten million Americans can be regarded as suffering from alcoholism, but this is probably an underestimation of the problem. More men than women are heavy drinkers, and the greatest prevalence is among those twenty-one to thirty-four years of age (Goodwin 1989). The National Institute of Alcohol and Alcohol Abuse (NIAAA), noted an increase in the number of women having problems with alcohol. It is most common between the ages of twenty-six and thirty-six and among those who are separated or divorced (NIAAA 1999). Fifty-four million people (26 percent of the population) are cigarette smokers, a decline from 29 percent in 1988.

The National Household Survey conducted by the Substance Abuse and Mental Health Services Administration has shown a decline in the number of people using illegal drugs from a peak of 24 million people in 1979, to 12.8 million in 1991, to 11.4 million in 1992. While more men than women use illegal drugs, the gap is decreasing (Ferguson and Kaplan 1994). The number of habitual cocaine users decreased from 1.9 million in 1991 to 1.3 million in 1992, down from a peak of 5.8 million in 1985. Illegal drug use correlates with education and employment. Highest rates were found among people eighteen to thirty-four years of age who had not completed high school and among the unemployed (U.S. Department of Health and Human Services 1993).

There has been a recent increase in the use of heroin, especially among people at higher socioeconomic levels. Its prevalence is somewhat greater on the West Coast than in the New York City area, and it appears to be increasingly attractive to groups who, in previous years, would have used cocaine—that is, the "fast track" young (Gabriel 1994).

Types of Substances

Because there is great variation among methods of use, tolerance levels, withdrawal symptoms, and intervention, each category will be discussed separately.

Substances that are prone to abuse generally fall into six categories: (1) sedatives and central nervous system (CNS) depressants, (2) opioid narcotics, (3) stimulants, (4) psychedelics or hallucinogens, (5) marijuana and hashish, and (6) PCP and ketamine.

Sedatives and CNS Depressants

These substances can be obtained legally and are commonly used. Their abuse is a cause of increased rates of suicide, domestic and other violence, and accidents.

Alcohol. Controversy exists over whether alcoholism is a disease. Those who do not regard it as a disease feel that labeling it as such makes it excusable, because it suggests that alcoholism is involuntary. It also rewards people for drinking, because the disease label suggests that the disorder is a disability, making alcoholics eligible for special benefits and protection under the Americans with Disabilities Act. The U.S. Supreme Court has consistently concluded that medical evidence does not show that heavy drinking is involuntary. Supporters of the disease model believe that if people who abuse alcohol see themselves as having a disease they will be more likely to abstain, seek intervention, obtain needed medical help, and assume responsibility for their actions. They and their families will also feel more hopeful about overcoming the disorder and will have a heightened sense of morale. Most treatment programs in the United States adhere to the disease model.

Alcohol is a hypnotic-sedative and anesthetic drug whose abuse can lead to many adverse physiological and psychological consequences. Users seek to control anxiety, feelings of anger, and release from inhibitions (particularly sexual inhibitions) as dependency occurs. Daily use is needed to prevent symptoms of withdrawal.

While the number of young women who have a problem with alcohol use has increased in the past decade, generally women drink less than men and have a lower rate of alcohol-use disorder. Women tend to use alcohol to alleviate depression; men use it in response to stress (Closser 1992).

Alcohol abuse is believed to contribute to many medical problems, including cancer, cirrhosis of the liver, heart failure, organic brain disorders, and other organ damage. In addition, each year thousands of children are born with fetal alcohol syndrome.

Sedatives.   Other sedative substances include short-acting barbiturates, some nonbarbiturate sedatives, and the benzodiazepines. These substances have been used over the past century and are likely to result in dependency and abuse. While often prescribed in fairly small dosages by a physician for insomnia, headaches, or anxiety, over time when tolerance occurs, the person feels a need to increase the dose. Sometimes people will self-medicate with these drugs and become so dependent that when it seems possible that a physician will refuse to refill a prescription, the addict will shop for doctors who will write prescriptions, steal the drugs from others, or resort to purchasing them on the street. In the past, glutethimide (Doriden) and methaqualone (Quaalude) were widely used, but now these drugs are less frequently encountered, and methaqualone is illegal in the United States. The benzodiazepines, especially diazepam (Valium) and chlordiazepoxide (Librium), used since the 1960s, were initially developed as antianxiety agents. They have been widely prescribed by physicians, often to cure insomnia, but they can cause serious physical dependence and a withdrawal syndrome that is difficult to treat. Use of these substances can impair psychomotor performance and concentration, and they are particularly dangerous if used in combination with alcohol.

Opioid Narcotics

Opium poppies can be seen in Greek drawings and on coins that antedate written Greek literature by at least one thousand years. Homer and Hesiod wrote of the medicinal effects of poppies that symbolized sleep, even death. The standard agent for euthanasia and suicide, which was given to Socrates, was a mixture of hemlock and opium. Poppy seeds contain substantial amounts of morphine and codeine, so much so that eating a poppy-seed bagel may produce a positive urine test for opiates. During the Middle Ages opium was used sparingly, but its popularity increased during the Renaissance as it was used in medications for pain, among them laudanum, which was used well into the nineteenth century. In the early nineteenth century, the alkaline base in opium was isolated, crystallized, produced commercially, and called morphine. While the medical benefits were enormous, addiction and abuse became equally large problems (Karch 1993). People who abuse morphine take it by intravenous, subcutaneous, or intramuscular injection, by sniffing it, or by ingesting it by mouth.

Two developments in the 1870s were largely responsible for the major problem of opiate abuse. Hypodermic syringes became available in the United States, and the morphine derivative heroin was discovered and synthesized. It was used initially to suppress coughing in tuberculosis patients and to help people sleep. Its ability to diminish psychic pain led to a serious and widespread problem of addiction. In 1920, on the advice of the American Medical Association, the importation, manufacture, and sale of heroin were prohibited. Illicit heroin use increased markedly during the Vietnam War, declined when cocaine use became epidemic, but is now once again on the increase. Heroin can be produced from opium or from semipurified morphine, and historically, it has been ingested through intravenous injection or through burning it and inhaling the smoke. A purer grade of heroin that can be inhaled like cocaine is increasingly available on the market. Tolerance to heroin develops quickly, and larger doses are required to obtain the desired effect. Use ranges from controlled use, once or twice a week by people whose personal and professional lives remain intact, to compulsive, self-destructive use by people who have lost the ability to do anything but support their addiction. People addicted to heroin then find that they need to snort several bags* a day to postpone withdrawal, and they turn to injection, which works more efficiently. The addict can thus use fewer bags per day, so injection provides a cheaper way to stay high (Treaster 1993a). Heroin use carries a greater danger of chronic dependency than does cocaine use.

Codeine and dilaudid are naturally-occurring alkaloids found in opium and were isolated about twenty-five years after morphine. They were frequently given to people for pain and can easily be abused. Because it is not difficult to get a prescription for codeine, people who become dependent or addicted may "shop around" and try to obtain prescriptions from several doctors and dentists.

Users of opiates often seek to relieve and control feelings of rage and aggression. They wish to feel calm and mellow. Daily use is necessary in

---

*In the 1970s a bag contained five to ten milligrams of heroin. In 1999 street heroin was much purer, approximately 40–60 percent heroin. The increased purity allows the same effect to be achieved through intranasal use, thus making the drug more usable for people who shun needles or who are educated about needle use. In 1999 a bag usually contained five or ten milligrams of heroin and cost ten dollars. A bundle (ten to twelve bags) cost about eighty dollars.

order to avoid or relieve withdrawal symptoms, which serve as a negative reinforcer. The euphoric aspects of opiates are a positive reinforcer, because they produce a pleasurable state in what may otherwise be a very difficult life. Endocarditis and AIDS are two diseases unequivocally associated with intravenous opiate abuse: both illnesses have a higher incidence among users than among the public in general. Recently there has also been an increase in the incidence of tuberculosis secondary to AIDS and the immunocompromised state. Two-thirds of drug-related deaths result from opiate abuse.

Methadone maintenance, begun in the 1960s and expanded in the 1970s, raises controversial issues among treatment providers and the general public. Methadone is a synthetic narcotic analgesic compound that has few side effects, does not affect daily functioning, and can be administered orally once a day. The drug prevents the withdrawal syndrome in those addicted to opiates and blocks the effects of opiates. Programs treat all socioeconomic populations and often vary with respect to the use of the drug, the program design, the outcome goals, and the funding sources. They are regarded as most effective when the use of methadone is only one component of a multiservice program including individual and family work, vocational help, housing, and participation in a self-help program. Those who are critical of methadone programs believe that they merely substitute one narcotic for another, but advocates see it as similar to the use of insulin by diabetics. Methadone maintenance therapy is used in almost every nation that has a problem with narcotics addiction (Lowinson et al. 1992).

Methadone blocks the effects of only opiates, not marijuana, cocaine, or alcohol, and as a result, many people in methadone programs will frequently seek "highs" through use of cocaine. When this occurs, it is important that the intervention treat both the abuse of the opiate and that of the cocaine. Higher doses of methadone may be required than if the person is abusing only opiates (Stine 1992), although this is a controversial approach. Higher doses are also needed to accommodate street heroin, which is more pure. Another problem, and a leading cause of failure or death among people in methadone maintenance programs, is alcohol abuse.

Additional "supplements" or "boosters" to enhance the high are likely to be "street" Elavil (amitriptyline) or Catapres (clonidine).

Synthetic opiates often prescribed for pain, which have serious potential for abuse, include meperidine (Demerol), propoxyphene (Darvon), oxycodone (Percocet), and fentanyl.

Stimulants

Cocaine. Evidence of cocaine together with nicotine has been found in three-thousand-year-old Egyptian mummies, although cocaine is generally believed to come exclusively from New World plants (Karch 1993). Andean Indians are said to have known for centuries about the stimulant effects of chewing coca leaves, and they apparently suffered few of the undesirable effects. In the nineteenth century, cocaine was used in England and in Europe as a stimulant and an analgesic. In addition, wines containing coca were produced in France and in Italy and became very popular. Elixirs containing cocaine were used for a variety of ailments and were viewed as "restorative and tonic," and manufacturers of patent medicines added cocaine extract to most of their products. In the late 1870s an American, John Styth Pemberton, tried to imitate the Italian wines with a product called "French Wine Cola," but it was not successful. The word *wine* was dropped and a new formula was concocted combining cocaine and caffeine to produce Coca-Cola (Karch 1993), which contained cocaine until 1903.

The first cocaine epidemic began in the United States with its introduction in 1885 as a cure-all and ended in the 1920s when it became regarded as the most destructive of all illicit drugs. Its use peaked around 1900 but declined after purified cocaine became more readily available and users recognized that its toxicity and its addictive properties outweighed its curative (and pleasurable) properties. From 1900 to 1914, it was dispensed primarily in over-the-counter medications, without many constraints, but with the implementation of the Harrison Narcotics Act on March 1, 1915 (Kosten and Kleber 1992), no cocaine was permitted in over-the-counter medicinal products. A new epidemic began in the 1970s as cocaine appeared on the illegal drug market and was favored by jet-setters and yuppies, who began to use it for recreational purposes and, in many cases, believed that it improved social and vocational functioning by inducing a heightened euphoria. Added to the mystique was the belief that cocaine is a powerful aphrodisiac (Jaffe 1992); there is, however, no research to support this claim, and with chronic use sexual performance is often impaired. Negative publicity and bad experiences led to a decline in the use of cocaine by people who still had some promise in their future.

Cocaine may be chewed, snorted, introduced through the genitals or rectum, injected intravenously, or smoked after it has been converted to the freebase form (crack). As recreational use deteriorates to abuse, greater tolerance requires increased dosage. There is usually a pattern of sleep disruption, and instead of increased social functioning, assessment reveals increased isolation as obtaining and using the drug become more and more important. People who become seriously addicted to cocaine will binge with higher dosages for days or weeks and often will switch from snorting the drug to the more potent forms of ingestion: smoking or injection. People often do not seek intervention until they are bingeing at least once a week, and then they seek help usually because of the discomfort of withdrawal, commonly termed *crashing*. Following a binge, the euphoric mood and the drug-induced feeling of energy decline with the crash. The person experiences agitation, depression, anxiety, fatigue, and a craving for sleep. Because the stimulant effects of the cocaine may not have worn off, he or she may find it impossible to sleep and may try to induce sleep through the use of alcohol, sedatives, opiates, or marijuana. Some people with a history of chronic high-dose use may experience paranoia, with symptoms of hypervigilance and fear that are usually not present when the cocaine is out of the system. Sleep, food, and time usually remove the symptoms of crashing. After a few days, the person may again experience intense boredom and binge again, repeating the cycle (Gawin and Kleber 1992). Other risk factors may include the company of others who use cocaine (social reinforcement), the use of alcohol, which impairs judgment, feelings of anxiety because of environmental stressors, and anticipation of a euphoric state, even if transitory. Before the early 1980s cocaine was used in the form of its hydrochloride salt, a product extracted from the coca leaf, but in the past ten years, crack, the freebase form, has increased in popularity.

The typical cocaine user is no longer an upper-middle-class, white male, intranasal user, and while general use has declined, heavy, chronic use in some inner-city populations has increased. The decline in the number of users is greater than the decline in the amount used, and cocaine remains the second most widely used illegal drug.

Crack.   Crack first appeared in the mid-1980s in New York City, where it is still found in much greater quantity than in any other part of the United States, although it previously had been found on the West Coast, where it was called "rock cocaine." Cocaine hydrochloride, the commonly available form of cocaine, decomposes when smoked. It can be purified and made into crack, which is an alkaline form more potent than powder cocaine. Crack can be made in any sink or in a blender by mixing powdered cocaine (which is now relatively cheap) with water and bicarbonate of soda. Ready-to-use crack can be packaged in quantities small enough to sell for as little as five dollars a vial. At that price, it is available not just to the powerful, chic, and wealthy, as cocaine originally was, but also to the poor and to adolescents (Wallace 1992). There is an upsurge in the number of cases of AIDS and syphilis in the population that uses crack and intravenous cocaine, because in crack houses it is not uncommon to indiscriminately exchange sex for the drug. Crack takes four to six seconds to reach the brain, and the high lasts three to twelve minutes; thus it requires more frequent smoking than is necessary to reach a high from heroin (Cohen and Levy 1992). Some substance abusers use "speedballs," a mixture of cocaine and heroin. In addition to the symptoms experienced when crashing from cocaine, people who use crack may experience acute psychotic states accompanied by extreme hostility and belligerence and leading to violent, volatile, or suicidal behavior. Some will use barbiturates or diphenhydramine (Benzedrine), diazepam, alcohol, or opiates to try to avoid crashing or to decrease paranoid symptoms and insomnia.

Amphetamines and Methamphetamine.   Ephedrine is a naturally occurring stimulant that was initially used to treat asthma. Its success led to concern about its availability and to research in the 1930s directed at synthesizing it. Eventually, drug companies were able to manufacture amphetamines and later methamphetamine. As happened with cocaine fifty years earlier, many claims were made for the effectiveness of amphetamines in treating a range of diseases and disorders, including schizophrenia (Karch 1993).

The introduction of amphetamines led to a decrease in the abuse of cocaine, as amphetamines were less toxic, cheaper, easier to obtain, and more socially acceptable. An inhaler containing diphenhydramine, developed to relieve nasal congestion, was found to increase alertness, relieve drowsiness and fatigue, and produce a sense of well-being, which led to its becoming a drug of abuse. The inhalers contained papers soaked with amphetamines. The papers were smuggled into prisons, where they were chewed. When this drug use was discovered, and amphetamine abuse was recognized as widespread, the inhaler was redesigned and finally restricted to prescription sales only. Soldiers in World War II were given amphetamines to help them stay alert, and many returned home addicted, resulting in laws that tightened distribution.

Amphetamines are used for stimulation and to reduce fatigue; paradoxically, some people feel calmer and less anxious when given amphetamines. This effect is probably related to differing personality types, such as those with variants of attention deficit disorders (ADD) who respond well to the drug. Currently, abuse of amphetamines is minor compared with cocaine abuse. While there can be physical problems, strokes, cardiovascular problems, and insomnia as a result of misuse, of major concern is the possibility of psychosis following heavy use at high doses, which can lead to incorrect diagnosis if a person is admitted through an emergency room without a thorough assessment of substance-use history. Generally, the psychotic symptoms will disappear within a few days of abstinence. Transient depressive or anxiety symptoms, as well as agitated, violent behavior and symptoms similar to those of schizophrenia or paranoia, are sometimes observed following withdrawal from amphetamines.

Most people abusing methamphetamine prefer to use the drug by intravenous injection or by pill, though sniffing also occurs. Tolerance develops quickly, requiring increasing frequency at higher doses. Ice, a smokable form of crystallized methamphetamine hydrochloride that is considered a "designer drug," is manufactured primarily in the Orient. Its use is greatest in Hawaii and on the West Coast. At 90 percent purity, it is very potent, and its effect can last as long as eight hours. Ice produces a state of euphoria and is relatively inexpensive, but tolerance soon develops. It has never become very popular outside of the West Coast because of its inaccessibility.

Caffeine. Caffeine is the most widely consumed psychoactive substance in the world. It is the most widely used stimulant drug in the United States, with an annual consumption of more than 100,000 tons (Karch 1993). Eighty percent of the adult population in the United States drink coffee or tea, and caffeine is present in many soft drinks and some medications. Very little is known about its chemical effects or its toxicology. The effects usually last about three to four hours, and heavy use may cause symptoms of anxiety or panic.

People generally do not generally think of caffeine consumption as a disorder. It often plays a part in one's social functioning—taking a coffee break or lingering over coffee after dinner, for example. There are, however, several disorders associated with caffeine: caffeine dependence, caffeine intoxication, caffeine withdrawal, caffeine-induced anxiety disorder, and caffeine-induced sleep disorder. A person who develops such disorders has usually been consuming at least a pint of caffeine daily.

To determine if caffeine intake constitutes a disorder, clearly a history of amount consumed must be taken. It should include not just coffee and tea but any other beverages and medications that contain caffeine.

Withdrawal symptoms include severe headaches, sleepiness, irritabililty, and, for some, anxiety and depression. To eliminate or at least reduce withdrawal symptoms, it is recommended that intake be tapered off, not stopped abruptly.

Psychedelics and Hallucinogens

Psychedelic drugs are substances with unusually wide-ranging psychological effects. The drugs produce vivid and unusual changes in perceptions, thoughts, and feelings, without much physical effect. In predisposed people, the drugs may produce hallucinations and may mimic psychosis. The best-known hallucinogens are two naturally found substances, mescaline and psilocybin, and the synthetic lysergic acid diethylamide (LSD). These drugs are used to stimulate fantasy and escape reality and logical thought processes; some users claim they enhance creativity. Most people who use psychedelic drugs do so for experimentation or merely out of curiosity, and long-term or frequent use is uncommon. Thus craving, withdrawal, and dependency are not likely.

The psychedelic drug experience generated by these substances is popularly referred to as the *trip*. Perceptions are intensified, attention is given to previously unnoticed detail, and one experiences the presence of dream-like imagery and a distorted sense of time and space. If the experience is unpleasant, it is called a "bad trip." A bad trip may result in acute anxiety or paranoid reactions, and sometimes it is accompanied by feelings of going insane. The length of the trip depends upon the drug, but with LSD, the longest trip usually ends within twenty-four hours. When the person is experiencing a bad trip, providing supportive reassurance, helping to talk the person down, and sometimes giving a mild tranquilizer or sedative are the most effective approaches. Occasionally, a bad trip will persist, and the person may need hospitalization. This occurs most frequently with people who have a history of serious emotional problems. Another adverse reaction can be a *flashback*, a transitory recurrence of the changes produced by the drug that may occur when the person is under emotional stress, has used psychedelic drugs repeatedly and has had many bad trips, or is abusing alcohol or other drugs, especially marijuana. The use of psychedelics may also accelerate an emerging psychological process or precipitate a full-blown schizophrenic episode. The flashback experience, however, need not always be unpleasant. If flashbacks are persistent the person may be suffering from a posthallucinogen perception disorder.

Mescaline.   Mescaline comes from the peyote cactus, which is used by Native Americans of the Southwest as part of their religious rites. While it can distort reality to the point of producing an artificial psychosis, it is rarely abused. Mescaline analogues, however, are part of a group known as "designer drugs" that are manufactured illegally and have become increasingly popular. The drugs are structurally related to mescaline and amphetamines (Jaffe 1989). They were first synthesized about 1920 and appeared as street drugs in the late 1960s and early 1970s. One of the most popular is called XTC, or Ecstasy (3,4,-methylenedioxymethamphetamine). Its effects last two to four hours and appear to precipitate intense feelings, self-exploration, and emotional openness. Use of the drug is often followed by feelings of fatigue and some anxiety, but rarely by psychotic reactions or flashbacks.

Psilocybin ("Magic Mushrooms").   Psilocybin is a substance found in three different kinds of mushrooms that produces psychedelic effects. Large quantities were grown for illegal distribution, and until the mid-1980s, when they were banned, kits with spores were available for homegrown crops.

LSD.   LSD (lysergic acid diethylamide) was first synthesized in Europe in the 1930s by Albert Hoffman to serve as a circulatory and respiratory stimulant. In 1943 he ingested some by accident, and his experience led to the beginning of the modern psychedelic age (Karch 1993). Psychiatrists were encouraged to try it in order to experience a psychotic state. The CIA was reported to have tried it, unsuccessfully, in some mind-control experiments. While there is not a large illegal consumer market for LSD, early on it did influence the direction of psychiatric research toward considering the chemical origins of emotional disorders.

The psychedelic age really began in the early 1960s, when Timothy Leary, doing research on psilocybin at Harvard, tried LSD, and immediately turned to research on this substance. His continuing use of LSD and his message, through the media, to "tune in, turn on, drop out" led to his dismissal from the Harvard faculty. Use of LSD resulted in psychic and perceptual symptoms. Some adverse reactions (bad trips) were acute panic reactions, flashbacks, and lapses of judgment that resulted in homicidal or self-destructive behavior. In the 1960s and early 1970s, some people who used LSD heavily saw themselves as members of a distinct subculture and referred to themselves as *acidheads* or *acid freaks*. In 1965 LSD was outlawed by the federal government. This prohibition, plus concern (which has never been documented) about possible chromosomal damage as a result of continued use, led to its decline, although it remains the most common psychedelic drug on the illegal market. Currently, there is believed to be an increase in LSD use, especially by high school students. LSD is inexpensive and easy to transport, hence its appeal to the young.

Cannabis and Hashish

Although cannabis, popularly known as marijuana, use is illegal, the substance is commonplace and is used regularly by millions. Millions more are occasional users, making it by far the most frequently used illegal drug. It is estimated that 62 million Americans have used it at least once; some use it occasionally, others use it once or twice a week, and a very small number smoke it daily (Jaffe 1989). Its active ingredient, Delta-9-Tetrahydrocannabinol, is found in the resin covering the flowers and top leaves of cannabis (hemp) plants. It is usually smoked in a cigarette ("joint") or pipe. Hashish, which is resin in its pure form, is also most frequently smoked. Both substances can produce a mildly euphoric mood and greater awareness of sights, sounds, and others, as well as a slowing down of time. Slowed reaction time can impair coordination and attention and thus can be hazardous. Adverse reactions include acute anxiety, paranoid thoughts, fears of death or of going insane, and, rarely, psychotic reactions.

There does not appear to be a serious problem of addiction to marijuana, as few report an urgent need to obtain the substance or to increase the dosage. Even heavy users do not experience severe withdrawal reactions, and dependency occurs much less frequently than for users of alcohol, cocaine, or heroin. The "stepping-stone hypothesis" suggests that using alcohol predates use of marijuana, which will then lead to the use of opioids or other illicit drugs, but research indicates that most alcohol users do not use marijuana and most marijuana users do not go on to use cocaine or heroin.

PCP and Ketamine

Phencyclidine.   Phencyclidine (PCP) was introduced in the 1950s as an anesthetic that produced few physiological problems, but a significant number of the patients became delirious and hard to manage following surgery. Recreational use began in California in the 1950s, and its abuse became prevalent in the 1970s and early 1980s (Karch 1993), distributed under the names *angel dust* and *crystal*. It has stimulant and hallucinogenic properties and can be taken orally, snorted, or injected intravenously, but usually it is smoked because the reaction is faster.

Some people using PCP become energetic and elated, others experience soothing euphoria and peace, and still others experience depersonalization and distorted body image. Mild depression may be experienced as the drug's effects wane. Chronic high-dose users may become anxious, confused, incoherent, paranoid, or violent, and may require hospitalization or the use of antipsychotic medication. Illicit use of PCP has declined, because of an increase in price and fears of antisocial, especially violent, behavior; however, it remains a serious problem for a small number of people, usually young men. It is used as an anesthetic by veterinarians.

Ketamine. Ketamine was first used in 1969 as a surgical anesthetic or analgesic. It was found to induce a usually pleasant dreamlike state, confusion, and occasionally delirium. It can produce a psychedelic experience in small doses, with a sense of dissociation, disconnection, and floating. It is not widely abused, although it is a popular "club" drug and widely used by people who frequent such settings.

Two additional addictions, nicotine and gambling, although legal, can cause many personal and medical problems.

Nicotine

There are about 50 million smokers and 40 million former smokers in the United States (Kleber and Conney 1994). Nicotine, the addictive component in cigarettes, is the most difficult drug to give up once a person becomes addicted, yet users report that it gives the least active pleasure. In 1988 U.S. surgeon general C. Everett Koop stated in a report that addiction to tobacco and cigarettes was equivalent in tenaciousness to addiction to heroin or cocaine. It is extremely difficult for people to stop smoking. It is estimated that in a given year, 90 percent of those who try to stop smoking fail; it often takes several attempts before success is achieved. Currently, smoking cigarettes is viewed by many as socially unacceptable, and smokers are sometimes treated like pariahs. Any substance that is smoked will potentially cause damage to the lungs, and nicotine increases the risk of cardiovascular disease. Tobacco smoking is the greatest cause of morbidity in the world, far greater than abuse of alcohol or other substances (L'Abate, Farrar, and Serritella 1992).

Addiction to nicotine develops quickly from a single incident of smoking to a pattern of several cigarettes in an hour. Dependence is easy to develop, as cigarettes are legal and used continually, rather than episodically. For most smokers, the stimulating, pleasurable sensation disappears in about half an hour. Withdrawal from nicotine may be experienced as craving, irritability, difficulty with concentration, anxiety, headache, and gastrointestinal problems.

Gambling

Compulsive gambling is a serious addiction that does not primarily involve drugs, although there is often secondary addiction to alcohol or drugs. There is usually no physiological danger. People may turn to gambling magically hoping that a win would relieve the depression and anxiety caused by the circumstances of their lives. Gambling may be a legal, socially acceptable addiction, and it is estimated that up to a third of the population gamble weekly. Forty-eight of the fifty states allow for some form of legal gambling.

It is an addiction that frequently begins, for men, in adolescence, and usually later for women, who may be seeking a way to make money in order to get out of a destructive relationship. A *big win*, defined as making at least 50 percent of one's annual income (Blume 1992), will often lead to escalating the habit. Self-esteem becomes related to making "smart" bets, and a tolerance is reached at which it takes more and more risk to try to win and to reach the desired state of euphoria. A compulsive gambler will continue to increase the stakes and the frequency of gambling. With greater betting risks comes deteriorating behavior, evidenced by excuses, denial, lying, forgery, and embezzlement, possibly leading to job loss or even jail.

AIDS and Substance Abuse

The existence of AIDS forced people working in the field of substance abuse to take a broader look at the implications of their clients' medical problems. The focus could no longer be simply on treatment for the abuse of a particular substance but also had to address such problems as intravenous drug use, needle-exchange programs, free needle distribution, education about needle cleaning, and, most especially, education about safe sex, often to resistant populations. At least 1 million people are infected with HIV, and the Centers for Disease Control (CDC) estimated a total of

285,000 to 340,000 deaths from AIDS between 1984 and 1993 (Cohen and Levy 1992). Intravenous drug users account for approximately 25 percent of all AIDS cases in the United States, and the percentage is increasing. The greatest concentration of cases of AIDS from intravenous drug use is in New York City, where the most common form of heterosexual transmission involves a male intravenous drug user passing the virus to a female heterosexual partner who does not inject. When children are born infected, it is almost always the result of intravenous drug use by the mother or her sexual partner. The CDC lists pediatric AIDS as a major cause of death among poor children, with as many as 2,000 HIV-positive babies born annually. Methadone maintenance programs have proved to be effective in reducing the incidence of intravenous drug use and sharing of unsterilized needles.

People who are chemically dependent and HIV-positive or have AIDS need services such as medical care, medication, nutrition counseling, psychotherapy, and access to residential medical and drug treatment programs. Twelve-step programs such as Positive Anonymous (PA) have been established to meet the special needs of this population. There is a high risk for relapse if the person becomes sicker, more anxious, depressed, or is in pain.

AIDS education should be routinely provided for participants in all inpatient and outpatient substance abuse programs, but particularly for those who are HIV-positive and may deny the implications for AIDS transmission, especially if they look and feel well.

Assessment

Assessment of a person with a substance abuse disorder can be very difficult, as the person usually uses the defense of denial, and it is difficult to get an accurate history of the abuse, the frequency, and the amount used. Often people who come to the attention of professionals in the field are there through coercion by an employer, a family member, or the legal system. In order to get an accurate picture of the type(s) of drugs used, the frequency of use, the progression of the disorder, and the effect on functioning, it may be necessary to obtain information from families, friends, and employers.

Assessment is essential in order to determine an appropriate plan for intervention. Motivation must be carefully assessed, and realistic goals set. The initial goal is detoxification and withdrawal from use of the substance, though many people are not ready for prolonged abstinence or for pursuing lifetime recovery. It is important to assess the person's personal and cultural feelings about substance abuse in order for the intervention plan to be effective. It is also important to be aware of the presence, or history, of emotional disorders. The person's physical condition must be assessed in order to determine what type of medical attention may be needed at the time of withdrawal and after. Urine analysis and blood studies may be needed as an adjunct to the psychosocial assessment. Assessment of the person's support system will indicate whether the person should return to the same environment if abstinence is to be maintained. Family history often reveals alcoholism; domestic violence; dysfunctional households; deception; physical, emotional, and sexual abuse; inconsistency, overstimulation, and antisocial behavior leading to low self-esteem, poor relationships, difficulty in identifying and handling feelings, and poor self-care. If possible, it is important to explore the person's feelings when he or she turns to substances, especially awareness of emptiness and boredom, and to try to identify what adaptive function the individual sought through the substance use.

Because there is no one treatment of choice for all people who suffer from substance use disorders, careful assessment is doubly important in order to tailor the plan for intervention to individual needs and beliefs. As well as identifying the type(s) of substances used, the assessment must take into account the individual's own personality, defenses, ego functioning, and life experiences and must take care to avoid stereotyping. Ego functions that may be impaired are judgment, regulation and control of affects, frustration tolerance, and capacity for object relationships. There is limited awareness of signal anxiety, and some may actually seek out self-destructive behavior.

Since clients who have problems with substance use may seek intervention for marital, financial, vocational, or relationship problems and may not mention or identify a substance use disorder, it is very important to include exploration of alcohol or drug history in any psychosocial assessment.

Assessing whether or not a person is suffering from a substance abuse disorder is accomplished through a much more directive approach than when assessing a person for other psychosocial problems. Direct questions are asked about:

- the age at which substance use began
- what substance was used initially and what subsequently
- pattern of use—daily, weekly, weekends, sporadically, alone, with others
- past attempts to stop and results of those attempts
- history of suicide attempts, incarceration, DWI

- physiological symptoms and problems, including "the shakes," blackouts, and delirium tremens
- psychiatric symptoms such as hallucinations and paranoia
- family relationships
- whether the person is annoyed when people talk about the substance use
- whether the person feels guilty about the substance use
- sources of income

Asking specific questions not only helps to direct the subsequent intervention but also can be helpful in reducing the person's denial of the severity of the problem. The social worker must, however, always remember that assessment is being made of a person, not merely of a substance abuser, and the worker must take care to make a thorough assessment that may reveal why the person abuses substances and what strengths and weaknesses exist in the environment that may help or sabotage efforts to overcome the disorder.

Intervention

The cocaine and crack epidemic of the 1980s challenged traditional alcohol and drug treatment programs, because it resulted in a significant number of people being addicted not only to cocaine or crack but also to alcohol. It pointed out the failure of a system that separates alcoholism and chemical dependency, and it increased the importance of a thorough assessment.

There are five basic models of intervention for substance abuse: moral, learning, disease, self-medication, and psychosocial. The moral model, most prevalent in the late nineteenth and early twentieth centuries, assumes that the abuser suffers from weakness, bad character, and a lack of will; the intervention approach is punitive, often religious, and aimed at strengthening willpower leading to abstinence. This model particularly stigmatized women, who were regarded as more moral than men. Thus, if they abused alcohol, they were viewed as more deviant (Rhodes and Johnson 1994). The learning model places less blame on the individual, suggesting that the person has learned bad habits, and the goal of intervention is increasing self-control and learning new, more adaptive coping skills. The disease model, probably the most widely accepted of the models, views substance abuse disorder as a disease without a cure, with complete abstinence as the goal of intervention. The self-medication model sees substance abuse as resulting from an attempt by the person to relieve symptoms of mental disorders or psychological stress by using substances, and intervention is aimed at the psychopathology. Finally, the psychosocial model sees substance abuse disorders as caused by external environmental factors such as family, poverty, peer pressure, or unemployment, and intervention is geared toward enhancing coping skills and altering the environment (Brower, Blow, and Beresford 1989). Clearly, each model has limitations, and optimal intervention should be guided by a thorough biopsychosocial assessment that leads to an individualized plan for intervention that might integrate several of the basic models.

Eighty percent of people who abuse substances go untreated, largely by choice (Cohen and Levy 1992). Thus a major issue is not so much what type of intervention but the failure of people to seek help or the failure of programs to reach them. Many people lack the motivation to give up the use of substances, seeing no reason to change, either because their lives are so unfulfilling or because they are so self-absorbed that they fail to recognize the impact of their disorder on others. Denial is another obstacle to intervention, as people fail to acknowledge that their substance abuse has gotten out of control and that they use substances to avoid painful feelings, as well as to temporarily enhance feelings of self-esteem and power. Lack of availability of services to special populations—for example, single mothers with few or no child care resources—can also prevent intervention.

Recovery from addiction always occurs in two stages, followed in some cases by a third stage. The first stage is detoxification, withdrawal, and abstinence, which allows the body to reach a new level of physiological homeostasis free of the drug or its by-products. This stage usually lasts five to seven days, depending on the type of drug, frequency of use and dosage, and general physical health, though there are often protracted withdrawal symptoms. The second stage, requiring abstinence, is a stage of continuing recovery and involves confronting self-defeating behavior, becoming aware of the consequences of the substance abuse, and identifying distorted thinking with respect to the substance use; many of these steps are now subsumed under the term *relapse prevention*. A third stage, which many never pursue, involves addressing the underlying social and emotional problems that may have led to the substance abuse.

The type and goal of intervention may depend on whether the clinician sees substance abuse as a disease requiring withdrawal and abstinence, as a symptom of an underlying emotional problem that must be addressed, or as a defense against feelings associated with inner or outer reality. The disorder, or disease, model can be therapeutically useful, as the clinician can make an analogy to common diseases such as diabetes or hypertension and can help the person with the disorder not to avoid its existence but rather to look at the possibility of taking joint responsibility with the clinician to formulate a plan to arrest it. Many drug abusers may use narcotics and hypnotics as a defense against feelings of rage, shame, and jealousy; stimulants, against depression and weakness; alcohol, against guilt, loneliness, and related anxiety; and psychedelics, against boredom and disillusionment (Wurmser 1992).

Inpatient treatment may be indicated if the person has been consistently abusing substances at high doses, if other forms of intervention are not accepted or have failed, if the person has been freebasing cocaine over a period of time, if the person is addicted to more than one substance, or if medical attention is needed. If the inpatient treatment extends beyond the stage of detoxification and withdrawal, much of the ongoing intervention combines individual and group work. Attempts are made to help the individual understand the past need to abuse substances and how challenging it may be to avoid relapse. High-risk factors that might lead to relapse should be identified, and strategies devised to help the person avoid people, places, and situations that might lead to renewed self-destructive behavior. Involvement with a twelve-step program often begins in an inpatient setting and continues on an outpatient basis, with the program serving to help alleviate isolation and guilt, meet dependency needs, give some structure, provide twenty-four-hour support, and eventually provide a chance to help others and thus enhance self-esteem. Inpatient intervention, including detoxification, is becoming shorter in duration because of insurance company directives: from five to seven days, occasionally two weeks, for crack/cocaine; one to three weeks for heroin; and fourteen to twenty-eight days for alcohol abuse.

In our present economy and with constraints on spending for health/ mental health care, inpatient treatment is going to be very limited. It will probably be reserved for only the most debilitated and seriously addicted people, especially those who need medical attention for malnutrition, AIDS, TB, or syphilis that probably resulted from the substance use, or for supervision in regulating methadone.

Therapeutic communities, staffed by former addicts and by professionals, where people stay for eighteen to twenty-four months are an intervention for high-dose, high-frequency substance users whose psychosocial functioning has significantly deteriorated. Many people in these facilities are unemployed, homeless, and have no relationships in the community except with other people who also abuse substances.

Highly structured, intensive outpatient treatment is viewed as being more cost-effective and gives the individual a chance to be abstinent within the day-to-day context of life. If this plan is used as a substitute for inpatient intervention, the person usually attends four or five times a week initially, tapering off over a period of months to one or two times a week (Tatarsky and Washton 1992). Most programs have an open-ended final phase. Intervention consists of individual, family, and group sessions, medical evaluation, educational meetings, urine testing, and attendance at twelve-step programs. An initial focus is on recognizing loss of control over substance use and getting through each day without using a substance in spite of craving and the existence of high-risk situations, such as having some extra money, passing a familiar bar, seeing drug paraphernalia, or meeting up with friends who are abusing substances. Total abstinence is desired, but many programs will continue to work with an individual who has an occasional "slip." The intensity of the treatment needs will depend on the degree of substance abuse, availability of support systems, motivation for abstinence, and general psychosocial functioning.

Twelve-step programs, begun in 1935 when Alcoholics Anonymous was founded, are readily available to people who suffer from substance use disorders and to their families. These programs see substance abuse as a spiritual and biological disorder. People may attend meetings while in inpatient or intensive outpatient treatment or they may go when they simply run out of excuses, recognize a problem, or a friend or family member suggests it. New members are encouraged to attend these programs daily for the first three months and to find a sponsor, a person who has been abstinent for a long period of time, who will be readily available to them. The programs enhance ego functioning. Step 1 introduces reality and the need for greater impulse control as the person acknowledges his or her powerlessness to control the substance use. Steps 4 through 10 further enhance reality testing, as the person must attempt to make an honest assessment of strengths and weaknesses and learn to understand and control feelings (Derby 1992). The person's capacity for object relations increases through permitting others to help and later helping others. The lessening of magical thinking and of the use of denial and projection, as well as the development of greater impulse control, frees energy for enhancing the autonomous ego functions. Because twelve-step programs are a very important intervention for many people with substance use disorders, clinicians should be familiar not only with the philosophy but also with the actual format of meetings. There are groups designed for specific populations, as well as more heterogeneous groups, and clinicians, as part of their training, should attend several different meetings. Self-help or mutual-aid groups have become an important source of health/mental health care. They are not limited to people with substance abuse problems but are organized for people who can identify with each other because of a disorder, a syndrome, or an experience that they have in common and who join together to fulfill a need, cope with a crisis, or support and educate each other in a common effort to overcome the shared problem.

Relapse is to be expected, and clinicians should consider this when they make their plan for intervention. Relapse is most common in the first six months following the start of abstinence, and intensive outpatient treatment during this period is often indicated. Most relapse prevention programs use psychoeducation about the biopsychosocial problems of substance abuse, together with a cognitive-behavioral approach involving confrontation of distorted beliefs and self-defeating behavior patterns, while introducing new problem-solving skills. Programs emphasize the need for change in values, attitudes, self-concept, possibly in living situation and support systems, and whatever else is needed to improve the quality of life. That these changes may be difficult and result in real losses needs to be recognized as a problem in establishing a drug-free identity. The clinician must guard against showing feelings of frustration when a person relapses. This phase of intervention involves showing acceptance, patience, and forgiveness while stressing the need to return to abstinence. It may be difficult for the clinician, particularly since it involves awareness of his or her own feelings about people who misuse substances.

In addition to relapse prevention programs there is also the "harm reduction" approach, which involves needle exchange programs and users of multiple substances agreeing to use only one substance or cutting down on use.

Insight-oriented psychotherapy may be sought after withdrawal and a period of abstinence. Many people with substance use disorders do not seek or want this final phase of intervention. Because clients who do seek psychotherapy often feel guilty and ashamed of their substance use and may have perceived themselves as criticized, stigmatized, deserving of punishment, and frequently misunderstood, the clinician needs to be able to show a good understanding of the problems of addiction and recovery and convey a nonjudgmental, understanding, respectful, and empathic approach. Support should be given for efforts to recognize and understand affects and to accept dependency needs. Denial of the extent and results of the substance abuse and ambivalence about total abstention must always be addressed. Efforts should be made to make substance abuse ego-dystonic.

Substance abuse affects the entire family, and intervention with the family, if possible, should be part of all inpatient and outpatient programs. Family assessment must look at the family's interactional pattern, and it is very important to determine if the family can be a potential source of support for, or an impediment to, the person's attempt at abstinence. The family may be frustrated, angry, and intolerant of the person's inability to stop the substance misuse, or they may be engaged in a codependent relationship in which they are caught up in, and react to, the person's substance abuse. Assessment should include looking at the importance of the substance abuse in the family's functioning. In some cases, it may be the organizing factor of family roles and functions, so that life is geared to adapting to the person who is abusing a substance; in this case, abstinence may be a threat to maintaining the family equilibrium. While intervention is needed to improve the general family functioning, the person who is abusing a substance may not be willing to stop, and the family will need help to make changes in their own behavior, which may have evolved around the person abusing the substance. They will need to set limits and to act to improve their self-image and well-being. In some cases, the family member who is abusing a substance will not change as the family changes, and it becomes clear that there is no choice other than to exclude this family member. In other cases, assessment may reveal a family that functions poorly and where interactions perpetuate the problem of substance abuse; here the person may need to separate from the family in order to maintain abstinence.

Families are seen as a unit or often in supportive multifamily groups. They need to have an opportunity to express their frustration, disappointment, anger, pain, helplessness, hopelessness, and feelings of being overburdened by the demands of the substance abuser and other family members. Twelve-step programs such as Al-Anon exist especially for family members. Some clinicians working with people who are actively abusing substances, or with their family members, will use a planned intervention in which family members and other significant people will come together with the clinician to confront the person about observed behavior and the need to follow the prescribed intervention.

Children raised in families where one or both parents are misusing substances need particular attention, for they are at risk for physical and sexual abuse, and for developing emotional and psychosocial problems, as well as for their own substance abuse. Boundaries between the family subsystems are usually weak, and parents may not be able to fulfill their roles. Children often take on roles to try to maintain an equilibrium, such as assuming parental duties, becoming the family scapegoat, or becoming the placater, who always attempts to fix things (Lewis 1992). Social workers in schools should be alert to children who miss a lot of school, appear sleepy and unkempt, are isolated, or appear depressed. These symptoms may be the result of substance abuse in their homes or their own misuse. Adults raised in homes where there was substance abuse can participate in ACOA (Adult Children of Alcoholics) twelve-step support programs.

Medications may play several roles in intervening with substance abuse. These include treatment of overdoses and acute intoxication with naloxone (Narcan) for opioids or flumazenil (Romazicon) for benzodiazepine or other sedatives; detoxification or withdrawal with benzodiazepines, clonidine (Catapres); blockage of drug reinforcement with naltrexone (Revia); development of responses to the abuse substance with disulfiram (Antabuse); and substitution agents to produce cross-tolerance and reduce drug raving with methadone. Detoxification is needed if antagonistic medications such as naltrexone for opioid dependence or disulfiram for alcoholism are to be used; however, agonist maintenance medications such as methadone or buprenorphine do not require detoxification before these medications can be used (Kosten 1997:750–51).

Medications are also sometimes used to help people with substance use disorders alleviate symptoms, such as depression and anxiety, that exist after withdrawal. Medications are often necessary in the detoxification phase, when minor tranquilizers are frequently used for alcohol or sedative-hypnotic withdrawal. Methadone should be used for opiate detoxification, and tapered off in two to three weeks. Clonidine (Catapres) is also useful for opiate detoxification. Methadone maintenance is believed by many to be essential for people who chronically abuse opiates, and the maintenance dosage, given orally, is generally between sixty and one hundred milligrams per day. This intervention is based on the medical model that postulates the development of a chronic "metabolic defect" as a result of unspecified metabolic changes in the body of a person following prolonged use of heroin and other opiates. These changes cause craving after detoxification, and methadone needs to be used to control the craving by substituting for heroin on the appropriate neurotransmitter receptor sites. Naltrexone (Revia), an opiate antagonist with few side effects, can also be used to block the effects of opiates, for interruption of the cycle of opiate addiction, and for maintenance of abstinence. (Cohen and Levy 1992; Gitlin 1990). A synthetic opioid antagonist, buprenorphine (Buprenex), may prove to be more effective than methadone for some people addicted to heroin, and to cocaine, as withdrawal from it is relatively easy and people experience satisfying feelings similar to those experienced with other opiates (Greenstein, Fudala, and O'Brien 1992). Many people who are alcohol-dependent are willing to take disulfiram (Antabuse), which provides negative reinforcement to continued alcohol use because it causes nausea and discomfort if alcohol is ingested. On December 30, 1994, the Food and Drug Administration approved the use of naltrexone, which has been used in the treatment of opiate addiction. It is a narcotic antagonist that reverses the effects of heroin overdose and blocks the action of opiates at the nerve receptor sites for forty-eight hours or more. Taken regularly, it prevents the craving side effect. It is marketed under the brand name Revia when used for alcoholism, preferably in conjunction with other psychosocial interventions, and has been shown to reduce craving. Studies have shown that it is effective in reducing craving, an alcohol-induced sense of euphoria, and subsequent relapse. It is not believed to be habit-forming, and the major side effect, experienced by only about 10 percent of those who take it, is nausea (Leary 1995).

Nicotine supplied through chewing gum (Nicorette) or a nicotine patch (Nicoderm) has been used by people attempting to give up cigarettes and has met with some success. It should be noted that medications are not particularly effective unless used as an adjunct to other types of needed intervention.

Those who are involved in planning treatment programs for people abusing substances need to look at the particular problems that women, especially single mothers, may have. Most treatment programs are designed for men; if there are programs for women, often there is no one who can care for children if the woman needs inpatient or intensive outpatient treatment: the fathers are often absent, and other family members may no longer be willing or able to help with child care after years of frustration. Transportation may not be available, or the person may not be able to afford it. Mothers also may fear that going to a program could result in their children's placement in foster care. Finally, many of these women feel ashamed and guilty about their drug use and possible sexual behavior, and they fear being judged. Social workers need to be attuned to the daily needs of these women; they should approach such clients with skilled, sensitive, nonjudgmental counseling. There is clearly a need for more programs designed specifically for women.

Dual Diagnosis

The term *dual diagnosis* refers to people in substance abuse programs who also have identified mental disorders, while the term *MICA* refers to clients seen in psychiatric programs who also have a chemical dependency problem (Beeder and Millman 1992). The mental disorder may be an affect, anxiety, schizophrenic, eating, or personality disorder, and the chemical dependency may be to any abusable substance. The Epidemiological Catchment Area Survey estimated that 50 percent of people addicted to a substance also have another mental disorder and that having a mental disorder nearly triples the risk of alcohol or other drug problems. It further estimated that 70 percent of people with schizophrenia have a problem with substance abuse and that the lifetime rate of substance abuse in people with antisocial personality disorder was 84 percent. The synergistic effect of substance use and mental illness is not clear, and many of these clients fall between the cracks of the alcohol, drug, and mental health systems. It is known that the presence of an emotional disorder may lead to drug abuse and dependence, since the person may try to self-medicate with alcohol or drugs. It is also recognized that impaired judgment can contribute to substance misuse. Alcohol and drugs can also cause mental disorders. There is obviously a need for comprehensive, integrated, holistic care based on good biopsychosocial assessment, and social workers can play important roles as case managers for these clients.

Obstacles to intervention for people with dual diagnoses, or MICA clients, include the separation of programs for alcohol abuse, drug abuse, and mental disorders, which require different funding sources and different licensing. The often conflicting philosophies of these different treatment providers may also present a stumbling block.

Many MICA clients obtain acute intervention through hospital emergency rooms when they seek relief of symptoms of one or more disorders. By age twenty-nine, the typical MICA client has had eight psychiatric hospitalizations, and those who continue to use mind-altering substances have an annual admission rate more than twice that of chronic psychiatric clients who are not substance abusers. However, their stays are usually shorter (Cohen and Levy 1992). MICA clients also are seen in medical clinics, as they are very vulnerable to contracting AIDS and other sexually transmitted diseases because their mental disorders may result in poorer ego functioning and fewer defenses, resulting in at-risk behavior, such as intravenous drug use and unprotected sexual contact. Minority clients are overrepresented among the MICA population and among the homeless, who have few of their daily needs met and are at high risk for substance abuse.

Assessment is crucial, as it will affect the plan and the setting for intervention, as well as the prognosis for abstinence. It is initially important to determine which disorder the client focuses on, and which, if any, he or she denies. One major problem is that the effect of the substance abuse on personality and mood may be underestimated, and the psychiatric problems may be mistakenly seen as preceding the drug use. Some common symptoms are low self-esteem, limited coping skills, isolation, and poor support systems. Careful assessment must be made of the client's thoughts, feelings, and behavior, as well as his or her psychiatric and substance use history, number and type of substances used, frequency and amount of use, and periods of abstinence, if any. Lifestyle, vocational history, housing, and social and economic supports must also be evaluated if possible, although it may be difficult to obtain data about long-term chronic users who have no collateral supports. It is most important to determine whether the symptoms of mental disorder were present before the substance abuse began or emerged as a result of substance use, and whether they are present following abstinence, as well as whether the substance abuse continues in the absence of symptoms of a mental disorder. Also important is whether there is a family history of substance abuse, mental disorders, or both.

In addition to getting information from family members about the presence of a coexisting mental disorder, it is best to wait until the person is abstinent for at least six weeks to be sure that the symptoms did not result from the abuse, from withdrawal, or from rebound abstinence effects. Unfortunately, it may not be possible to wait this long. Family information must be evaluated with caution, as the family may deny or be prejudiced about one or the other disorder. Relapse may be prevented if a coexisting disorder is assessed and treated. As there has been greater acceptance of the existence of dual diagnoses, twelve-step "double-trouble" meetings have proliferated. Good plans for intervention have been hindered by the difference in approach to intervention by mental health and chemical dependence providers, and also by funding, which often provides money for intervention for mental disorders or substance use disorders, but not both.

Although substance abuse disorders were separated from personality disorders in DSM-III, clinicians recognize a strong relationship between substance use and Axis II personality disorders. People with cocaine or opiate use disorders have unusually high rates of comorbid Axis I depressive and anxiety disorders, as well as alcoholism (Rounsaville and Lithar 1992). In addition, clinicians often uncover an Axis II disorder, which most frequently is an antisocial, borderline, or passive-aggressive personality disorder (Kleinman et al. 1992).

Symptoms of mental disorders may perpetuate substance abuse, and substance abuse may precipitate initial or recurrent symptoms of mental disorders. Thus there is often improvement in the mental disorder as a result of abstinence, and there is a need for education about the effects of substance misuse. Generally, the success or failure of intervention for substance abuse depends as much on the severity of the substance abuse as on the severity of the mental disorder.

Substance abuse is a major public health and criminal justice problem. Recent data show a sharp increase in emergency room visits, the most expensive form of medical care, by chronic, heavy users of marijuana, heroin, and cocaine (Treaster 1993b). This information indicates that in addition to the need for social workers to play a greater role in rehabilitation programs and case management, there is also an important role for them in developing programs for primary and secondary prevention. Primary prevention would identify people, particularly children, who are at risk and would offer education about substance use as well as training to help them develop good problem-solving and refusal skills. Children need help in defining their needs, in overcoming the difficulties of living with a person who abuses substances, and especially in finding ways to cope with emotional stress without drugs. An additional public health problem is the increase detected in the incidence of unprotected sex among young gay men. This is partially attributed to the increased use of recreational drugs, which relax inhibitions and present a problem particularly for young men who have come of age at a time when debilitation and death from AIDS is less visible than earlier and thus they ignore the perils of unsafe sex. Secondary prevention would involve providing help for those who are using substances, but where the process appears to be reversible. Unfortunately, thus far, funding has always been inadequate for prevention programs, partly because it is difficult to evaluate the effectiveness of such programs.

Progress in developing effective intervention has always been hampered by punitive, very costly policies based on law enforcement, culminating in the recent War on Drugs. Fear of arrest, prosecution, incarceration, and for women, the fear of losing their children, have resulted in users' avoiding intervention and rehabilitation even if they were aware of the need for it. As noted above, the separation of programs for people with mental disorders from those for people with substance abuse disorder has also hampered effective intervention.

Social workers trained in the ecosystems perspective should be concerned with making a thorough assessment of any client with a substance abuse problem. The worker should look for causes as well as try to determine what type of intervention would be most helpful, given the person's history, life circumstances, and available or potential supports. In January 1997 NIAAA published the results of a five-year randomized large-scale clinical trial, Project Match (Project Match Research Group 1997), which was designed to look at interaction of different interventions and client characteristics to determine what variables can be used to effectively match clients with interventions. The interventions used were a twelve-step program, motivational enhancement therapy, and cognitive-behavioral coping skills therapy. Clients were chosen from outpatient settings and from a group receiving aftercare following inpatient treatment for alcoholism (NIAAA 1993). While this is a good start, it is limited, and clearly there is a need for social work research that would refine the assessment process for people with substance abuse disorders so that they can be matched with the appropriate form(s) of intervention, given the range of possibilities.

8   Eating Disorders

Concern with eating disorders is relatively new and is found primarily in countries where abundance of food creates options of self-starvation or excessive eating. The media in the United States have stressed the desirability of thinness for women, as models, ballet dancers, and actresses are invariably very thin. Author Tom Wolfe, in *The Bonfire of the Vanities*, referred to the women of the "Jet Set" as "social x-rays." In the last two decades, being thin has come to be associated with success and happiness and, for some, has become the basis of self-esteem. Women's magazines are filled with "new and exciting diets," and well-known restaurants offer "light fare." The more intense the social pressure to be thin, the more likely it is that a young person with low self-esteem will develop an eating disorder.

Bingeing and purging was socially acceptable in the Roman Empire, when the elite would interrupt banquets of up to twenty courses to purge. During the Middle Ages, persons were encouraged to purge to rid themselves of sins and reduce sexual desire (Giannini 1993). When historians describe people such as Henry VIII and William Howard Taft, they are not said to be obese; they simply had "healthy appetites."

The change in perception of women's bodies can be seen by looking at art from past eras, where it often appears that a degree of plumpness was seen as desirable for women's breasts, hips, thighs, and abdomens. In some societies, where there was uncertainty about food supply, a tendency for the family to be overweight implied that the husband or father was a good provider (Abraham and Llewellyn-Jones 1992).

DSM-IV includes criteria for anorexia nervosa and bulimia nervosa, but does not include obesity as an eating disorder, stating that the evidence does not support consistent association of obesity with a psychological or behavioral syndrome (American Psychiatric Association 1994). While concern may initially begin with a tendency to be underweight or overweight, these concerns become disorders as physical and mental health is affected. For people suffering from anorexia or bulimia, day-to-day living may revolve around their patterns of eating. While some theorists see eating disorders as similar to substance abuse disorders, an important distinction needs to be made. Intervention with people suffering from substance abuse disorders stresses the need for abstinence, which is not possible when the substance is food. The goal must instead be controlled use.

Definitions

Anorexia nervosa is a term with Greek and Latin roots, first used in 1873 by Sir William Gull, an English physician, to refer to loss of appetite due to nervous symptoms. Gull used it to describe a "want of appetite" attributable to a "morbid mental state" (Slaby and Dwenger 1993:9). The main symptom is significant weight loss, resulting from severely restricted eating or starvation, which may be accompanied by excessive exercising and purging. Weight is at least 15 percent below what is considered to be normal, and it may fall to a level that is life-threatening, although persons with this disorder tend to deny the grave medical risks. They experience an extreme fear of gaining weight and a distorted body image. *DSM-IV* includes in its criteria amenorrhea, the absence of a minimum of three consecutive menstrual cycles (American Psychiatric Association 1994). Most persons with anorexia nervosa are of normal weight before the onset of the disorder and become underweight through a combination of dieting and exercising. About 50 percent of people with anorexia nervosa will use starvation and purging for weight control, thus incorporating symptoms of both anorexia nervosa and bulimia nervosa (Williamson 1990).

Bulimia nervosa, defined as oxlike hunger of nervous origin, was considered to be an atypical symptom of anorexia nervosa until 1979, when it was recognized as a disorder that shares some symptoms with anorexia but is characterized by binge-purge cycles. Some people with anorexia nervosa binge, and a small group of people with bulimia nervosa develop anorexia nervosa. Most people who suffer from bulimia are within 10 percent of normal weight. Some are overweight, and some are underweight, but like people with anorexia nervosa, they have a morbid preoccupation with body shape and weight. The most salient aspect is a binge-purge cycle characterized by a compulsion to eat, at least twice a week, large quantities of calorie-rich food over a short period of time, usually about two hours, followed by vomiting, abuse of laxatives, diuretics, or amphetamines, or a period of rigorous fasting. *DSM-IV* requires that this pattern persist for three months or longer in order to warrant the diagnosis of bulimia nervosa (American Psychiatric Association 1994).

Obesity is not considered an eating disorder but rather a medical condition defined as having an excess of fat tissue and a weight at least 20 percent higher than what is considered normal for age and build (Williamson 1990). Mild obesity is defined as 5–39 percent over ideal weight, moderate obesity is defined as 40–99 percent over ideal weight, and severe obesity is 100 percent or more over ideal weight (Wadden 1993). Obesity is further defined by appearance, circumferential measurements of the body and its parts, and skin-fold tests. Obese persons are at increased risk for many serious medical conditions and for social stigmatization.

Binge eating is rapid consumption of an excessive amount of calorie-rich food.

Laxative abuse is using at least twice the recommended dosage of a laxative one or more times a week for a minimum of three months (Abraham and Llewellyn-Jones 1992).

Assessment

People suffering from anorexia nervosa or bulimia nervosa have rigid, distorted attitudes about weight, eating, and fatness. Assessment often reveals an extreme interest in the preparation and planning of meals. Many will shop very carefully and take great pleasure in the preparation and presentation of meals, even if, in the case of those who suffer from anorexia, they will not partake of the meal. They are often very good and knowledgeable cooks.

Adolescents are always concerned with their changing bodies, and many are displeased with how they have developed. This is a particularly difficult time for young women, and it is at approximately age fourteen that many symptoms of anorexia nervosa begin, although there have been people as young as nine with this disorder. People with anorexia nervosa do not lack appetite and they are often hungry, but they refuse to eat normally, fearing a loss of control over their eating, which will result in weight gain that will subvert their relentless determination to be thin. They have a morbid fear of weight gain and becoming fat and tend to look at parts of their bodies rather than the whole, which results in their seeing areas of fat even when they appear skeletal to others. They vehemently deny their thinness. They are preoccupied with food and weight control, like to cook and to serve others, but will cut their own food into tiny pieces, pocket it, or throw it away. They often develop obsessional rituals related to eating and are compulsive about exercising. Assessment often reveals negative attitudes, or at least misunderstandings, about puberty, menstruation, genital anatomy, contraception, sexual relations, pregnancy, and childbirth. Young women with anorexia nervosa are often very intelligent, somewhat shy, serious, conscientious, perfectionistic, obsessive, hypersensitive to rejection, conformist, and dependent on the approval of others, especially family. Compulsive fasting and exercising appear to give the person a sense of control over self and others and a false sense of independence. Families are often successful, concerned with appearance and physical fitness, and eager to present as solid and harmonious.

In general, people with bulimia nervosa are more aware of having an eating disorder than are people suffering from anorexia nervosa. They are often outgoing, impulsive, and emotional people. Assessment often reveals that food may have been forced on them as children, used to quiet them, or perceived as a substitute for love. They recognize as ego-dystonic their love of food, fear of not being able to stop eating, and fear of fatness. They are concerned with their body shape and weight, but if they seek intervention, their stated concerns are about their loss of control over their eating and the effects of laxative abuse and vomiting on their physical health. Much careful planning may have gone into following a pattern of bingeing and purging, which may have been kept secret from family and even those they are living with. Careful assessment can often identify sources of anxiety, unhappiness, or stress that result in binge eating in an attempt to temporarily escape from the emotional discomfort. The bingeing, however, may cause a feeling of fullness, shame, or guilt, and the person will induce vomiting in order to increase a sense of well-being. People with bulimia nervosa do not appear to have the concerns over their sexuality experienced by those with anorexia nervosa, but the need to binge and purge dominates their lives and often impedes the establishment of long-term relationships. An ego assessment often indicates that poor impulse control is a major problem for people with bulimia nervosa, evidenced not only by binge eating but also by substance abuse and promiscuity.

Controversy exists about whether or not obesity should be considered an eating disorder, and it does not appear in *DSM-IV*. Severe obesity is, however, a habitual disturbance in eating patterns, and people with this problem often lack the motivation to lose weight by permanently remaining on a diet.

In making an assessment of whether a person is suffering from an eating disorder, the initial step, of course, is to establish the relationship between the person's current weight and what is considered normal weight, based on age, body type, and state of physical health. Before asking any questions, the clinician can obtain some information by evaluating appearance: Is the person obviously overweight or underweight? Are clothes apparently chosen to attempt to disguise a weight problem? Do teeth look damaged or discolored? Is there any puffiness that may be related to bingeing and purging?

The clinician making the assessment should expect the client to use denial and to withhold information when asked questions about eating habits and weight, as this has been the way to cope with the eating disorder over a long period of time. Questions that need to be asked include the following:

What is the person's current weight and what could be accepted as a desirable weight range?

How are the person's present weight and body perceived?

What is the most, or the least, the person has weighed and what weight would the person like to achieve?

Has there been a history of anorexia, bulimia, or obesity?

Does the person really want to change existing eating habits?

Has the person ever stabilized weight for a period of six months to a year without effort? When was this?

What attempts has the person made in the past to establish a normal weight and better eating habits? What were the results?

Is the person currently on a diet?

How frequently does the person go on a diet?

What changes are anticipated if the person's weight changes significantly?

What is the response of family and friends to the person's weight?

Does the person's occupation affect weight?

Questions need to be asked about meals, such as:

Who shops for and prepares the food?
What kinds of foods constitute a normal meal?
What kinds of foods are avoided?
How many meals are eaten daily, at what times? Alone or with others?
Does the person snack between meals or fast or diet during the day?
Does the person want to change eating habits?

People who binge and purge are usually very guarded about their behavior, and this area needs to be assessed carefully and with sensitivity. Questions should include:

Does the person feel that the urge to binge can be controlled or is
    uncontrollable?
How frequently and under what circumstances does bingeing occur?
What activities and thoughts precede the binge, and what follow?
Is the food readily available, or must the person shop in anticipation
    of a binge?
What foods are usual chosen?
Does the person vomit after a binge? Does this need to be induced
    or has it become automatic?
When does the person vomit, during or after the binge? If after, how
    long after?
Does the person use laxatives, diuretics, or appetite suppressants? If
    so, which ones, at what dosage, and how often?
Does the person exercise or feel hyperactive after bingeing and
    purging?
How does the person imagine life will change if bingeing and purg-
    ing is no longer, or at least is less of, an important part of life?
Is the person afraid to stop? Why?

Questions should be asked about menstrual and sexual history, such as:

Age of onset of menstruation?
How was the girl prepared?
What has been the pattern of menstruation?
What are the feelings about menstruation and amenorrhea?
What are the thoughts and feelings about sex? (if appropriate)

What has been the pattern of sexual relationships?
Is there any history of sexual abuse or trauma?

Assessment needs to include information about the person's psychosocial functioning, such as:

Does the person live alone? If not, with whom does the person live?
Is the person in school or employed?
What is the highest level of educational achievement?
How does the person estimate functioning in comparison to peers?
Does the person see friends regularly? Sporadically?
Does the person confide in friends or family?
Whom does the person seek out for support?
What characterizes the person's relationships with parents and
    siblings?
How good is the person's reality testing in general?
Is the person excessively self-critical?
Is reasoning "black or white"?
Is there a history of impulsivity?
Is there a history of any sort of abuse or trauma?

Assessment should include speaking with family members, especially if the person is an adolescent living at home or is in a stable relationship with another person. Questions should include:

What are family relationships and interactions like?
Is there a family history of emotional, eating, or substance abuse
    disorders?
What phase of the life cycle is the family in?
What are family members' perceptions about the family's function-
    ing as a unit?
How are anger, tension, and conflict dealt with within the family?
What are the family expectations?
Is the immediate family isolated or involved with extended family
    and friends?
Who in the family knows about the eating disorder?
Who knows about the bingeing and purging? How long have they
    known?

What is the reaction to the eating disorder? Who is particularly con-
cerned? Who denies it?
Is the eating disorder a family secret?
What needs to be done to solve the problem?
What has the family done to seek help?
Are there any other identifiable family problems?

These questions should indicate the degree to which family intervention is indicated and may give some information about what role the eating disorder plays in the family dynamics.

Assessing areas of ego strengths and deficits is essential for intervention planning. People with eating disorders often have deficits in ego functions such as judgment, impulse control, reality testing, autonomous functioning, object relations, defensive functioning, and frustration tolerance, and thus they have a poor sense of mastery and competence. Eating disorders nearly always are related to other emotional problems, so careful assessment is needed to determine other problem areas, the extent of their impact on the individual, and the implications for intervention. Some of the problems that may be identified are depression, anxiety, mood swings, self-destructive be-havior, substance abuse, stealing food, assuming responsibility for family or marital problems, and stress resulting from unrealistic personal expectations. Recent research estimates that 20 to 50 percent of people suffering from bulimia nervosa have been sexually abused (American Psychiatric Associa-tion 1993). Exploration geared to identifying other problem areas may also yield information about what issues the person seeks to avoid or deny by continuing to have an eating disorder.

Answers to the above questions will be helpful in planning intervention, especially in assessing motivation to change, extent of the use of denial, existence of other problems, and whether or not goals are realistic. It is notable that people with eating disorders seem to have a pervasive sense of being ineffective in controlling most areas of their lives and see their eating and their weight as the only possible area under their sole control. They also appear to have difficulty in correctly interpreting their body's response to eating, as well as in tolerating feelings of anxiety, depression, loneliness, and boredom. Problems of self-esteem and identity are common.

Epidemiology

It is estimated that up to 95 percent of people with anorexia nervosa or bulimia nervosa are women, and between 1 percent and 4 percent of adolescent and young adult women suffer from these disorders. Most of these women are white and upper middle class. Prevalence is increasing, especially among men, minorities, and women in other age groups (American Psychiatric Association 1993).

Anorexia nervosa is fifteen times more common in women than in men and is conservatively estimated as affecting 0.1 percent of women who are between thirteen and twenty-five years of age, and 0.5 percent of women who are between fifteen and eighteen (Abraham and Llewellyn-Jones 1992). It is possible that there is a greater prevalence of anorexia nervosa in men than is generally assumed, because amenorrhea, part of the *DSM-IV* criteria, is obviously not a symptom for men, and the psychoanalytic theory of the etiology of anorexia nervosa as a fear of oral impregnation (except possibly in fantasy) also cannot refer to men (Andersen 1992). The sociocultural expectation is also that this is a disorder of women and not of men.

It is estimated that 1 to 2 percent of women suffer from bulimia nervosa, but it is very probable that the prevalence is greater, for many people do not seek intervention for this disorder and may be misdiagnosed as having gynecological or gastrointestinal problems or depression. Bingeing can begin as early as mid-teens or as late as the thirties, but it is most prevalent in late adolescence or early adulthood, after the person leaves home.

Thirty-five percent of men and 40 percent of women are considered to be obese, 23 percent of men and 30 percent of women are overweight, and 0.5 percent fall into the severely obese range (Hodge and Maseelall 1993). The prevalence of obesity, or at least overweight, increases with age and peaks between ages fifty-five and sixty-five. Within this age group, 24 percent of women and 17 percent of men are estimated to be obese (Abraham and Llewellyn-Jones 1992). There is a strong correlation between race and obesity in women: higher rates are found among African American women, Southwest Native American women, and Hispanic American women (Brown 1993). The prevalence of obesity is six times greater in lower socioeconomic classes than in upper classes (Lomax 1989).

Clinical Course

The line between dieting and suffering from an eating disorder is not always clear, and if a clinician simply follows the *DSM-IV* criteria, recognition of the extent of the problem may be delayed. A person may be losing significant weight but continue to menstruate; some people suffering from obesity may binge without purging; people may have a binge-purge cycle that is not as frequent as twice a week. Knowledge of any of these behaviors should alert the clinician to the possibility of an eating disorder. Twenty-five percent of people with anorexia nervosa and 40 percent of those with bulimia nervosa were actually overweight before the onset of these disorders (Hsu 1990). Thus overweight must be considered a possible risk factor.

People suffering from anorexia nervosa or bulimia nervosa see themselves as overweight in spite of evidence to the contrary; initially they may try to control their weight by increasing their exercise, avoiding snacks between meals, or visiting "fat farms," efforts that may be praised by family and peers at first. These behaviors, however, are then followed by excessive dieting, fasting, and in some cases vomiting or abusing laxatives and diuretics.

Anorexia Nervosa

As noted above, anorexia nervosa usually begins to develop in the early teens. People suffering from anorexia usually begin restricting foods that are high in carbohydrates, then fatty foods, and ultimately all foods, as they move further toward self-starvation. Continual weight loss is viewed as success, and maintaining a consistent weight without loss may cause the person to experience panic and despair. Although as many as 40 percent of people with anorexia nervosa will, in time, binge-eat, most people with bulimia nervosa will not develop anorexia nervosa. The most common disorder suffered by people whose symptoms suggest recovery from anorexia nervosa is bulimia nervosa (Hsu 1990).

Anorexia nervosa is a psychosomatic disorder whose physical symptoms, in addition to dehydration, vitamin deficiencies, and electrolyte imbalance, may include slow heart rate, low blood pressure, dry skin, brittle nails and hair, constipation, edema, loss of bone, swollen joints, drop in hormone levels, and the presence of a layer of soft, downy hair on arms, back, and face. Twenty percent of persons suffering from anorexia nervosa will die from a combination of dehydration, malnutrition, and starvation.

Bulimia Nervosa

Bulimia nervosa usually develops after age eighteen, with initial concern about appearance and being overweight. Many people with this disorder try fad diets or starve themselves, do not feel satisfied, and turn to binge eating.

Following the onset of a binge, they will then feel full, have had their binge interrupted by others, or become anxious about the calories they have consumed, will induce vomiting during or at the end of the binge, and also use laxatives between or after binges. As the disorder becomes more severe, patterns of behavior develop. The person may secretly prepare for a binge by hoarding food or, in contrast, will keep very little food in the house and then frantically go shopping for "forbidden foods," such as ice cream, cake, cookies, peanuts, or chocolate, which are consumed immediately upon returning home. The amount of food eaten when bingeing can represent up to thirty times the person's usual intake, although most do not eat all of the food they have assembled for the binge. Some will gulp the food frantically, others will savor it slowly. Often there is a specific time, usually evenings or weekends, when bingeing is most likely to take place. Most people binge in private, although some binge to induce guilt in others with whom they are in conflict. Individual patterns vary, with 50 percent bingeing at least once a day (Vanderlinden, Norre, and Vandereycken 1992), some bingeing several times a day, some several times a week, and others going on extended periods of bingeing that may last days or even weeks. For some, a cycle develops during which they initially may feel anxious, depressed, empty, angry, rejected, or lonely; will binge to feel better; and will then feel guilty or anxious about possible weight gain. These feelings of tension and discomfort will induce another binge.

People suffering from bulimia nervosa will often abuse laxatives, diet pills, or diuretics, causing physical problems such as dehydration, electrolyte imbalances, seizures, and renal damage. Vomiting will also cause dehydration, dental problems, and damage to the esophagus. Other medical complications can include menstrual and endocrine disorders and risk of stomach rupture. Twenty percent of people suffering from bulimia nervosa also abuse alcohol or other chemical substances, further increasing the risk of health problems. Studies have shown that people with bulimia nervosa who have had a history of anorexia nervosa have a poorer prognosis than those who have never had anorexia. Other factors negatively affecting the prognosis are long duration of the disorder, assessment of a coexisting personality disorder, and a family history of emotional disorders (Vanderlinden, Norre, and Vandereycken 1992). Review of outcome studies with five- and ten-year followups showed a decline in bingeing and purging in direct relation to the duration of the follow-up. At the end of ten years 70 percent were in remission, 11 percent still met most criteria for bulimia nervosa, and 0.6 percent met the criteria for anorexia nervosa. Thirty percent acknowledged some bingeing-purging activity, and 18 percent met the criteria for eating disorder not otherwise specific. The same study showed that substance abuse was related to a poorer prognosis (Keel et al. 1999).

When women suffering from anorexia nervosa or bulimia nervosa become pregnant, symptoms often remit because they are afraid of producing a damaged infant. Some will express hope that the pregnancy will make them "well" and are able to recognize the positive changes in their appearance. Good eating habits are more likely to be established throughout the pregnancy and while the woman is nursing, but relapse is a risk when the woman no longer feels that her eating habits affect the baby and she reverts to viewing herself as fat, in spite of evidence to the contrary.

Obesity

Most people suffering from obesity simply need to change their eating habits, eat less, and exercise, but this is often quite difficult, especially if the person views eating as particularly pleasurable. Because of the difficulty that many people have in losing weight and keeping it off, they often lack the motivation to do anything about their obesity unless they experience related physical problems. Diseases that are affected by obesity are diabetes, respiratory problems such as shortness of breath, gallbladder disease, bowel or rectal cancer, coronary heart disease, hypertension, and stroke. Prejudice and discrimination affect people who are obese, and such reactions to them can cause withdrawal, poor self-image, and depression. Children who are obese may be teased, and studies have shown that obesity negatively affects hiring and even college acceptance (Wadden and Stunkard 1993). The earlier the onset of obesity, the poorer the response to intervention (Bruch 1973) and the more likely that personality disorders are present.

Differential Diagnosis

Because the symptoms of anorexia nervosa and bulimia nervosa are so distinctive, there is usually not a problem with differential diagnoses. Weight changes, however, may indicate medical problems. To rule these out, it is essential that any person thought to have an eating disorder have a very thorough physical examination, including a review of any medications he or she may be taking. AIDS, cancer, and tuberculosis may affect appetite and cause significant weight loss, while brain tumors or endocrine problems can cause obesity. Some medications, such as neuroleptics and some anti-depressants, also affect weight. A physical examination is always essential to determine what kinds of physical damage may have occurred from what may have been years of poor nutrition.

Depression can also account for changes in eating patterns and thus in weight. Conversely, depression may be a response to the eating disorder, especially in people suffering from bulimia, who may experience intense dysphoria after a binge-purge cycle. Questions need to be asked about feelings of sadness, hopelessness, thoughts about suicide, loss of interest and motivation, lessening of sense of self-worth, and changes in sleep patterns. If, upon assessment, the person generally does not appear to feel depressed and is functioning well in other areas, then the primary problem is probably one of abnormal eating rather than depression, and the depression will lessen when normal eating is reestablished. Other problems often experienced by people with eating disorders include anxiety, personality disorders, obsessive-compulsive disorder, family problems, and substance abuse. There is a high comorbidity of eating disorders and personality disorders, especially the cluster B disorders, borderline or histrionic; or the cluster C disorders, avoidant, obsessive-compulsive, and dependent (Wonderlich and Mitchell 1992). If the person fails to improve after seeking intervention for an eating disorder, the primary disorder may be another problem rather than the eating disorder. If so, the focus of intervention needs to change. If a person suffering from bulimia nervosa also has a significant problem with substance abuse, the latter ought to be the initial focus of intervention, since binges may occur when the person is under the influence and out of control.

Bulimia nervosa in some cases responds to antidepressant medication, even if the person has not reported feeling depressed. Some people, however, do identify depression, and if there is family history of depression, comorbidity is suggested. The onset of depression following treatment for bulimia nervosa suggests that it is the result of having the disorder rather than the cause.

Diagnosis is made easier by the fact that when a physical or emotional disorder is the primary cause of weight changes, the person usually is realistic about weight and body image.

Etiology

The etiology of eating disorders appears to be multifactorial, with no single event or factor identifiable as the cause. Dieting, or difficulty in controlling overeating, can lead to acquiring an eating disorder. Factors that may influence the development of an eating disorder include society's emphasis on the desirability of thinness; adolescent concerns with attractiveness, self-concept, body-concept, and sexuality; genetic predisposition; neurotransmitter dysfunction; individual personality; and comorbidity of another mental disorder such as an anxiety, affective, or personality disorder.

While studies show that first-degree relatives of people with anorexia nervosa have higher rates of some kind of eating disorder than does the general public, and twin studies show a higher rate of anorexia nervosa and bulimia nervosa in monozygotic than in dizygotic twins, the genetic component is not considered significant in the etiology of these disorders. Genetic evidence does, however, suggest possible vulnerability. Studies have shown low concentrations of serotonin in the hypothalamus, which is involved in appetite regulation, in people with anorexia and bulimia nervosa, which suggests a biological cause. Dopamine and norepinephrine are other neurotransmitters involved in appetite regulation.

Psychoanalytic theory postulates that anorexia nervosa results from unconscious fantasies about oral impregnation, i.e., pregnancy resulting from eating. Freud regarded the disorder as resulting from a failure to master sexual excitement, a refusal to grow up, and overprotective mothering (Slaby and Dwenger 1993). The individual was fixated at the oral phase of development and suffered an accompanying fear of object loss, a sense of maternal overcontrol, and the equation of food with love. It was also believed that people with anorexia nervosa had unresolved oedipal conflicts resulting from preoedipal fixation (Wilson, Hogan, and Mintz 1992).

A psychodynamic explanation of anorexia nervosa would state that a major task of adolescence is accepting one's sexuality and that the eating disorder is a symptom of a personality defect based on a fear of growing up and thus becoming physically and sexually mature. By appearing emaciated and asexual, and either never beginning, or ceasing, menstruation, the adolescent girl is able to avoid confronting her sexuality and suppress associated feelings. The tasks of accepting and integrating into her relationships her genital sexuality while also negotiating more independence from her family can be very threatening to the adolescent who feels ill-equipped to control most of her life. Anorexia nervosa delays physical maturity while giving a false sense of control.

Bruch (1973) sees anorexia nervosa as a disturbance in body image resulting from underlying deficits in developing self-esteem, a sense of individual identity, and a sense of autonomy. She believes that something went wrong in the experiential and interpersonal processes associated in the early years with nutrition and that it impairs the ability to recognize both hunger and satiation, resulting in the inability to distinguish between hunger and other signs of discomfort, physical or emotional. Inconsistent and inappropriate responses to a child's needs further result in difficulty in seeing oneself as separate and in establishing a sense of identity. Later, the adolescent feels ineffectual, powerless, and helpless and seeks to make herself perfect, through gaining a sense of competence and approval by appearing thin. The adolescent uses weight loss to establish a sense of identity, control, purpose, and uniqueness. Eating is misused in an attempt to solve or camouflage problems of living. The parents, who have imposed their own wishes without recognizing the child's needs and wants, cannot exercise control over eating, and the adolescent may, for the first time, feel autonomous and in control. Thus the goal of self-starvation is to be in control of one's life and to have a sense of identity.

The family model of the etiology of anorexia nervosa suggests that it is a symptom of dysfunctional family interaction. It postulates that young women suffering from this disorder usually come from higher socioeconomic families with higher than normal rates of depression and eating disorders, especially among the mothers. Family interactions are characterized by parental control, overprotectiveness, rigidity, high expectations, and a high degree of parent-child dependence. Tensions and conflicts are rarely acknowledged. When the girl reaches puberty, the family has difficulty in moving to this stage of the family cycle and establishing new rules for interaction. The girl tends not to perceive herself as having needs that may differ from those of the family, and she fears abandonment if she acts independently. Fasting is an attempt to act independently by assuming control over eating and weight, and therefore not letting others impose their will. Family assessments of people with bulimia nervosa have shown a higher than normal prevalence of affective disorders, substance abuse, and eating disorders (American Psychiatric Association 1993), possibly resulting in a stressful environment in which relief from tensions is sought through bingeing and purging. Assessment often reveals that initial bingeing is precipitated by a stressful event such as a family argument, an illness or death, the end of a relationship, school or vocational problems, or feeling lonely or bored.

The feminist model (Orbach 1986) places eating disorders in a broader sociocultural context. Thinness, and a related wish to look young, as a magic route to a happy and successful life is viewed as not only unrealistic but destructive. Disturbed eating behavior is viewed as a symptom of underlying intrapersonal and interpersonal conflicts related to society's inhibiting a woman's recognition of her needs and desires.

Object relations theory suggests that anorexia nervosa develops as a result of a deficit in development of object relations, starting in the oral incorporative stage, resulting in difficulties in developing a sense of self and of object constancy. The mother has been incorporated as controlling, and self-starvation is an attempt to establish a separate identity. There has been little clinical evidence to support this explanation (Hsu 1990). Self-psychology theorists also see the etiology of anorexia as resulting from a disturbance in the early mother-child relationship with the child then lacking an internal sense of well-being and security and thus feeling ineffectual, out of control, and empty.

Psychoanalytic theory postulates that, for people who develop bulimia nervosa, the fantasy of becoming pregnant is expressed through overeating (Pope and Hudson 1989). Biological theories suggest that because antidepressant medication can help to reduce bingeing, a cause of bulimia may be found in the part of the brain that affects eating. Some risk factors have been identified: parental problems resulting from impoverished relationships (Chassler 1998), high expectations and family history of psychiatric disorders, perceived or real risk for obesity, abuse, and premorbid psychiatric disorders (Fairburn et al. 1997).

Assessment of men suffering from anorexia nervosa or bulimia nervosa often reveals a history of preadolescent obesity, dieting begun to attain some athletic goal or avoid a sports injury, or dieting out of fear of getting a familial medical illness. Psychodynamic theory suggests that the abnormal eating with resultant weight loss is a defense against sexual thoughts, feelings, and behavior (Andersen 1992). Like women, these men experience an external loss of control over their lives except with respect to eating.

Obesity, or at least a tendency to be significantly overweight, can run in families who will describe themselves as having "healthy appetites," as being "just large people" or who "get enjoyment from eating." In modern industrial societies, there is an abundance of food high in fats and calories, and in some cultures providing and sharing food is the focus of social life.

Statistics show that when both parents fall into the range for obesity, 80 percent of the children will also be considered obese; when one parent is obese, 40 percent of the children will also have this disorder; in families in which the parents are normal weight, only 10 percent of the children develop this disorder (Hodge and Maseelall 1993). Twin and adoption studies have yielded evidence of a genetic tendency, especially for childhood obesity. While there are genetic and environmental factors that contribute to obesity, the most widely accepted theory is that it is caused by the imbalance between energy intake (calories) and energy output (exercise) regulated by the hypothalamic system (Keesey 1993). Obesity results when the energy intake through eating exceeds the energy output as a result of the person's metabolism or inactivity (Williamson 1990). It is believed that further research is needed to better understand the causes of obesity, especially with respect to fat oxidation and the effects of altered fat intake (Ravussin and Swinburn 1993). It is probable that obesity results from "nature and nurture," as a genetic vulnerability may make the person at risk when coupled with an environment that promotes obesity.

Bruch (1973) saw obesity as stemming from underlying conflicts similar to those of anorexia nervosa. She felt that people who develop obesity were "elected" by the parents to compensate for their own disappointments and frustrations. The parents often denied the child's individuality and saw themselves as providing "the best of care" through supplying food. People who become obese have a poor sense of self and of autonomy, as well as a basic problem in correctly judging how much has been eaten; they feel there is always "room for more," and they tend to eat more when they are tense, anxious, or lonely.

Psychodynamic theory about obesity suggests that obese people eat as a way to compensate for feelings of being unloved, emptiness, sadness, insecurity, or loneliness. Food is believed to provide comfort. Psychoanalytic theory regards obesity as resulting from fixation at the oral stage of development (Hodge and Maseelall 1993), in which food was used as a pacifier and led to a passive, dependent personality with problems of anxiety, depression, and separation.

Intervention

Although eating disorders are potentially life-threatening, people with these disorders usually do not seek out mental health professionals for intervention unless they have been urged to do so by their internists or concerned family and friends, or if they are experiencing related problems of anxiety, depression, or low self-esteem. Most people with eating disorders like food, and the problem is one of control of eating: rigid overcontrol by those suffering from anorexia nervosa, lack of control by those suffering from bulimia nervosa or obesity.

In order for intervention to be successful, the person must perceive an eating problem as affecting lifestyle, possibly affecting physical health, and as possibly serving to avoid other problem areas. People with bulimia nervosa more often seek intervention as they experience their symptoms as egodystonic, while people with anorexia nervosa often do not recognize a problem; for an intervention to be successful, they need to become motivated. Many people diagnosed as obese may be unhappy and initially want to look better but later decide not to significantly alter their weight because failure to do so, after several attempts, may only increase their already vulnerable sense of self-esteem. Working with people seeking intervention for eating disorders usually involves prolonged and intense interaction. The clinician needs to be supportive and understanding, accepting of relapse, and able to maintain a positive attitude toward the possibility of change, presenting the problem as soluble while at the same time being aware that feelings of hopelessness, anger, frustration, and being manipulated may emerge in the course of the intervention. Good prognostic indicators for intervention with people who have anorexia nervosa include early age of onset and weight gain within two years after the beginning of the intervention. Poorer prognosis is indicated with later onset, comorbidity with personality disorders, a history of psychiatric hospitalizations, and poor family relationships (Waldinger 1990).

Hospitalization

Hospitalization, if possible on a unit specializing in eating disorders, is indicated when the person with the eating disorder is in danger of dying from starvation, is at risk from a variety of medical problems related to or stemming from the disorder, is a suicide risk, has not responded to outpatient intervention, or cannot control weight loss or break the cycle of bingeing without supervision. Since control is a major factor in these disorders, however, outpatient intervention, which gives the person more responsibility for progress, would be the intervention of choice. In the hospital, these people need close supervision, as they tend to store food in their mouths, napkins, or under the table to avoid eating it; those who are likely to binge need controlled portions of food, to make bingeing impossible. Food consumption and use of the bathroom are supervised, at least initially. Weighing is usually done daily, at the same time, and precautions are taken to see that the person does not drink water, avoid emptying the bladder, or wear clothing or jewelry that might falsely yield a higher weight. Many inpatient programs use cognitive positive reinforcement by allowing the person greater privileges if weight is gained and requiring bed rest or even tube feeding if weight is lost in the hospital. A team approach is used, including family education and involvement, individual psychotherapy, and educational groups often involving a dietitian. Intervention is aimed at beginning the process of stabilizing the person's weight, improving the general physical condition, understanding the need to change eating habits, correcting distortions about weight and body shape, and helping to identify problems that may impede recovery. Good discharge planning must determine the outpatient interventions needed to prevent relapse. Since the temptation to resume former eating habits, or to discontinue intervention, will be great, the person should be connected with outpatient resources before leaving the hospital.

Managed care has resulted in more day programs or partial hospitalization, which is believed to be more cost-effective than inpatient hospitalization. The person is provided with structure, especially at mealtime, while continuing to face the challenges, triggers, and problems with social supports in their home environment (Garner and Needleman 1997).

Psychotherapy

If a person seeks intervention, an immediate goal—whether treatment is provided on an inpatient or an outpatient basis—is to stabilize weight, and since people with eating disorders express a range of feelings related to their eating habits, an initial approach may be cognitive-behavioral, in which the person is asked to keep a diary of moods, feelings, and eating patterns in order to try to establish and recognize associations. Development of socialization skills is stressed to improve social interaction, especially while consuming meals. Programs using this approach also include an educational component geared to a greater understanding of nutritional requirements, as well as to dispelling misconceptions about food and weight. Tasks include preparing shopping lists that specifically eliminate certain foods, attempting to eat slowly, planning activities to fill the time when compulsive eating may be tempting, and planning rewards to be enjoyed if bingeing has been avoided. For people suffering from obesity, an eating program based on eating less food, especially those foods containing fats and carbohydrates, and increasing the amount of fairly strenuous exercise is essential.

Establishing a well-balanced eating pattern is the first step. Three meals a day are encouraged, plus snacks if the person is underweight, so that the person will feel satiated and not as likely to binge. Portions should be small enough not to arouse fear of "getting fat" and should be nutritionally balanced. The clinician should be aware that as some weight is gained, the person needs to be encouraged to discuss fears about this, about perceived or real changes in body shape, and especially about losing control. Since people who binge and purge cannot realistically be expected to suddenly stop this behavior, the initial goals are to lessen the frequency, limit the quantity of food consumed, begin to integrate some "forbidden foods" into the regular diet in moderation, and urge the person to try not to vomit, or at least try to delay it until the food is probably absorbed and regurgitation is thus senseless. In addition to establishing better eating patterns, the initial phase of intervention must focus on the person's resistance to, or ambivalence about, change, as well as feelings about relapse, which usually occurs to some degree.

Supportive psychotherapy is very important after the crisis is past and the person is beginning to try to alter eating habits. Morbid fears need to be addressed, whether they have to do with weight gain, in the case of people with anorexia nervosa, or with losing control over eating, which can lead to bingeing or other forms of overeating. The person must be helped to find more effective, less painful ways to cope with the problems of daily living, beginning with increasing recognition and awareness of feelings, needs, and impulses, which often in the past have been dictated by external sources. An important goal is to decrease reliance on others for affirmation, direction, and self-esteem. Establishing a relationship is slow, as the person will fear that the clinician will be unreliable or controlling, as significant people in his or her life may have been, and the clinician must combat this fear by being consistent and empathic, establishing boundaries, and focusing on the person's own thoughts, feelings, and needs. Giving up the perceived power that comes with the symptoms of the disorder may be difficult, and the worker needs to be aware that relapse is a real probability and to be non-judgmental and realistic in dealing with the client, who may feel shame, guilt, and a sense of failure. A major goal in working with people suffering from obesity is to increase self-esteem, especially if significant weight loss is not a realistic goal.

For people with anorexia nervosa, intervention should support attempts at independence. In addition, two areas need to be approached: (1) issues relating to weight, exercise, dieting, and bingeing, and (2) the psychological problems of self-esteem, self-concept, perfectionism, interpersonal functioning, and family conflicts. Both address errors in reasoning, dysfunctional thinking, and distorted assumptions. Psychoeducation is also very important for both the person and the family.

For people with bulimia nervosa or obesity, intervention should provide assistance in developing a greater sense of self-control, in order to help increase self-esteem. Cognitive-behavioral therapy (CBT) is more effective for bulimia than for anorexia and is regarded as the first-line intervention (Wilson, Fairburn, and Agras 1997). Often this intervention involves a twenty-week, three-stage, manual-based intervention. Stage one (weeks 1–8) involves self-monitoring of food intake and of bingeing-purging episodes, including the thoughts and feelings that trigger these episodes. Weight is checked weekly, and efforts are made to normalize eating habits aand restrict dieting through menu planning. Persons try to identify self-control strategies, especially with respect to foods that ought to be avoided, and there is the beginning of cognitive restructuring, aimed at distorted thoughts about eating and weight. Stage two (weeks 9–16) focuses on eliminating dieting, identifying problems, and teaching new problem-solving skills. In the final stage (weeks 17–20), geared to termination and relapse prevention, future potential problems and new ways to cope are identified, realistic goals are established. and sessions are tapered off from weekly to biweekly.

Interpersonal therapy (IPT) is also used to intervene with persons suffering from bulimia nervosa, usually following CBT if that has not been successful. Others will use IPT as part of a relapse prevention program. This approach is also a three-stage program: (1) identification of interpersonal problems that have led to developing and maintaining the eating disorder, (2) therapeutic work on interpersonal problems, and (3) termination.

In summary, CBT and IPT are two different pathways toward effective intervention for persons suffering from bulimia nervosa. CBT is aimed at improvement in eating habits, which will lead to improved interpersonal functioning, while IPT is aimed at improving interpersonal functioning, which will then lead to improved eating habits (Garner, Vitousek, and Pike 1997).

Careful assessment is needed to determine whether the goal of intervention for people who are suffering from obesity should be weight stabilization rather than weight loss, for the latter might result in despair and increased depression if the goal is unrealistic. Achieving and maintaining a weight less than the lowest the person has weighed for a period of at least a year since becoming an adult is probably not realistic (Wadden 1993). Cognitive-behavioral treatment is sometimes effective in stabilizing obese persons who experience episodes of binge eating (Garner and Needleman 1997).

Women who are suffering from obesity, according to a recent study following a large sample from adolescence to adulthood, experience social and vocational discrimination. They are less likely to marry and more likely to face rejection in the job market. Men who are obese were also found to be less likely to marry, but apparently were not affected vocationally (Gortmaker et al. 1993). Thus, especially with women suffering from obesity, low self-esteem, depression, and hopelessness need to be addressed as part of the intervention.

Problems underlying preoccupation with weight and eating need to be addressed in ongoing intervention. Some of the common problems are sense of inadequacy, impaired awareness of feelings and bodily responses, self-doubts, a perceived need to be perfect, and self-worth that is dependent on others. Permission needs to be given for the person to recognize and artic-ulate individual needs and wants. The clinician needs to challenge misper-ceptions, introduce realistic goals for achieving success, and support appro-priate independent thoughts and decisions.

The feminist model of etiology advocates participation in a women's group to identify common underlying conflicts and to dispel the socially learned notion that self-denial is a positive female attribute. It focuses on sociopolitical themes and addresses role conflicts, identity confusion, sexual abuse, and victimization, especially that involving sexual abuse, as causes of eating disorders (Garner and Needleman 1997). The groups also focus on interpersonal relationships, identifying the inequitable position of women in society and societal demands to conform to culturally defined norms of physical attractiveness and attraction (Dare and Eisler 1997). Sociocultural expectations are particularly important during adolescence, which is when anorexia nervosa usually develops.

The formation of groups of people with a similar disorder has been found to be somewhat useful as an adjunct intervention. The groups may be based on a longer-term psychodynamic approach or a shorter CBT model. The benefits are that people with these disorders can feel less isolated, get feed-back, learn new ways of coping, and get a heightened sense of self-esteem and control through helping others. Group participation may help in un-derstanding the need to alter eating patterns as well as to offer suggestions about meal planning and nutrition. A problem can occur if the group par-ticipants become competitive about their weight gain or loss, which could lead some group members to drop out. People suffering from obesity have particularly benefited from mutual-aid or self-help groups, which dissemi-nate nutritional information and often require weight checks.

As indicated above, family assessment is important, particularly for fam-ilies of people suffering from anorexia nervosa, who, because of the early age of onset, are often living at home. Family members may have participated in denial of the disorder and may choose to view the weight loss as only a resistance to eating, which could be easily remedied, or they may see thinness as desirable and thus need education about the severity of the disorder and its possible relationship to family and environmental stresses. Some theorists feel that the disorder is a symptom of a problem the adolescent is having in becoming independent from a family that may be rigid and overprotective and thus foster dependency. Other families may be chaotic, disorganized, or present a range of psychosocial problems, and the client perceives that concern over the eating disorder deflects attention from other family problems and serves to keep the family together. Intervention should include helping the client to separate and individuate and to make independent decisions about all aspects of life, thus diminishing the family's overinvolvement and helping the family to support the client's need for autonomy. Studies have indicated that while there appears to be a pseudo-mutuality in families of people with anorexia, families of people with bulimia are more overtly hostile, neglectful, and marked by conflict (Hsu 1990).

Couple counseling may be indicated if the symptoms appear to be affecting a relationship or if there is evidence that the person suffering from the eating disorder feels that her only control over the relationship is through needing to have her partner concerned about her weight and health. It is also important to assess the partner's feelings about weight and how these may be influencing the problem and the intervention. If the woman becomes pregnant, working with both partners can reinforce the importance of the person's having regular, nutritional meals as well as supporting the improvement in appearance, thus dispelling fantasies that only thinness is attractive.

Medication

Medication is not often used for people with anorexia nervosa, although low doses of neuroleptics have been used to relieve marked obsessional, anxious, or psychotic thoughts. Some reasons not to use medications when a person has a very low weight are the danger because of metabolic and biological changes caused by the weight loss, heightened sensitivity to side effects because of increased sensitivity to changes in body or feelings, and danger of noncompliance if taking medication is equated with loss of control and autonomy (Gitlin 1990) or results in weight gain as a side effect. If there is comorbid depression, antidepressant medications should be considered. Trials of fluoxetine (Prozac) have also reported weight gain (Kaplan and Sadock 1996).

Antidepressant medications such as imipramine (Tofranil), desipramine (Norpramine), trazodone (Desyrel), and fluoxetine (Prozac) have helped to reduce the binge-purge cycle of bulimia nervosa as well as the binges of people suffering from obesity. The effectiveness of high doses of fluoxetine suggests that an increase in serotonin may result in feelings of satiation and that it has an antibulimic property independent of its mood-stabilizing effects. Fluoxetine appears also to help with obsessional thinking and compulsive behaviors associated with eating disorders. Fenfluramine (Pondimin), a serotonin antagonist, is sometimes used as an appetite suppressant to produce satiety in people with bulimia nervosa or obesity.

Intervention outcomes for people with eating disorders are better for people with anorexia nervosa than for people with bulimia nervosa or obesity. Less than 50 percent of people with anorexia nervosa have a full recovery; 70 percent show significant improvement, although they will probably always be thin, but the death rate on follow-up was 15–20 percent (Yager 1992). Only 40 percent of people with bulimia nervosa have what is regarded as a good outcome (Abraham and Llewellyn-Jones 1992), and relapse is not uncommon when the person is under stress. Some degree of chronic bulimia nervosa or obesity appears to be more the rule than the exception in those with a history of these disorders. Positive outcome appears in part to depend on motivation, ability to feel autonomous, self-awareness, optimism, self-acceptance, and high self-esteem. Hindrances appear to be strong use of denial, pessimistic thinking, impulsivity, unrealistic expectations, poor self-esteem, and a tendency to view any weight gain as a catastrophe.

Research into the etiology, epidemiology, and intervention outcome has been marred by underdiagnosis, high dropout rate after intervention begins, inadequate follow-up that probably underestimates relapse, and the fact that clinicians and clients may differ on what constitutes a favorable outcome. Research is also needed into the comorbidity of personality and eating disorders and the implications for intervention.

Social workers, especially those working with young women, should be alert to appearance and ask questions about eating habits. Education is needed about nutrition to correct false beliefs about food, to discourage rigid dieting, and to encourage eating with others rather than alone. Exercise should be put in perspective, stressing the general health benefits while also indicating that it is maladaptive if used only out of fear of "fatness." This educational approach might serve as prevention against the media's influential preoccupation with thinness and the seductiveness of "fast food."

9 Personality Disorders

Personality disorders both fascinate and frustrate mental health professionals. They have proved to be highly resistant to definition, to classification, and to consensus as to etiology and best approaches to intervention. People with personality disorders are frequently viewed as difficult clients and because of the problem of definition, the term has been used as a "wastepaper basket" when diagnosis is unclear.

The study of personality has always been of interest, because our personality defines who we are, in terms of both how we see ourselves and how others see us. Much has been written about abnormal personality. One of the earliest sources was Theophrastus, in the fourth century B.C. (Perry and Vaillant 1989). In 1801 Philip Pinel identified people whose behavior was irrational, though their intellect appeared intact. Other nineteenth-century psychiatrists wrote of "moral insanity" and "psychopathic inferiority" as they described what are now regarded as personality disorders (Perry and Vaillant 1989).

In the twentieth century, Kraepelin, while writing about what he regarded as manic-depressive "insanity," described what is currently similar to *DSM-III-R* and *DSM-IV* criteria for a diagnosis of borderline personality disorder (Millon 1992, 1996). Freud, Alexander, and Reich all tried to explain personality disorders in psychoanalytic terms, and in 1938 Adolph Stern first used the label *borderline*.

In 1952 *DSM-I* brought "personality disorder" into the classification literature, and the first two editions of the *DSM*, in classifying personality disorders, were deeply influenced by the psychoanalytic model. *DSM-III*

introduced the concept of Axis II, which allowed the separation of personality and developmental disorders from the clinical syndromes of Axis I. Axis
II refers to long-term, more or less stable handicaps, while Axis I refers to
disorders that are episodic or can become progressively worse unless intervention takes place. Critics have questioned the reliability and validity of the
DSM-III-R classifications of personality disorders, for there is considerable
overlap in diagnostic criteria, thus leaving room for confusion in the diagnosis and the resulting plan for intervention. While *DSM-I* identified twenty-
seven personality disorders, *DSM-II* reduced the number to twelve, and
DSM-III-R includes eleven, broken into three clusters. It is not clear why,
in *DSM-II*, some of the clinical features were included, and there is a confusing mix of personality *traits* and more specific *behaviors*. Personality disorders continue to be misunderstood and controversial, and many feel that
they represent a spectrum of one disorder rather than separate disorders.
DSM-IV excludes the former cluster C category of passive-aggressive personality, stating that there was need for further research to refine criteria for
inclusion.

Cultural context must also be considered. Whether or not behavior is
dysfunctional may depend on whether or not it meets social expectations
and value norms. It may not be considered abnormal unless, or until, it
interferes with functioning (Paris 1998).

Definitions

In describing people, several words are commonly used and require definition, as do the types of personality disorders most commonly observed.

Personality (character) implies the conscious and unconscious ways in
which a person more or less consistently interacts with the environment and
with other people. Factors considered in assessing character may include
interests, attitudes, intellectual ability, talents, and style of interaction. Most
people are capable of some adaptive flexibility of character.

Personality traits may be ego-syntonic or ego-dystonic, They are the individual's pattern of relating and thinking about oneself and one's environment. They often represent the individual's largely unconscious attempt to
adapt to stress. Traits may be the result of developmental conflicts, overt
manifestations of defenses, or learned behavior. In combination, personality
traits make up one's personality.

Personality disorders exist when the traits that make up one's personality are inflexible and impair one's ability to interact with the environment and with others. People with personality disorders usually respond poorly to changes and to stress and exhibit deficiencies in their capacity for relationships and, often, for work. There is, however, a danger in stereotyping, for the line between personality types is not clear, nor is it simple to draw a distinction between *normal* and *abnormal*. *Pathological* behavior may only be behavior that is experienced by others as excessive or repetitive but does not cause significant impairment. Personality disorders begin to be observable in adolescence or early adulthood and are stable over time.

Paranoid personality disorder is characterized by a pervasive, long-standing, groundless suspiciousness and distrust of others. People with this disorder are constantly vigilant and view the intentions of those they interact with as malevolent. They are often hostile, irritable, and angry, yet they refuse to take responsibility for their feelings, instead attributing them to others.

Schizoid personality disorder is the term used for people who have a lifelong history of being socially withdrawn and introverted, may be isolated, and are ill at ease with people but do not exhibit the disordered thinking seen in people with schizophrenia. They do, however, restrict emotional expression, and their affect is bland and constricted. Others see them as eccentric, isolated, and lonely, even though this is not their own self-image.

Schizotypal personality disorder is a term given in *DSM-III* for what was formerly called simple or latent schizophrenia. People with this disorder frequently appear to be odd, behave strangely, and have a very active fantasy life. They may experience magical thinking, ideas of reference, illusions, and derealization (Kaplan and Sadock 1996). There is a pattern of interpersonal deficits based on discomfort with, and reduced capacity for, close relationships.

Histrionic personality disorder is not to be confused with people whose behavior is characterized as *hysterical*. While both may appear dramatic, extroverted, attention-seeking, and excitable, persons with a histrionic personality disorder have a much greater problem in relating to others, and they function at a lower level (Kernberg 1992). They tend to be emotionally manipulative, with low frustration tolerance.

Narcissistic personality disorder characterizes people who have severely unrealistic concepts of their own self-worth, often appearing grandiose, lacking in empathy, and enraged. These behaviors cover a fragile sense of self-worth, and such people are very vulnerable to threats to their self-esteem.

Antisocial personality disorder (sociopathic) is often incorrectly thought to be synonymous with criminal behavior. It more accurately describes behavior, usually first noticed in childhood or adolescence, that has a pattern of violating the rights of others without apparent concern. It may be referred to as psychopathy or sociopathy. Persons with this disorder often exhibit lack of empathy, arrogance, and glib, superficial charm.

Borderline personality disorder is characterized by impulsivity, and instability of mood, relationships, and self-image. People with this disorder may experience brief psychotic symptoms when under perceived stress.

Avoidant personality disorder refers to a pattern of social withdrawal caused by an extreme fear of rejection in people who would like to have relationships. People with this disorder are extremely sensitive to criticism, timid, inhibited, feel inadequate, and may seem indifferent.

Dependent personality disorder describes a pattern of pervasive and extreme dependency on others to take responsibility for one's life and to make decisions. Behavior includes submissiveness, clinging, fear of separation and abandonment, and a strong need to be cared for. People with this disorder appear to be docile and self-deprecating and will avoid a show of anger at any cost.

Obsessive-compulsive personality disorder is characterized by perfectionism, rigidity, orderliness, stubbornness, inflexibility, and emotional constriction. People with this disorder often have difficulty making decisions and seem to be excessively moralistic. They often have strong, rigid defenses and tend to use intellectualization, separating thoughts and feelings.

Passive-aggressive personality disorder (negativistic personality disorder), included in *DSM-III-R* but excluded as a cluster C category in *DSM-IV*, refers to a pattern of passive resistance to demands, authority, and responsibilities made by others or by society in general. This resistance may be manifested by obstructionism, inefficiency, or procrastination.

Assessment

Diagnosing personality disorders is a very difficult task. They represent the least-understood and most-controversial categories of mental disorders, and it is possible that they are overdiagnosed. There is significant overlap in the criteria for specific personality disorders, and it is sometimes difficult to determine whether the behavior is really impairing the individual. An individual's core personality can possibly be changed if the person is suffering from chronic depression or substance abuse (Axis I), but change is less likely if the person suffers from a personality disorder (Axis II). People with a personality disorder usually have problems in both relationships and work. They respond poorly to stress and to change, but a lack of self-awareness further complicates the diagnostic process. Since people with personality disorders often do not see anything wrong with themselves, but see the problem as being with "the world," the diagnosis may be a judgment call by the mental health professional, who determines what constitutes "inflexible," "maladaptive," or "impaired" character traits.

The clinical syndromes that are given Axis I diagnoses usually have the following characteristics: a defined collection of symptoms, a family history or environmental experience, stability over time, and a fairly predictable clinical course (Perry and Vaillant 1989). For personality disorders, these conditions do not usually exist. Thus it would appear that diagnosis of personality disorder is far less systematic and based more on intuitively chosen groups of associated character traits. The process is fuzzy, with few clear lines between different personality disorders, as well as lack of clarity about what constitutes normal or abnormal behavior. Mental health professionals need to be especially careful not to stereotype when using these diagnoses, especially since there is a pejorative aspect to them.

Assessment of people with personality disorders is complicated by a general lack of self-awareness and the fact that presenting symptoms often are insufficient for a diagnosis. Self-reports about the past are often distorted by present moods and circumstances, and thus it is helpful to get additional information from significant others. It is sometimes difficult to tell whether the trait described is habitual or transitory. In addition, the assessment may yield information suggesting the presence of more than one type of personality disorder. Different behaviors or traits may be observed at different times, or the same traits may be seen in different personality disorders. Family and sociocultural factors are also important variables, since individual personalities often reflect the family system, and behavior that may be unacceptable in some segments of society may be acceptable in others.

Some characteristics appear to be common in people with personality disorders and can be detected through assessment:

1. Repetitive, inflexible, and maladaptive responses to stress that are often self-defeating
2. Problems in interpersonal relationships and at work

3. Generally in touch with reality
4. Annoying or attention-seeking behavior that may result in rejection by others, including mental health professionals
5. Limited ability to see that they have problems and thus they may have to be coerced into seeking intervention

In making an assessment—since if the diagnosis is of a personality disorder, the person probably has not changed abruptly—it is important to determine "Why now?" Why has the person only now come to the attention of a mental health professional? This determination will help the clinician to evaluate the nature and severity of the stress as well as to get a sense of the motivation for intervention.

Given what is known about the etiology of some of the personality disorders, it is important that assessment include information about the following areas:

1. History of intimate relationships
2. History of abuse, rape, or other trauma
3. Family losses through death, divorce, or abandonment
4. Head injury, other bodily injury, or birth complications
5. Family history of mental disorders, especially schizophrenia, depression, antisocial or severe personality disorder, or of substance abuse
6. School and work history
7. History of psychiatric hospitalizations and suicide attempts
8. An evaluation of areas of successful functioning

A valid diagnosis should be enduring for at least two different points in the person's history (Perry 1991).

DSM-III attempted to organize the personality disorders into clusters based on some common characteristics. People with cluster A disorders appear odd or eccentric; those with cluster B disorders appear dramatic, emotional, or erratic; and those with cluster C disorders appear fearful or anxious (American Psychiatric Association 1987). DSM-IV uses the same clusters but excludes passive-aggressive personality disorder.

All people suffering from cluster A personality disorders characteristically have problems in relating to others and thus lead isolated lives. People with a paranoid personality disorder present at assessment as hypervigilant, mistrustful, and possessed by a deep sense of foreboding. Intervention is rarely sought, for although their fears are groundless, they view the actions of others as personally hostile and threatening. They will not acknowledge any responsibility for what may have transpired and show no awareness of projecting onto the world unconscious feelings that are threatening. Because they fear intimacy, the interviewer should remain concerned but distant, tolerant of the amount of detail that is given to justify the concerns, and initially accepting of rather than challenging their perceptions, which at times may appear delusional. Such people may be litigious, experience extreme jealousy, or be bigoted, and can elicit negative feelings in the interviewer. If a consent form is required, or a session taped, the reasons and ramifications must be clearly explained, since they are innately suspicious.

People with a *schizoid personality disorder* usually will give a lifelong history of being socially withdrawn and lacking interest in close relationships. Such people present as shy and somewhat bland, usually are involved in solitary activities, and seek employment in settings that involve very little human interaction. They usually do not seek out intervention and may come to the attention of mental health professionals because family members are concerned about their lifestyle. Childhood history may show them to have been solitary, rigid, and hypersensitive. They often have rich fantasy lives that they can share only when they can feel comfortable enough to attempt a therapeutic relationship. Acceptance of the person's lifestyle, which in some cases may be quite satisfying to him or her, is essential in the early stages of exploration; otherwise, the client will not continue. Often the person is quite resigned to his choices and is not unhappy.

Some clinicians see *schizoid* and *schizotypal personality disorders* as being at the healthier end of a spectrum of schizophrenic disorders (Waldinger 1990). In contrast to people having a schizoid personality disorder, who may appear merely to be socially withdrawn, those with a schizotypal personality disorder may appear odd in behavior and appearance. On assessment, some evidence of a thought disorder will be found. They have an excessively elaborate fantasy life. At assessment, they may resemble people with schizophrenia, yet usually are higher functioning. It is diagnostically important to ask about a family history of schizophrenia, for it is not uncommon among people with a schizotypal personality disorder to be related to a person with schizophrenia. The interviewer must be careful to be nonjudgmental, as people with this disorder may reveal some very odd beliefs that should not be challenged initially. The clinician must also be patient, as responses to questions may seem vague or abstract. Again, these people usually do not seek out intervention and often do not recognize the existence of a problem; thus assessment may be very difficult.

People with cluster B personality disorders do not overtly withdraw from others but have severely disturbed interpersonal relationships. They frequently appear to be dramatic, emotional, angry, exploitative, impulsive, self-centered, and erratic in behavior. A fear of intimacy is present in relationships, and this, coupled with a tendency to devalue others, can exacerbate the problems of evaluation.

People with a *histrionic personality disorder* may present as warm, flamboyant, concerned with appearance, excitable, and highly emotional. Upon exploration, it can be seen that there is a shallowness in emotions and in relationships. They may appear seductive, but this is largely directed toward seeking attention, and sexual relationships are devalued and unsatisfactory. In an assessment interview they appear to like the attention and may try hard to please, but seem not to be in touch with their real feelings and are very vague about details. Many recognize that they have problems in relationships but tend not to recognize their own role in the difficulties. Some report somatic symptoms, with hypochondriasis being a further attempt to be cared for and nurtured, but if physical symptoms are presented, assessment should include a medical examination to rule out any organic problems.

Narcissistic personality disorder is a term that is frequently used inaccurately to describe people who are thought to be "self-centered" or "full of themselves." Characteristics attributed to people with this disorder are similar to those seen in people with a borderline personality disorder. Some clinicians view these two disorders as being at opposite ends of a spectrum, with narcissistic at the healthier end (Adler 1985). People with the latter disorder will initially present as well groomed, talented, grandiose, entitled, omnipotent, and often successful. Exploration, however, will reveal great concern for how others regard them and a very unstable sense of self-esteem. They often tend to set unrealistic goals for themselves that are doomed to failure, evoke an internal response of rage, and further injure their sense of self-worth, or they may have fantasies of success and an undue sense of uniqueness. Family history often shows that these people were unrealistically regarded by one or both parents as having unusual talent, good looks, or high intellect. Relationships are highly problematic, for their initial idealization and envy of people is followed by devaluation and hostility when the formerly desired person fails to meet dependency and intimacy needs. They may seek intervention because of experiencing some depression, and though they may be aware that they are unable to maintain positive relationships, they have very limited insight into their responsibility and view others, and society, as not fully appreciating their qualities. It should be noted that a degree of narcissism can be healthy, especially in performers such as actors and athletes. In excess, however, it impairs judgment as well as professional and personal relationships.

Antisocial personality disorder has frequently been used to describe substance-abusing, minority members of the population. This, however, is unjustly limiting, as people with this disorder can be found at all levels of society, with the affluent and powerful among them more protected and harder to identify. The true roots of this disorder can be recognized in early childhood behavior, not in the inner city. There is often a history of impulsivity in childhood, with the first signs of antisocial behavior observed as early as age eight in boys and twelve in girls. Antisocial behavior may be overt or it may be very subtle. People with an antisocial personality disorder will usually not seek out intervention because they are not concerned about their behavior; they usually come at the demand of the courts, an employer, a school, a spouse, or the department of social services. Often the request is for documentation that they have come, or if mandated, that they will continue to come. Sometimes recognized as "con artists," they can present as charming, ingratiating, and seductive, while in fact they are highly manipulative and demanding. They will give a history of a rebellious, problematic childhood and adolescence, during which they began a continuing pattern of activities harmful to, and violating the rights of, other people and often those of animals as well. Many have a history of substance abuse and suicide threats. What is striking in assessing these people is the apparent lack of depression, anxiety, or guilt as they describe behavior that may impair all areas of their lives. Since they may underplay the extent of their antisocial activities, it is helpful to interview close, dependable relatives and obtain records from referral sources, if any. Family history often reveals substance abuse and antisocial behavior by one or both parents and a chaotic home life. Many of the clients with antisocial personality disorder who come to the attention of mental health professionals are mandated. Thus it is important that after assessment, a mutually agreed-upon area for intervention is identified, even if the goals are minimal, because this could lead to a significant intervention if the person can begin to overcome the distrust of closeness. The interviewer needs to convey acceptance of the *person* but not of the *behavior*.

The term *borderline personality disorder* is frequently used, inaccurately, to describe any observed form of personality disorder. It has also been subjected to a range of definitions over the years and is one of the most controversial personality disorder diagnoses. Questions have been raised about its relationship to the Axis I diagnoses of schizophrenia or affective disorders. It often coexists with major depression, yet the relationship between the two is unclear. What is agreed on is that it is characterized by a history of ambivalence, very unstable and intense relationships and moods, erratic and often self-destructive behavior, fear of abandonment, poor impulse control, chronic feelings of boredom, and poor self-image. People with this disorder can, when under stress, exhibit transient psychotic symptoms that will disappear within hours or, at most, days. In an assessment interview, the person may be able to acknowledge relationship problems and report feelings of emptiness, of being alone, and of depression. Even in the initial interview, the interviewer may be able to observe extremes of affect ranging from anger and devaluation to warmth and idealization. The clients will try to project the blame onto others for poor relationships or for problems at work, where they are usually underachievers. They appear to lack a sense of identity and may exhibit strong dependency needs and clinging behavior. Assessments should include inquiry into history of substance abuse and of self-destructive acts, including self-mutilation and suicide attempts. Theories of the etiology of borderline personality disorder support the need to get a history of early separation and loss, as well as a family history of physical, sexual, and verbal abuse. The interviewer needs to guard against an impulse to meet the presenting dependency needs, as well as against negative feelings that might be induced by the client's erratic reaction to the content of the interview and to the interviewer. Because of fear that closeness will lead to abandonment, although an initial session may seem to go well, the person with a borderline personality disorder may elect not to return. Another reason that intervention may be abruptly terminated is the tendency of a person with borderline personality disorder to split rather than integrate, initially idealizing (the good object) and later devaluing (the bad object) the clinician.

People with cluster C personality disorders tend to be anxious, fearful, and introverted. Unlike people with cluster A disorders, they would like to be involved with others, but like people with cluster B disorders, they fear rejection and seek out relationships that may be problematic but that they pursue to meet their needs for social interaction.

People with *avoidant personality disorder* have a great fear of rejection, which can be observed in the assessment interview, as they appear anxious, timid, eager to please, and lacking in self-confidence. They will give a history of relationships, primarily with family members or a few very close friends whom they regard as accepting and not likely to criticize them. They are afraid, in relationships, to be assertive or to express their own needs, and they tend to seek employment in areas that do not require them to assume leadership roles. They focus on trying to please. They describe their lives as revolving around situations, tasks, and relationships in which they can avoid calling attention to themselves for fear of embarrassment and rejection. The interviewer must be accepting, nonjudgmental, and understanding in phrasing questions and comments, remembering that this type of client is hypervigilant for perceived criticism.

People with *dependent personality disorder* need and want social relationships but lack self-confidence, especially in asserting their own needs. They are often brought to the attention of mental health professionals because people close to them feel stifled by their demands. People with this disorder will present as helpless, and they will give a history of manipulating others to take responsibility for them, while stating that they place the needs of others ahead of their own. They fear rejection and abandonment and will agree with the ideas of others to avoid criticism and rejection, or will "do for others" in order to be needed and thus have their own dependency needs met. The dependency needs are often so great that they will tolerate almost any behavior on the part of people who seem to meet these needs. It is important to inquire during assessment whether there is a history of past or present abuse.

People with *obsessive-compulsive personality disorder* are more apt to seek intervention on their own than are people with other personality disorders. While they may have a stable marriage or relationship and a solid job, they usually are aware that they have few friends and that they live rather constricted, joyless lives. In assessment they show some awareness that their preoccupation with detail, order, and doing things in their own, inflexible way tends to alienate others. There may be a family history of obsessive-compulsive personality disorder. The patterns that they follow are more ego-syntonic than those of people with the anxiety disorder, obsessive-compulsive disorder. People with obsessive-compulsive personality disorder, though appearing unemotional, are often more aware of their feelings than are people with other forms of personality disorder, but they fear that the expression of warm feelings might lead to rejection. They tend to be perfectionists, fearful of making mistakes, and can appear quite indecisive. It can be tedious to assess people with this disorder, as they are so preoccupied with details and circumstances that the assessment process can be quite lengthy. Use of intellectualization as a defense is quite common.

The term *passive-aggressive* is unfortunately overused, more often pejoratively than to describe a type of personality disorder. As a disorder, it is characterized by controlling, usually oblique, behavior in which anger is covertly manifested through procrastination, obstructionism, and inefficiency. A history will show that people with this disorder have strong dependency needs but then find fault with those on whom they depend and behave in ways to alienate those around them. They have great difficulty expressing their own needs. Frequently such people come to the attention of mental health professionals when marital therapy is indicated. It is often difficult to engage them. In assessment and subsequent sessions, there is a pattern of anger at a partner for "not knowing my needs" and assuming that they are entitled to a partner who would meet those needs, even if the needs are not articulated and appear to be insatiable. Seen individually, people with this disorder may speak of "taking revenge," feeling that they are doing the best they can at home and at work, yet are unappreciated. They show little awareness of their negative behavior, and when things repeatedly go wrong, it is "only" a mistake. Though their anger is usually apparent even in an initial interview, they do not usually recognize it themselves. Anger at the clinician for not meeting dependency needs as well as needs to be "understood" may be manifested by delay in paying for sessions or by paying in small installments.

Epidemiology

Because of the elusiveness of diagnosis, it is difficult to get accurate epidemiological data. It is also possible that the recognition of these disorders may depend on the orientation of the person making the assessment, as well as the setting in which the client is seen. The fact that many people with personality disorders never come to the attention of mental health professionals also skews the data. It has been estimated that 5 to 15 percent of the general population and a third to a half of all psychiatric patients have personality disorders (*Harvard Mental Health Letter* 1987).

People with cluster A personality disorders (paranoid, schizoid, and schizotypal) are very unlikely to seek intervention, and a review of the literature yielded little epidemiological data. No data were found on prevalence of people with paranoid personality disorder. It has been estimated that prevalence of schizoid personality disorder is 2 percent (Waldinger 1990) and that schizotypal personality disorder has a prevalence ranging from 2 percent to 6 percent (American Psychiatric Association 1987; Waldinger 1990). It must be noted, however, that the last two disorders are considered by some to be part of a spectrum of schizophrenia disorders, and thus prevalence data are rather soft. Paranoid and schizoid personality disorders are more frequently diagnosed in men than in women (Perry and Vaillant 1989). No sex ratio data were found for schizotypal personality disorder.

The literature yielded little hard data on the epidemiology of cluster B disorders (antisocial, histrionic, narcissistic, and borderline), with the exception of antisocial personality disorder, for which there is an estimated lifetime prevalence of 5.8 percent in males and 1.2 percent in females (Kessler et al. 1994). As would be expected, there is a higher prevalence of people diagnosed as having an antisocial personality disorder in prison populations than in the population at large. Research suggests that diagnoses of borderline, narcissistic, or histrionic personality disorders are fairly prevalent, but this appears to be inferential. It has been estimated that 20 percent of people seen in psychiatric treatment have a diagnosis of borderline personality disorder (Gunderson 1989). Sex ratio estimates suggest sexism in the absence of any real conclusive studies. It is postulated that more women are found to have borderline and histrionic personality disorders, while narcissistic personality disorder is more prevalent for males.

The limited epidemiological data for cluster C personality disorders (avoidant, dependent, and obsessive-compulsive) may be the result of their resemblance to anxiety disorders and the fact that dependency traits are observed in people with a range of diagnoses. It is estimated that 0.5–1 percent of the population suffer from avoidant personality disorder and 1–3 percent from obsessive-compulsive disorder (Staff 1996). Again, sex ratio estimates suggest sexism, as they postulate that avoidant and dependent personality disorders are more common for women, while obsessive-compulsive personality disorder is more common for men. Greater use in research of diagnostic rating scales, such as the Personality Disorders Examination (Loranger 1988), might be useful in obtaining more epidemiological data on these disorders.

There is a clear need for rigorous epidemiological research on personality disorders, but this is contingent on greater reliability and validity of diagnostic criteria.

Clinical Course

As noted above, many people with personality disorders never come to the attention of mental health professionals and, if they do, frequently do not follow a suggested course of intervention. The traits that compose a personality disorder are so pervasive that the person may not see them as causing a problem. Most personality disorders appear to emerge in adolescence, although identifying behavior may be detected in childhood; this is especially true with people with an antisocial or a schizoid personality disorder. There is also some evidence that as people get older, even though the diagnosis of a personality disorder is still applicable, the degree of impairment seems less apparent. It is not clear whether there is some yet undetermined cause for the change or whether with maturation the person learns more acceptable adaptive techniques or simply adjusts to the lifestyle pattern.

Long-term studies on people with cluster A personality disorders apparently do not exist. Because people with paranoid personality disorder usually do not complain, they rarely seek intervention. Generally clinicians view the disorder to be intractable. While some people with these disorders deteriorate and develop a primary diagnosis of schizophrenia, that progression is not generally the case. Some show improvement with intervention, while still retaining the characteristic traits to some degree. Studies show that people with a schizotypal personality disorder often function better later in life than people with a diagnosis of schizophrenia, but not as well as people with a borderline personality disorder who have sought intervention (Perry and Vaillant 1989).

A problem in evaluating the clinical course of people with cluster B personality disorders is that even if they seek intervention, many are lost to follow-up because of their tendency to abruptly terminate the intervention, to change therapists, and, especially in the case of people with borderline personality disorders, to commit suicide. In general it is believed that people who have this cluster of disorders show improvement with age. For people with a histrionic or an antisocial personality disorder, it may be that society does not provide them with the same self-destructive opportunities as it did when they were younger. In any case, antisocial behavior appears to go somewhat into remission when the person reaches the thirties, although this is less true for those who may have been more aggressive and less socialized. People with narcissistic personality disorders tend to remain somewhat the same, but may establish more realistic goals or may experience a midlife crisis that precipitates abrupt vocational changes or inappropriate love affairs. People with borderline personality disorders also show improvement in functioning as they mature, although for them and for people with an antisocial personality disorder, there seems to be a higher incidence of depression and alcoholism in later years, which may increase the risk of suicide. In a longitudinal study of people with borderline personality disorders who had been hospitalized, the prognosis was poorest for those who had a history of parental physical abuse or intergenerational incest (Stone 1990). Despite the tendency toward improvement by people with borderline personality disorders, it must be remembered that they suffer from a serious, severe illness that has a high suicide rate (Docherty 1992).

People with cluster C personality disorders may come to the attention of mental health professionals because they are aware of their loneliness and problems with others, or because the people on whom they are dependent have difficulty coping with their needs. Most of these disorders will remain fairly persistent. People with dependency disorders or passive-aggressive personality disorders are at risk for depression and alcoholism if there is disruption in the relationship with the person on whom they depend. The course of people with obsessive-compulsive personality disorder appears to vary. They are particularly vulnerable to unexpected changes. Some seem to show less rigid behavior as they get older, but others are at risk for increased depression and psychosomatic problems.

Longitudinal studies of persons with personality disorders, regardless of diagnosis and length of follow-up, show that the majority continue to have significant symptoms and impairment in social functioning. Thus it can be concluded that Axis II disorders have a more serious social impact than many of the Axis I disorders (Perry 1993).

Differential Diagnosis

As has been noted above, there is considerable overlap in the criteria for personality disorders, and people may have more than one. In addition, some of the personality disorders are associated with vulnerability to certain symptom (Axis I) disorders, further confusing the diagnosis—for example, the relationship of schizotypal personality disorder to schizophrenia, or dependent personality disorder to depression, perhaps suggesting a continuum between some Axis I and some Axis II disorders. Personality disorders precede the onset of clinical (Axis I) syndromes and can make a person much more vulnerable to stress. Certain personality disorders, such as borderline, even tend to create stressful situations, resulting in depression, anxiety, and, at times, psychosis (Millon 1999).

Cluster A personality disorders all involve limited or no social relationships. People with paranoid personality disorders can be differentiated from people with paranoid schizophrenia by the lack of hallucinations, delusions, or any other formal thought disorder. They differ from people with borderline personality disorder in that they are rarely physically self-destructive and tend not to be involved in stormy relationships. They differ from people with an antisocial disorder because they have no history of deviant behavior, although they can be perceived as threatening. Because paranoid symptoms or traits can be induced by a high level of stimulant substances, such as cocaine, it is important in assessment to obtain a substance abuse history, past and present. People with a schizoid personality disorder usually can be differentiated from people with schizophrenia or with schizotypal personality disorder because usually they are capable of better functioning at school or work. Also, there is usually not a family history of schizophrenia. They are often even less involved with others than are people with a paranoid personality disorder, who are aware of others, even if only to be suspicious and mistrustful. People with avoidant or obsessive-compulsive personality disorders (cluster C) differ from those with schizoid disorders in that they have some sustained relationships and are aware of feeling lonely, while a person with a schizoid personality disorder may be quite content to be solitary. Finally, a person with a schizotypal personality disorder may be hard to differentiate from a person with schizophrenia, because of odd appearance, perceptions of the eccentricity of their behavior, and the idiosyncrasies of their communication patterns. For the most part, there is, however, an absence of psychosis. Schizotypal personality disorder is sometimes confused with borderline personality disorder, but the latter assumes greater involvement with others, even if that involvement is grossly impaired.

The criteria for diagnosis of cluster B disorders overlap so much that differentiation is difficult and a person may appear to have, or may actually have, more than one disorder. Often people with cluster B disorders are believed to have a dual diagnosis of histrionic and of borderline personality disorder, but those with primarily a histrionic disorder appear less empty, have a better sense of identity, and fewer, if any, psychotic episodes. They are warmer and more concerned about others than are people with narcissistic personality disorder. If the person complains of physical symptoms, the differential diagnosis of somatization disorder should be considered, after physical diagnoses have been ruled out. People with narcissistic personality disorders may resemble those with a borderline disorder and, as mentioned above, may represent the healthier end of the spectrum of cluster B disorders. They are usually less anxious, less dependent, less impulsive, and tend to show less regression in treatment. They are usually less impulsive than people with antisocial personality disorders. There is also a resemblance to people with histrionic personality disorders, but they are more distant toward others and more concerned with their sense of self-esteem than with meeting their dependency needs. A person with an antisocial personality disorder is clearly differentiated by the age of onset: the disorder can be traced to conduct disorders in childhood. This is particularly important in differentiating it from a narcissistic personality disorder, in which the person may seem to disregard the rights of others but does not have a history of childhood violence. People with antisocial personality disorder also have greater superego pathology, and there is an absence of guilt or remorse. Because there are similarities between people with an antisocial personality disorder and people who are abusing substances, it is important to get a good history to determine whether the abuse of substances predated antisocial behavior, in order to establish a primary diagnosis. People with antisocial personality disorder have high rates of affective disorders and substance abuse. They are less dependent than those with a histrionic disorder and usually less impulsive than people with a borderline disorder, who also have a greater capacity for experiencing guilt. Finally, while a person with a borderline personality disorder may resemble those who have other cluster B disorders, a greater sense of emptiness and impulsivity may be observed. In addition, the clinician will observe a more demanding quality in relationships and more self-destructive behavior and gestures that may be attempts at manipulation. It is estimated that as many as 50 percent of people with this disorder also suffer from a major affective disorder (Waldinger 1990), and there is also a high rate of substance abuse.

The disorders making up cluster C do not have the flamboyant, demanding, and impulsive characteristics of cluster B personality disorders. People with an avoidant personality disorder are not as demanding as people with borderline, histrionic, or dependent personality disorders. They are more responsive to others than are those with a schizoid personality disorder. They may resemble people with an anxiety disorder, and it is possible that some people will have an Axis I as well as an Axis II diagnosis. Dependency is a characteristic found in many people suffering from mental disorders, and a diagnosis of dependent personality disorder may be comorbid with another diagnosis. Traits may be similar to those recognized in people with borderline, histrionic, and avoidant personality disorders. With respect to cluster C personality disorders, it is often hard to differentiate between people with dependent personality disorder and people with passive-aggressive personality disorder. Therefore, a decision was made to exclude passive-aggressive personality disorder from cluster C in *DSM-IV*. People with a dependent personality disorder can be differentiated from those with agoraphobia, for the former are immobilized by feelings of incompetence and the latter by fear. The degree of impairment in functioning differentiates people with obsessive-compulsive personality disorder from those with obsessive-compulsive disorder: people with the personality disorder appear more impaired and present symptoms that are more ego-syntonic. These people may appear to be paranoid when anxious, but they do not have a history of mistrust. They can be differentiated from people with schizoid personality disorder because many find their lives unsatisfying.

It must be remembered that people with mental disorders may have more than one diagnosis on Axis I and Axis II, only one per axis, or a diagnosis on only one axis. Comorbidity is widespread and can be confusing when planning interventions. People with personality disorders often have a mood or anxiety disorder, or schizophrenia. Substance abuse and somatization frequently are comorbid with Cluster B and C personality disorders (Tyrer et al. 1997). People with borderline, histrionic, dependent, or avoidant personality disorders often have a major depression. Anxiety disorders frequently are found in people with borderline or antisocial personality disorders (Fiester et al. 1990). In addition, some organic disorders may look similar to personality disorders and thus require careful assessment, including physical, and possibly neurological, examination. The clinician should rule out temporal lobe epilepsy and frontal lobe dysfunction in clients who exhibit high emotionality and impulsive, inappropriate behavior; and Huntington's chorea, Parkinson's disease, and multiple sclerosis where personality changes may be the first symptoms noted. Obtaining a family history of physical and mental illness as well as specific testing may be needed to ascertain diagnosis. People with AIDS may experience personality changes, disturbance of affect, and cognitive dysfunction that may be evident before the onset of physical deterioration (Welch 1990).

Etiology

As has been indicated above, little is known with certainty about the etiology of personality disorders, although it may be assumed that there are

biological, social, cultural, and psychological influences on their development. Although research has been limited, it is thought that there may be
genetic and environmental factors that may cause a predisposition for personality disorders. A study of 15,000 pairs of twins showed a concordance
rate for personality disorders in monozygotic twins several times higher than
for dizygotic twins (Perry and Vaillant 1989). All formulations have stressed
the importance of family environment. As noted above, culture must be
considered when assessing what is "normal" or "abnormal" behavior.

There is stronger, albeit still weak, evidence for a genetic component in
the development of cluster A personality disorders than there is for those in
the other clusters. This is greater for those with schizotypal personality disorder than for people with paranoid personality disorder. Little is known
about the effect of family and early environment on the development of
cluster A personality disorders, but social learning theory would suggest that
children raised in homes with aloof, distant parents who themselves led
isolated lives might have a predisposition for these disorders. Some theorists
believe that people with paranoid personality disorder are projecting onto
others the anger that their parents may have projected onto them.

The etiology of cluster B personality disorders, especially borderline personality disorder, has interested many clinicians. Again, there are little hard
data and there is some disagreement. Little is postulated about the etiology
of histrionic personality disorders, although some research suggests that there
may be a relationship between histrionic and antisocial personality disorders
that is similar to the relationship between borderline and narcissistic personality disorders. The etiologies of all cluster B disorders suggest a problematic
family situation, especially in the early years, often with inconsistent parenting. Several theories about the etiology of these disorders, particularly
borderline and narcissistic, have been formulated and will be summarized.

Mahler (1971) saw what she identified as the rapprochement subphase
in the separation-individuation process as the point where the child's "narcissism" is most vulnerable. If the parental figure cannot support the child's
need for autonomy, this will threaten the child's sense of omnipotence, and
the attainment of self and object constancy will suffer. She believed that the
result is a search for perfection in the self and others, intolerance of ambivalence, sensitivity to perceived setbacks, conflicting self-images of omnipotence and inferiority, and vacillation in object relationships between controlling and withdrawing.

The conflict model, developed by Otto Kernberg from an object-relations
perspective, states that the origins of histrionic personality disorders lie in
the preoedipal period. In Kernberg's view, people with this disorder come

from dysfunctional families where there is profound and chronic mother-child conflict and often severe personality disturbance in the mother. He sees this disorder as similar to the borderline personality disorder in the use of splitting and other primitive defense mechanisms (Kernberg 1992). Kernberg sees people with antisocial personality disorder as very similar to people with narcissistic personality disorders, with the difference that the former have specific pathological superego functioning. He feels that people with this disorder did not integrate the good and bad aspects of parental objects and saw them as omnipotent and cruel. Often they report observing and experiencing violence in childhood. The person devalues the "good" as weak and destructible and views the "bad" as powerful and able to survive. Kernberg sees antisocial behavior, at times, as an adaptation to a highly pathological social environment, such as a "gang culture," and believes that it needs to be looked at in terms of the general level of superego functioning (Kernberg 1992).

Most of Kernberg's work has centered on borderline and narcissistic personality disorders. He uses a conflict model to explain borderline personality disorders and believes that the origins lie in disturbance during the rapprochement phase of separation and individuation. The disorder arises when the environment fails to meet basic needs, especially support of individuation. His work is based on psychoanalytic metapsychology and is influenced by the British analysts Klein, Fairbairn, and Winnicott, and by Margaret Mahler. Kernberg believes that the personality organization of a person with borderline personality disorder results from preoedipal conflicts stemming from severely pathological relationships with the parental object that do not permit integration of the good and bad aspects of the object and subsequently of the self. It is a problem related to the drives and to inadequate defenses. The intrapsychic conflicts result in fixation at an early stage of development, with splitting and associated defenses, such as primitive idealization, projective identification, omnipotence, denial, and devaluation, as the primary, ego-weakening defenses. These defenses are used to protect the good self and the good object.

Kernberg believes that people with borderline personality disorder have an excess of aggressive drive that may be genetic, or may be the result of excessive frustration in early childhood that must be defended against by the use of splitting (Druck 1989). The defenses are mobilized against the anxiety generated by these aggressive impulses toward the self and others. Kernberg feels that the sense of emptiness, the difficulties with object constancy, and the difficulties in development of the psychic structure are consequences of the excessive aggression. People with borderline personality disorders are unable to deal with others as separate and individuated because they would hate and envy "the other" if separation is acknowledged. The excessive aggressive drive fails to be integrated with the person's libidinal strivings. Kernberg sees splitting as the essential cause of ego weakness and subsequent inadequate superego development.

To Kernberg, narcissistic personality disorder has an etiology similar to that of borderline personality disorder, in that both have their roots in poor childhood object relations. He believes that people with narcissistic personality disorders usually experienced unempathic, cold, sometimes spiteful parenting, yet the parental object(s) saw something special in the individual that received attention. This may account for a somewhat better cohesion of self.

Masterson and Rinsley (1975), like Mahler, see the origins of borderline personality disorder as the inability of the person to separate and individuate during the rapprochement phase. There was a lack of "good enough mothering." The mother was perceived as threatening to withdraw love if the child tried to separate, while rewarding clinging behavior and thus continually undermining the child's development. Independence and autonomy were perceived as leading to abandonment. The child had ambivalent needs for mothering and for individuation, and the cause of the later development of the disorder was the lack of support for the need to individuate. Rinsley (1989) feels that the development of a narcissistic personality disorder is similar in etiology to that of a borderline personality disorder, but that the former is more advanced developmentally.

Representational deficit/self-deficit models are used to explain the etiology of borderline and personality disorders based on the assumption of object-relations deficits in the course of personality development. Kohut's (1971, 1977) self-psychology model repudiated Freud's drive and structural theories and postulated the self as a psychic structure equal to the id, ego, and superego. For people with borderline and narcissistic personality disorders, the deficit is a fragile self, and it is greater in people with borderline personality disorder. People with narcissistic personality disorder have established some sense of self that could be self-soothing, so the deficits are less entrenched. Kohut believed that the character pathology of the parents of a person with a narcissistic personality disorder made them unable to empathize and respond with acceptance to the child's grandiose exhibitionistic (mirroring) needs, idealizing (merging) needs, and twin or partnership needs (alter ego), leading to a poor sense of self-worth and unrealistic goals and resulting in persistent needs for approval and perfection that were then frustrated. This frustration, in turn, led to further deficits in self-esteem. The excessive aggression often observed was seen as narcissistic rage, with its roots in the lack of true parental empathy, and represented a profoundly angry reaction to frustration and to injured self-esteem. Kohut's work focused on failure of attachment, and aggression was secondary to disappointment in the self-object relationship.

Adler and Buie (Adler and Buie 1979; Buie and Adler 1982) attributed the experience of aloneness as core to borderline pathology and related this to the person's inability in childhood to maintain a positive internal, soothing image of a loving, caring object. As a result, the world is experienced as empty and ungratifying. The person's early needs to be held and nurtured by an idealized object had been frustrated, resulting in a susceptibility to separation anxiety. Such people do not develop the capacity to self-soothe and must rely on others for soothing and psychological holding. They are susceptible to disappointment and intense separation anxiety, panic, and rage. They have not developed the internal resources needed to cope with separation. Buie and Adler recognize a person's legitimate need for relationships with others and feel that narcissistic rage results when these needs have been frustrated. The healthy needs become distorted, resulting in unrealistic demands that cause greater frustration and anger. People with borderline personality disorder will first idealize a person whom they feel will meet their needs, then experience disappointment, followed by anger, a sense of aloneness, and an inability to maintain a positive image of the person.

The ego-deficit model suggests that borderline personality disorder is caused by a deficit in the development of ego functions during the rapprochement phase of separation and individuation. This is attributed to the parental object-child relationship that may be characterized either as pushing the child away or pulling the child too close. It is a model that focuses more on ego functions and less on the development of object constancy.

Biological researchers see borderline personality disorders as belonging within the spectrum of affective disorders and as caused by an endogenous metabolic defect (Millon 1992). They support their position by pointing to the positive response of some people with borderline personality disorders to antidepressants. Neurobiologists postulate a correlation between the negative effects of childhood brain dysfunction and the development of borderline personality disorder. The hyperactivity, distractibility, confused cognition, poor affect regulation, and poor impulse control seen in childhood are later seen in characteristic borderline symptoms (Millon 1992, 1996), such as poor impulse and affect control and limited frustration tolerance.

Family factors, as noted above, are considered important in the development of personality disorders. For cluster B disorders the focus has, for the most part, been on family interaction in the very early years of life. People with antisocial personality disorder often have relatives who display antisocial behavior, and thus it may be learned behavior.

A study by Norden et al. (1995) of the home environment of persons with antisocial personality disorder revealed significantly poor maternal and paternal relationships and often physical abuse. There is also a high rate of anxiety disorders among first-degree relatives (Fiester et al. 1990).

In giving histories, people with borderline personality disorders will often report early separations and losses that led to neglect and deprivation. The losses were more often due to divorce, abandonment, or hospitalization than to death. Histories also frequently show mental illness or substance abuse as problems for one or both parents, thus suggesting failure, or at least impairment, in adequate parenting. When a hostile and conflictual relationship developed to its extreme, it took the form of physical or sexual abuse. The abusing parent might be overinvolved, infantalizing, and intrusive, or emotionally cold, indifferent, and neglectful.

The vulnerability to developing a borderline personality disorder is greater in families with high expressed emotion, i.e., in families in which many critical comments are made about the person, where hostility is evident, and where the atmosphere is highly emotional. A study by Laporte and Guttman (1996) of women with personality disorders showed that while 74 percent of those with other personality disorders suffered from some form of early separation or abuse, this occurred in the lives of 93 percent of women with borderline personality disorder.

A study by Herman, Perry, and van der Kolk (1989) showed a strong association between the trauma of childhood abuse and the development of a borderline personality disorder. It was, however, felt that the trauma was greatest for those with more vulnerable temperaments or with fewer protective relationships. Because sexual abuse of girls is more prevalent than of boys, the results may help explain the higher rate of borderline personality disorders in women. Recent work on the relationship of sexual abuse to the development of borderline personality disorder yielded a significant result only where the abuse involved penetration (Paris 1994). Both studies also showed that risk for developing borderline personality disorder increases significantly in direct relation to frequency of abuse.

The cultural changes of the last few decades may contribute to the greater prevalence of borderline personality disorder. The greater mobility of people, the economy, technology, and the increased rates of separation and divorce affect patterns of childrearing, family cohesion, and lifestyles. Customs and institutions are more fluid, and there is an absence of community and of consensual values. This cultural instability may affect people who are vulnerable to developing borderline personality disorder. There is a breakdown of extended families, with less access to people such as grandparents, older siblings, and long-term neighbors. In addition, the social networks such as school or church that might in the past have served as protection or substitutes when parent-child relationships were problematic are today more fragile (Paris 1998).

As noted above, most clinicians have focused attention on the etiology of cluster B personality disorders. There has been little work on the etiology of the cluster C, anxiety-type personality disorders. There are suggestions that the root of avoidant personality disorder may lie in fear of strangers and separation anxiety in the early years that may have been attributed to shyness. Some clinicians feel that dependent and passive-aggressive personality disorders may result from childhoods in which expression of independence or of aggression was discouraged. The Baker, Capron, and Azorlosa (1996) study of the families of origin of persons with dependent personality disorder (N 15) found that the families scored low in independent functioning, low in cohesion, and high in control. It is also possible that people with these disorders copied the behavior of close family members. There is some evidence of a genetic predisposition for developing obsessive-compulsive personality disorder (Waldinger 1990). Freudian theory suggested that the disorder is rooted in rigid, controlling parenting, especially concerning issues of toilet training. Erikson's developmental theory saw obsessional defenses developing in order to deal with anger at unmet needs for dependency and affection.

The etiology of personality disorders is controversial, and little systematic research is available. It is possible that given the problems of definition, diagnosis, and treatment, it would be impossible to conduct such research.

Intervention

As noted above, many people with personality disorders do not seek treatment, because they do not recognize that there are problems. Often, if they do come to the attention of mental health professionals, it is not by choice, and a struggle between client and clinician ensues. Therefore, intervention can be very difficult. An additional problem is the lack of clarity about etiology and diagnosis. There is no real intervention of choice. What occurs will depend on how ego-syntonic the behavior is, cultural factors, personality and training of the clinician, time frame, social supports, and cost.

There are some general obstacles to successful intervention. The defenses used by people with personality disorders, especially denial and projection, and in the case of people with borderline personality disorder, splitting, can be very strong, protecting the person from underlying, unconscious anxiety and depression. These people can be chronically angry and hostile and very quick to take offense. They may appear contemptuous and demanding of the clinician, and they have a high rate of leaving treatment abruptly. If coerced into coming for intervention, they may regard efforts to help them change behavior as punishment or brainwashing, and resist the clinician's efforts to make them see their behavior as self-destructive. Since the problems are mainly ego-syntonic and there is always a problem in relating to others, it is difficult, and sometimes impossible, to form a relationship.

It is important in working with people who have these disorders to show acceptance of the person, but not of the person's behavior, to point out the consequences of self-destructive behavior, and to help the person see that these actions function as maladaptive defenses against unwanted feelings and impulses. The person should be discouraged from blaming others or "life," and the intervention should focus on the observed behavior, and the possibility for change, not on explanations or justifications. Social workers are trained to recognize the importance of a mutually agreed-to plan for intervention, and this tool is particularly important with this population, who are fearful of the motivations of others.

Structure and control are essential components of intervention with a person who has a borderline personality disorder. Structure and an atmosphere of acceptance are important in order to confront the defenses and to allow people to think about the immediate and long-term consequences of their behavior. Control is exercised through maintaining clarity and consistency with respect to rules about appointments, fees, and especially in response to self-destructive thoughts and behaviors. If possible, the client should be seen regularly in the same office.

While being empathic and concerned, the clinician must be very careful not to encourage dependency that the person may want but also fears. Some clients may evoke rescue fantasies on the part of the clinician, and overtreating must be avoided. In addition, clinicians also have to be careful not to appear moralistic, punitive, or exasperated. Because of the impulsivity found in some people with personality disorders, especially those with cluster B disorders, it is important to try to agree on a plan on how to manage self-destructive impulses, to be prepared for crises and chaos, and to hospitalize the person if necessary.

Psychotherapy

People with cluster A personality disorders do not often seek intervention. A person with a paranoid personality disorder will find it difficult to trust, and the clinician needs to be patient, sensitive, empathic, and somewhat distant, and to respect the client's need for autonomy. Openness and honesty are essential, and the clinician must reinforce for the patient the confidential nature of their sessions. Confrontation would be very threatening, and it is helpful to sympathize with the pain and distress the person is experiencing, while slowly trying to convert the paranoid symptoms into depression (Meissner 1987) and helping to increase awareness of projecting thoughts onto others. When an alliance has been achieved, gentle reality testing can be useful. Group treatment is usually too threatening. Families may need to be helped to learn not to ridicule or challenge the person's distorted thinking.

As would be expected, forming a relationship with people who have schizoid or schizotypal personality disorders is very difficult, but once established there is usually sharing of the person's fantasy life. Since a goal is to increase the person's capacity for intimate relationships, that capacity needs careful assessment, and the clinician must avoid showing disappointment if this proves impossible. It may also be necessary to accept whatever relationship the person has been able to establish, even if it appears immature or, sometimes, self-destructive. Some people with schizoid personality disorder have responded to behavioral social skills training and, though there is usually limited participation, to the social context of a group. Families may need help in accepting the lifestyles chosen by these people or, in the case of people with a schizotypal personality disorder, their oddities of thought and appearance.

Much of the literature on intervention with people with personality disorders concentrates on intervention with people who have cluster B disorders, especially borderline disorder. These are the people who more frequently seek intervention. People with these disorders have had poor early relationships with parents and fear intimacy, thus they are leery of a treatment relationship. They may come for help, yet expect abandonment and annihilation. Psychoanalytically oriented psychotherapy is the treatment of choice for people with histrionic personality disorder, with the goal being clarification of the person's inner feelings, with which they are rarely in touch. Since there is always a show of emotion, the clinician must cautiously differentiate between real emotion and emotion that is being displayed for effect. Group treatment can also be helpful, as the peer pressure may force the individual to be less superficial, will challenge the person's seductiveness, and can discourage destructive acting out.

If a person with an antisocial personality disorder comes for intervention, it is often through coercion, and a relationship is hard to form. If the person is mandated to continue to come to sessions, what may emerge is considerable anxiety and sensitivity to rejection, which has been defended against through inappropriate behavior and apparent unconcern. An immediate goal is to show acceptance of the person but not of the behavior, to strongly hold the person responsible for the behavior, and to reach mutual agreement on how to establish control over impulsive behavior. Self-help groups in which limits are set by peers have been helpful. Families need to be involved in order to help them recognize that they may be at risk due to the behavior of the family member and to help them learn to protect themselves without experiencing guilt. They also need to be helped to set consistent limits and to avoid both minimizing and ignoring the behavior.

Given the variety of theories of the etiology of borderline and narcissistic personality disorders, there are obviously different approaches to intervention. People with these disorders lack a coherent sense of self and others, and cannot present in a focused, integrated way. They may seek intervention in order to be taken care of, yet fear that the clinician will tire of them and betray or abandon them. To help with identity development, the focus of intervention should be on the self and not on others, i.e., "How do *you* feel?" The debate with respect to intervention is between an interpretive, insight-oriented approach and a supportive, structured intervention environment.

Kernberg, using the conflict model to explain etiology, sees the central concern as the defenses organized around splitting that do not permit the person to neutralize the primitive drives, particularly aggression, and thus do not permit the individual to achieve realistic, comprehensive self and object representations. He advocates a modified psychoanalytic approach using the techniques of confrontation and interpretation within the evolving transferential relationship aimed at modifying the core pathology. He confronts the early apparent idealization of the analyst as underlying hostility and focuses on interpreting the negative aspects of the transference through which the person experiences the self as a frightened child and the analyst as a punitive parent. Confrontation of the ego-syntonic and ego-weakening defenses to make them ego-alien is viewed as essential for integration. Clarification is another frequently used technique, as the client may present material in a poorly organized and contradictory manner. Kernberg sees his clients two to four times a week and sets firm rules with respect to regularity, time, cost, and length of appointments. He does not use supportive techniques. In order to help protect the client from self-destructive impulses, Kernberg allows no verbal abuse in sessions, thus hoping to develop the observing function of the ego and support delayed impulse gratification. If the client becomes suicidal, Kernberg chooses not to manage this in outpatient sessions but requires hospitalization. In order to maintain neutrality, in addition to his own intervention Kernberg may have the client see a social worker for concrete services and reality-based day-to-day issues. So as not to enhance splitting, he makes the client aware that the two clinicians will be in close contact.

Masterson and Rinsley also adhere to the conflict model of etiology. Their model of intervention is more supportive than Kernberg's, offering "better parenting" by encouraging and congratulating the person for attempting individuation. The client's feelings and behavior are interpreted early in the intervention process, and there is confrontation of self-destructive, regressive behavior. Attempts are made to make defenses and acting-out behavior ego-dystonic, to interpret and work through early feelings of rage and depression resulting from perceived (or real) abandonment, and finally to allow separation and individuation. As with Kernberg's model, this is a long-term intervention, requires structure, and may involve hospitalization.

Adler and Buie base their intervention on the deficit model and focus on aloneness as the core problem for people with borderline personality disorder. The experience of isolation and emptiness can turn into panic and desperation, feelings that are projected onto the world, which then seems empty and without purpose. The developmental failure is in the lack of ability of the person to hold and soothe the self. In this more experiential model of intervention, the clinician becomes the holding self-object and provides what the person cannot provide by becoming the good parental caretaker—a stable, consistent, nonpunitive person who can survive the person's rage and destructive impulses, and will continue to be there to provide a "holding" environment. The clinician takes an active role and tries to establish a collaborative atmosphere to help alleviate loneliness and establish a relationship that can lead to exploration at a later date. Because the person with the disorder may actually not be able to remember the clinician between appointments, or may fear that the clinician will forget appointments or not return from a vacation, Buie and Adler, recognizing a legitimate need for a "transitional object," advise calling clients, giving them a tape of the clinician's voice to play at home, and sending postcards to clients when on vacation. Unlike Kernberg, they do not emphasize the hostility behind idealization of the clinician; they do acknowledge the longing for a "perfect" caretaker and permit positive feelings to emerge. As the process continues, the person becomes more able to see the difference between the idealized and the actual clinician and develops insight into unrealistic feelings. Adler and Buie acknowledge the legitimate need for a holding introject and intercept threats to such introjects that may be caused by the person's anger, fear of incorporation, guilt, and other dynamic factors. Confrontation is used to point out realistic dangers caused by actions based on unconscious fantasies, and if the person's primitive rage becomes too overwhelming, hospitalization may be indicated. This model is supportive, self-enhancing, and, when successful, results in the formation of sustaining, holding introjects and superego maturation.

Clinicians who see borderline personality disorder as caused by deficits in ego functioning deemphasize use of transference, interpretation, or examination of internal conflicts. The emphasis is on ego building through examination of the person's behaviors and motivations. Self-confrontation is viewed as ego building. The assessment phase is particularly important, in order to identify the areas of ego deficit. As in Buie and Adler's model, clinicians are active and available for support between sessions; they do not try to be the "good parent," but rather represent a needs-gratifying object in the adult person's life. This is a highly supportive approach that overtly recognizes the person's strengths, helps to differentiate affects, encourages verbalization rather than acting out, and builds up adaptive defenses.

Kohut's work was primarily with people who have narcissistic personality disorder. He viewed the cause of the disorder to be lack of empathic responses from the mother and other love objects who did not provide the person with "empathic mirroring . . .and a responsive target for [their] idealizing need" (Kohut 1977:274). This lack of empathic response resulted in primary structural defects in establishing the self, which emerged in a lack of healthy grandiosity and exhibitionism. Intervention begins with exposing the defects of the self, identifying compensatory structures, and rebuilding and strengthening the structure of the self toward greater self-cohesion. The clinician functions as an empathic observer, a "holding self-object" (Kohut 1977), and a respondent who is fairly active. While being supportive and validating, the clinician avoids overwhelming the client with too much praise or encouragement. Much of the focus is on the client's subjective experience. The reparative process seeks to reactivate the person's need for an empathic response, resulting in replacing destructive behavior with healthier, more competent behavior. The more cohesive self will be able to pursue goals and aspirations with the hope of fulfillment and happiness and the absence of fear of disintegration; a form of narcissistic homeostasis is reached.

Marsha Linehan developed a model specifically for the treatment of persons with borderline personality disorder, although this has subsequently been modified as an intervention for persons with other mental disorders. The model, called Dialectic Behavioral Therapy (DBT), is based on the biosocial theory of personality functioning, with borderline personality disorder viewed as primarily a dysfunction of the emotion regulation system, resulting from biological irregularities as these interact with certain dysfunctional, invalidating environments in persons with high emotional vulnerability who are unable to regulate emotions (Linehan 1993a). What follows is a description of DBT on an outpatient basis, although it may have begun in an inpatient setting.

DBT is based on the principles of cognitive behavioral theory, but is also influenced by Linehan's study of the practice of Zen meditation and Eastern spirituality emphasizing the importance of a balance of acceptance and change. Linehan defines "dialectics" as "the reconciliation of opposites in a continual process of synthesis . . .the most fundamental dialectic is the necessity of accepting patients just as they are within a context of trying to teach them to change" (1993a:19). She defines "dialectic thinking" as requiring "the ability to transcend polarities and . . .to see reality as complex and multifaceted; to entertain contradictory thoughts and points of view and to unite and integrate them; to be comfortable within flux and inconsistency" (1993a:121). The goals are to enhance thought patterns and cognitive functioning while helping clients to change extreme behaviors so that they respond in a more integrated, balanced manner.

The core of the intervention is standard cognitive behavioral techniques such as problem solving, skills training, contingency crisis management, cognitive modification, and, when indicated, exposure. The intervention is begun with:

1. Assessment
2. Data collection on *current* behavior
3. Definitions of targets for intervention

4. Formation of a *collaborative* client-clinician relationship
5. Education about DBT
6. *Mutual commitment* to goals

The clinician must be warm, responsive, flexible, willing to self-disclose when appropriate and to validate the client's sense of emotional desperation. Telephone calls between sessions are encouraged if the client feels the need for help in applying newly learned skills to everyday living, in resolving interpersonal crises or in averting suicidal gestures or attempts. The clinician believes in the client's desire to grow and to change.

DBT is a very structured intervention. Each client has an individual clinician who is the primary therapist on the team and whom the client must continue to see even after starting group sessions. Individual sessions are usually held weekly for sixty minutes. If the person is in crisis, twice weekly may be indicated for a limited period of time, and if trauma work is done involving exposure, the sessions may extend to an hour and a half or two hours. After the initial orientation to DBT and the setting of goals in individual sessions, the client must be in a structured skills-training group for the first year. The groups usually consist of six to eight persons with a different clinician than the one involved in the individual sessions. After the year is completed, some people choose to join an ongoing support group, but they must also be involved in individual treatment or in a case management program.

The skills-training intervention is presented in a manual and involves three hierarchical stages. Clients and therapist make a strong commitment to the process, and a client absent for more than four consecutive sessions must leave the group. Validation is given to the person's pain and desperation, but self-destructive behavior is viewed as maladaptive problem-solving behavior. The emphasis is on skills training, construction of alternate behaviors, development of contingency plans, regulation of emotions, tolerance of stress, and cognitive restructuring to help the person view the environment as not black *or* white. Clients are provided with skills-training handouts and are responsible for monitoring their skills through the use of daily diary cards and homework sheets (Linehan 1993b).

The three stages are as follows (Linehan 1993a):

Stage One
1. Decreasing suicidal behaviors such as suicide crisis behavior, parasuicidal acts, suicidal ideation and communications,

suicide-related expectations and beliefs about the effect on others, and suicide-related affect
2. Decreasing therapy-interfering behaviors and increasing behaviors that have a positive effect on the therapy
3. Decreasing quality-of-life-interfering behaviors such as substance abuse, promiscuity, dysfunctional interpersonal or work-related behaviors, or noncompliance with treatment recommendations
4. Increasing behavioral skills
    a. Core mindfulness skills include observing, describing, and participating, as well as being nonjudgmental, focused, and effective
    b. Interpersonal effectiveness skills are similar to assertiveness training and problem-solving skills and are geared to keeping appropriate relationships and maintaining self-respect
    c. Emotion regulation is an essential change for persons with borderline personality disorder whose emotions are always intense and labile
    d. Distress tolerance involves the ability to tolerate and accept distress that is necessary for change
    e. Self-management skills are needed to reduce maladaptive behaviors and to learn and maintain new adaptive behaviors

Stage Two
Decreasing posttraumatic stress if the person has experienced unresolved, untreated trauma, neglect, or significant losses. The phases of the work at this stage are
1. "Uncovering" the trauma, which may be readily available to the client or may have been repressed and thus emerge slowly
2. Grieving the reality of one's life and accepting the facts of the trauma
3. Reducing self-blame and stigmatization

Stage Three
Increasing self-respect and achieving individual goals
1. Sessions may be spaced out instead of weekly
2. Therapist must reinforce the patient's self-respect independently of the clinician's promoting self-validation, self-soothing, and increased problem-solving skills.

Because persons suffering from borderline personality disorder are very frustrating to work with, and they have is a tendency to "split" their clinicians into "good and bad," case conferences involving consultation and supervision including both the individual therapist and the group clinician are mandated. Linehan has continued to modify this core model, and since it is structured, is presented in a manual, and involves homework, it has lent itself well to empirical research.

Because lengthy psychodynamic intervention is problematic, now, given the long time commitment and the cost, some programs are trying to supplement this approach with some cognitive-behavioral techniques. Heller and Northcut (1996) discuss three of the rationales for this:

1. *Theoretical controversies.* There is agreement about the descriptive features, affective experiences, and interpersonal difficulties of the person with borderline personality disorder. Psychodynamic intervention recognizes the importance of transference and the complexity of the borderline experience, but does not provide the tools that could be acquired from a cognitive-behavioral approach.

2. *Practice characteristics and constraints.* Cognitive behavioral therapy with its emphasis on structure, goals, and problem solving makes it very effective for crisis intervention involving dangerous or self-destructive behaviors. Thus it can be expeditious to include this even in a longer-term psychodynamic intervention.

3. *Influence of trauma history on treatment.* The prevalence of early trauma in the history of persons with borderline personality disorder has been generally accepted. Cognitive-behavioral techniques may be clearer to the client than working within the transference as in psychoanalytic models. They can be used to enhance a sense of mastery over chaotic and frightening interpersonal and behavioral problems, as well as to help identify and internalize missing ego functions.

It will not be easy to merge these two approaches, but clearly each could augment the other. Research needs to look at how this can be accomplished to provide the most helpful intervention for this difficult population.

Group psychotherapy, when used, is usually an adjunct to individual therapy for people with borderline or narcissistic personality disorders. One problem may be that these people can be disruptive and demanding, but a benefit is that the transference to the clinician is diluted by the group, which serves as a buffer. The group can be helpful in identifying maladaptive patterns of social interaction, controlling impulsivity, and generally providing feedback.

It is very important to involve the family of people with narcissistic and, especially, borderline personality disorders in the assessment process. The client and therapist often view the family as the locus of the problem, and they may seem to perpetuate it, but in some cases they can be mobilized as a resource to help the person. Assessment needs to be made of family conflicts and tensions; whether family members are denying, overcontrolling, or intrusive; the severity of hostility directed toward the person; and whether family behavior is contributing to the severity of the disorder or is a response to the behavior of the person. Families need education about *degree* of *appropriate* involvement with the client. If the disorder develops in adolescence, the family must be evaluated to see what unconscious motivations and fears may be affecting the development of the disorder and whether the adolescent should remain in the home or, if hospitalized, return to the home. When there is a history of abuse or loss, the impact needs to be assessed and part of the intervention directed at resolving the aftermath individually or with the family. Since living with people who have these disorders can be very difficult, psychoeducation is sometimes offered to families, particularly if the person enters a hospital. Information is provided about the illness, suggestions are made as to how to cope with the person's behavior, and advice is given about consulting with the clinician and about recognizing the potential for self-destructive behavior and management of such behavior. When family intervention is indicated, it is usually an adjunct to individual intervention for the client, who may or may not be included.

Clinicians sometimes intervene with borderline couples, people who alternately merge and distance themselves and thus seem not to be able to live together and/or live apart. They are often locked in a chronically bad marriage, and although verbalizing a wish to end it, rarely take any action. Despite what may appear to be a volatile and chaotic relationship, these marriages may be tightly, if maladaptively, regulated and provide security to both participants. Both often came into the marriage with impaired capacity for object relations, and neither is capable of meeting the insatiable needs of the other; thus there is repetition of the early trauma of unmet needs. Intervention may be very difficult, as change, or the possibility of abandonment, may be feared and thus motivation limited. The focus must be on the here and now and on increasing individual autonomy and self-esteem. Assessment needs to be made about whether to initially see the couple individually or together and whether by the same or different therapists, or with cotherapists (Goldstein 1990). People with narcissistic personality disorder often experience marital and parent-child problems, as they may blame, or be disappointed in, their partner or child for not meeting their needs. Others try to present as part of "the perfect family," and when thwarted they may respond with physical or emotional abuse.

Finally, when a person who has a borderline personality disorder has a history of sexual abuse, there is a greater risk of self-mutilation, substance abuse, depersonalization, and recurrent illusions (Links 1990), and thus intervention initially may need to be geared toward dealing with the trauma.

With the exception of people with obsessive-compulsive personality disorders, people with cluster C disorders usually do not seek intervention and, if they do, often do not continue. Because of their fear of rejection, hypersensitivity to perceived criticism, and their anxiety, it is difficult to engage people with avoidant personality disorders. If successfully engaged, they are capable of insight into how they project onto others their self-criticism. Groups can be helpful in letting people see how their extreme sensitivity affects others. Assertiveness training and social skills training groups are sometimes recommended. However, the assignments must be carefully structured so that individuals will not experience failure and leave the group. Behavioral techniques to manage anxiety can also be helpful.

Intervention with a person who has a dependent personality disorder must be handled carefully to avoid being directive and making decisions for the person. Insight into the effect of the dependency on others is helpful, as are techniques related to decision making. Assertiveness training can be used as an adjunct to individual work. The clinician must always be aware of the person's need for attachment, since that affects the intervention. The clinician must also avoid being critical of, or urging termination of, a seemingly needed relationship that may be destructive. It can be very discouraging when the person chooses to leave treatment rather than to leave an abusive relationship. People in abusive relationships often fear being alone, but in addition, reality may make them feel that they cannot leave. Rather than pushing the client to leave, the social worker would be better advised to help the person prepare for leaving at a later date by pursuing educational or vocational opportunities and looking at alternate places to live. Short-term intervention can be helpful for people with dependent personality disorder who are in crisis because of a loss. The length of time needed for intervention must always be considered so that the dependency needs do not get projected onto the clinician, with termination never in sight. It is useful, when possible, to include in the assessment the people on whom the dependent person relies, to evaluate any possible secondary gain, to see the effect the dependency is having on the relationship, and to evaluate the potential effect on others if the dependency is reduced.

People with obsessive-compulsive personality disorder may seek intervention because they are not happy with their lives. Because of the nature of the disorder, intervention can be lengthy, and moving the person away from using the defense of intellectualization can be difficult. Group work can be helpful in cutting into the pattern of obsessive thinking seen in ambivalence, and in the person's need for perfection. Behavioral techniques can be used to help interrupt compulsive behaviors.

Intervention with people who have passive-aggressive personality disorder is difficult, for if their dependency demands are met, their disorder is supported; if the demands are refused, they feel rejected and will withdraw from treatment. In working with these people, it is useful to challenge their behavior or what they report they wish to do in terms of what the consequences will be. It is also useful to set some limits on unacceptable behavior. Group therapy can help the patient to realize the effects of the oppositional behavior on others.

Hospitalization

People with personality disorders, other than borderline or narcissistic personality disorders, are rarely hospitalized. Some people with antisocial personality disorder who are also substance abusers can be found in rehabilitation facilities or therapeutic communities. When hospitalization is indicated, it is usually because the self-destructive impulses of the person with a borderline personality disorder cannot be controlled on an outpatient basis. Because of the cost of hospitalization and limited insurance coverage, most hospital stays are now short-term and geared to resolving the crisis that resulted in hospitalization. Short-term hospitalization, usually of two to four weeks' duration, is indicated when there is acute decompensation with self-destructive behavior, a brief psychotic reaction, or the need for, or an adverse reaction to, medication. The goal is that, after remission of the acute symptoms, the person will return to the pre-crisis level of functioning. Intervention is then continued on an outpatient basis. Short-term hospitalization is less regressive than long-term hospitalization, but some clinicians feel that chronically self-destructive people, or people for whom less-intensive intervention has failed, need a long hospitalization in order to begin to modify behavior significantly and to provide the structure needed to change adaptive functioning. Long-term hospitalization affords opportunities for individual, family, and group intervention, as well as training in skills of daily living and supervised trials of medication. It is difficult to treat a person with a severe personality disorder, and hospitalization has the advantage of providing the benefits of a team approach. Social workers, as part of the team, are usually responsible for family assessment and treatment, identify the resources needed, and often serve as discharge planners and case managers. However, long-term hospitalization is prohibitive for most people, and there is controversy over its effectiveness. Other alternatives may be more-restrictive quarter-way or less-restrictive halfway houses or day treatment.

Assessment of the need for inpatient hospitalization should include consideration of the comorbidity of an Axis I diagnosis, the presence of more than one Axis II diagnosis, and an assessment of ego functioning with emphasis on capacity for reality testing, sense of identity, and type and use of defense mechanisms (Peters 1990).

Medication

Most people who have no Axis I diagnosis but do have an Axis II diagnosis probably would not benefit from medication. Thus, when medication is given to people with Axis II disorders, it is usually to treat the comorbid Axis I diagnosis (Gitlin 1990), especially if there is a symptomatic crisis. As noted, there is significant overlap in criteria for symptom-based (Axis I) and personality (Axis II) disorders, and careful assessment is essential to determine the presence of an Axis I diagnosis that might respond to medication. If intervention has been directed by a diagnosis of a personality disorder and the person fails to respond, it is possible that there is an Axis I diagnosis. If there is comorbidity of Axis I and Axis II diagnoses, the Axis I disorder will not be as responsive to medication as it would be if no personality disorder was present. When medication is effective, it gives relief from mood, anxiety, or thought disturbances and makes the person more amenable to psychotherapy. The most common Axis I disorder seen in people with personality disorders is depression. In addition, panic disorders may also be present in people with avoidant or dependent personality disorders. Medication is particularly useful for persons whose Axis II diagnosis is similar to an Axis I diagnosis, such as schizotypal personality disorder, which is similar to schizophrenia; avoidant personality disorder, similar to social phobia; and borderline personality disorder, similar to mood disorders (Kapfhammer and Hippius 1998). Medication is usually of value in the short term.

Although social workers cannot prescribe medication, they can be helpful in educating the person and the family about what to expect from medication and what the possible side effects may be. It is particularly important with these clients to be sure that there are no unrealistic expectations and no hope for a magic cure. Medication will only treat some targeted symptoms; it alone will not change personality. Because people with personality disorders, especially cluster B disorders, tend to idealize or denigrate interventions, clarity about the goal of medication therapy is essential. Assessment needs to evaluate the person's tendency to split, and it may be indicated that medication should be prescribed by a psychopharmacologist who takes part in no other aspects of the intervention.

When medication is indicated for cluster A disorders, low-dose antipsychotics are most often prescribed, usually for people with schizotypal personality disorder. People with paranoid personality disorder are usually mistrustful and are reluctant to use any medication. Antianxiety and antidepressant medications are occasionally prescribed if symptoms warrant.

Antidepressant medications, usually MAO inhibitors or SSRIs, are the medications most often prescribed for people with cluster B personality disorders, to modulate impulsive or aggressive behavior (Kaplan and Sadock 1996). Depression often accompanies borderline personality disorder, and it will respond to antidepressants. The medications must be dispensed carefully, because of the propensity for suicidal acting out. Low-dose antipsychotics may also be used if a person with a severe borderline personality disorder experiences a brief psychotic episode. Stimulants are sometimes used for people with antisocial personality disorder to combat symptoms that resemble attention deficit disorder, although these must be monitored, as they may be abused. These stimulants also have street value, and some people may sell them rather than use them (Gitlin 1990). There is little information about using medication for people who have histrionic or narcissistic personality disorders, although lithium sometimes is used if people with narcissistic personality disorder have prominent mood swings. People with narcissistic personality disorder often see the need for medication as a personal failure, a "narcissistic blow," and choose not to take it. People with histrionic personality disorder, because of their tendency to somatization, may report more side effects of prescribed medication than are actually experienced.

People with cluster C personality disorders, especially avoidant disorder, may experience concomitant anxiety in the form of panic disorder, with or without agoraphobia or social phobia. In addition, there may be depression, especially if there is a loss of people on whom they depend. The most frequently used medications are benzodiazepines for the anxiety and antidepressants for the depression. Some people with obsessive-compulsive personality disorder may also have the Axis I anxiety diagnosis of obsessive-compulsive disorder and may have responded to clomipramine (Anafranil) and fluoxetine (Prozac). Any medication prescribed for people with passive-aggressive personality disorder may become part of the struggle between clinician and client: the patient may fill the prescription and not use the medication or may self-medicate rather than following the prescribed directions.

There is still much to learn about the etiology, epidemiology, and assessment of personality disorders, as well as how to intervene most appropriately. Not everyone can, or wants to, work with people who have these disorders, especially those with borderline personality disorder. Their behavior may be hard to tolerate and will arouse negative feelings. It is essential that clinicians constantly monitor their own feelings and set realistic expectations so as to avoid allowing themselves or their clients to suffer disappointment.

It is also important, because of the interest in these disorders, not to overlook the possibility that there are comorbid Axis I disorders. In addition, given the complex etiologies of personality disorders, a careful biopsychosocial assessment should help indicate areas where intervention could be most useful in enhancing personal and vocational functioning.

In this era of managed care, long-term intervention, which has been favored for people with personality disorders, will be almost impossible, and the emphasis will need to be on short-term episodes of service. Social workers who see people who have these disorders may function as clinicians, case managers, or advocates, and they will need to determine the appropriate focus at any given time, even when confronted with a range of possibilities for intervention.

10   Delirium, Dementia, and Amnestic and Other Cognitive Disorders

The term *organic mental disorders*, used in *DSM-III-R*, was changed to *delirium, dementia, and amnestic and other cognitive disorders* in *DSM-IV*. These disorders can be devastating for the person afflicted, as well as for the sufferer's friends and family. Changed behavior and impaired cognitive functioning are consequences of brain dysfunction that may be reversible, as in the case of delirium, or irreversible, as in the case of degenerative organic mental disorders. Ability to communicate, to comprehend, and ultimately to care for oneself may become increasingly impaired. In the most severe forms, these disorders attack the very core of the person and may alienate the person from self and others. Ego strength and coping are reduced in all cases of dementia, as the person loses the ability to connect with others, to concentrate, to remember, to test reality, to assume personal and family responsibilities, and, in some cases, to control impulses.

The term *dementia* derives from the Latin *de* (out of) + *mens* (mind) + *ia* (state of) and suggests being out of, or deprived of, one's mind (Weiner, Tintner, and Goodkin 1991). The first reference to senile dementia appears in the second century A.D., in the writing of Aretaeus, who used the term *dotage* to describe a disorder characterized by impaired cognitive functioning. Pinel and Esquirol in nineteenth-century France also described cases of dementia. Prichard, in 1837, recognized that dementia might be a primary disorder or secondary to other disorders and developed a four-stage description of its progression. Kraepelin, in 1913, further refined the definition, recognizing a form of brain damage that was acquired rather than congenital. Bleuler, in 1924, used the term *organic psychosyndrome* to describe symptoms of what is now recognized as chronic organic mental disorder, and found that not all cognitive functions were equally affected. Efforts in recent years have been directed toward devising more precise diagnostic definitions (Weiner, Tintner, and Goodkin 1991).

Organic mental disorders are often difficult to diagnose, because although they look as if they have psychological roots, in fact they represent a breakdown in brain functioning because of a range of somatic problems that affect brain tissue. They represent the most neglected and underresearched area of mental disorders. No one specific disease can be identified as the cause: the condition may result from a tumor, an infection, endocrine disease, hypertension, nutritional deficits, drug or alcohol toxicity, or degenerative brain disease. Thus organic mental disorders are not synonymous with aging and may be observed in people of all ages. Aging is, however, a major determinant of dementia, as people become more vulnerable to systemic and cerebral diseases and to acute and chronic psychosocial problems. People of all ages with AIDS frequently suffer from dementia, and they, in addition to the increasing numbers of frail elderly, represent a major problem for health and mental health providers and program planners.

Definitions

Perhaps no other mental disorder has had more confusion in terminology, with terms used inaccurately and interchangeably.

Organic mental syndrome involves the presence of a constellation of behavioral symptoms with one or more cognitive deficits that may have a variety of causes and appear in varying combinations. Assessment of the rate of onset is important in trying to assess cause and prognosis.

Organic mental disorder is a particular organic mental syndrome with known or presumed etiology that is emotional or physical, usually identified on either Axis I or Axis III.

Rapid-onset brain syndrome involves sudden, dramatic changes in cognition and behavior. The most frequent causes are acute medical disease and drug or alcohol intoxication and withdrawal. This syndrome is frequently reversible once the cause is identified.

Slow-onset brain syndrome is much harder to detect, as it is more insidious. Often it is irreversible, and the exact cause may be unknown.

Amnestic disorder (amnesia) involves severe decline in orientation to time and place, and in recent memory, especially the ability to retain any new information. An uncommon disorder, it interferes with social and occupational functioning but does not exhibit any other significant impairments in cognitive functioning. While there is memory deficit, associated features such as aphasia, agnosia, and apraxia are not present (Frierson 1997). It often results from a general medical condition or from persistent substance use. Blackouts and Korsakoff's syndrome are amnestic disorders, and head injuries may also cause amnesia.

Delirium is a state of profound cognitive and personality disruption that usually has an acute onset of hours or days, is of brief duration, and is usually reversible. There is a clouding of consciousness, the person may be lethargic or agitated, and there is fluctuation in cognitive abilities, which differentiates delirium from dementia, although they can coexist. It is a syndrome, not a disease. There may be hallucinations, illusions, emotional lability, psychomotor disturbances, and alternations in sleep-wake cycles (Stoudemire et al. 1998).

Dementia is not a disease per se, but a functional diagnosis manifested by a cluster of symptoms involving deterioration or impairment of cognitive, emotional, and behavioral functioning that is severe enough to result in impaired social and vocational functioning. It involves a diffuse disorder of the brain, impairing the function of nerve cells in the cerebral cortex (Waldinger 1990). Onset is usually insidious. Dementias may have a variety of etiologies, including the physiological effects of a general medical condition or the persistent abuse of a substance. It may be reversible or irreversible, though it is usually chronic.

Vascular dementia (in DSM-III-R, multiple infarct dementia) is a rapid-onset form of dementia resulting from arteriosclerotic changes in the blood vessels of the brain. It is irreversible. Multiple infarcts are a series of small strokes that, when cumulative, affect a large area of the brain, causing dementia.

Alzheimer's disease is an irreversible organic mental disorder and is the most common cause of dementia. It involves widespread, progressive destruction of brain cells, and its etiology is unknown. It is characterized by memory loss, personality change, and impaired cognition. Diagnosis can be confirmed only following autopsy.

Presenile dementia implies onset of dementia before age sixty-five.

Senile dementia implies onset of dementia at age sixty-five or over.

HIV-related dementia occurs in 40 to 50 percent of persons with AIDS and is observed as neurological complications. It is a result of the direct effects of the virus on cells that enter the central nervous system and of the neurological conditions that opportunistically affect the person (Frierson 1997). There is impairment of the cognitive, behavioral, and motor systems. It may be the *primary* symptom of the illness, appearing before any systemic signs of immunosuppression.

Epidemiology

It must be noted that organic mental disorders can emerge at any age. Head injuries are the most likely cause in childhood and adolescence, substance abuse in adulthood, and systemic disease in the elderly. Dementia resulting from HIV infection or AIDS can occur at any age. Studies indicate that 5 percent of people over sixty-five have severe dementia, and 10 percent are suffering from mild to moderate cognitive impairment (Cummings 1992).

Organic mental disorders account for more than 50 percent of initial inpatient psychiatric admissions for people over fifty-five. Ten percent of people over sixty-five have senile dementia, and 20 percent of people over eighty-five suffer from dementia. Approximately 3.75 million people have Alzheimer's disease, which accounts for 70 percent of all cases of dementia. It is a disease that affects mainly the elderly. Less than 5 percent of people with Alzheimer's disease are under sixty-five years of age. It affects 1 percent of people between sixty-five and seventy-four, 7 percent of those seventy-five to eighty-four, and 25 percent of those over eighty-five (Gregg 1994). The incidence and prevalence increase with age, and while early-onset Alzheimer's disease is more prevalent for women, the gender difference is reduced after age sixty-five (Sutker and Adams 1993), although there are still more women than men with Alzheimer's disease, as women tend to live longer. Fifteen percent of people suffering from dementia have vascular dementia, and 18 percent have a combination of Alzheimer's disease and vascular dementia. The prevalence is greater for men than for women, as men are more at risk for hypertension and heart disease. Ten percent of people with symptoms suggesting senile dementia actually have reversible forms of dementia.

Delirium is probably the most common neuropsychiatric syndrome found in general hospital inpatient units. It is more common in people over sixty and may exist concomitantly with dementia.

HIV-related dementia, formerly called AIDS dementia complex, is found in 30 to 50 percent of people who have late-stage AIDS.

Assessment

Since the majority of people who will be assessed for organic mental disorders will be elderly, it is important to keep in mind that certain changes are expected with normal aging. There may be diminished hearing and sight that may make perceptions less accurate, sleep patterns may change, physical changes may limit some activities, life changes may result in some depression or anxiety, and some forgetfulness of names and dates is not unexpected.

Most people seen for assessment for organic mental disorders are brought to the attention of health/mental health professionals by family or friends who are concerned with apparently deteriorating cognitive functioning. A small number, who usually are self-referred, are the "worried well," who may be unnecessarily concerned with normal changes in cognitive functions that begin in middle age. A third group has had a history of deteriorating functioning that the family can no longer accept, as the person has increased inability to manage activities of daily living such as dressing, eating, and toileting independently, or the caregiver can no longer assume as much responsibility. This last group may need referral to a day program or to nursing home care.

As noted above, the presenting symptoms of organic mental disorders may appear to be psychological in origin but actually have an organic base that involves a breakdown in the functioning of the brain. If misdiagnosed, the ensuing improper intervention will cause frustration in the family and for professionals, and the person may suffer residual disabilities or even die. The setting in which the person is assessed can influence the clinical observations, and it is particularly important to recognize this when assessing people with dementia or delirium, in which psychological symptoms may mask whatever organic process is involved. In addition to obtaining a personal history from the person and the family, a careful, comprehensive assessment should include a medical, and possibly neurological, evaluation as well as a review of prescribed and over-the-counter medications taken by the person. History taking must be done slowly and gently to diminish feelings of anxiety, embarrassment, and fear because of awareness of impaired cognitive functioning. Attention should be given to:

1. The onset and progression of the illness
2. What areas of functioning are impaired
3. What changes have occurred in personality or emotional responses
4. What social and environmental supports exist

A mental status examination and some simple pencil-and-paper psychological tests can be helpful in establishing the diagnosis.

Assessment of language may reveal problems in:

fluency
articulation
comprehension
naming familiar people and objects
delay in finding the correct word
in the later stages, use of neologisms

Other areas requiring assessment are problems with:

memory
orientation
reasoning
judgment
motility
ability to carry out routine, simple tasks

If assessment is made in the earlier stages of onset, the person suffering from an organic mental disorder may be very sensitive to changes and may attempt to cover up deficits. The ability to hide deficits, however, decreases as the disorder progresses. These disorders can profoundly affect family members. It is important to interview the family separately from the person with the disorder to assess the impact on family functioning, as well as to assess how much denial is operating and how much tension has been created as the family has tried to adjust to the disorder. Families may also give information about the presence of paranoid thinking, hallucinations, and difficulties with activities of daily living that the person has not revealed. When the onset is insidious, it may be helpful to ask about employment: What job does the person have? What are the usual requirements, and what difficulties are being experienced? If the person has retired, was this because of company policy, the person's desire, or because of awareness of difficulties in job performance?

Delirium can be recognized by its acute onset, which can occur in hours or days, and its brief duration, usually lasting days or, at the most, weeks. The person and family will report rapid, acute, profound cognitive and personality disorganization and fluctuation, with clouding of consciousness. The clouding of consciousness is what differentiates delirium from dementia. Delirium frequently occurs when the ego is impaired through being overwhelmed by internal and external stimuli (Weiner, Tintner, and Goodkin 1991), and it is almost always associated with an underlying medical disorder such as infection, dehydration, electrolyte imbalance, or the cumulative effects of alcohol or drugs. It can be a medical emergency, as it may be caused by a life-threatening illness such as heart, liver, or kidney failure, myocardial infarction, or a drug overdose. Assessment will reveal profound impairment of cognitive and attentive functions, hyperactivity or hypoactivity, disruption of sleep cycle, and heightening of symptoms at night. "Sundowning" is not uncommon, with symptoms often worsening in the afternoon or evening as it gets darker outside. Reasons for this phenomenon may be the dimmer light or a lessening of ability to cope with stress because of fatigue or overstimulation.

To make an assessment of dementia, there should be no history of similar symptoms, and in most instances the symptoms should have developed after the age of fifty-five. There should be no readily identifiable stressors, and the disorder may have emerged with or without explanation. It is important to include family and close friends in the assessment and to assess the impact on the family. To correctly understand what is happening, it is good to obtain from them a baseline measure of the person's abilities before onset of the disorder. If the disorder is dementia, there will be a steady decline in intellectual functioning, a symptom that is not seen with delirium. One of the most difficult problems in assessment is to distinguish between what is pathological cognitive impairment and what may be within the normal range for the person's age. People who have cognitive impairment, but who are not suffering from dementia, usually have little or no diminishing of vocabulary, general information, or ability to recall personal history and major historical events. Significant cognitive impairment, usually in more than one area, such as in abstract thinking, use of language, recognition of formerly known people, and memory loss, differentiates dementia from stroke damage, amnesia, or normal forgetfulness.

The most common form of reversible dementia is the result of medication "intoxication"; therefore, a comprehensive review of medications is needed. Since many older people take several medications and, in addition, may be more sensitive to dosage, there is potential for misdiagnosis. If the person or family reports sudden onset of cognitive or emotional disturbance, medication may be the cause. Some of the medications often taken by older people may cause side effects that suggest the presence of organic mental disorders. For example, anti-inflammatory drugs may cause depression; diuretics may result in fatigue, apathy, and depression; and antianxiety drugs or sedatives tend to be less quickly metabolized in the elderly and may cause cognitive deficits. Cinetidine hydrochloride (Tagemet), prescribed for stomach disorders, including ulcers, can cause delirium or psychotic symptoms, and digitalis, prescribed for people with heart disease, must be carefully prescribed to avoid toxicity (Taylor 1990).

If a person, or a family member, reports disorientation, speech defects, visual hallucinations, change in headache patterns, changes in motility, lapses in conversation, shifting levels of consciousness, endocrine disorders (including diabetes and hypoglycemia), sleepiness, recent memory impairment, or diminishing problem-solving skills, organic mental disorder must be considered. Equating psychotic behavior with schizophrenia obviously is a serious error in assessment, but it is not uncommon and it is important to note that such behavior is most frequently caused by an organic disorder. Thus, in the absence of a *documented* history of schizophrenia or bipolar disorder, psychotic behavior should be considered as organic in etiology (Taylor 1990). Paranoia, depression, and mania can also be caused by organic diseases or medications.

Assessment of a person with rapid-onset organic mental disorder is not difficult, as the history will show a sudden, readily observable change. The person will be disoriented to time and place and appear to be confused, there will be a severe deficit in *recent* memory, activity may be increased and frenzied or withdrawn and apathetic, insomnia or reversed sleep patterns may be observed, simple problem solving is impaired, and visual hallucinations may be present. The most telling characteristic, however, is a shifting level of consciousness: the family will report that the person has been confused, disoriented, and illogical, followed by a period in which the person is calm, logical, and "normal." A person with this type of disorder is usually more distressed toward evening or at night. Vascular dementia has a rapid onset, and the medical history usually reveals cardiovascular disease, hypertension, or diabetes, as well as a history of small strokes.

Assessment of slow-onset organic disorder is much more difficult. Often the person and the family have resisted recognition of the extent and implications of the problem. The person, somewhat aware of a decline in cognitive functioning, may have begun to avoid tasks that involve recent memory and problem solving, and also may have withdrawn from social interaction except with people in the household. History should be obtained from the person, but even more important for accuracy, information should also be gathered from family and close friends. Indicators of the presence of slow-onset organic disorders are loss of recent memory, disorientation, poor judgment, decline in problem-solving skills, difficulty with abstract thinking, and decline in personal hygiene. The most serious disorder of this type is Alzheimer's disease, which to date is irreversible. Because its etiology is unknown, it is a diagnosis of exclusion, confirmed only on autopsy. The insidious onset of Alzheimer's distinguishes it from the other common irreversible organic mental disorder, vascular dementia, which has a rapid onset and in which deterioration is stepwise. In addition, defects in motor function, which frequently occur in people with vascular dementia, are uncommon for those suffering from Alzheimer's disease.

Amnestic disorder is a fairly well-circumscribed disorder and thus is easier to assess. Although the person can respond to an immediate situation or problem-solving activity, recent memory is severely impaired. The person may not know how a certain destination was reached nor remember having recently met some other person. Amnesia may be caused by a stroke, head trauma, chronic alcoholism (Korsakoff's syndrome), oxygen deprivation, or nutritional deficiency, such as insufficient thiamine (vitamin B-1).

People infected with AIDS are especially vulnerable to organic mental disorder, and the majority of them exhibit some neuropsychiatric symptoms, including poor concentration, slowing down of cognitive processes, memory deficits, motility problems, and emotional and personality changes. Relatively rapid onset of mania, depression, or paranoia in people at risk for AIDS may be the first symptoms of an undiagnosed HIV infection. The majority of people suffering from advanced AIDS will develop dementia (Weiner and Svetlik 1991), with no predictable pattern. Two-thirds of people with AIDS will develop HIV-related dementia, a subacute encephalitis, caused by HIV infection (Weiner, Tintner, and Goodkin 1991), which manifests itself in insidious deterioration in motor, affective, and cognitive functioning, ultimately affecting occupational and personal activities.

Particular care must be used when assessing a person with an organic mental disorder, especially an elderly person, because it is easy to make an inaccurate assessment and to miss forms of this disorder that are reversible.

Clinical Course

Before the onset of delirium, the person may appear unusually anxious, restless, and irritable, and will experience sleep pattern disruption. A problem with assessment is the fluctuation in behavior: the person may appear quite lucid at times, followed by a period of confusion. The person may be apathetic, confused, or agitated and hypervigilant. There may be disorientation to time and place, but rarely to person. Memory is impaired while delirium is present, with amnesia for this time following recovery. Misperceptions of what is heard and visual hallucinations are not uncommon. The majority of people experiencing delirium will recover fully. Some, however, will become stuporous or comatose and may develop chronic brain damage or die.

Reversible dementia can occur in people of all ages. Most frequent causes are drug or medication intoxication or withdrawal, vitamin deficiencies, subdural hematoma, normal pressure hypocephalus, diminished sensory activity, and chronic inflammatory conditions.

While people age differently, certain processes are fairly standard. There is physiological deterioration that may affect brain functioning, the person is more prone to chronic disease, falls that may result in head injuries are more likely, and the older person is more sensitive to medications. Adverse reactions to medications, whether because of the adverse synergistic effect of medications prescribed by more than one doctor, or improper dosages, or substance abuse, are the main cause of reversible organic mental disorder. As noted above, organic mental disorders may have a rapid or an insidious onset.

Alzheimer's disease is irreversible and so insidious that it is only in retrospect that one can identify its onset. This disorder may be noted as early as age forty-five, and there is progressive deterioration until death. People with Alzheimer's disease may live anywhere from two to twenty years. The initial symptoms are usually personality changes or failing memory and disorientation. Initially, events of recent weeks or months are forgotten, and as memory deteriorates memory is lost for events of the preceding days, hours, or even minutes. Suspicion of others may increase and may resemble paranoia. As memory deteriorates, often the person will not read, watch TV, or listen to the radio. The world becomes limited to the immediate event and may become increasingly unpredictable and frightening, thus increasing paranoia. In its most severe form, a person with Alzheimer's disease will no longer be able to recognize family members and ultimately will not be able to dress, eat, and use the toilet independently. Incontinence, emotional lability, and nocturnal wandering are additional problems at this stage. In the final stage, lasting from months to years, the person may become mute and unresponsive to family and environment. Symptoms of vascular dementia are very similar to those of Alzheimer's disease; however, deterioration is stepwise, with more dramatic periods of decline.

As these disorders progress, the primitive defenses, denial, delusional projection, and distortion are frequently observed. Regression is seen, as the person may fear strangers, have tantrums, and be inappropriately dependent, attention-seeking, and clinging. Hypervigilance as a way to compensate for ego impairment may deteriorate to paranoid thinking. Delusions may include believing that spouse or other close relatives are impostors, that home is unfamiliar, that deceased friends and relatives are alive, and that others, not present, are in the house. Hallucinations, common in people with delirium and dementia, are most often visual, involving children and small adults running in and out of the house, or tactile, involving the sensation that insects are crawling over the body (Weiner, Tintner, and Goodkin 1991). The person suffering from the disease may become depressed with increasing awareness of impaired cognitive functioning. As memory further deteriorates, however, the person becomes less aware of the deficit and depression lifts.

HIV may enter the brain through two types of immune cells even before opportunistic infections or carcinomas develop. The resulting disorder is the most common neurological complication of AIDS. In its mildest form it is called HIV-associated motor-cognitive disorder. As the severity of the disorder increases, it may be called HIV-associated dementia, HIV encephalopathy, AIDS-related dementia, and finally, in the last stage, AIDS dementia complex (ADC) (Staff 1999:2).

If the person develops HIV-related dementia, early manifestations may include loss of concentration, forgetfulness, loss of balance, and apathy. At the most severe, symptoms may include psychomotor retardation, mutism, ataxia, weakness, incontinence, tremors, and a greater risk of seizures. The prognosis is very poor, and survival following diagnosis is usually under eight months (Weiner, Tintner, and Goodkin 1991).

People with AIDS who develop organic mental disorder often find that the first symptom is a difficulty in concentration. Thought processes may be slower, problem solving becomes more difficult, there are memory deficits, and following routines may be confusing. Energy level diminishes, and the person may become apathetic and withdrawn and have little or no sexual interest. Motor coordination deteriorates, and the person may suffer from tremors or other involuntary movements. Emotional responses may appear blunted or inappropriate. Depression may be present, is significantly greater in people positive for HIV or those who have AIDS, and may be a response to these diagnoses. People with AIDS have been found to be very sensitive to psychotropic medications, and dosages must be carefully monitored. In addition, some of the medications used to treat secondary complications may also produce neuropsychiatric symptoms.

Etiology

Organic mental disorders may be the result of infections, seizure disorders, brain tumors (benign or malignant), head injuries, subdural hematoma, substance abuse, or a degenerative process of unknown origin. Some chronic diseases, such as Huntington's, Wilson's, hypertension, diabetes, cardiac problems, kidney disease, liver disease, and chronic obstructive pulmonary disease, can all influence neuropsychiatric functioning and may also produce symptoms of dementia. Acute onset suggests vascular, traumatic, or functional origin; subacute (developing over days or weeks) suggests infection (including AIDS and neurosyphilis), toxicity, metabolic disturbance, or neoplastic origin; and insidious onset suggests that the cause is a degenerative disease (Tintner, Weiner, and Bonte 1991).

People who have had heart surgery or who suffer from severe burns are at high risk for experiencing delirium. Others at risk are people with pre-existing brain damage, those withdrawing from alcohol or benzodiazepines, and people suffering from sleep deprivation, sensory deprivation, or overload. "Sundowning" is a phenomenon observed in medically hospitalized patients over sixty-five, who may appear delirious during the night. This is probably because of a combination of sleeping medication, waking in unfamiliar surroundings, and a lack of stimulation.

Delirium affects 90 percent of people with advanced AIDS and is the most frequent neuropsychiatric complication (Wise and Brandt 1992). People with AIDS may develop organic mental disorder either from the HIV attacking the central nervous system (primary), as a result of opportunistic infections resulting from immunosuppression (secondary), or iatrogenic resulting from treatment or its sequelae (Markowitz and Perry 1992).

The etiology of Alzheimer's disease remains unknown, although research has indicated the possibility of a genetic defect. There is stronger evidence of a genetic component in early-onset Alzheimer's disease than in late-onset. Researchers believe that an abnormal gene on chromosome 14 or on chromosome 21 accounts for most early-onset familial Alzheimer's disease but have been unable to identify the gene. If one parent has this defective gene, a child has a 50 percent chance of inheriting it, but may not be afflicted with the disease (Gregg 1994). Some family studies have shown an increased prevalence of dementia in people whose parents (10–14 percent) or siblings (4–13 percent) have Alzheimer's disease (Malaspina, Quitkin, and Kaufmann 1992). Vascular dementia, however, is known to be caused by arteriosclerotic changes in the blood vessels to the brain and is often associated with a history of high blood pressure and heart disease.

Differential Diagnosis

Most people with mental disorders are not disoriented. Recent memory is intact, and except during acute episodes, there is capacity to solve simple problems. Sensory impairment is not significant unless a person experiences auditory hallucinations. Core cognitive functioning is intact, although the person may be somewhat inattentive. Thus the presence of significantly impaired cognitive functioning is an important consideration in making a differential diagnosis of organic mental disorder. Organic brain disorders can be differentiated from mental retardation, since loss of cognitive functioning is acquired rather than innate.

Some guidelines do exist in distinguishing organic mental disorders from other mental disorders. The confusion, disorientation, and possible memory loss seen in people with schizophrenia are usually of short duration and result from the person's problems with concentration; when these symptoms are observed in a person suffering from irreversible dementia, they are more persistent. In addition, symptoms of psychosis that emerge for the first time after age thirty are almost never because of schizophrenia. Psychotic behavior resulting from drug overdose can also resemble schizophrenia. Visual hallucinations are also more typical in people who have an organic mental disorder, while auditory hallucinations are more common in people with schizophrenia.

Interesting differences can be seen in how people perceive others. A person suffering from functional psychosis may perceive a familiar person as unfamiliar and may have paranoid feelings toward that person, while a person with an organic psychosis, trying to compensate for memory impairment, may respond to a stranger as if that person were familiar (Taylor 1990).

People with organic mental disorders may at times seem like caricatures of themselves because of exaggeration of personality traits. For example, a person with a compulsive personality trait may become rigid and obstinate.

Though there may be lability of affect, the person's facial expression may remain the same throughout, and the reaction may fluctuate rapidly (Taylor 1990). Apathy, withdrawal, and a sense of helplessness may resemble depression, and increased suspiciousness and jealousy may resemble paranoia, but careful assessment will show that these personality changes occur together with increasing cognitive deficits. People who are suffering from depression will, when talking to mental health professionals, often identify the symptoms, while people with Alzheimer's disease will cover them up or pay little attention to them. If cognition is impaired, a person with depression will acknowledge not knowing or remembering, while a person with Alzheimer's will make significant mistakes or confabulate. When depression is the primary disorder, the person will usually respond to antidepressant medication and some of the symptoms will diminish or disappear.

Some chronic diseases produce symptoms similar to those of organic mental disorders. These include Parkinson's, Pick's, Wilson's, Huntington's, liver disease associated with alcoholism, and multiple sclerosis. Some symptoms of delirium may actually be complications of diabetes, hypertension, intracranial bleeding, decreased blood pressure, meningitis, or a reaction or exposure to poisons or certain drugs (Wise and Brandt 1992).

Intervention

Following assessment, if a treatable medical condition has been identified, it, obviously, must receive the first attention in the intervention. In addition, people should bring in all medications, prescribed or over-the-counter, in order to have an evaluation of whether some medications ought not to be taken together and whether prescribed dosages are correct given the person's age and medical history. Often a person taking medications will not report taking medication for physical problems to a psychiatrist prescribing medications for emotional problems or vice versa, and health professionals may not ask, thus causing organic symptoms because of synergistic effects that may increase or diminish the effects of individual medications, particularly in the elderly. Discussion of nutrition is also indicated to find out if there are any deficiencies in diet, and if supplemental foods and vitamins and minerals are included in the person's diet when certain medications are taken, such as potassium when diuretics are taken.

Delirium may be caused by a medical illness such as heart disease, urinary tract infection, or pneumonia, or by the effects of medications, and thus initial intervention should be geared toward first treating the medical problem or adjusting the medication. Further intervention with people suffering from delirium focuses on frequent orientation of the person to time and place. Physical contact with familiar people, such as holding a hand or touching an arm, is helpful, as are photographs of close friends and family, and even some objects from home, if the person is hospitalized. Having a clock, a calendar, or other familiar objects may help with reorientation. Adequate light, a predictable schedule, and glasses or hearing aids, if needed, are also useful. An optimal level of stimulation, neither too little nor too much, should be arrived at to reduce clouding of consciousness. Medication may be necessary if the person is very agitated. It is very important to help a family understand that the acute, and fluctuating, change in behavior may be frightening to the person and to stress the importance of being calm and comforting when around the person with delirium.

Intervention planning will depend on whether or not the disorder is reversible, the age and lifestyle of the individual, and the availability of supports. People who have reversible dementia can be helped with supportive and behavioral intervention, although the results may be improvement, but not necessarily a return to the premorbid level of functioning. Traditional psychotherapy, based on an ability to communicate verbally, to remember, and to be able to abstract, is not appropriate for many people who are suffering from dementia. Because of the nature of the impairments, during a session it is helpful to sit closer to the client than would be usual, and even to touch an arm or a shoulder to help reinforce the connection and stimulate attention. It is important to challenge the person until he or she is functioning at the highest level that can be expected. Help can be directed toward stimulating the attention and concentration necessary to relearn some cognitive and ego functions. While the goal is to help the person to function as independently as possible, tasks should be geared to avoid failure, which might increase feelings of depression over what has been lost.

While some dementias are irreversible, many of the symptoms are amenable to intervention. If the symptoms are fixed and show little improvement over a period of a year or two, the intervention focus should shift from challenging the person to improving the environment to better meet the person's needs. Certainly this includes helping families to have realistic expectations. There is no intervention that will halt the downhill course of Alzheimer's disease, and care is costly, estimated by the surgeon general to be $17.7 billion annually (Pear 1999).

AIDS is an out-of-sync disease in that it results in youthful dementia and death, which are traditionally thought to affect the elderly. Therefore, in

addition to experiencing feelings similar to those of older people when affected with organic mental disease, the person afflicted with AIDS experiences additional rage and frustration, as he or she is no longer able to function socially and vocationally on an appropriate age level. There is also the
need to confront the process of deteriorating and dying at an age when peers
may be planning for, and working toward, a future. The person's sense of
self-worth may suffer, and it is important to approach people with AIDS with
acceptance and concern, and to acknowledge their value to themselves and
to others.

Those afflicted with AIDS may be faced with revealing aspects of their
lives that they may have wanted to keep secret. They may fear or experience
shame, guilt, stigma, and rejection over personal histories of homosexuality,
bisexuality, promiscuity, intravenous drug use, or prostitution. The family,
from whom the person may have been estranged, may once more become
involved, resulting in resurgent or new family tensions.

People with AIDS are usually young and have been able to function
independently. As dementia is common in the later stages of AIDS, dependence on others must increase, and the person may become increasingly
sensitive and angry as power and control over daily functioning and life
decisions decreases. Social workers should be available to listen to these
feelings and concerns, and to serve as case managers, locating and providing
needed resources while recognizing the need to support, as much as possible,
the person's sense of autonomy and dignity.

Family

The role of social workers following assessment of irreversible organic
mental disorder is primarily with the caregivers, who bear the responsibility
for most aspects of the ongoing care of the ill person. Alzheimer's disease,
the most severe form of irreversible organic brain disorder, affects the entire
family. It must be recognized that caring for someone with dementia is often
more stressful than caring for a person with a physical illness. If the onset is
slow, sessions with the person suffering from the disorder, and with close
family members, should focus on the loss of status within the family that the
person may be feeling, and on the need to come to terms with the prospect
of further deterioration. A goal should be the maintenance of equilibrium
within the family to the extent possible, in spite of inevitable changes in
roles. The person should feel safest with the family unit, and be able to
experience the most security, care, and love. Most of what can be done for

the person will depend on the understanding and availability of supportive caregivers. Changing demographics and mobility patterns have resulted in many older people, and more men, becoming the primary caregivers, as extended families are no longer geographically near and close young women relatives are most often employed full-time or part-time in addition to having responsibilities to their own husbands and children. A study in Great Britain showed that 37 percent of caregivers for people with dementia are over seventy, and the average age was sixty-one (Bloom 1993).

Assistance is needed for the emotional problems of caregivers, and they should be provided with suggestions and concrete services. Education about the assessment, the illness, and the prognosis is important, especially if caregivers have been denying the extent and implications of the illness. Exploration of financial and social supports and of availability of resources must take place early in the intervention. Plans need to be made about supervision of the person with the illness, about coordinating medical appointments and consulting with the doctors, and about how decisions about the person's care will be made.

The caregiver may withdraw, as has the person with the disorder; caregivers need to understand that the person cannot help this behavior and that physical contact and assistance in compensating for deficiencies would be most helpful. Caregivers frequently complain that the person repeatedly asks the same questions, often in quick succession. Succinct answers, attempts to redirect the conversation, or engaging the person in a distraction are possible solutions. If the person has poor memory and poor judgment, caretakers may need to ensure that sharp instruments are not readily available, that there is a way to shut off the gas, that toxic household products are hidden, and that precautions are taken so that the person cannot leave the house without others knowing. Demands on the person with respect to activities of daily living need to be reduced in number and complexity, and choices should be limited. Efforts should be made to keep the environment as consistent and predictable as possible. In some ways, it may seem as if the adult must be treated like an infant, which may anger, frustrate, or embarrass family members, but these steps must be taken, even while preserving the dignity of the afflicted person. It also must be kept in mind that people suffering from severe dementia have greater difficulty than infants in finding the environment consistent and in ability to self-soothe.

The physical and emotional demands on caretakers are very difficult and may evoke feelings of anger, frustration, loss, and guilt. Whenever possible, there should be a plan to give the caregiver some respite, either on a regular daily or weekly basis or for long enough to enable the caregiver to take a vacation. Regular attendance at a day program or a senior citizens' center can provide some free time for the caregiver if supervision is needed. Meals on Wheels is a resource if the person can be home alone during the day but cannot cook. In order to minimize fears of abandonment, the person with an organic mental disorder needs to be psychologically prepared for any prolonged absence of the caregiver. If possible, the person should remain at home with a familiar person, but it may be necessary to find temporary foster care or institutional accommodations.

Caregivers need an opportunity to talk about their feelings about the person and the illness. Feelings of anger, sadness, shame, abandonment, and guilt are common and need to be recognized as normal and appropriate. They need help in balancing their own needs against those of the person with the disorder, especially if the caregiver is elderly and ill or is an adult child with a young family. Caregivers should be encouraged to follow their own interests and to have outside companionship and enjoyable activities in order to lessen feelings of resentment and self-denial. Declaring a relative incompetent is often very painful for a caregiver, especially if the person had been a well-functioning, independent individual. Much support is needed if a decision must be made that the person can no longer be maintained at home. This usually occurs when the person becomes incontinent and when sleep disturbance affects the life and endurance of the caregiver, when the verbal abuse from the person becomes too frequent to be acceptable, or when the caregiver no longer feels able or capable to care for the person. Frequently, this is more difficult for the caregiver and other family members than for the person suffering from dementia. Feelings of guilt, embarrassment, and loss will emerge. Caregivers will need help with these emotions, and with accepting the way the nursing home will provide care. Nursing home visits initially should be short, as longer ones will be overstimulating for the resident and emotionally stressful for the visitor. Complaints by the person that possessions have been "stolen" should be investigated with care, as the person has probably forgotten where he or she put the missing item.

Ethical issues may emerge as dementia progresses. Because of the interest in learning more about dementia, particularly Alzheimer's disease, families may be approached for consent to involve the person in antemortem or postmortem research. Life supports may be a consideration if the dementia progresses to a comatose state. Families need help in understanding the differences and implications of living wills, health care proxies, informed medical consent, DNR (do not resuscitate) orders, powers of attorney, competency hearings, and the need to "spend down" so that the family resources are not wiped out should the person need nursing home care. While specific information needs to be given, it is important to remember that taking control of the life of another person has many emotional implications, and caregivers should be given a chance to explore and discuss their feelings. Social workers also need to monitor the care of people with severe organic mental disorder, and occasionally it may be necessary to alert Adult Protective Services. Although incidences of abuse of these people are infrequent, they do occur, particularly if they are elderly.

Caregivers of people with AIDS face some unique problems. Parents may resume care of their adult children and may have learned for the first time of a lifestyle with which they are not familiar and of which they may disapprove. In other situations, parents may be too old, live too far away, or have responsibility for an ailing spouse, and thus be unable to help the person with AIDS. Social workers can help the person and the family to handle their feelings, including those of guilt and rejection.

Some families will refuse to help, out of shame or a fear of contagion. In some cases, one parent or family member will accept the person and the disease, while others will respond with rejection, thus causing a rift within the family. Social workers can be most helpful to the relative who is offering support and who may be faced not only with losing the person who has AIDS but also with losing other family members because of prejudice and ignorance. Reconciliation of a person who has AIDS with the family of origin may not be possible, and the social worker must be careful to accept this and not pursue a "fantasy" of reconciliation.

Stress and conflict may emerge between the partner of the person with AIDS and the family of origin. The wishes of the person with AIDS must be the primary consideration, and the social worker may need to help the family understand that the partner is the one the person wants as caregiver and the one who is best able to provide a familiar surrounding and routine. Anger that the family may feel toward the person with AIDS and toward the disease may be projected onto the partner. How the person has acquired AIDS and how the family may view the method of transmission must be secondary to planning for the comfort and care of the terminally ill person. It is important to see that the partner receives regular testing for HIV or the necessary care if AIDS develops. Whether the partner is HIV-positive, HIV-negative, or has AIDS, help should be given with respect to anticipatory grief and to planning for what may be a long life without the person who will succumb to AIDS.

Groups

Some people with irreversible organic mental disorders can benefit from socialization groups. Some enjoy participation in a reminiscence group, which often is a nursing home activity. These groups may use photographs or recordings of old popular music in order to try to stimulate memories of past relationships and events.

People with HIV and early-stage AIDS may benefit from bereavement groups as they experience the loss of friends and partners. Cognitive-behavioral groups can also be helpful in increasing communication skills, skills in decision making, and self-confidence.

Caregivers often benefit from support groups. Among the well-organized agencies offering support and educational groups are the Alzheimer's Association, the Alzheimer's Disease and Related Disorders Association, the National Stroke Association, the Huntington's Disease Society of America, the National Head Injury Foundation, the Parkinson's Disease Association, and Partners of People with AIDS. Other resources for information include the American Association for Retired People, the National Institute on Aging, and state offices for the aging.

Medications

There are no medications specifically for organic mental disorders, but medications such as antidepressants, minor tranquilizers, and antipsychotics are sometimes used to alleviate secondary symptoms. They must be very carefully prescribed because of the increased sensitivity of elderly people and people with AIDS to these medications and to their interaction with other necessary medications.

With increasing longevity and thus a greater number of elderly people, who are more prone to dementia, there will be greater prevalence of irreversible, impairing, organic mental disorders. The cost, at the micro and macro levels, to families and to society will make this a significant public health problem. Currently, it is estimated that the national cost for people with Alzheimer's disease in nursing homes is $20 billion, and for those receiving home care, $38 billion. These costs do not include the cost to family caregivers in time and lost wages (Gregg 1994).

It is projected that early in the twenty-first century, at least 20 percent of the population of the United States will be over sixty-five. This population will require needs assessments and provision of a range of services. There should be a range of employment possibilities for social workers, especially those who do not regard aging as a disease but rather as a developmental stage, are not threatened by awareness of their own mortality, and can be creative in trying to help elderly people receive appropriate respect and the optimal quality of life.

No cure has been found for AIDS, which now afflicts an increasing number of women and children. Entire families may develop AIDS, and the responsibility for caregiving will increasingly need to be assumed by social and health agencies. A person in the last stages of AIDS may be homebound. Social workers who work with these people and take on the role of case manager will need extreme compassion and flexibility in order to be available on a case-needed basis and most often be willing to work away from an office.

11   Psychological and Neuropsychological Assessment

John F. Clarkin, Eric Fertuck, Stephen W. Hurt, and Steven Mattis

The contemporary use of psychological assessment is influenced by the current diagnostic system in psychiatry (*DSM-IV*) (American Psychiatric Association 1994), the specific referral question that psychological assessment can clarify that other forms of assessment cannot, and the ability of psychological assessment to contribute to the priorities of the current health care system (e.g., cost containment and quality assurance). Psychological assessment has evolved under these influences, resulting in a diversification of this unique form of assessment.

This chapter discusses the objectives, forms, and utility of psychological assessment and provides an outline for considering the main areas of assessment. A review of the most valid and established tests within this structure and a clinical decision tree that relates both to the referral of patients for testing and to the selection of appropriate tests are provided. The chapter also includes a review of recent developments in the use of psychological testing in managed care and "evidence-based" mental health treatment.

Indications for Referral

With the costs of medical care soaring, in part because of an indiscriminate use of laboratory tests, clinicians should be clear about the precise areas for assessment before referring a patient for testing. Likewise, the clinical psychologist should pursue the testing with efficiency and utilize instruments that will answer the referral questions with precision, reliability, and validity. Social workers, psychiatrists, and psychologists should utilize a clinical decision tree that informs their differential therapeutic procedures.

We suggest that in referring a patient for assessment the clinician already have completed a semistructured interview (or methodological clinical interview) that provides knowledge of which *DSM-IV* criteria (on both Axis I and Axis II) the patient meets. With this diagnostic information, the clinical psychologist can pursue questions about the patient along any one axis or along a mix of the axes that we describe in this chapter—symptoms, personality traits, cognitive functioning, psychodynamics, and environment and social adjustment—by the selection, administration of tests, interviews, and rating scales with the overall goal of informed differential therapeutics. Which of the five axes the psychologist pursues will depend on which *DSM-IV* criteria the patient meets and the nature of the pathology that needs further explication.

Referral Questions: Objectives and Forms of Assessment

Psychological assessment currently takes many forms. Depending on the objective of the assessment, one can decide the types of tests, the number of tests, and the level of expertise required to complete the assessment. By *level of expertise*, we mean whether the assessment can be done by a clinician who is not a psychologist or requires the training and expertise of a psychologist. The most common forms of assessment include screening, diagnostic/treatment planning assessment, and neurocognitive/neuropsychological assessment. More recently, psychological testing has also been used to assess patients or clinicians, and groups of both within a system of care.

Psychological screening is typically done with self-report instruments during the initial evaluation and periodically during and after the treatment process to assess the severity, complexity, and type of distress in an quick, cost-effective manner. The scoring and interpretation of these instruments are straightforward and can be done with reliability and validity by most clinicians. The Hopkins Symptom Checklist (SCL-90) (Derogatis 1977, 1983) is commonly used and recommended for initial and periodic screening in psychiatric settings. If a screening and standard psychiatric interview does not adequately clarify the referral question, referral to a psychologist for more elaborate assessment may be recommended.

The indications for assessment vary with the setting in which the assessment is conducted and the typical patient encountered in such a setting. In clinical psychiatric settings, assessment is most often requested to aid in reducing uncertainty regarding diagnosis and in evaluating the severity of specific symptoms or symptoms complexes (e.g., depression, suicidal intent, or thought disorder). Such an assessment plays an important role in providing information on patients that can be generalized by facilitating comparisons between patients or by tracking the severity of symptoms under the impact of treatment. This assessment may form the basis for recommended treatments, help in establishing goals for the general treatment plan, or help in determining treatment progress and the need for further intervention.

Different levels of clinical care often have referral questions unique to their setting. Inpatient settings have historically focused on the questions of differential diagnosis. In day hospital settings, referrals often emphasize the need for assessment of specific cognitive, vocational, and social assets that can be adaptively employed in helping the patient return to full participation in community life.

In general outpatient settings, psychological assessment can uniquely address a variety of clinical issues. Common referral questions include:

1. Does this patient exhibit a thought disorder indicative of a diagnosis of psychosis? The answer to this question will clarify whether medication may be required and if so, what type, as well as the form of psychosocial intervention that is optimal.
2. What is the cognitive ability of this patient? This will inform clinicians as to whether the patient may require special education and/or whether he or she has the intellectual capacity to utilize typical psychosocial interventions that usually require at least average intelligence.
3. What type of personality characteristics does this patient have and how might these characteristics affect his or her ability to utilize treatment—in particular, psychotherapy? Such factors as the presence of a personality disorder, a treatment-resistant personality profile, a tendency toward deception, and the level of psychological sophistication can predict treatment dropout, adherence, and success rates.

These types of assessment usually require the administration of several tests (a battery) in a reliable and standardized manner. Further, the scoring, interpretation, and synthesis of the information requires supervised training.

Therefore, these assessments, unlike screening assessments, require the expertise of a clinical psychologist.

Neurocognitive and neuropsychological assessment are an increasingly valuable form of assessment that measures impairment in how patients process information and how this impairment might be affected by brain-behavior relationships. In neurology clinics, referral for assessment is frequently made in order to identify the nature, degree, and localization of impairment more specifically, particularly in children and in elderly persons. Because the symptoms overlap, common questions for referral are:

1. Is this geriatric patient suffering from dementia or depression? Depending on the answer to this question, quite different treatment approaches may be indicated.
2. Is this patient's cognitive profile indicative of possible brain damage, such as from a stroke?
3. Does this patient have a learning disability that affects his or her ability to perform academically?

Because of the training in administration, scoring, and interpretation required for this type of assessment, it requires the expertise of a clinical psychologist or clinical neuropsychologist.

Psychological testing in the context of outcome assessment within a system of care typically utilizes standard, brief, self-report instruments that can be routinely administered and scored, usually by a computer. We discuss this type of assessment in more depth later in the chapter.

Objectives of Psychological Assessment
1. To clarify diagnostic and other treatment-relevant questions to aid in treatment planning
2. To assess barriers to learning for educational planning
3. To screen for psychological disturbance
4. To monitor the impact of treatment over time
5. To assess the quality and cost-effectiveness of systems of care

Specific Psychological Tests

The most common psychological tests will be summarized in this chapter. This review is not meant to be exhaustive. It is intended to provide a broad overview of the major and most valid instruments in each particular domain of patient functioning and symptomatology. Three types of instruments are currently utilized in this kind of assessment: psychological tests, rating scales, and semistructured interviews.

Psychological tests are standardized methods of sampling behaviors in a reliable and valid way (Anastasi 1982). *Reliability* is defined as the degree to which two or more observers can agree on what they are observing or to which the same test administered at two different times will demonstrate similar results. *Validity* is defined as the degree to which a test measures what it is intended to measure. The test stimuli, the method of presenting those stimuli, and the method of scoring the responses are carefully standardized so as to ensure reliability. The actual test stimuli can be constructed in numerous ways. For example, test items on the recently revised Wechsler Adult Intelligence Scale (WAIS-III) (Wechsler 1997), a widely used intelligence test, include factual questions (e.g., What does *ponder* mean?) and the answers are scored 2 (e.g., to contemplate), 1 (e.g., to wonder), or 0 (e.g., fret). Items on the Minnesota Multiphasic Personality Inventory-2 (MMPI-2) (Butcher et al. 1989), a highly developed and popular symptom and personality test, are questions about presence or absence of feelings, thoughts, and experiences in a true/false format. Test stimuli on a popular projective test of personality styles and characteristics such as the Rorschach Inkblot Test (Rorschach 1949) are amorphous inkblots. The patient is asked to tell the examiner what it looks like or what it reminds him or her of. The response is recorded verbatim and scored with a standardized system.

Behavior rating scales are standardized devices that allow various informants or observers (e.g., therapist, nurse on a clinical inpatient unit, relatives, trained observers) to rate the behavior of the patient in specified areas. In order to aid the observer in a reliable rating of the behavior, anchor points are provided in one of several ways. For example, on the Brief Psychiatric Rating Scale (BPRS) (Overall and Gorham 1962), somatic concern, defined as "degree of concern over present bodily health," is rated by the interviewer on a seven-point scale from *not present* to *extremely severe*. Other rating scales include the Hamilton Rating Scale for Depression (HRSD) (Hamilton 1960, 1967), and the Katz Adjustment Scale (KAS) (Katz and Lyerly 1963).

Semistructured interviews are standardized by controlling the questions, including specifying what kind of probes can be used, and standardizing the scoring of the patient's response. These interviews have been developed for research, but they have clinical usefulness in the reliable assessment of diagnostic criteria. Useful semistructured interviews include the Schedule for

Affective Disorders and Schizophrenia (SADS) (Spitzer and Endicott 1977), the Structured Clinical Interview for DSM-IV Diagnoses (SCID) (First et al. 1995), and the International Personality Disorders Examination (IPDE) (Loranger 1995). The science of assessment depends upon the development of instruments that meet certain standards. Chief among these standards are reliability and various types of validity.

Assessment of Axis I Constellations and Related Symptoms

As psychiatric nomenclature has undergone revision, assessment tools have been developed that rely on interviews and self-reports that provide data that are immediately relevant to diagnosis. Utilizing the semistructured interview format and item-rating procedures, Spitzer and his associates (First et al. 1995; First et al. 1996) have developed the Structured Clinical Interview for DSM-IV Diagnoses (SCID), which directly orients the diagnostic process to the Axis I and II categories of *DSM-IV*.

With an explicit focus on psychiatric classification, the SCID has problems inherent in adopting the present psychiatric nomenclature as the reference point for assessment. Chief among these difficulties is the insufficient validation of the diagnostic categories themselves. As tools for investigating the range, severity, frequency, and duration of symptomatic disturbance and for training in the formal interview assessment of psychopathology, however, they are important tools in the assessment armamentarium.

Omnibus Measures of Symptoms

There are a number of self-report instruments that have been developed for the assessment of a wide variety of symptoms. These measures depend on either self-report or interview methods for obtaining data.

Minnesota Multiphasic Personality Inventory

The Minnesota Multiphasic Personality Inventory (MMPI) (Hathaway and McKinley 1967) and its recent successor, the MMPI-2 (Butcher et al. 1989), are probably the most widely used assessment instruments in existence. Reasons for their extensive use include efficiency (the patient spends one to two hours taking the test, which can be scored by computer), the extensive data accumulated, the normative base, and the use of validity scales that indicate the patient's test-taking attitude. Although labeled as a personality test, the MMPI was constructed to assess *DSM-II* Axis I conditions and to a lesser extent a few dimensions of personality that are not represented in *DSM-II* Axis II.

Beginning with a large pool of items, the authors of the test used the method of contrasting criterion groups to construct several psychopathological scales. For example, a hypochondriasis scale measuring the degree of concern with bodily health was developed based on items frequently endorsed by patients with hypochondriasis uncomplicated by psychosis or other psychiatric disorders. Responses to the MMPI items were contrasted with those of friends or relatives who visited the University Hospitals in Minneapolis. Using this method of criterion-keyed scoring, the authors constructed nine clinical scales: hypochondriasis (Hs or Scale 1), depression (D or Scale 2), hysteria (Hy or Scale 3), psychopathic deviance (Pd or Scale 4), masculinity-femininity (Mf or Scale 5), paranoia (Pa or Scale 6), psychasthenia (Pt or Scale 7), schizophrenia (Sc or Scale 8), and mania (Ma or Scale 9). Items were worded so that persons with an elementary-school education could take the test, and norms were established for determining the degree of disturbance typical of psychopathological groups.

In addition to the clinical scales, validity scales assess the test-taking attitudes of the patient. McKinley, Hathaway, and Meehl (1948) focused on the assessment of defensiveness or minimizing symptoms and problems ("faking good") and of maximizing or exaggerating problems ("faking bad"). Validity scales were constructed to evaluate these dimensions, which are helpful in interpreting the severity of symptomatic complaints on the clinical scales.

The MMPI was revised and restandardized as the MMPI-2 (Butcher et al. 1989). Revisions include the deletion of objectionable items and the rewording of other items to reflect more modern language, as well as the addition of several new items focusing on suicide, drug and alcohol abuse, Type A behavior, interpersonal relations, and treatment compliance. Restandardization of the norms was based on a randomly solicited national sample of 1,138 males and 1,462 females.

Current clinical interpretation of the MMPI-2 is not, however, simply a matter of noting a scale that is highly relative to these norms and assigning that diagnosis to the patient (e.g., a patient with a high Sc or Scale 8 score would not necessarily be diagnosed schizophrenic). Instead, relying on an extensive clinical database, typical symptomatic and personality dysfunctions are described, based upon two-point and three-point codes (Dahlstrom, Welsh, and Dahlstrom 1972; Marks, Seeman, and Haller 1974; Greene 1991). For example, individuals with a 2–4–8 three-point code (scores above 70 on Scales 2, 4, and 8) are described as distrustful of people, keeping others at a distance, afraid of emotional involvement, utilizing projection and rationalization as defenses, argumentative, sensitive to anything that can be construed as a demand, and unpredictable and changeable in behavior and attitudes (Marks and Seeman 1963). Research has indicated that many patients with this code are classified by *DSM-III-R* as suffering from a borderline personality disorder (Hurt et al. 1985).

The MMPI and the MMPI-2 are good examples of psychological tests, since both were developed with careful attention to issues of reliability and validity. Moreover, they provide information on the response style of the individual taking the test, a personality attribute that is essential in interpreting the clinical scales.

Personality Assessment Inventory

The Personality Assessment Inventory (PAI) (Morey 1991) focuses on clinical syndromes that have been staples of psychopathological nosology and still retain their importance in contemporary diagnostic practice. Items were written with careful attention to their content validity, which was designed to reflect the phenomenology of the clinical construct across a broad range of severity. The instrument consists of 344 items covering four validity scales, eleven clinical syndromes, five treatment planning areas, and the two major dimensions of the interpersonal complex. All items are rated in a four-point Likert-type response format.

Hopkins Symptom Checklist-90

The Hopkins Symptom Checklist (SCL-90) (Derogatis 1977, 1983) is another example of a self-report instrument designed to provide information about a broad range of complaints that are typical of individuals with psychological symptomatic distress. It is briefer than the MMPI-2 and the PAI, containing only ninety items, and can be administered in thirty minutes and scored by computer. These items are combined into nine symptom scales:

1. Somatization
2. Obsessive-compulsive behavior

3. Interpersonal sensitivity
4. Depression
5. Anxiety
6. Hostility
7. Phobic anxiety
8. Paranoid ideation
9. Psychoticism

In addition, three global indices are compiled:

1. General severity
2. Positive symptom distress index
3. Total positive symptoms

A companion instrument, the Hopkins Symptom Checklist (HSCL) (Derogatis et al. 1974), can be used to rate material obtained through direct interview of the patient on each of the nine symptom dimensions of the SCL-90. No structured interview procedure is associated with the HSCL, so formal training in the interview assessment of psychopathology is essential to the accuracy of the assessment. Eight additional dimensions are covered in the interview.

Brief Psychiatric Rating Scale

Another widely used rating scale for a range of psychiatric symptoms is the Brief Psychiatric Rating Scale (BPRS) (Overall and Gorham 1962), which was developed mainly for the assessment of symptoms with an inpatient population and involves a clinical interview. Areas rated include somatic concern, anxiety, emotional withdrawal, conceptional disorganization, guilt, tension, mannerisms and posturing, grandiosity, depressive mood, hostility, suspiciousness, hallucinatory behavior, motor retardation, uncooperativeness, unusual thought content, blunted affect, excitement, and disorientation. There are a number of rating scales for the assessment of general areas of psychopathology that can be used most efficiently in inpatient settings by personnel who make routine observations of patient behavior (Raskin 1982). The best-known scales of this type are the Inpatient Behavioral Rating Scale (IBRS) (Green et al. 1977), patterned after the BPRS, and the Nurses' Observation Scale for Inpatient Evaluation-30 (NOSIE-30) (Honigfeld and Klett 1965).

The MMPI-2, PAI, SCL-90, HSCL, and BPRS represent efforts to develop procedures for the general assessment of psychopathology that meet standards of test construction. These procedures provide coverage of symptomatically distressing areas that are independent of psychiatric classifications. Through their extensive use in psychiatric settings, however, a large body of literature has developed that relates the findings of these tests to diagnostic categories.

Specific Areas of Symptomatology

In addition to the omnibus measures of symptomatology, there are a number of instruments that assess one area of symptomatology in depth. The major constellations of symptoms that may require assessment are (1) substance abuse, as well as abuse of food; (2) affects, including anxiety, elation, and depression; (3) thought disorders; and (4) suicidal intentions/behaviors.

Substance Abuse

Psychological distress and dysfunction arising from the abuse of a wide variety of substances is one of the chief reason for seeking psychological or psychiatric treatment. The cost for treatment of, and income lost from, alcoholism, drug abuse, and eating disorders combined probably consumes more health dollars than any other group of mental disorders. Thus, the identification of these disorders deserves careful attention. Efforts to deal with these disorders have also relied on a wide variety of behavioral, cognitive, somatic, and social treatments, which have generated their own assessment techniques.

The need for the assessment of substance abuse is reflected in omnibus symptom rating scales such as the MMPI-2, which contains the MacAndrew Alcoholism Scale (MacAndrew 1965) for identifying patients with histories of alcohol abuse, or for identifying patients with the potential to develop problems with alcohol (Hoffman, Loper, and Kammeier 1974). A more thorough instrument, the Alcohol Use Inventory (AUI) (Horn, Wanberg, and Foster 1986), is a self-administered test standardized on more than 1,200 admissions to an alcoholism treatment program. It contains twenty-four scales that measure alcohol-related problems, and it considers the subjects' responses in four separate domains: benefits from drinking, style of drinking, consequences of drinking, and concerns associated with drinking. Other substance abuse instruments include the Addiction Severity Index (ASI) (McLellan et al. 1980) and the Time Line Follow-back Assessment Method (TL) (Sobell et al. 1986). This last measure was adapted to drugs of abuse as well as alcohol and was integrated with the ASI drug and alcohol section to form the Substance Abuse History Interview (SAHI). The TL was developed to collect information about subjects' drinking histories during a specific time period. It provides information about frequency and quantity of alcohol consumption.

Garner has developed an inventory to assess attitudes and behaviors associated with anorexia nervosa. The Eating Disorders Inventory-2 (EDI-2) (Garner 1992) consists of ninety-one items rated on six-point frequency scales. The items were chosen to reflect important clinical aspects of anorexia and were retained if they successfully discriminated between anorexic, normal weight, and obese males and females.

Affects

The content, range, and management of emotional expression constitutes a symptomatic area of focus for the evaluation of psychopathology and is important in the differential diagnosis of a wide variety of psychiatric disorders. The main affects of interest are anxiety, depression, and elation. As one factor in the larger context of the total personality, anxiety can be assessed with the Sixteen Personality Factor Inventory (16-PFI) (Cattell, Eber, and Tatsuoka 1970), the Eysenck Personality Inventory (EPI) (Eysenck and Eysenck 1969), and the Taylor Manifest Anxiety Scale (TMAS) (Taylor-Spence and Spence 1966), a scale derived from the MMPI. Other instruments, which assess only anxiety or other forms of fearfulness, may be more clinically useful as dimensional measures of the severity of anxiety or the identification of specific situational anxiety that will become the focus of intervention. The Anxiety Status Inventory (ASI) is a rating scale for anxiety developed for clinical use following an interview guide, and the Self-Rating Anxiety Scale (SRAS) is a companion self-report instrument, both developed by Zung (1971). Both scales assess a wide range of anxiety-related behaviors: fear, panic, physical symptoms of fear, nightmares, and cognitive effects. These scales are recommended for the serial measurement of the effects of therapy on anxiety states. Hamilton (1959) has devised an anxiety-rating scale parallel to the one for depression but less frequently utilized.

The State-Trait Anxiety Inventory (STAI) (Spielberger, Gorsuch, and Luchene 1976) is a self-report instrument that asks the patient to report on anxiety in general (trait) and at particular points in time (state). The Endler S-R Inventory of Anxiousness (Endler, Hunt, and Rosenstein 1962) is a self-report measure of the interaction between the patient's anxiety and environmental situations, such as interpersonal, physically dangerous, and ambiguous situations. This instrument has been widely used as a therapy outcome measure, and it is recommended as an instrument that may be helpful in tailoring treatment to the specific circumstances of the patient's anxiety. Assessment procedures for the treatment of individuals suspected of having agoraphobia will serve as a model of a combined assessment and treatment approach (Barlow and Waddell 1985). A semistructured interview, the Anxiety Disorders Interview Schedule (ADIS) (DiNardo et al. 1983), is used to differentiate subcategories of anxiety disorders, as well as to rule out affective disorders and other major problems. From a differential treatment point of view, it is important to distinguish between agoraphobia with panic, generalized anxiety disorder, and panic disorder, as they are optimally treated with different therapeutic approaches. Once the initial classification is determined, a clinical interview is utilized to obtain a behavioral analysis, to assess the degree of reliance on safe places and/or safe persons, to assess the pattern of avoidance behavior over time, and to assess the presence or absence of depersonalization or derealization. In addition to the structured interview, a number of self-report measures are utilized to assess important ancillary areas and to rate progress during treatment.

The Fear Questionnaire (Marks and Mathews 1979) is a brief paper-and-pencil instrument that yields scores on scales of agoraphobia, social phobia, and blood and injury phobia. The Beck Depression Inventory (BDI-II— Beck, Steer, and Brown 1996; BDI—Beck, Ward, and Mendelson 1961) is also administered, as many patients with agoraphobia are also depressed. Finally, the Dyadic Adjustment Scale (DAS) (Spanier 1976) is administered to assess the marital context of the agoraphobia, an important clinical factor. In addition, the patient is asked to keep a weekly record for the purpose of self-monitoring the type and amount of outside activity on a daily basis.

The BDI (Beck, Ward, and Mendelson 1961) is probably the most widely used self-report inventory of depression. The original scale was administered in an interviewer-assisted manner, but a later version is completely self-administered. The twenty-one items of the inventory were selected to represent symptoms commonly associated with a depressive disorder. The rating of each item relies on the endorsement of one or more of four statements listed in order of symptom severity. Item categories include mood, pessimism, crying spells, guilt, self-hate and accusations, irritability, social withdrawal, work inhibition, sleep and appetite disturbance, and loss of libido. The content of the BDI emphasizes pessimism, a sense of failure, and self-punitive wishes. This emphasis is consistent with Beck's cognitive view of depression and its causes. The BDI has recently been revised (Beck, Steer, and Brown 1996) and preliminary results suggest that the revision has led to improved psychometric properties (Dozois, Dobson, and Ahnberg 1998). This BDI is frequently used in conjunction with the Hamilton Rating Scale for Depression (HRSD), which allows a clinician to rate the severity of depressive symptoms during an interview with the patient. In contrast to the BDI, the HRSD is more systematic in assessing neurovegetative signs.

The Manic-State Rating Scale (MSRS) (Beigel, Murphy, and Bunney 1971) is a twenty-six-item observer-rated scale that is useful with bipolar patients. Eleven items reflecting elation, grandiosity, and paranoid-destructive features of manic patients have produced the most consistent results and have been applied successfully in the prediction of inpatient length of stay (Young et al. 1978). The scale has demonstrated adequate reliability, concurrent validity, and reflection of clinical change (Janowsky et al. 1978). Secunda et al. (1985) have used similar item content from several instruments employed in the NIMH Clinical Research Branch Collaborative Program on the psychobiology of depression to develop indices for responsiveness to lithium treatment in manic patients. A newer instrument, the Internal State Scale (ISS) (Bauer et al. 1991), is a self-report instrument that allows individuals to rate the present state of seventeen items reflecting bipolar symptomatology on a hundred-millimeter line.

Aggressive behavior, including aggressive imagery and hostile affect, are important areas in treatment planning both for the individual patient and for the general concepts that the inventory assesses. The Buss-Durkee Hostility Inventory (Buss and Durkee 1957) is a seventy-five-item self-report questionnaire that measures different aspects of hostility and aggression. There are eight subscales: assault, indirect hostility, irritability, negativism, resentment, suspicion, verbal hostility, and guilt. Some norms exist for clinical populations. Megargee, Cook, and Mendelsohn (1967) developed an overcontrolled hostility scale using MMPI items. A review (Greene 1991) of the number of studies using this scale suggests that it can be used to screen for patients displaying excessive control of their hostile impulses and being socially alienated. Spielberger has developed a State-Trait Anger Expression Inventory (STAEI) (Spielberger, Gorsuch, and Luchene 1976; Spielberger et al. 1983; Spielberger 1991) that takes about fifteen minutes to complete. This forty-four-item scale divides behavior into state anger (current feelings) and trait anger (disposition toward angry reactions), and the latter area has subscales for angry temperament and angry reaction.

Suicidal Behavior

The suicidal potential of patients has obvious treatment and management implications for the clinician. Suicidal threats, suicidal planning and/or preparation, suicidal ideation, and recent parasuicidal behavior are all direct indicators of current risk and should be assessed thoroughly and specifically in the clinical interview. In addition, self-report instruments that focus specific and detailed attention on known predictors of suicidal behavior are sometimes clinically useful. The Suicide Intent Scale (SIS) (Beck, Schuyler, and Herman 1974), the Index of Potential Suicide (IPS) (Zung 1974), and the Suicide Probability Scale (SPS) (Cull and Gill 1986) are three widely used instruments. A complementary approach has been taken by the development of a Reasons for Living Inventory (RFL) (Linehan et al. 1983). Of practical interest is that the fear of suicide subscale in the RFL differentiated between those who had only considered suicide and those who had made previous suicide attempts. Individuals scoring high on reasons for living and with high scores on subscales measuring survival and coping skills, responsibility to family, and child-related concerns were less likely to attempt suicide.

Thought Disorders

One approach to the reliable assessment of cognition is the use of semistructured interviews such as the SADS and the SCID. The presence or absence of disorders of thinking, such as thought derailment, frank hallucinations, or delusions, is determined during the course of an extensive interview. There are obvious problems with this approach. Many individuals may not wish to reveal frank delusional experiences, or they may be unaware of the presence of more-subtle varieties of disordered thinking. To avoid these pitfalls, the interviewer may take an alternative approach of obtaining a sample of the thought process. The test most widely used in examinations for thought disorders has been the Rorschach Inkblot Test, which was developed by the Swiss psychiatrist Hermann Rorschach. In this test, a relatively ambiguous stimulus (a colored or achromatic inkblot) is used, and, without additional instruction, individuals are asked to state what the blot looks like to them. Responses are scored for location (the area of the card that elicits a response), determinants (form, movement, color, and shading), form quality (the degree to which percepts are congruent with the area chosen), and content (e.g., human, animal, object). Exner (1974, 1978) has developed a scoring system that attempts to integrate the best aspects of prior systems.

In its present version, the Thought Disorder Index (Hurt, Holzman, and Davis 1983; Johnston and Holzman 1979; Solovay et al. 1986) considers twenty-two forms of thought disturbance ranging across four levels of severity as the basis for a total score. The total score has been found to distinguish psychotic from nonpsychotic patients, and more severe forms of thought disorder have been most frequently associated with schizophrenic disorders.

In addition to the work of Holzman and his colleagues, Harrow and associates have developed another battery of three tests to quantify thought disorder. This work has considered patients with clinical diagnoses of schizophrenia, affective disorder, and schizoaffective disorder.

Assessment of Cognitive Functioning

The development of clinical assessment procedures for the investigation of brain-behavior relationships has been an active area of psychological investigation. Because impairment to different areas of the brain results in disorders in higher cortical functions in human beings, clinical neuropsychology has been able to develop assessment procedures that consider both the localization and the degree of functional impairment as the focus for test development. In recent years the assessment of less clearly anatomically-based functional disorders characteristic of clinical psychiatric populations has occurred.

These procedures are sensitive to abnormalities of brain function because of the direct alteration of brain tissue. For example, among chronic schizophrenic patients, the degree of neuropsychological dysfunction has been found to be correlated with structural abnormalities on computed tomography (CT) scans (Seidman 1983). In other psychiatric groups where the evidence for structural abnormalities is less clear, the degree to which these disorders interfere with performance on these tests by mechanisms other than structural abnormalities of brain tissue is as yet unclear. There is increasing evidence that some schizophrenic and affective disorders traditionally considered functional psychoses may result from as yet poorly understood abnormalities of brain biochemistry (Barchas et al. 1977), and modern imaging techniques such as positron-emission tomography (PET) and magnetic resonance imaging (MRI) scans have begun to produce evidence of alterations in brain functioning that may be relatively specific to traditional functional psychiatric diagnoses. The relationships between these biochemical and neurophysiological findings and the quality and severity of functional impairment identified through neuropsychological assessments remain to be clarified.

In general, one assesses specific cognitive abilities in psychiatric patients for two reasons: (1) to document disorders in cognitive skills referable to primary or concomitant neurogenic disorder, e.g., discriminating between a thought disorder and a language disorder or the mnemonic deficits of a depression versus a dementia; or (2) to document a specific disorder in cognition referable to a specific class of psychiatric disorders, e.g., intrusion into thought of task-irrelevant items in patients complaining of delusional or obsessive ideation or disturbances in recall in patients with major affective disorders. Common clinical questions in a psychiatric setting with a neuropsychological focus include (1) dementia in the elderly, (2) toxicity in substance-abusing individuals, and (3) specific learning disabilities in children, adolescents, and adults. In clinical psychiatric populations, the possibly confounding influences of behavioral impairment because of the nature and severity of the emotional disturbance and the impact of concurrent pharmacological treatments must be carefully considered in order to reduce the rate of false positive diagnoses of organic mental disorder. These factors should be carefully considered in the context of scheduling the timing of the assessment and in interpreting the results of the assessment. Heaton and Crowley (1981) have provided a thorough review of the literature on neuropsychological testing and organic mental disorder in psychiatric patients that considers the above issues. Their review is particularly useful because of its attention to the issue of the effects of somatic treatments on neuropsychological functioning in psychiatric populations.

Although the fields of cognitive and experimental psychology may offer an almost limitless number of different cognitive functions capable of being defined and measured in the adult, only a finite number appear to be clinically useful. In one form or another, most neuropsychological assessments of cognitive processes evaluate the presence of disorders in the following abilities: general intelligence, attention and concentration, memory and learning, perception, language, conceptualization, constructional skills, executive-motor processes, affect. In many clinical settings, the areas of higher cortical functions of interest are assessed by a formal battery of tests. Two such standardized batteries are the Halstead-Reitan (Boll 1981) and the Luria-Nebraska (Golden, Hammeke, and Purisch 1978) neuropsychological batteries. In its present form, the Halstead Neuropsychological Test Battery consists of five tests that yield seven summary scores and a total impairment index. The five tests are a category test, a tactile perception test, a speech sounds perception test, the seashore rhythm test, and a finger oscillation test. A group of tests referred to as the allied procedures are frequently included as a part of the total examination. The entire examination typically takes from four to six hours, depending on the number of ancillary procedures (i.e., intelligence and academic performance) included. The reliability and validity of the tests are well established, and normative data for most comparisons of interest in clinical psychiatric populations are available. The major neuropsychological instruments are reviewed below. For a compendium of these and other neuropsychological tests, we recommend the recently updated Spreen and Strauss (1998).

In its present form, the Luria-Nebraska covers rhythm (and pitch) skills, tactile and visual functions, receptive and expressive speech, writing, reading, and arithmetic skills, memory, and intelligence. The complete examination consists of 269 items that yield raw scores in each of eleven areas. Three additional scores for right and left hemisphere impairment and a pathognomonic score are also computed. These fourteen raw scores are plotted as T-scores for the purposes of interscale and interindividual comparison. Both of these batteries are oriented toward an extensive evaluation of neuropsychological functioning, and in clinical practice they are typically supplemented with instruments that allow a more flexible test approach and a more intensive focus on areas of possible dysfunction. The neuropsychological areas of interest and appropriate assessment procedures for detailed examination of these processes follow.

Premorbid Intelligence

A number of inferences as to the presence of neuropsychological deficits are based on observed discrepancies between present functioning and estimated premorbid abilities. Premorbid intelligence may be estimated by assessing those cognitive abilities that do not rapidly deteriorate with dementing processes, such as the general fund of information and vocabulary subtests of the WAIS-III or reading recognition as measured by the Wide Range Achievement Test Reading subtest (Jastak and Wilkinson 1981) or the Nelson Adult Reading Test (Nelson 1982), which has new North American norms and has recently demonstrated reasonable validity. It is also common to estimate premorbid intelligence on the basis of educational and vocational background. The validity of a number of different estimates of premorbid intelligence based on demographic data has been demonstrated (Karzmark et al. 1985).

General Intellectual Abilities

The most frequently used instrument, the WAIS-III (Wechsler 1997), is the revision of the WAIS-R. The revision has updated the norms, has expanded the age range from sixteen to eighty-nine, and has been constructed to be used concurrently with the Wechsler Memory Scale (WMS-III) and the Wechsler Individual Achievement Test. There is now a version of this test for abbreviated intelligence testing, which can estimate cognitive abilities in fifteen to thirty minutes (WAIS). Briefer measures may be employed, including the Ammons Quick Test (Ammons and Ammons 1962) or the Shipley-Hartford Test (Shipley 1946).

Most tests of general intellectual abilities obtain normative data from an unimpaired population and therefore are sensitive instruments in detecting individuals whose performance lies at the extremes of the normal range. Such instruments lose sensitivity to discriminate among patient populations whose performance falls outside this range. There are a number of instruments in broad use for the assessment of general cognitive abilities in patient populations. All such instruments have skewed distributions in normal populations, i.e., a decided floor effect, but they distribute well in the atypical population. Perhaps the most commonly used instrument in a psychiatric setting is the Mini-mental Status Exam (MMSE) (Folstein, Folstein, and McHugh 1975), a ten-minute test generating thirty points on which a score below twenty-four is considered to be good evidence of clinically significant cognitive impairment. A commonly used instrument is the Dementia Rating Scale (Mattis 1988), a twenty- to thirty-minute instrument generating 144 points, with greater sensitivity at the upper levels and better ability to detect progressive changes of dementia over several years (Haxby et al. 1992).

Within the neuropsychological literature exists a vast armamentarium of tests of specific neurocognitive processes validated within neurologic and neurosurgical populations. A smaller number of instruments are useful in a psychiatric setting, but even so, there are too many to itemize here. Research concerning the neuropsychology of psychiatric disorders is relatively new. It should therefore be noted that the tests presented below are examples of widely used measures of cognitive processes, not an exhaustive list, and are expected to be replaced as new data are accrued.

Attention Disorders

Attention disorders are among the most common findings in psychiatric patients, since attention and concentration will be affected by both psychologically determined processes such as anxiety, depressive mood, and/or rumination and neurogenic compromise of the brain stem and limbic structures because of toxic-metabolic disorders or direct structural impairment. Attention processes are most commonly measured by the WAIS-III subtests constituting the "distractibility" triad—digit span, mental arithmetic, and digit symbol. In digit span the patient is asked to repeat a string of digits of increasing length and then, in a separate administration, repeat a string of digits in the reverse order in which they are presented. The digit string cannot be repeated by the examiner, so that lapses in attention by the patient result in repetition of only the shorter strings. In the arithmetic subtest, the patient is asked to solve arithmetic problems of increasing difficulty without the aid of pencil and paper. Selection and monitoring of the appropriate arithmetic operation while storing partial solutions are easily disrupted by alterations in arousal and attention. The digit symbol subtest presents the patient with the digits 1 through 9 and gives each digit a separate, very simple geometric design. The digits are then randomly sequenced in rows across the page, and the patient must draw the appropriate design beneath each digit. The number of designs correctly drawn in ninety seconds is noted. This task is not only affected by impairment of the attentional system but is very sensitive to fine-motor tremor and extrapyramidal impairment secondary to neurotoxins. In addition, a number of variants of these procedures and specialized procedures are in common practice. Cancellation tasks are available, in which the patient is required to cross out a given letter or design presented within rows of randomly distributed other letters or designs (Mesulam 1985). An advantage of such tasks is that they can be strung together to form a lengthy continuous performance task of ten to fifteen minutes and variation in accuracy across discrete twenty-second epochs can be determined.

With increasing use of computer-assisted examinations, a popular continuous performance test developed by Rosvold can be employed (Mirsky and Kornetsky 1964). In this task, the patient is presented with a randomly selected letter in midscreen at fixed intervals and directed to push a button (or press the space bar) when a given letter is presented. One notes the number of correct responses (hits), misses, false alarms (the number of times the bar is pressed in response to a nontarget item), and correct rejections. The advantage of this computer-assisted approach to the measure of attention lies in its flexibility and the accuracy with which responses can be recorded and stimuli presented. One can measure reaction time of each response and note fluctuations in reaction time over the duration of the task. One can systematically alter stimulus characteristics such as stimulus duration, speed of presentation, size of target, and duration of task. A good deal of clinical research has been conducted using such a procedure to explore the attentional characteristics of children with Attention Deficit Hyperactivity Disorder (ADHD).

Research in attention processes has demonstrated the efficacy of a procedure called dichotic stimulation (Kimura 1967), which presents dissimilar auditory stimuli simultaneously to each ear and requires the patient to report both stimuli. Thus the patient might hear the number "one" in the right ear and the number "four" in the left at the same time. Strings of three such pairs might be presented to adults and the patient asked to report all six digits. The competing stimuli can be matched for such stimulus characteristics as time of onset, offset, peak amplitude, and so on, making it a very difficult speech sound discrimination task as well as an attention measure.

Memory Disorders

The memory disorder of particular interest to the clinician is the one that affects recent memory and is generally referable to impairment of limbic system functioning. Operationally, one seeks to present the patient with a specific set of information or events, then divert attention so that it cannot be rehearsed, and then require the patient to demonstrate that the target information has been encoded and stored by either reproducing the material or recognizing it among distractor items. Thus recall of brief paragraphs or reproduction of geometric designs from memory are often used to assess mnemonic processes. Among the most commonly used standard tests of memory are the Wechsler Memory Scale-III (Wechsler 1997), which presents both verbal and nonverbal material as the to-be-remembered items, and the Benton Test of Visual Retention (Benton 1955), which presents only geometric designs. Free recall of recent events has been found to be among the most sensitive of memory processes. Unfortunately, in many instances free recall has been found to be quite fragile and vulnerable to disruption because of affective arousal, depression, and motivational factors, and therefore it may present many "false positives" when discriminating between neurogenic and psychogenic diagnostic considerations.

It has been suggested that mechanisms other than free recall might be employed to assess the integrity of encoding and storage processes. Recognition memory techniques, in which the patient is asked to detect a recently presented word or design from among distractor items, have been successfully used to discriminate patients with major affective disorders from those with organic amnesias such as progressive dementia. In patients presenting with a major depression, for example, free recall might be quite consonant with that of patients with Alzheimer's disease, but recognition memory remains relatively intact. The well-designed instruments assessing both recall and recognition memory generally present the patient with a list-learning task requiring free recall. Subsequent to that, the patient is given a recognition memory probe, in which he or she must detect the target from distractor items. Most of the instruments introduce either an interpolated list or a significant time delay before presentation of the final recall and recognition trials. Among the most widely used instruments are the Rey Auditory Verbal Learning Test (Rey 1964; Geffen et al. 1990) and the California Verbal Learning Test (Delis et al. 1987). Several instruments have multiple forms useful in serial examination of patients, e.g., the Hopkins Verbal Learning Test (Brandt 1991) and the Mattis-Kovner Verbal Learning Test (Mattis, Kovner, and Goldmeier 1978).

It should be noted that neurologic patients with focal lesions might present only a verbal or nonverbal recent memory defect, depending on the locus of the lesions. It is therefore only in patients with bilateral or diffuse neurogenic impairment that one finds amnesic disorders in both realms. Thus verbal and nonverbal memory must be assessed independently, with the finding of asymmetric dysfunction strongly suggesting focal neurologic impairment.

Perceptual Disorders

There is very little evidence for a significant prevalence of perceptual deficits in a psychiatric population when care is taken to exclude significant problem-solving components from the task and exclude the presence of concurrent toxic metabolic disorders in the patients. Nonetheless, it is probably a good idea to rule out the presence of perceptual deficits. Visual perceptual processes can be assessed with tasks such as the Benton Line Orientation

Test (Benton, Hannay, and Varney 1975), which requires the patient to match a target line at a given orientation to true vertical with alternative lines presented at various orientations. Another such test is the Benton Face Recognition Test (Benton and Van Allen 1968), in which a photograph of a face is presented as the target and the patient is requested to detect this face from alternatives. In this task the correct face is presented as an identical photograph as well as the same individual in various profiles. Both of these tests have good validation as measures of the integrity of posterior cerebral, primarily nondominant-hemisphere, functioning.

Auditory perception tends to be difficult to assess without hardware. Now-adays, however, the fidelity available in personal tape recorders with ear-phones affords the clinician a wide range of excellent auditory stimuli. Tests such as the Goldman-Fristoe Test of Speech Sound Discrimination (Gold-man, Fristoe, and Woodcock 1976) allows for the assessment of the efficiency of speech sound detection with and without background noise. The use of dichotic stimulation tests as measures of speech sound discrimination has been mentioned above. Subtests of the Seashore Battery of Tests of Musical Abilities (Seashore, Lewis, and Saetveit 1960), especially the timbre discrim-ination and tonal memory subtests, have been used as measures of auditory perception of nonverbal material.

The study of disorders of somatosensory perception have a long history in the field of psychophysics, and the techniques evolved from this early literature constitute a large part of the standard neurologic examination for peripheral and central nervous system disorders. Measures of pressure thresh-old (Von Frey hairs and Semmes-Ghent-Weinstein pressure esthesiometer), two-point discrimination, joint position sense, finger agnosia, finger order and differentiation, graphesthesia, and stereognosis are common assessment procedures for the presence of disorders of parietal lobe functioning.

Perhaps the most specific index of neurogenic impairment is the presence of a language disorder. For almost all right-handed individuals and half of left-handed individuals, focal or diffuse impairment of the left hemisphere is likely to result in an aphasis, i.e., a disorder of language comprehension and/or usage. The relationship between the nature of the aphasis, e.g., fluent versus nonfluent, and locus of cerebral impairment is among the most well documented of brain-behavior relations (Mesulam 1985). Thus, the exam-ination for aphasis can provide the "hardest" evidence in the mental status exam of the presence and locus of brain impairment. In general, the aphasis examination will consist of specific measures of disorders of linguistic pro-cesses well correlated with focal brain lesions. Most such batteries will contain measures of verbal labeling or word-finding skills, language comprehension, imitative speech, and motor-expressive speech. Many such tests also include specific measures of reading and writing. Among the most commonly used multifactorial instruments is the Multilingual Aphasis Examination (Benton and Hamsher 1976).

Conceptualization Disorders

The question as to whether the patient can assume an abstract attitude is often critical to diagnosis and treatment planning. The question arises most often when the differential diagnostic considerations include diffuse brain damage, and to some degree, schizophrenia. Perhaps the most direct measure of abstract or categorical thinking is the similarities subtest of the WAIS-R, which presents the patient with perceptually dissimilar items and asks him or her to determine the category to which both belong, e.g., "How are North and West alike?" Proverb explanation has a long history in the psychiatric mental status exam as a task designed to measure abstract reasoning and is included among the items of the comprehension subtest of the WAIS-R, e.g., "Shallow brooks are noisy." However, some consider explanation of proverbs too dependent on general intellectual abilities and sociocultural factors to be a specific measure of concretization of thought. Analogistic reasoning can also be gauged using such tasks as the Conceptual Level Analogies Test (Willner 1971) for verbal reasoning and the Raven Progressive Matrices (Raven 1960) for nonverbal or spatial analogistic reasoning.

Two measures of concept formation arising from the neuropsychologic literature have recently been applied to psychiatric patients. The data to date indicate that schizophrenic patients, like patients with frontal lobe lesions, have particular difficulty with the Booklet Categories Test (DeFillipis, McCampbell, and Rogers 1979) and the Wisconsin Card Sorting Test (Berg 1948; Heaton 1981). Both tests require the patient to induce a concept or rule of organization from patterned visual stimuli. In the Wisconsin test, which has received the most recent programmatic research attention, the patient is shown a pack of cards depicting colored geometric figures and required to match the top card with one of four cards that vary in color, number, or form. As the patient matches his card to one of the alternatives, the examiner informs him as to the "correctness" of his sort, and the patient then attempts to match the next card correctly. The "rule" of sorting that the examiner reinforces in color, form, or number is changed after the patient correctly sorts ten cards in a row (indicating he has grasped the rule). One notes the number of concepts correctly induced and the number of perseverative errors in matching.

Constructional Disorders

Perhaps the quickest estimate of the integrity of the central nervous system can be obtained by asking the patient to draw a complex figure. Posterior sensory, central spatial, and anterior planning, monitoring, and simple motor skills must all be intact, integrated, and appropriately sequenced for this task to be successfully completed. One can alter the degree to which psychological and dynamic factors and initiative or executive planning play a role by modulating both task structure and design complexity. For example, asking the patient to draw a person or to draw his family requires a maximum level of planning, initiative, and decision making, does not put any limit on the degree of complexity of the figures, and chooses a subject matter fraught with complex feelings and attitudes. Patients without structural impairment but with conflictual feelings about family or disordered thinking affecting planning and execution will have difficulty on such tasks. However, asking a patient to draw a clock, setting the hands to a specific time, e.g., ten to eleven, also requires complex planning and initiative but without the conflictual overlay. Similarly, asking the patient to copy a complex design, e.g., the Rey-Ostereith figure (Rey 1941) minimizes initiative, limits (but does not eliminate) planning, but maintains assessment of high levels of spatial constructional skills. Contrasting the patient's figure drawing to his clock and copy of geometric figures often allows valid inferences as to presence and locus of CNS impairment and the degree to which affective and psychiatric factors impair otherwise intact cognitive skills. Quite often, construction tasks other than drawing, such as the block design and object assembly subtests of the WAIS-R, are used for the same assessment goals.

Disorders of Executive-Motor Skills

In general, in assessing disorders in executive skills, one is alert to the presence of perseveration in motor activity, thought, and affect. Perseveration of motor activity is often elicited by starting the patient on a simple repeated task and then altering one of the motor components. Thus having the patient perform a simple diadochokinetic task such as alternating palm up, palm down and then presenting as the next task palm up, palm down, fist, may result in repeated performance of only two components of the task. Similarly, asking the patient to write, in script, alternating *m*'s and *n*'s will also elicit simple motor perseveration. Perseveration of thought or set is often quickly elicited by shifting task instruction. For example, in a task developed by Luria (1966) for the assessment of frontal lobe dysfunction, the patient is told, "When I raise one finger, then you raise one finger, and when I raise two fingers, you raise two fingers." After a number of successful completions, the patient is told, "Now when I raise one finger, you raise two fingers, and when I raise two fingers, you raise one." Patients with dorsal lateral frontal lobe lesions have a great deal of trouble with such tasks. The Trail Making Test (Lezak 1969) is a "connect the dots" type of task in which the patient must first connect the dots in ascending numerical order (trails A) and then connect the dots in alternating sequence of numbers and letters, e.g., 1 to A to 2 to B to 3 to C, and so on (trails B). Note is made of both the time to completion and the number of errors. Disorders in evolving or shifting more complex ideas can also be measured quite accurately. Concept formation tasks such as the Category Test (DeFillipis, McCampbell, and Rogers 1979) and the Wisconsin Card Sorting Test (Berg 1948; Heaton 1981) differ in specific directions and stimuli, but both present a series of specific examples of a class of events and require the patient to induce the concept or rule of which they are an exemplar. The rule changes over time. Thus, one might observe that the patient fails to induce the first concept or perseverates the same rule well past its utility. The number of perseveration errors is among the scores obtained on both tests.

Disorders in Motor Skills

Disorders in simple motor skills are among the common concomitants to most toxic-metabolic disorders and structural lesions to both the extra-pyramidal and the pyramidal systems. Examination is usually exceptionally brief and the results quite reproducible and valid. One can measure line-quality parameters of copied geometric drawings (Mattis, French, and Rapin 1975). One can, in addition, present simple fine-motor coordination tasks such as the Purdue Pegboard (Costa, Vaughn, Levita, and Farber 1963) or the Grooved Pegboard (Klove 1963). The Purdue Pegboard measures the number of slim cylinders (pegs) one can insert in a row of holes in thirty seconds. One notes the number of pegs placed with the right hand alone, left hand alone, and pairs of pegs placed using both hands simultaneously. The number of pegs placed simultaneously has proved to be a sensitive measure of frontal dysfunction. The grooved pegboard uses pegs that contain a flange on one side so that the pegs fit into a keyhole-shaped hole. The keyholes are placed in differing orientations on the board. One notes the total time required to place all the pegs with each hand alone. Given the greater fine-motor component to the grooved pegs, the Grooved Pegboard tends to be a more sensitive measure of tremor than the Purdue Pegboard.

Assessment of Personality Traits and Disorders

In developing a treatment plan, the clinician must assess personality traits for various reasons: personality traits or disorders may be the focus of intervention, personality traits may exacerbate or be related to the incidence of certain symptoms (e.g., depression), and personality traits may either help or hinder the development of a therapeutic relationship with the patient.

Dimensional Assessment of Personality

Several widely used and psychometrically sound instruments are available for the assessment of personality. Such tests include the Sixteen Personality Factor Inventory (16 PFI) (Cattell, Eber, and Tatsuoka 1970), the Eysenck Personality Inventory (EPI) (Eysenck and Eysenck 1969), the California Psychological Inventory (CPI) (Gough 1956), and the Personality Research Form (PRF) (Jackson 1974). These instruments were designed for the validation of personality constructs rather than for the assessment of psychopathology, although they have been employed in clinical settings with limited success. These instruments and their designers, however, have not been oriented toward psychopathology, and there is no explicit theory of personality disorder that underlies the interpretation of results from these tests.

The NEO Personality Inventory-Revised (NEO-PI-R) (Costa and McCrae 1992) provides a measure of the five facets of personality: neuroticism, extroversion, openness, agreeableness, and conscientiousness. Each of the facets also includes six subscales. For example, the six facets of neuroticism include anxiety, anger/hostility, depression, self-consciousness, impulsiveness, and vulnerability. The revised version completes the earlier instrument by providing facet scales for agreeableness and conscientiousness.

In this era of managed care, some consideration should be given to the use of screening instruments that can be administered rapidly to assess for the potential for personality disorders, disorders that retard and complicate the treatment of Axis I disorders. Four screening instruments deserve consideration: the International Personality Disorder Examination DSM-III-R Screen (IPDE-S) (Lenzenweger, Korfine, and Neff 1997), the Iowa Personality Disorder Screen (Pfohl and Langbehn 1994), the Self-Directedness subscale from the Temperament and Character Inventory (Cloninger, Svrakic, and Przybeck 1993; Svrakic et al. 1993), and a screen for personality disorders developed from the Inventory of Interpersonal Problems (IIP) (Pilkonis et al. 1996).

Interpersonal Aspects of Personality

One particular school of personality research that has concerned itself with pathological expressions of personality factors has focused explicitly on interpersonal behavior. Adherents to this view of psychopathology emphasize the centrality of the problems that people experience with others, because this is an area in which all symptoms are activated, reinforced, and (for some) caused. The assessment of interpersonal behavior can be central both for understanding the patient's social world, with its pleasures and disappointments, barriers to success in love and work, and as a forecast of the kind of relationship the patient will form with the clinician.

This interpersonal tradition dates back to psychologist Timothy Leary's circumplex model (Leary 1957). Underlying the expression of all interpersonal styles are the two major orthogonal axes of power and affiliation. Each interpersonal style is seen as involving varying degrees of the expression of power and affiliation, leading to sixteen modes of interaction. These sixteen modes are organized along the circumference of a circle defining eight broad categories that are used in interpersonal diagnosis: ambitious-dominant, gregarious-extroverted, warm-agreeable, unassuming-ingenious, lazy-submissive, aloof-introverted, cold-quarrelsome, and arrogant-calculating.

The system is more than merely descriptive. Theoretically, the system is able to predict not only the kind of interpersonal style that the patient expresses but also the kind of behavior that this style tends to elicit from others. Behavior on one side of the circle tends to elicit behavior from others on the opposite side of the circle.

Several instruments have been developed from this basic interpersonal theory. In a series of investigations, Lorr and McNair (1965) have generated the latest version of the Interpersonal Behavior Inventory (IBI). The IBI has been judged to be psychometrically sound and a useful clinical device for the assessment of patient characteristics and therapy outcome (Wiggins

1982). The instrument is a clinical rating by professionals but in principle could be employed in a self-report format. The Interpersonal Style Inventory (ISI) (Lorr and Youniss 1973) is a self-report instrument for those fourteen years of age and older. Three hundred true-false statements are employed to assess interpersonal involvement, socialization, self-control, stability, and autonomy. Techniques of rational scale construction were employed, including validity factor analyses. Norms have been established based on 1,500 college and high school students.

Also in the same tradition, Benjamin (Benjamin 1974) has developed an instrument for the assessment of interpersonal behavior, the Structural Analysis of Social Behavior (SASB), and a computer-based scoring system marketed under the trade name INTREX, which is self-administered. The SASB can also be used by clinicians to record their impressions about the patient. A related coding scheme has been developed to be used by trained observers to record the patient's actual interactions with others, such as family members, during the course of treatment.

Assessment of Personality Disorders

A relatively new approach to the assessment of personality disorders is to construct instruments, either self-report or semistructured interviews, that evaluate the presence or absence of specific personality traits described in Axis II of DSM-IV. The most promising instruments of this type include the Personality Diagnostic Questionnaire—4th Edition (PDQ-4—Hyler et al. 1992; PDQ—Hyler, Rieder, and Spitzer 1978; Hurt et al. 1984), the Millon Clinical Multiaxial Inventory (MCMI-III) (Millon 1994), the SCID-II (First et al. 1996), the IPDE (Loranger 1995), and the Structured Interview for the DSM-IV Personality Disorders (SIDP-IV) (Pfohl, Blum, and Zimmerman 1997).

The PDQ-4 is a self-report inventory of Axis II traits, and the test yields scores on each of the thirteen personality disorder categories of DSM-IV. Preliminary investigation of the instrument suggests that patients typically report a number of traits and will often meet criteria for several diagnostic categories, but the PDQ may be useful for screening (Hurt et al. 1984).

The Millon Clinical Multiaxial Inventory (MCMI) (Millon 1983) is a 175-item true-false, self-report instrument that yields scores on eleven personality disorder dimensions closely related to the personality disorder diagnoses of DSM-III Axis II. The instrument also provides information on nine clinical syndromes. Probably the major difficulty with this instrument is psychometric in nature, as there is much item overlap in the scales (Wiggins 1982). The MCMI-III (Millon 1994) is a revision of the MCMI-II scale. The instrument incorporates new items and an improved weighting system. The revision includes additional scales that are tailored to assess *DSM-IV* personality disorders and ten other clinical syndromes.

There are three semistructured interviews that are constructed to assess, via the patient's report and the clinical judgment of the interviewer, the presence of Axis II disorders: the International Personality Disorders Examination (IPDE), the Structured Interview for the DSM-IV Personality Disorders (SIDP-IV), and the Structured Clinical Interview for DSM-IV Axis II (SCID-II).

The IPDE (Loranger 1995) is a semistructured interview that yields both dimensional and categorical scores for *DSM-IV* Axis II criteria. An important feature of this semistructured interview, which takes approximately two hours to administer, is that the criteria are assessed in related clusters such as self-concept, affect expression, reality testing, impulse control, interpersonal relations, and work. The interview goes beyond a simple listing of the criteria and provides, in many cases, multiple questions designed to help the interviewer gain a broad appreciation of the criterion under assessment. A parallel version of the interview has been constructed to use with informants, recognizing that information from patients themselves, especially around personality issues, may be distorted. Initial reliability data are impressive, and validity studies are under way. The instrument is likely to be widely used, and it has been translated into several languages and was used in an international study approved by WHO/ADAMHA (Loranger et al. 1991). The interview now includes a self-administered screener questionnaire that takes approximately fifteen minutes to complete. This screener can be used to identify individuals who may or may not require the full interview (Lenzenweger, Korfine, and Neff 1997).

The SIDP-IV (Pfohl, Blum, and Zimmerman 1997) consists of a semistructured interview form that provides questions pertinent to the diagnostic criteria of Axis II of *DSM-IV*. The questions are organized into assessment areas such as low self-esteem/dependency, egocentricity, ideas of reference, magical thinking, and hostility/anger. The questions are keyed to the *DSM-IV* criteria for Axis II disorders. A rating form provides a rating scale for each of the criteria. Ratings are based on the clinical assessment of the interview data. The authors recommend that the interview be used in conjunction with a general psychiatric interview in which major (Axis I) psychiatric disorders have been diagnosed so that lifelong personality traits can be distinguished from episodic psychiatric disorders. The authors also recommend gathering information from an informant who knows the patient well.

The Structured Clinical Interview for DSM-IV Axis II Personality Disorders (SCID-II) (First et al. 1996) is a semistructured diagnostic interview that can also be used to obtain Axis II diagnoses. Previous studies with the *DSM-III-R* version of the SCID have shown adequate reliability. This is a recommended scale for clinician use; it is easier and briefer, but it does require clinical expertise in noticing clinically relevant criteria.

Finally, there are several self-report questionnaires assessing personality pathology that have been carefully constructed with attention to psychometric properties. These instruments include the Schedule for Nonadaptive and Adaptive Personality (SNAP) (Clark 1993) and the Dimensional Assessment of Personality Pathology—Basic Questionnaire (DAPP-BQ) (Schroeder et al. 1994).

Assessment of Psychodynamics

The assessment of factors relevant to psychodynamic and psychoanalytic theory and treatment approaches has a long history in the clinical psychological literature. The development of the "standard battery," including the Wechsler-Bellevue, Rorschach, and Thematic Apperception Test (TAT), has its origins in the efforts of clinical psychologists to provide an assessment of such psychodynamic factors as drives, unconscious wishes, conflicts, and defenses. For those committed to the psychodynamic model, assessments that focus exclusively on overt behaviors will be less than totally satisfactory.

The importance of providing information about personality dynamics and structure that is outside the conscious awareness of the examinee has been the single most important rationale for the continued use of projective tests. In part, therefore, the value of such assessments varies directly with the degree to which maladaptive and symptomatic behaviors are presumed to be beyond the conscious control of the examinee. A second rationale for the continued use of these tests is that the unstructured nature of the tests themselves provides a singular opportunity to assess the degree to which organization of behavior is dependent on a high degree of structure in the examination procedure itself. The assessment of both of these factors is of clear relevance to a treatment method that attempts to explore and alter unconscious determinants of behavior and that depends for its success on introducing as little structure into the treatment as is realistically possible.

The most widely used assessment procedure to examine patients for a range of ego functions and dynamic factors is the Rorschach Inkblot Test described earlier. Scoring systems have been developed by many authors, and more recently Exner has developed a scoring system that attempts to integrate the best aspects of the previous systems. From these scores inferences are drawn concerning the patient's self-image, identity, defensive structure, reality testing, affective control, amount and degree of fantasy life, degree of thought organization, and potential for impulsive acting out.

The Thematic Apperception Test (TAT) is another widely used projective process for assessing the patient's self-concept in relation to others. Originally developed by Murray (1943), the test consists of a set of thirty pictures depicting one or more individuals. The stories generated by subjects were scored for the individual's needs as reflected in the feelings and impulses attributed to a major character in the story and the interactions with the environment leading to a resolution. As currently used, the stories are most often examined for the patient's self-other concepts as revealed in the interaction and outcome of the story line.

Assessment of Environmental Demands and Social Adjustment

The interaction between the patient and the pressures of the environment is now acknowledged in the standard diagnostic system (*DSM-IV*) by a rating on Axis IV. The investigation of expressed emotion (EE) and its influence on the course of schizophrenia is probably the area that has generated the most substantial amount of empirical data indicating the impact of the patient-environment interaction. This work suggests that certain elements in the home environment of a schizophrenic patient can adversely affect the course of the illness.

In measuring both stress and coping with stress, one can assess the stimuli, the individual's response to the stimuli, or the interaction of the person with stressful stimuli. The Jenkins Activity Survey (JAS) (Jenkins, Rosenman, and Friedman 1967) is the prototype of an interaction measure of stress, since it focuses on the cognitive and perceptual characteristics of the individual that mediate responses to stress. This instrument has shown predictive validity in studies of reaction to coronary heart disease. The Derogatis Stress Profile (DSP) (Derogatis 1982) is useful in assessing stimuli from work, home, and health, as well as characteristic attitudes and coping mechanisms.

We use the term *social adjustment* to indicate the skill of the individual in handling interpersonal situations, whether at home, in school, or at work. The term has been used more narrowly to indicate the community and social adjustment of diagnosed psychiatric patients, often with severe illnesses such as schizophrenia and major affective disorder (Weissman and Sholomskas 1982). Notable assessment instruments in this area include the Social Adjustment Scale—Self-Report (SAS-SR), the Dyadic Adjustment Scale (DAS), and the Katz Adjustment Scale.

The Katz Adjustment Scale—Relative's Form (KAS-R) (Katz and Lyerly 1963) is a self-report inventory from a relative of the patient that describes the patient's symptomatic behavior and social adjustment in the community. The scale has sections on symptoms and social behavior, performance of socially expected tasks, the relative's expectation for the performance of these tasks, the patient's free-time activities, and the relative's satisfaction with the performance of free-time activities.

The Social Adjustment Scale—Self-Report (SAS-SR) (Weissman and Bothwell 1976) contains forty-two questions covering instrumental and affective qualities in role performance, social and leisure activities, relationships with extended family, marital role, parental role, family unit, and economic independence. Norms are available for nonpatient community samples, acute and recovered depressed outpatients, schizophrenics, and drug addicts.

Marital adjustment is relevant to treatment planning for married individuals with psychiatric disorders such as phobias and affective disorders (Clarkin, Haas, and Glick 1992), as well as those couples who present with marital difficulties. Among several useful self-report instruments in this area are the Dyadic Adjustment Scale (DAS) (Spanier 1976) and the Marital Satisfaction Inventory (MSI) (Snyder, Willis, and Keiser 1979).

Assessment of Therapeutic Enabling Factors

Based on a review of psychotherapy and treatment outcome research (Beutler 1983; Beutler and Clarkin 1990; Gaw and Beutler 1995), several nondiagnostic factors have demonstrated relevance to state-of-the-art treatment planning. Psychological tests can be useful in assessing these factors. One can isolate five areas of assessment: (1) problem severity, (2) motivational distress, (3) problem complexity, (4) resistance potential or reactance level, and (5) coping style. These areas are discussed in the following paragraphs.

Problem severity is defined as a continuum of functioning ranging from little impairment to incapacitation. Instruments reviewed in this chapter for assessing symptoms and general functioning are appropriate measures of problem severity. Motivational distress is one aspect of problem severity and is defined as the degree of subjective disturbance experienced by the patient in reference to his/her problems. Motivational distress is important because it marshals help-seeking activity such as psychotherapy to reduce discomfort. The Global Severity Index (GSI) of the Brief Symptom Inventory (BSI) (Derogatis 1992) is an efficient method of assessing aspects of a patient's subjective distress level. It is suggested that when the GSI value exceeds a T-score of 63, a treatment that is designed to reduce subjective distress is indicated (Derogatis 1992). If distress levels are low, the clinician must consider confronting the patient with the contradiction of low distress in the face of impairment. The MMPI-2 can also be used to assess motivation distress (Graham 1990).

Problem complexity relates to the pervasiveness and the chronicity of the problem. The BSI offers data on the degree to which the problem spreads across several areas, as this is one aspect of complexity. The MMPI-2 two-point code types (Graham 1990) and the Axis II indicators from the MCMI-II may also inform clinicians on the breadth and pervasiveness of problems.

Reactance, a construct that comes from social psychology, indicates how oppositional or open a patient may be to advice, suggestion, and recommendations from authority figures such as clinicians. One of the most promising tests for assessing reactance is the Therapeutic Reactance Scale (TRS) (Dowd, Milne, and Wise 1991). It is a twenty-eight-item self-report instrument, and there have been two normative studies.

Coping style is defined as the way a patient regulates and modulates anxiety, anger, and other emotions. The MMPI-2 is helpful in identifying the patient's coping styles along an internalizing-externalizing continuum. Externalizing patterns are indicated by the Hy, Pd, Pa, and Ma scales. Internalizing coping styles are indicated by the Hs, B, Pt, and Si scales.

Cultural Factors in Psychological Assessment

The results from the psychological tests described previously must be carefully considered in the context of the culture, subculture, gender, age, and linguistic competence of the patient. The Multicultural Assessment Procedure (MAP) (Ridley, Li, and Hill 1998) has been developed as a flexible and pragmatic clinical procedure that allows clinicians to incorporate cultural data into the assessment process. The principles of the procedure can be applied to all clinical data, from a standard interview or from psychological testing. The four phases of MAP are as follows:

1. Identify Cultural Data. Data obtained during the initial interview include the following cultural variables: level of acculturation, economic issues, history of oppression, language, experience of racism and prejudice, sociopolitical issues (e.g., citizenship status and level of political activity), methods of child-rearing, religious and spiritual practices, family composition, and cultural values (e.g., attitudes toward time, property, family, work, gender, sexuality, and leisure).
2. Interpreting the Cultural Data. The clinician arrives at a working hypothesis regarding the impact of cultural variables on the patient's clinical presentation. The working hypothesis requires a careful consideration of the relative contributions of the patient's current stressors, clinical presentation, experience with discrimination, psychiatric history, and reality testing.
3. Incorporate Cultural Data. The working hypothesis is measured against additional data and criteria. This can include medical evaluation, psychological tests, and DSM-IV diagnostic criteria.
4. Arrive at a Sound Assessment Decision. Once the working hypothesis has been tested with additional data, one can assert an assessment and treatment plan that has meaningfully and fairly incorporated the cultural data. In this manner, the clinician can guard against cultural bias continuously during the assessment process.

Despite the importance of cultural factors in the assessment process, few tests have been adequately developed to address the test biases that could influence such important clinical decisions as diagnosis, severity of psychopathology, and intelligence/achievement levels. However, the MMPI-2 is an instrument that has been restandardized and normed on adolescents, ethnic minority groups, non-English cultures, and the elderly (Butcher 1998). It is recommended in personality assessment within diverse cultures. Also, intelligence can be assessed in a culturally and linguistically fair manner by using nonverbal tests of intelligence or by utilizing an interpreter during the testing process.

In order for a test to be valid across culturally diverse patient populations, the test should exhibit the following psychometric properties: translation from English to the patient's native language, subsequent norms and validation of the translated test, and demonstration of relevance to the new cultural group (Geisinger 1994).

Psychological Assessment in the Contemporary Health Care Climate

Because of its methodological rigor and psychometric sophistication, psychological assessment has the potential to become central to the mental health care system. In response to rapidly escalating health care costs of the last forty years, businesses, legislators, and consumers have identified cost containment as a top priority (Fonagy 1999; Moreland, Fowler, and Honaker 1994). In the United States, managed care, with its utilization reviews and profit-oriented focus, has moved in to address the cost-containment needs with jarring speed and mixed success. For better or worse, third-party payers are demanding that services become time-limited, problem-focused, and "medically necessary." By these standards, traditional psychological assessment has come to be viewed as a superfluous and unnecessary cost and has therefore had to change significantly in focus.

Psychological assessment has survived in this era, and it will continue to do so, insofar as it contributes to cost-containment mechanisms, quality improvement, and consumer satisfaction in health care settings (Moreland, Fowler, and Honaker 1994). Consequently, the following areas, which assessment has begun to address in systematic and rigorous ways, are the hallmarks of sound psychological assessment: (1) treatment planning, (2) ongoing assessment of the impact of treatment and outcome assessment, (3) quality assurance within and across institutions, and (4) screening for psychiatric disturbance (Ben-Porath 1997; Berman and Hurt 1999; Fonagy 1999).

In treatment planning, psychological assessment can systematically inform clinicians and reviewers about the most cost-effective treatment. This relates to such questions as "What level of care is most appropriate for this patient at this time — inpatient, partial hospital, intensive outpatient, or outpatient?" For example, a nonpsychologist clinician may, if familiar with them, use such instruments as the Beck Depression Inventory (BDI) and the Reasons for Living Scale (RFL) to assess a patient's suicide potential and then use the results of these tests to articulate what level of care is needed to address this patient's suicidality.

Once treatment has begun, routine, standardized psychological assessment can track the progress and impact of treatment among individuals and groups. Many efficient, easy-to-administer, omnibus measures have been developed that, with computerized databases, can quickly assess changes in patients' symptoms, behaviors, quality of life, and functional levels during the treatment process. With these data, the mental health professional can make informed decisions as to whether the current treatment is having an effect or whether another approach should be considered. Take, for example, the depressed patient with a BDI score of 24 and few Reasons for Living at the outset of treatment. If these measures were administered by the clinician at monthly intervals, that clinician would have reliable and valid indicators of the impact of treatment. These data would allow for convincing communication to reviewers as to the continued need for treatment and as to the effect of the current treatment.

Related to the ongoing impact of treatment, outcome assessment addresses the immediate and long-term stability of improvements in patients and groups. At the end of treatment and after, psychological assessment can be utilized to address such questions as "How permanent are the patient's improvements in symptoms of depression? And, with improvements in mood, has the patient's ability to work and have relationships improved (functional level)?" Insofar as recidivism, relapse, and short-term treatment effects are a major financial drain, any health care system that is serious about containing costs must grapple with long-term outcome on functional level after treatment has ended, even if patients appear to improve symptoms and behavior adequately in the short term.

Quality assurance appears at this time to be defined primarily by the satisfaction of the health care consumer; it can be argued, however, that this alone is an inadequate measure of quality. Regardless, psychological assessment has the ability to systematically track patient satisfaction for accrediting agencies, such as the Joint Committee on Health Care Accreditation, that require this information. Ideally, these data can be observed along with other outcome data such as symptoms, behaviors, and quality of life.

Within the last several years, mental health tracking systems have been developed to collect data that are useful for clinicians (treatment planning), administrators (efficiency of clinicians in delivering care), and third-party payers, employers, and accrediting agencies (patient satisfaction and outcome assessment). The Integra outpatient mental-health tracking system called Compass, one of the most well-developed tracking systems, is based upon a model of patient treatment response (Howard, Lueger, and Maling 1993). The Menninger Clinic has implemented its own system, originally started in Britain (Fonagy 1999), which is a computerized online health information record that is methodologically and psychometrically sophisticated. By gathering systematic and sequential data, these systems provide information for utilization review regarding the need for additional treatment. They can also be used to assess the clinicians' performance in relation to cost and to identify clinicians who are efficient or inefficient in intervening with different types of individuals. These systems focus on patient processes and outcomes that are of interest to employers as well, among them alleviation of symptom distress, reduction of health care expenses, and reduction of absenteeism.

In summary, psychological assessment in the health care system of the twenty-first century will likely become more prominent in determining the cost-effectiveness of treatments for mental and physical health as the demand for rigorous and systematic documentation of treatment effects remains a priority. One can thus predict that psychological assessment will continue to evolve to address individual, group, and institutional variables, will become more rapid and focused, will rely heavily on computerized administration, scoring, and database management, and will address not just symptoms and behavior in the short term but also functional level and quality of life in the long term. In addition, psychological and biological assessments will continue to become more integrated through neuropsychological assessment. Finally, considering these trends, nonpsychologist clinicians will need to become better acquainted with, and trained in, the principles and uses of rigorous, empirically sound psychological assessment.

12 Psychotropic Medications

Sharon Hird

The increased availability and variety of psychotropic medications over the last half century have advanced our ability to treat a wide range of mental disorders with good results, in a generally safe way, and have given the clinician the ability to offer hope to clients who otherwise might continue to experience uncomfortable symptoms, including dysfynctional behavior. If one medication fails, it is quite likely that there is another that may work. The clinician needs to be aware of when to suggest that medications be considered and should have a general idea of what medications are available, how they work, and, ultimately, what common side effects may emerge during treatment.

Basic Brain Science

The brain is composed of billions of nerve cells, neurons, which communicate with each other via electrical impulses. On the basis of the type of communication received, the neuron is triggered to release a neurotransmitter, which will, in turn, communicate with another neuron at a designated site, where it will bind to a receptor. There are many classes of neurotransmitters, which are responsible for regulating different functions either by exciting or activating brain activity or by inhibiting activity. The quantity, quality, and availability of these neurotransmitters affect mood states, reality perception, and states of arousal and alertness. Psychotropic medications target neurotransmitters either in a broad way, affecting more than one type, or in a specific way, targeting one particular neurotransmitter.

As can neurotransmitters, receptors can be regulated to treat psychiatric conditions through the use of medications that enhance binding, or that block binding, of neurotransmitters or other substances. The body has an inherent mechanism of receptor regulation that is dependent on over- or underuse of receptors, resulting in having more or fewer receptors available on cells for binding. Some medications, called dopamine receptors, work at the receptor site, which allows control of symptoms associated with psychotic processes. Other medications, such as methadone, for substance use disorders act at the receptor site. With the advent of improved technology, knowledge of specific receptors is growing, allowing for the development of medications that act in very selective ways.

After binding to a receptor and initiating an action, the neurotransmitter is released into an area between cells for "processing." Either the neurotransmitter is taken up into neurons via the reuptake pump and repackaged for subsequent release and use, or it is converted to a less complex chemical compound (degraded) by enzymatic activity inside the cell after reuptake. Several psychotropic medications act by either inhibiting the reuptake of neurotransmitters or inhibiting the enzymatic degradation of the neurotransmitter. Both of these actions permit continued activity at receptor sites by increasing the availability of neurotransmitters.

In summary, psychotropic medications work at multiple levels of the brain's architecture and sites of activity. The complexity of brain activity is both challenging and frustrating. The good understanding of the biology of many mental disorders that currently exists allows for selection of appropriate medication(s). Information can be conveyed to clients and to families in a way that makes taking medication less of a stigma. Brain science is an exploding field, and in the future, DNA activity may be regulated, making treatment more effective.

Biological Treatments for Mental Disorders

Psychotropic medications are often necessary additions to psychotherapeutic interventions. Use of psychotropic medication helps to alleviate symptoms that accompany such disorders as major depression, schizophrenia, bipolar disorder, obsessive-compulsive disorder, and anxiety disorders. Without the use of medications, psychotherapy often cannot proceed in a viable or timely manner. It is difficult to engage a patient in treatment when the symptoms interfere. A person with even subtle psychotic symptoms may not be able to concentrate during sessions or follow through with suggestions. Without medication, the depressed patient may not be able to participate in behavioral change during a cognitive-behavioral treatment or to deal with issues of self-worth during insight-oriented therapy. Similarly, a patient suffering from anxiety, especially panic or phobic disorders, may not even be able to keep appointments regularly. Consequently, it is important for all clinicians to know when to seek a medication consultation as well as have some knowledge of the various available psychotropic medications.

The following sections will provide a brief overview of medications that are commonly used in the treatment of various mental disorders. This discussion is not meant to be comprehensive. Rather it permits a general acquaintance with a number of frequently used medications that could be prescribed if a consultation is requested, and it discusses what positive and negative side effects might be expected.

Depressive Disorders and Antidepressant Medication

Although treatment with antidepressant medication is indicated for several mental disorders, it is especially useful in decreasing or eliminating symptoms of a major depressive episode, a dysthymic disorder, or the depressed phase of bipolar disorder. According to the fourth edition of the *Diagnostic and Statistical Manual of Mental Disorders* (DSM-IV) (American Psychiatric Association 1994), a major depressive episode is characterized by a persistently depressed mood or marked loss of interest or pleasure in most usual activities daily for a period of at least two weeks and representing a change from previous functioning. It is accompanied by at least four of the following symptoms:

appetite disturbance, which may result in a significant weight change
sleep disturbance
psychomotor agitation or retardation
fatigue or loss of energy
feelings of worthlessness or excessive guilt
difficulty concentrating or indecisiveness
frequent thoughts of death or suicide
possibly delusions or hallucinations

If left untreated, the average depressive episode lasts from six to thirteen months; most treated episodes resolve within three months. Fifty to 75 percent of affected persons have a second episode, often within the first six months after the initial episode. The average number of depressive episodes over a twenty-year period is five to six. Alarmingly, 10 to 15 percent of persons with depression eventually commit suicide (Kaplan, Sadock, and Grebb 1994). Given the natural course of depression and the frequency of recurrences, the clinician must be prepared to enter into discussion about maintenance therapy. Often, as a person begins to feel better on medication, he or she feels ready to stop the medication; it is generally believed, however, that medication should be continued for at least six months after the depression appears to subside. Some persons, in the course of the depression, may require more than one medication to achieve adequate control of symptoms, and clinicians must help the person to avoid viewing this as a failure on the part of either the person or the clinician. The client, and the family, need to be informed about the natural course of depression and the need to stay on medication in order to prevent another episode.

Dysthymic disorder, although not as severe in intensity as a major depressive disorder, may be just as disabling, given the chronicity of the condition. In some aspects, dysthymia may be more disabling, in that the person may have no recall for feeling anything other than dysthymic and may consider this state "normal." In addition, because there is no dramatic change in function or feeling with dysthymia, people may not recognize the existence of a disorder, and as such, may be very resistant to discussing medication. Clinicians need to be sensitive to this and need to recognize that it may take many sessions to educate the client, and the family, about the need for a medication consultation. The DSM-IV criteria for dysthymia include a depressed mood, more days than not, of at least two years' duration, accompanied by at least two other symptoms such as sleep disturbance, appetite disturbance, fatigue, poor self-esteem, indecisiveness, poor concentration, or feelings of hopelessness.

Pharmacological intervention for depression is targeted at the neurotransmitter system and interacts at a variety of levels with different neurotransmitter receptors. Depending on the site of action, a variety of classic responses and side effects can be expected. In working with clients who are on medication, the clinician must be aware of some basic information to ensure safety, improve compliance, and be able to have effective discussions about the client's progress with the consulting psychiatrist. In general, it is important to know about all medications that the person is taking, including nonpsychiatric medications, as well as the client's general medical status. It is possible that this information could contraindicate the use of some psychotropic medications. It is not uncommon for a patient to experience symptoms that are consistent with depression but that are in fact a side effect of another medication, such as medications to control high blood pressure. It is also not uncommon for the client to share information with the primary therapist that was not shared with the consultant, because of either anxiety or resistance. While the consultant will manage drug-drug interactions, the primary clinician should be kept informed of changes in nonpsychotropic medications made by any of the person's health care providers, and the client should be reminded to inform the consulting psychiatrist. Communication of this information helps alert the therapist to possible mood changes and the possibility that another medication review may be needed. The primary clinician probably spends more time with the client than the consultant does, and thus may be more aware of changes that may indicate the need for dosage adjustment. Often, once the patient is stabilized on a given dose of medication, the consultant will decrease the frequency of visits with the client and will rely on the primary therapist to recognize changes in mood. Medications often reach an effective plateau at a given dose, and there is no way to predict if and when this will occur; it is important, however, to be aware that it usually will occur. If a client who had been doing well on a medication begins to present with signs and symptoms similar to those experienced in the untreated state, the clinician must consider whether the dose needs adjusting, the medication needs to be changed, or the client has stopped taking the medication. People stop taking medication for a variety of reasons. Most frequently, negative side effects are responsible for noncompliance. Negative side effects can be something as minimal as dry mouth; something annoying and potentially difficult to discuss, such as sexual dysfunction; or something disabling, such as the emergence of anxiety symptoms or insomnia.

A large number and variety of antidepressant medications are available, including tricyclic and heterocyclic antidepressants, monoamine oxidase inhibitors (MAOIs), selective serotonin reuptake inhibitors (SSRIs), and several atypical agents. Controlled studies have shown these medications to be 60 to 80 percent effective in nonpsychotic depressions, and often clients who fail to respond to an adequate trial of one medication do respond when treated with an antidepressant from a different class. The cause of treatment nonresponse may actually result from an inadequate dose of the medication given for too brief a period of time for a response, since antidepressants generally require two to four weeks to take effect. Sometimes patients report improvement almost immediately, an event that can be considered a placebo response; the newer medications, however, can in fact begin to be effective before the expected two-week mark. Choosing an antidepressant depends on several factors, such as previous response to a particular medication, a family member's response to this medication, side effects, and safety. On occasion, an antidepressant will be chosen because of a particular side effect, such as sedation, which can be useful for patients with insomnia or agitation as part of their depressive symptomatology. Table 12.1 shows the currently available antidepressants, their major site of action, and their potential side effects.

There has been much media coverage about people becoming violent, even homicidal or suicidal, or having a personality change, as a result of taking antidepressants. Patients who have been severely depressed with poor self-esteem, thoughts of death and suicide, and very low energy can become "activated," with more energy from taking the medication, and they may be at risk for destructive behavior. This *possibility* is true for any class of anti-depressant, and the clinician must be sensitive to this phenomenon, although such a reaction is infrequent.

Personalities, per se, do not change as a result of using antidepressants. However, when a dysthymic individual, who by definition experiences chronic low-grade depression, is successfully treated and has an improved mood with a higher level of functioning, it may be experienced as a "personality change." While the core personality is generally stable, the ability to make decisions, think with clarity, concentrate, and have improved self-esteem may enable the person to achieve goals that he or she previously thought of as unattainable.

Educating the person and the family about the symptoms of depression and the expected effects of medication, and maintaining contact with the consultant while providing psychotherapy will offer the person the best chance for successful management of depressive disorders.

Electroconvulsive Therapy (ECT)

No chapter on biological treatments for psychiatric disorders would be complete without a discussion of electroconvulsive therapy (ECT). ECT is an effective treatment for acute episodes of severe depression and may also provide prevention against its recurrence. ECT yields a quicker therapeutic response and may have fewer adverse effects than treatment with antide-

TABLE 12.1 Antidepressant Medications

Medication class and name	Major mechanism of action	Potential side effects
Tricyclics (TCAs): Amitriptyline (Elavil) Doxepin (Sinequan) Desipramine (Norpramine) Protriptyline (Vivactil) Imipramine (Tofranil) Clomipramine (Anafranil)	Inhibit the reuptake of neuro-transmitters, primarily norepinephrine and serotonin. Results in increased availability.	Sedation, orthostatic hypotension (a sudden drop in blood pressure on standing up), dry mouth, increased heart rate, blurred vision, constipation, urinary retention, and cardiac dysrhythmias. Cardiotaxic side effects may be fatal in overdose.
Monoamine Oxidase Inhibitors (MAOIs): Phenelzine (Nardil) Tranylcypromine (Parnate) Isocarbolxazid (Marplan)	Block the enzymatic degradation of norepinephrine and serotonin. Results in increased availability.	Hypertensive crisis resulting from interaction with food containing tyramine (aged cheeses, aged or processed meats, pickled or salted herring, fava beans, sauerkraut, liver) or certain medications (stimulants, decongestants, other antidepressants, narcotics). Also, decreased blood pressure, postural hypotension, weight gain, sedation or agitation, insomnia, impotence, and anorgasmia.

pressants does. Since the primary risks are minor and tend to be related to anesthesia, it can be the safest treatment in certain circumstances, including pregnancy and old age, for persons who are at high risk for suicidal behavior

TABLE 12.1 Antidepressant Medications *(continued)*		
Medication class and name	**Major mechanism of action**	**Potential side effects**
Selective Serotonin Reuptake Inhibitors (SSRIs): Fluoxetine (Prozac) Sertraline (Zoloft) Paroxetine (Paxil) Citalopram (Celexa) Fluvoxamine (Luvox)	Selectively block the reuptake of the neuro-transmitter serotonin.	Anxiety, restlessness, insomnia, tremor, headache, nausea, diarrhea, weight loss, inhibition of ejaculation, anorgasmia.
Atypical Agents: Trazodone (Desyrel) Nefazadone (Serzone) Venlafaxine (Effexor) Bupropion (Wellbutrin) Mirtazapine (Remeron)	Combination of receptor blockade and serotonin reuptake inhibition.	orthostatic hypotension, dizziness, dry mouth, sedation, appetite increase or decrease with weight gain or loss, seizures, dangerously low white blood cell count.

Many of these agents are completely unrelated and therefore not all side effects are associated with each medication; and side effects can be dose-dependent; consult with the administering MD or the PDR.

and for those who are rapidly deteriorating physically and/or psychologically from depression. Delusional or psychotic depressions, when the response to antidepressants alone is poor, are particularly responsive to ECT. Depressions with features of melancholia and markedly severe symptoms, such as psychomotor retardation or agitation, early-morning awakening, symptoms that are worse on awakening and improve later in the day, and decreased appetite with weight loss, are also most likely to respond well to ECT.

The main side effect of ECT is a treatment-related amnesia for events occurring during the course of the treatments. Unless there is an underlying dementia, in almost all cases full memory returns in a few weeks following the final treatment. The average course of treatment is a total of six to twelve weeks, usually three times per week and ideally as an inpatient. Maintenance ECT for prevention against recurring depression, usually for the elderly, generally is once a month as an outpatient, as memory loss is in most cases not a problem.

In addition to major depression and dysthymia, other indications for ECT include mania, schizophrenic disorders, catatonia, and mood disturbances secondary to an underlying organic process.

Bipolar Disorders, Cyclothymia, and Mood Stabilizers

According to DSM-IV, mania is a distinct period of abnormally and persistently elevated, expansive, or irritable mood of at least one week's duration that significantly impairs occupational and social functioning. The period of mood disturbance is also accompanied by three or four of the following symptoms:

inflated self-esteem
decreased need for sleep
a pressure to keep talking
flight of ideas or racing thoughts
distractibility
increased social, work, or sexual activity or psychomotor agitation
excessive involvement in activities that can lead to distressing conse-
    quences, such as spending sprees, reckless driving, foolish busi-
    ness decisions, or sexual indiscretion
possibility of psychotic features such as auditory hallucinations, delu-
    sions, or paranoid ideation

Hypomania is similarly defined, except that the episode is not severe enough to cause marked impairment in functioning or necessitate hospitalization. The hypomanic period may not occur as a discrete episode of mania. Similar to dysthymia, hypomanic states may be somewhat chronic and viewed very much as a personality disorder. The hypomanic patient may be the classic example of someone with "high energy" or individuals we regard as "overachievers." Unlike manic episodes, which represent a clear-cut need for pharmacological intervention, hypomania may not require medication. The clinician may suggest medication consultation for hypomania if the associated behaviors escalate in nature, if there is a change in behavior, or if the client finds the condition to be distressing.

When manic or hypomanic states occur with a past history of depressive illness, the condition is classified as a form of bipolar disorder or cyclothymic

disorder. Untreated manic episodes can last three to six months, with significant rates of recurrence. Over a lifetime, an individual may have from
two to thirty episodes of mania, with an average of nine recurrences. Eighty
to 90 percent of people with mania eventually experience a full depressive
episode, and at least 10 percent of people with bipolar disorder commit
suicide. There is also a very high association of bipolar disorder with substance abuse and dependence.

To meet criteria for a diagnosis of cyclothymia, alternating symptoms of
hypomania and depression must occur over at least a two-year period. It is
more common for persons with cyclothymia to seek treatment with complaints of marital problems, unstable relationships, or career difficulties than
with a complaint about mood states.

It can be extremely difficult to encourage persons with hypomania to seek
medication consultation, and equally as difficult to keep manic individuals
compliant. People often feel "good" when experiencing mania or hypomania
because these states, when not out of control, offer times of high productivity,
creativity, increased feelings of self-worth, and a sense of general well-being.
It is not uncommon for a person with bipolar disorder, stabilized with medication, to complain of feeling dull or numb on medication, or to feel less
productive at work or even dysthymic. Sometimes these feelings are a result
of the stark contrast between affect states, and the individual needs time to
adjust; at other times these feelings are quite real. Such complaints very
often lead to medication noncompliance and ultimately to recurrence of
dangerous states. Without intervention, clients often seek situations or substances that reproduce a manic-like state. It is helpful to work with the consulting psychopharmacologist to adjust medications so that the client can
feel a little energized without becoming manic, but achieving this balance
is often a difficult task.

A number of excellent mood stabilizers are available to treat bipolar disorder. With the exception of lithium, they are anticonvulsant medications,
which the person may need to take for life. All of them can have distressing
and sometimes dangerous side effects, and they require careful monitoring.
Clients with bipolar disorder may require more than a mood stabilizer: often
an antidepressant is used in low dose, or an antipsychotic for delusions or
paranoid ideation may be required during an acute state. It is useful to know
that these adjunct medications may be needed for only a short period and
can be tapered off or discontinued when called for, or used as part of maintenance therapy. It is prudent to have reevaluations or new consultations for
people who have been on polypharmacy regimes for long periods. It is not

uncommon for people who have been on many medications to remain on medication because they are viewed as very sick and in need of polypharmacy by virtue of using polypharmacy. Some clinicians may be reluctant to change medications, fearing a recurrence, but with a careful review of symptoms adjustments can be made that reduce side effects and keep the patient stable. Table 12.2 outlines the important mood stabilizers and their side effects.

Other disorders that may respond to mood stabilizers, either as the primary therapy or as part of a treatment complex, include schizophrenia, depression, schizoaffective disorder, intermittent explosive disorder, and personality disorders characterized by loss of impulse control. Mood stabilizers, primarily the anticonvulsants, are also used for pain syndromes, and are beginning to be used as part of the treatment for substance abuse disorders.

Schizophrenia, Psychotic Disorders, and Antipsychotics

The primary indication for use of antipsychotics is the presence of psychosis in a number of conditions, including schizophrenia, schizoaffective disorder, delusional disorder, brief psychotic disorder (which may be present in a number of personality disorders), mood disorders with psychotic features, or psychotic disturbance secondary to an underlying medical condition or substance use disorders, resulting from severe intoxication or during withdrawal.

Schizophrenia can be viewed as the prototypical psychotic disorder, certainly when considering psychotic symptoms and medication intervention. For purposes of this discussion, the symptoms associated with the schizophrenic process and the medications available for treatment will serve as the model. The salient features of this disorder and the medications used to treat those symptoms will be reviewed. Persons with schizophrenia will require at least low doses of medication for life to prevent recurrence.

Schizophrenia is a disorder of unknown etiology, but with a genetic and possibly a viral origin. It is characterized by psychotic symptoms that significantly impair the ability to function and that involve disturbances in feeling, thinking, and behavior. *DSM-IV* describes the condition as being present for at least six months, during which there is a deterioration in functioning in work, school, self-care, and interpersonal relations. During the active phase of the disorder the classic positive symptoms of delusions, hallucinations, disorganized thoughts and behavior are observable. Negative symptoms include flat affect, poverty of speech, lack of motivation, and social

TABLE 12.2 Mood Stabilizers		
Medication class and name	**Major mechanism of action**	**Potential Side effects**
Salt or Carbonate: Lithium	Effects calcium activity, which changes cellular electrical charge, affects neurotransmitter release, and stabilizes cell membranes.	Thirst, increased urination, nausea, diarrhea, hand tremor, renal damage, electrolyte imbalance, hypothyroidism, seizure activity, and cardiac toxicity. Blood levels must be monitored, as toxicity is level-dependent and can be fatal.
Anticonvulsants: Carbamazepine (Tegretol) Valproate (Depakote) Gabapentin (Neurontin)	Exact mechanism unknown.	Both Tegretol and Depakote can have toxic effects on liver and bone marrow and require blood level monitoring. They can both cause nausea, vomiting, and sedation. Tegretol can cause blurry vision, ataxia, and dizziness. Depakote can cause hand tremor, weight gain, and hair loss. Both may cause birth defects. Neurontin can cause fatigue, sedation, dizziness, and ataxia; does not require blood monitoring

withdrawal. It is these negative symptoms that have been the most difficult to treat pharmacologically. The older, more traditional antipsychotic medications effectively treat the "positive" symptoms, but have little impact on the "negative" symptoms, which keep the person unable to function well after the resolution of the "positive" symptoms. Now, a number of new "atypical" antipsychotics are more effective in treating the "negative" symptoms without introducing the severe side effects of the earlier antipsychotic medications.

These older, typical antipsychotics bond to, and block, dopamine neurotransmitter receptors. They are generally classified by their potency and the side effects related to this. The low-potency antipsychotics, such as chlorpromazine (Thorazine), thiroidazine (Mellaril), and mesoridazine (Serentil), have the side effects of sedation, orthostatic hypotension, dry mouth, blurred vision, constipation, and increased heart rate. A high dose is needed to obtain the desired clinical effect, necessitating multiple doses during the day, which allows for increased noncompliance. Often, the low-potency medications are used for their sedating qualities in situations when the patient is agitated or aggressive. Commonly prescribed high-potency medications include haloperidol (Haldol), fluphenazine (Prolixin), and pimozide (Orap). Mid-potency medications include perphenazine (Trilafon), thiothixene (Navane), and trifluoperazine (Stelazine).

The mid- and high-potency medications can produce such side effects as muscular stiffness, spasms, fixed gaze, difficulty in swallowing; slowness of motion, rigid muscles and movements, shuffling gait, masklike face; subjective feeling of restlessness with the need for pacing and other signs of agitation. Many of these side effects can be mistaken for mental conditions, particularly the blunted affect, slowness of motion (which can be associated with depression), and restlessness and agitation (which can easily be confused with anxiety). Some of these side effects can be ameliorated with the use of additional medications, by adjusting the dose, or by switching medications.

One of the most serious side effects associated with typical antipsychotics is NMS, neuroleptic malignant syndrome, which can be life-threatening. It develops rapidly over a few days and is characterized by high fever, marked stiffness of muscles, blood pressure instability, rapid pulse, and change in mental status, which can lead to stupor. NMS is more associated with the high-potency medications, occurs most often early in treatment, and requires immediate medical attention. Another serious side effect of the older antipsychotics is tardive dyskinesia (TD), which can occur after prolonged use of medication. This side effect consists of involuntary movements of the tongue, jaw, lips, face, upper and lower extremities, trunk, or various muscle groups involved in breathing or swallowing. It may be reversible, but it usually persists for years even if medication is discontinued. Persons with chronic schizophrenia may be faced with the difficult choice of either suffering from symptoms of the disorder *or* developing tardive dyskinesia.

Persons who have been in the psychiatric system for any length of time or who have had uncomfortable reactions to antipsychotic medications in the past may be extraordinarily reluctant to see a consultant for medications. The clinician may hear of "allergies" that clients have to the above medications or realistic fears of developing severe side effects. Knowledge of the newer, "atypical" medications can be useful at this point, as many of the classic side effects are not associated with this group. It is important to work with consultants who are comfortable prescribing the newer medications. Physicians often "grow up" with a certain cluster of medications—that is, they have been using medication class "X" for years, have had generally good results, and may be reluctant to work with new medications. Thus matching clients and consultants can be a challenge. The referring clinician must take into account personality styles, schedules, and some degree of flexibility about medication in both the client and the consultant.

The newer, atypical antipsychotics, often not used enough as "first line" because of the expense, have changed the face of treating schizophrenia and other psychotic disorders. The side effects are fewer, and very often the same drug can treat both the positive and the negative symptoms. Some of these medications, such as risperidone (Risperdal) and olanzapine (Zyprexa), work at both the dopamine and the serotonin sites, thus treating negative symptoms. Others, such as clozapine (Clozaril) work on very select dopamine receptor sites. Because of the decrease in uncomfortable side effects as well as broader treatment of symptoms with these medications, there is a likelihood of greater medication compliance and potential for a higher level of functioning. Ironically, some patients are uncomfortable without the presence of psychotic symptoms. Chronically ill individuals often compensate for the illness by accommodating to the symptoms, structuring their behaviors and daily activities around the symptoms, such as sleeping during the day and staying awake at night when some symptoms are worsened by the quiet and the dark. Some patients even miss their auditory hallucinations, for when the voices are no longer present, there is a sense of loss of companionship. Working with a creative consultant on such cases is vital, as is offering a supportive, structured, and consistent environment for the patient. Table 12.3 provides an overview of the major antipsychotics and their side effects.

One advantage of some of the older antipsychotic medications is their availability in injection form. Thorazine, Haldol, and Prolixin can be used intramuscularly during acute situations that require fast relief of symptoms.

TABLE 12.3 Antipsychotics	
Medication class and name	**Potential side effects**

Low potency:
  Chlorpromazine (Thorazine)
  Thioridazine (Mellaril)
  Mesoridazine (Serentil)
	Sedation, orthostatic hypotension, dry mouth, increased heart rate, blurred vision, constipation, urinary retention, cardiac toxicity.

Medium and high potency:
  Perphenazine (Trilafon)
  Thiothixene (Navane)
  Trifluoperazine (Stelazine)
	Acute dystonic reactions, Parkinsonian symptoms, akathisia, lactation, neuroleptic malignant syndrome, tardive dyskinesia.

Also Halperidol (Haldol)
  Fluphenazine (Prolixin)
  Pimozide (Orap)
	Some of the side effects associated with low-potency medications (dry mouth, constipation, blurred vision)

Receptor Selective: Clozapine (Clozaril)	Agranulocytosis, dangerously low white blood cell count, which requires monitoring with weekly expensive blood tests to determine whether the medication can be safely continued. Also, orthostatic hypotension, sedation, increased salivation, seizures, NMS and TD

Atypical medications:
  Risperidone (Risperdal)
  Olanzapine (Zyprexa)
  Quetiapine (Seroquel)
  Sertindole (Serlect)
	Acute dystonic reactions, Parkinsonian symptoms, insomnia, anxiety, dizziness, headaches, dry mouth, sedation, increased appetite and weight gain (with Zyprexa).

Additionally, Haldol and Prolixin are available in a long-lasting form allowing for injections to be administered monthly for Haldol and every two weeks for Prolixin. This is an excellent form of medication delivery for the severely ill and noncompliant patient. Manufacturers of some of the atypical antipsychotics are currently working on creating similar forms of these drugs.

Anxiety Disorders, Benzodiazepines, Buspirone, and SSRIs

Anxiety disorders are a group of disorders characterized by a feeling of dread, and often accompanied by physical complaints. The five types of anxiety disorders include panic disorder, generalized anxiety disorder, phobic disorders, obsessive-compulsive disorder, and posttraumatic stress disorder. Additionally, depression can have associated features of anxiety as part of the symptom complex. Anxiety is a normal and appropriate response to many situations in its nonpathological form. We have all experienced anxiety, with increased heart rate, sweating, abdominal cramps, insomnia, and mildly obsessive thoughts during times of heightened stress, such as taking exams, getting married, buying a house, fearing a physical illness, or interviewing for a job. When the anxiety state occurs in extreme proportions, without an external stimulus, or for prolonged periods, thus interfering with function, the need for medication may arise. Usually medication is continued for three to six months after symptoms subside.

Panic disorder is characterized by the sudden and recurrent onset of massive anxiety in the form of panic attacks that have no precipitating factor. A panic attack is a discrete period in which there is an unexpected onset of intense apprehension, terror, and feelings of impending doom. Symptoms such as shortness of breath, palpitations, chest pain, choking, and fear of losing control or "going crazy" may be present. There may or may not be associated agoraphobia, a fear of being in open spaces, going outside the home alone, or being caught in a crowd. Because of the unexpected nature of the attacks, there is often secondary anticipatory anxiety, which may lead to avoidance behaviors, which further limit the individual's ability to function.

Generalized anxiety disorder, which may or may not be accompanied by panic attacks, is characterized by at least six months of persistent and excessive anxiety and worry. It is distinguished by at least three of the following symptoms: restlessness or feeling on edge, fatigue, trouble concentrating, irritability, muscle tension, and sleep disturbance.

Phobic disorders are marked by intense anxiety provoked by the thought of exposure to a feared object or situation, resulting in the need to avoid it. The two types of phobic disorders are specific and social. Specific phobia is characterized by a marked and persistent fear of a clearly discernible, circumscribed object or situation. The fear is excessive and unreasonable, and exposure, or the thought of such exposure, to the phobic stimulus provokes an immediate anxiety response. Social phobia is excessive fear of social or performance situations, such as attending school, going to a party, or performing in public, which the person fears will result in embarrassment.

Obsessive-compulsive disorder is characterized by recurrent obsessions or compulsions that are severe enough to be time-consuming, cause distress, or result in significant impairment in functioning. Obsessions are persistent, often intrusive, and repetitive ideas, thoughts, impulses, or images that are experienced as inappropriate and uncomfortable but recognized as the product of one's own mind as opposed to hallucinations. Compulsions are repetitive behaviors, such as hand washing or checking locks and appliances, or mental acts such as praying or counting, with the goal of preventing or reducing anxiety or distress resulting from the obsessions.

Posttraumatic stress disorder is characterized by the reexperiencing of a traumatic event, either recent or remote, and is generally associated with intrusive images or thoughts of the event, flashbacks, illusions, or hallucinations. It is also often accompanied by symptoms of increased arousal manifested by a hypersensitivity to sounds or sights and avoidance of stimuli associated with the trauma.

It is clear from the above descriptions that anxiety disorders can be severely incapacitating. Symptoms can be so severe that the individual cannot even seek help. Avoidance behaviors, though maladaptive, can be very powerful in reducing anxiety, making it more difficult to treat. Patients often self-medicate with alcohol or drugs in order to obtain immediate relief of symptoms, thus further compounding treatment difficulties. A variety of effective medications exist that can treat the anxiety disorders generally, as well as medications approved for specific anxiety disorders. As with most other mental disorders, the anxiety disorders may require long-term or maintenance pharmacotherapy to be alleviated. Also as with other mental disorders, the combination of psychotherapy with psychopharmacology is the most effective intervention. This may be particularly true when anxiety disorders are treated with a combination of medication and cognitive-behavioral therapy.

When medication is indicated, the clinician needs to know that some medications work faster than others but are potentially addictive. Some take weeks to work and therefore do not offer quick relief of symptoms, which may make the patient more anxious, and some have side effects, which paradoxically increases anxiety. Overall, the benzodiazepines work almost immediately, but they may require higher and higher dosages as patients reach tolerance of the effect, and they should be used cautiously with patients who have a history of alcohol or drug dependence. Generally, the short-acting benzodiazepines, such as alprazolam (Xanax) and lorazepam (Ativan) are the most addictive, while the longer-acting options, such as clonazepam (Klonopin), are better tolerated. Though a full knowledge of all the many benzodiazepines available is not necessary, the clinician should be aware of the potential side effects: sedation, impaired concentration and memory, lack of inhibitions, depression, addiction and withdrawal syndromes, and the need to avoid use of benzodiazepines when consuming alcohol or operating heavy machinery. Generally, the benzodiazepines are a safe and effective treatment and can be used on an as-needed basis or for maintenance.

Buspirone (Buspar) is a nonbenzodiazepine antianxiety medication that has been shown to be as effective as the benzodiazepines for generalized anxiety disorder. It has no immediate impact on anxiety and needs to be taken regularly for several weeks before results are achieved. It may not be as effective for individuals who have been treated with benzodiazepines in the past, and it is not a first-line medication for panic. It is, however, an excellent primary or adjunct choice for people with a substance use disorder. Possible side effects include dizziness, nausea, headache, nervousness, lightheadedness, and excitement, but it is generally a safe medication.

The tricyclic antidepressant clomipramine (Anafranil) also offers effective treatment of the anxiety disorders. The selective serotonin reuptake inhibitors (SSRIs) fluoxetine (Prozac), sertraline (Zoloft), paroxetine (Paxil), and fluvoxamine (Luvox) all treat anxiety disorders, generally at higher doses than are required for treatment of depression, except for fluvoxamine, which is specifically approved for obsessive-compulsive disorder treatment as well as for depression. With these medications there is a time lapse before decrease in symptoms, and the client may need more frequent visits, support, education, and reassurance during this period. Refer to table 12.1 for mechanisms and side effects when using these medications.

On occasion, anxiety can reach such intense proportions that an antipsychotic is temporarily needed. This may be especially true for clients who suffer from obsessive-compulsive disorder. In addition, the primary clinician should be aware of the fact that individuals who are in the midst of difficult periods in their lives may benefit from a consultation and a short course of antianxiety medication. These are generally clients who are high-functioning individuals who would not ordinarily need medication, but who are experiencing life events that are better tolerated, and have less potential of becoming an impairment, with a brief trial of medication.

Psychiatric Consultation

One of the hallmarks of being a good clinician is knowing when to ask for help. This refers not only to seeking consultation for medication, but in general to evaluation of psychiatric disorders, particularly when a client may be at risk for destructive behaviors. Shifts in mood, sleep and eating patterns, work performance, and interpersonal relationships may indicate the need for medication. Consultation might involve clarification of a diagnosis, evaluation of a medication, or assessment of suicidal or homicidal risk or the need for hospitalization. Making a good referral or obtaining a good consultation can strengthen the alliance with the client and can enhance the support system that may be needed.

It is important to have a good relationship with psychiatric consultants. This involves an open dialogue with frequent updates about the client so that both clinicians are working with the same information. The primary clinician and the consultant should inform each other of any changes in behavior or medications. The consultant should be used as part of the treatment team — or as another treatment modality available to the client.

Epilogue

This is a book about mental disorders written by a social worker for social workers. It is hoped that the reader will come away with a greater awareness of the need for careful psychosocial assessment, which considers the multiplicity of psychosocial variables and is based on individualizing the client, the client's environment, and the client's experiences. Classification systems can never replace assessment obtained through the "fluid, personal process of exchange between people" (Meyer 1993:130).

Kirk and Kutchins (1994) in "Is Bad Writing a Mental Disorder?," a *New York Times* editorial piece criticizing *DSM-IV*, used as an example of the psychiatric thrust to categorize "actions or traits . . .[as] possible symptoms of some disorder" (code 315.2: Disorder of Written Expression). The example supports the premise of this book that classification without assessment is useless for intervention planning. Poor writing skills might be a symptom of a mental disorder, but they are more likely to be found, on assessment, to be the result of a range of social problems, including family; English as a second language; lack of space and other conditions conducive to writing; poor schooling; physical problems; or simple lack of ability. Intervention could be effective only after a thorough assessment had been completed, which might include psychological testing and a physical examination.

Managed care and third-party carriers, with their emphasis on cost-cutting and accountability, seem determined to limit assessment, and thus intervention planning, to decisions made on the basis of classification systems. In addition, with very short medical, or psychiatric, inpatient stays and reim-

bursement for outpatient intervention for persons with mental disorders limited to very few sessions, the time needed to make a thorough biopsychosocial assessment has been greatly reduced. *DSM-IV* may be useful in listing
the symptoms that will suggest what mental disorder may be present, but it
is not contextual and tells nothing about "why" a disorder is present, nor
about "how" to improve adaptation and coping. Thus schools of social work,
together with the training agencies, must respond by teaching students to
make rigorous assessments in as short a time as possible and must avoid
allowing them to be seduced by the simpler, less accurate, parsimonious
process of classification. Time constraints will limit the amount of information that can be obtained, and thus it is essential to develop the skills
necessary to determine what is salient and relevant for the social worker to
learn about in order to understand the person-in-environment.

Besides gathering data by interviewing a client, social workers should
consider adding graphic representations. Meyer (1977) introduced the eco-
map, the first graphic assessment tool, which focuses on the client's present
situation. Additional tools, such as the genogram, which gives a "picture" of
the client's family history, have been developed. Computer graphics have
enabled the development of increasingly sophisticated visual assessment
tools (Mattaini 1993), and it is anticipated that as social workers become
more familiar and comfortable with them, these tools will be most helpful
in enabling the clinician, together with the client, to assemble and consider
the data and plan for the intervention. Graphic depictions can present the
complexity of the case in a simpler way, in that "seeing" the case often makes
it easier, and quicker, to comprehend than reading about it does; it is not
suggested that graphic images replace written assessment, but rather that
they be used, in most cases, as an adjunct.

It is difficult to integrate social work assessment, with its emphasis on
individualization, with classification systems that are often closely linked to
research. Systems such as *DSM-IV* do not lend themselves to consideration
of such important variables as age, ethnicity, gender, culture, and socioeconomic status, which social workers know must be taken into account in order
to understand the whole case and to determine effective interventions.
Tucker (1998) cautions that *DSM* diagnoses have become the main goal of
clinical practice, and thus may be ruining the essence of it. Meyer, noting
the highly complex nature of social work cases, sees "developing social work
classificatory models . . .[as an] enormously difficult task" (1993:106) that
lies ahead. Social workers may find the work of psychiatric epidemiologists
more useful in understanding case phenomena, and in directing future re-

search, than a medically oriented classification system, as the field refines the necessary knowledge base needed to make inferences from case data.

It is hoped that social workers will accept the idea that no classification system can substitute for rigorous psychosocial assessment. An effort has been made in this book to look at how mental disorders develop and what can be done to help the person with a mental disorder (and the person's family) cope and adapt better. The social work profession makes a unique contribution in the provision of mental health services that focus on person and environment. We need to feel pride in this and let our mission guide our practice and our research. Social workers must also be concerned about the approach of managed care, which violates our Code of Ethics by not permitting self-determination with respect to choice of clinician and violates our respect for confidentiality by making information available to up to seventeen persons (many of whom are not professionals) in the review and authorization process (Austrian 1998:326). These concerns present a difficult challenge in today's society, which does not put a premium on the welfare of all its members.

Glossary

Acting out. Use of behavior, rather than words, to express strong feelings in a self-destructive or maladaptive manner.

Agnosia. Deficits in recognition and understanding. Involves failure to recognize changes in oneself and one's functioning in spite of overwhelming evidence. It is usually related to brain damage, with the person seemingly unaware of the illness.

Agonists medications. Drugs that interact with appropriate neurotransmitter receptors with the ability to produce the maximum effect possible by stimulating the receptor.

Akathisia. A state of motor restlessness or an internal sense of restlessness. The sufferer moves constantly—shifting around when seated, crossing or uncrossing legs, shifting from foot to foot—and has a stated inability to relax.

Akinesia. A state of reduced voluntary, spontaneous movement, such as arm swinging or crossing one's legs. There are few spontaneous facial expressions, muscular rigidity, and often tremor.

Alexthymia. Difficulty in describing or recognizing one's emotions, which may be experienced as somatic symptoms or behavioral reactions rather than as thoughts. This *may* be a personality trait.

Alogia. Poverty of speech content or spontaneous speech.

Anhedonia. Inability to derive pleasure from previously pleasurable activities, resulting in loss of interest and withdrawal.

Antagonist medications. Drugs that occupy a receptor and cause inhibition of the actions of a specific agonist.

Aphasia. Impairment in the use and understanding of language, most often seen as a difficulty in finding the correct word.

Apraxia. Inability to perform motor activities that require sequential steps; a disturbance in gait.

Ataxia. Loss, partial or complete, of coordination of voluntary muscular actions.

Attribution. Taking credit for what has or has not been done. May be positive or negative.

Behavior therapy. Therapy based on the hypothesis that maladaptive behavioral patterns result from a person's receiving little positive feedback from others, which when addressed, results in the person's learning to function in ways to receive positive reinforcement.

Blood alcohol level. Percentage of alcohol in the bloodstream in relation to total blood volume; detected by a blood test or a breathalyzer; percentage to be considered as intoxication may vary by state.

Chronic fatigue syndrome. Condition experienced as lethargy, diminished energy, fatigue, and apathy and believed to be associated with anxiety, family or work problems, and especially depression.

Clanging. Fixation on the sound of a word, which results in the person's using a string of similar-sounding words (for example, *mad, sad, glad*).

Cognitive restructuring. An attempt to identify and change dysfunctional patterns by addressing thinking styles, cognitive errors, dichotomous thinking, core beliefs, and behaviors.

Cognitive therapy. A focus on cognitive distortions, including selective attention to the negative aspects of circumstances and unrealistic morbid inferences about consequences; identifies sets of dysfunctional attitudes, cognitions, and images, as well as learned helplessness.

Comorbidity. Presence of more than one disorder, either *concurrent* or *lifetime*. The disorders may be on Axes I, II, or III.

Countertransference. Attitudes and feelings of the therapist toward the client, often based on past experiences or significant people in the therapist's past; may be positive or negative and needs to be identified by the therapist so that it does not impede the intervention; may be conscious or unconscious.

Defenses. Specific unconscious behaviors used by the ego to defend against impulses, feelings, and situations that produce anxiety. Repression underlies most defense mechanisms. While defenses are often maladaptive, they can also be adaptive.

Detoxification. Process of removing drugs or alcohol from the body to restore adequate physiological functioning; accomplished by withholding the substance and providing medication to diminish withdrawal symptoms. Can be accomplished in an outpatient setting, though inpatient is preferable.

Dual diagnosis. Term most commonly used to describe the coexistence of substance and psychiatric disorders; can also mean that a person has more than one diagnosis of any type or that there is poly drug abuse.

Echolalia. Parrotlike repetition of words or phrases of another in a nonsensical, semiautomatic manner.

Echopraxia. Repeated mimicking of the movements of another.

Eco-map. Diagram illustrating reciprocal relationships between the client, the client's family, and environmental influences that affect the client's life.

Ecosystems perspective. View that emphasizes understanding the individual and the impinging environment, particularly understanding the transactions of person-in-situation. It is a *perspective* and thus directs the thinking about the case, but not the model or method of intervention.

Ego-dystonic (ego alien). Term describing behaviors or characteristics that are not acceptable to the individual, where there is awareness of the need to change; may also be referred to as *ego alien*.

Ego ideal. A person's goals, values, and aspirations *or* a person whom the individual may want to emulate.

Ego-syntonic. Term describing behavior that is acceptable and not distressing to the person, although it may adversely affect others.

Epidemiology. Study of the frequency and distribution of a specific disease in a population group during a given period.

Extrapyramidal. Side effects that are disturbances in the motor systems of the brain and are manifested as spasms, abnormal muscle tension, Parkinsonian symptoms, and tardive dyskinesia.

Feminist therapy. Therapy directed toward helping the client overcome psychological problems resulting from sex discrimination or sex role stereotyping, using consciousness-raising groups that focus on commonalities of women's problems and political influences.

Flight of ideas. Rapid movement from one thought or association to another without apparent connection.

Flight to health. Clients' symptoms and problems *suddenly* cease, with client wanting to terminate the intervention or change the focus of attention.

Flight to illness. As termination approaches, client raises new symptoms related to the presenting problem in order to extend the intervention. Similar to "doorknob therapy," characterized by the client's bringing up important issues just as a session ends.

Genogram. Diagram to illustrate using symbols for family relationships spanning at least three generations.

Grief work. A series of stages that an individual goes through following a major loss; results in acceptance, adjustment, and developing new supports.

Halfway houses. Transitional facilities for persons with mental or substance abuse problems who require supervision and support following inpatient stays.

Huntington's chorea. A genetic disease resulting in mental deterioration and often ending in dementia.

Iatrogenic effects. Harmful effects inadvertently caused by the clinician or the intervention.

Illusions. Misperceptions of sensory stimuli.

Imagery reconstruction. An alternative used when a trauma experience cannot be reexperienced in vivo; tries to replay the sequence of thoughts and feelings and thus become aware of the interdependence of reactions and symptoms.

Incident rate. Number of cases in a given period.

Insight. Awareness and understanding of one's feelings, behaviors, and problems.

Insight therapies. Interventions geared to helping the client become more self-aware about feelings, behaviors, motivations, and thought processes.

Interpersonal therapy. Intervention that focuses on one or two of a person's current interpersonal problems (grief, role dispute, role transition, or interpersonal deficits), based on the assumptions that current interpersonal problems have roots in early dysfunctional relationships and that current interpersonal problems are likely to be involved in precipitating or perpetuating the current symptoms (usually depression).

Kaposi's sarcoma. A form of cancer that is a major symptom of HIV infection or AIDS.

Lifetime prevalence. Reference to those individuals who, up to current age, have met diagnostic criteria at some point in their lives.

Lifetime risk. Proportion of individuals who would develop a disorder if all lived to a designated age.

Linear perspective. A cause-and-effect view of problems and behavior, similar to a medical model and considered narrow compared with the ecosystems perspective.

Living will. A formal document specifying the person's wishes about the management of illness and death, which should be executed when the person is well and competent and, together with a Health Care Proxy, should designate person(s) to execute decisions if the client is not able to do so.

Magical thinking. The perception, often seen in persons with schizophrenia and paranoia, that one's thoughts or desires influence events and the environment.

Medical model. Approach that looks at the individual's symptoms with little or no concern with the environment and then applies specific diagnostic labels.

MICA. Mentally ill and chemical abuser. The psychiatric diagnosis is primary, with alcohol or drug addiction secondary.

Milieu therapy. Therapy involving the whole staff and the environment of a closed setting, such as an inpatient service or a therapeutic community.

Neologisms. Words that a person makes up, usually using condensation, with the meaning known to the client but probably not to others.

Neurasthenia. Condition characterized by a wide range of symptoms, including fatigue, joint pain, weakness, headaches, palpitations, and concentration difficulties; disorders are defined by subjective symptoms, with no objective criteria or consistent organic explanation, but are debilitating.

Parasuicide. Nonfatal, intentional self-injury resulting in bodily injury, illness, or risk of death, including ingesting drugs or other substances with the intent of bodily harm or death. This is similar to what is commonly referred to as "suicide gestures."

Perseveration. Persistence of one reply or one idea in response to various questions *or* inability to stop a motor activity.

Point (or current) prevalence. Proportion of individuals who have the disorder being studied at a designated time.

Prevalence rate. A measure of the total number of cases with a particular problem.

> **Point prevalence.** Number of cases measured at one point in time.
>
> **Period prevalence.** All cases occurring in a specific time frame, usually a year.

Projective identification. A very complicated defense mechanism involving the projection by the client onto another of an unacceptable impulse or feeling so that the client perceives it as the other's impulse or feeling, induces the other to behave in accordance with the projection, and thus the client becomes the victim and fears the other.

Psychoactive drugs. Drugs that change the client's mood, cognitive ability, or perceptions. Can be psychotropic *or* illegal drugs.

Psychoanalytic theory. Theory that focuses on the role of the libidinal and aggressive drives and their management through the use of unconscious material and transference.

Psychoanalytically oriented therapy. Therapy with the goal of effecting changes in a personality structure or character rather than simply alleviating symptoms.

Psychodynamic therapy. Therapy that focuses on working with the emotional and cognitive processes that motivate behavior, both conscious and unconscious.

Psychosocial assessment. Assessment of the person-in-situation, focusing on the strengths and weaknesses in the individual and the environment and resulting in a plan for intervention. While initially the assessment is rapid, it is also an ongoing process as new data emerge.

Psychotropic drugs. Drugs used to help alleviate symptoms of emotional distress and often to make the client more amenable to psychotherapy aimed at change.

Respite care. Temporary care for a person requiring home care in order to give the primary caregiver a change of scene or a rest.

Right to refuse treatment. A legal right (may vary state by state) to refuse intervention unless the person is a danger to self or to others even if the person is institutionalized.

Right to treatment. Legal right of an individual confined to an institution to receive treatment necessary in order to have a chance to leave the institution and function in the outside environment; established in the *Wyatt v. Stickney* decision.

Secondary gain. The *perceived* advantages of being ill in order to attract attention that a person may receive only when ill. Playing the "sick role" may enable the person to avoid responsibilities and receive sympathy and support without being blamed or feeling like a failure. May be experienced physically or as a mental disorder.

Survivor guilt. Feelings of guilt, shame, and even regret if a person does not experience the danger that affects others. Sometimes seen in relatives of persons subjected to physical or sexual abuse and those who survived war or torture.

Tarasoff. A 1976 California Supreme Court ruling in *Tarasoff v. Regents of the University of California* stating that under certain conditions a clinician must warn a potential victim if the client states a wish or makes a plan to do harm. Has been upheld in most states.

Transference. Unconscious displacement onto the therapist of feelings, attitudes, and expectations about persons or situations from the past.

References and Additional Readings

Abraham, S., and D. Llewellyn-Jones. 1992. *Eating Disorders.* New York: Oxford University Press.

Adler, D. A., ed. 1990. *Treating Personality Disorders.* San Francisco: Jossey-Bass.

Adler, G. 1985. *Borderline Psychopathology and Its Treatment.* New York: Jason Aronson.

Adler, G., and D. H. Buie. 1979. Aloneness and borderline psychopathology: The possible relevance of child development issues. *International Journal of Psychoanalysis* 60:83–96.

Akhtar, S. 1989. Narcissistic personality disorder. In O. F. Kernberg, ed., *The Psychiatric Clinics of North America* 12 (3): 505–30. Philadelphia: Saunders.

American Psychiatric Association. 1987. *Diagnostic and Statistical Manual of Mental Disorders.* 3d ed. rev. Washington, D.C.: American Psychiatric Association.

———. 1989. *Treatment of Psychiatric Disorders: A Task Force Report of the American Psychiatric Association.* Washington, D.C.: American Psychiatric Association.

———. 1993. *Practice Guidelines for Eating Disorders.* Washington, D.C.: American Psychiatric Association.

———. 1994. *Diagnostic and Statistical Manual of Mental Disorders.* 4th ed. Washington, D.C.: American Psychiatric Association.

———. 1998. Outpatient commitment pilot in New York shows program works. *Psychiatric News,* July 3, 15.

Ammons, R. B., and C. H. Ammons. 1962. The Quick Test (QT): Provisional manual. *Psychological Reports* 11:111–61.

Anastasi, A. 1982. *Psychological Testing.* 5th ed. New York: Macmillan.

Ancill, R. J. 1993. Depression in Alzheimer's disease: Confusing, confounding, but treatable. In G. K. Wilcock, ed., *The Management of Alzheimer's Disease,* 87–95. Petersfield, Hampshire, U.K.: Wrightson Biomedical.

Andersen, A. E. 1992. Males with eating disorders. In J. Yager, H. E. Gwirtsman, and C. K. Edelstein, eds., *Special Problems in Managing Eating Disorders,* 87–118. Washington, D.C.: American Psychiatric Press.

————, ed. 1990. *Males with Eating Disorders.* New York: Brunner/Mazel.

Anderson, C., D. Reiss, and G. Hegarty. 1986. *Schizophrenia and the Family.* New York: Guilford.

Anderson, L. P. 1992. Differential treatment effects. In L. L'Abate, J. E. Farrar, and D. A. Serritella, eds., *Handbook of Differential Treatments for Addictions,* 23–41. Boston: Allyn and Bacon.

Anonymous. 1990. My name is Legion, for we are many: Diagnostics and the psychiatric client. *Social Work* 35 (5): 391–92.

Anthenelli, R. M., and M. A. Schuckit. 1992. Genetics. In J. H. Lowinson, P. Ruiz, and R. B. Millman, eds., *Substance Abuse: A Comprehensive Textbook,* 39–50. 2d ed. Baltimore: Williams and Wilkins.

Arana, G. W., and S. E. Hyman. 1991. *Handbook of Psychiatric Drug Therapy.* 2d ed. Boston: Little, Brown.

Austrian, S. 1998. Clinical social work in the twenty-first century: Behavioral managed care is here to stay. In R. Dorfman, ed., *Paradigms of Clinical Social Work,* 2:315–36.

Austrian, S. G., L. Linn, and R. S. Miller. 1981. DSM-III: A guide to a holistic approach. Paper presented at the annual meeting of the American Public Health Association, November, Los Angeles.

Baker, J. D., E. W. Capron, and J. Azorlosa. 1996. Family environmental characteristics of persons with histrionic and dependent personality disorders. *Journal of Personality Disorders* 10:82–89.

Ballenger, J. C. 1990. *Clinical Aspects of Panic Disorder.* New York: Wiley.

Barchas, J. D., P. A. Berger, R. D. Ciaranello, and G. R. Elliott. 1977. *Psychopharmacology: From Theory to Practice.* New York: Oxford University Press.

Barlow, D. H. 1988. *Anxiety and Its Disorders.* New York: Guilford.

Barlow, D. H., and C. L. Lehman. 1996. Advances in the psychosocial treatment of anxiety disorder. *Archives of General Psychiatry* 53:727–35.

Barlow, D. H., and M. T. Waddell. 1985. Agoraphobia. In D. H. Barlow, ed., *Clinical Handbook of Psychological Disorders*, 1–68. New York: Guilford.

Barsky, A. J. 1989. Somatoform disorders. In H. I. Kaplan and B. J. Sadock, eds., *Comprehensive Textbook of Psychiatry*, 1009–27. 5th ed. Baltimore: Williams and Wilkins.

Bartlett, H. 1970. *The Common Base of Social Work Practice*. Washington, D.C.: National Association of Social Workers.

Bartlett, J. G., and A. K. Finkbeiner. 1993. *The Guide to Living with HIV Infection*. Baltimore: Johns Hopkins University Press.

Bauer, M. S. 1997. Bipolar disorders. In A. Tasman, J. Kay, and J. A. Lieberman, eds., *Psychiatry*, 2:966–89. Philadelphia: Saunders.

Bauer, M. S., P. Crits-Cristoph, W. A. Boll, E. Dewees, T. McAllister, P. Alohi, J. Cacciola, and P. C. Whybrow. 1991. Independent assessment of manic and depressive symptoms by self-rating. *Archives of General Psychiatry* 48:807–12.

Beck, A. 1967. *Depression: Clinical, Experimental, and Theoretical Aspects*. New York: Harper and Row.

Beck, A. T., D. Schuyler, and I. Herman. 1974. Development of suicidal intent scales. In A. T. Beck, H. L. P. Resnick, and D. J. Lettieri, eds., *The Prediction of Suicide*. Bowie, Md.: Charles.

Beck, A. T., R. A. Steer, and G. K. Brown. 1996. *Beck Depression Inventory Manual*. 2d ed. San Antonio: Psychological Corporation.

Beck, A. T., R. A. Steer, and M. S. Garbin. 1988. Psychometric properties of the Beck Depression Inventory: Twenty-five years of evaluation. *Clinical Psychology Review* 8:77–100.

Beck, A. T., C. H. Ward, and M. Mendelson. 1961. An inventory for measuring depression. *Archives of General Psychiatry* 4:561–71.

Beck, A. T., and J. E. Young. 1985. Depression. In D. H. Barlow, ed., *Clinical Handbook of Psychological Disorders*, 206–44. New York: Guilford.

Becker, R. E., and E. Giacobini. 1990. *Alzheimer Disease: Current Research in Early Diagnosis*. New York: Taylor and Francis.

Beeder, A. B., and R. B. Millman. 1992. Treatment of patients with psychopathology and substance abuse. In J. H. Lowinson, P. Ruiz, and R. B. Millman, eds., *Substance Abuse: A Comprehensive Textbook*, 675–90. 2d ed. Baltimore: Williams and Wilkins.

Beigel, A., D. L. Murphy, and W. E. Bunney. 1971. The Manic State Rating Scale: Scale construct, reliability, and validity. *Archives of General Psychiatry* 25:256–62.

Benjamin, L. S. 1974. Structural analysis of social behavior. *Psychological Review* 81:392–425.

Benson, D. F. 1985. Aphasia. In K. M. Heilman and E. Valenstein, eds., *Clinical Neuropsychology*, 7–48. New York: Oxford University Press.

Bentley, K. J., and J. Walsh. 1996. *The Social Worker and Psychotropic Medication*. Pacific Grove: Brooks/Cole.

Benton, A. L. 1955. *Visual Retention Test*. New York: Psychological Corporation.

Benton, A. L., and K. Hamsher. 1976. *Multilingual Aphasia Examination*. Iowa City: University of Iowa.

Benton, A. L., H. J. Hannay, and N. R. Varney. 1975. Visual perception of line direction in patients with unilateral brain disease. *Neurology* 25: 907–10.

Benton, A. L., and M. W. Van Allen. 1968. Impairment in facial recognition in patients with cerebral disease. *Cortex* 4:344–58.

Benton, A. L., and O. Spreen. 1969. *Neurosensory Center Comprehensive Examination for Aphasia*. Victoria, B.C.: University of Victoria.

Ben-Porath. Y. S. 1997. Use of personality assessment instruments in empirically guided treatment planning. *Psychological Assessment* 9 (4): 361–67.

Berg, E. A. 1948. A simple objective test for measuring flexibility in thinking. *Journal of General Psychology* 39:15–32.

Berman, W. H., and S. W. Hurt. 1999. The implication of clinical outcome systems: Conceptual and practical issues. In E. Mullen, ed., *Outcomes in Behavioral Health, Child Health, and Social Service Settings*, 21–97. Washington, D.C.: National Association of Social Workers Press.

Bernstein, B. E., and M. F. Weiner. 1991. Legal and ethical aspects of dementia. In M. F. Weiner, ed., *The Dementias: Diagnosis and Management*, 201–15. Washington, D.C.: American Psychiatric Press.

Beutler, L. E. 1983. *Eclectic Psychotherapy: A Systemic Approach*. New York: Pergamon.

Beutler, L. E., and J. F. Clarkin. 1990. *Systemic Treatment Selection: Toward Targeted Therapeutic Interventions*. New York: Brunner/Mazel.

Black, D. W., and N. C. Andreasen. 1994. Schizophrenia, schizophreniform disorder, and delusional (paranoid) disorder. In R. E. Hales, S. C. Yudofsky, and J. A. Talbott, eds., *Textbook of Psychiatry*, 411–68. 2d ed. Washington, D.C.: American Psychiatric Press.

Black, D. W., R. Wesner, W. Bowers, and J. Gabel. 1993. A comparison of fluoxamine, cognitive therapy, and placebo in the treatment of panic disorder. *Archives of General Psychiatry* 50 (1): 44–50.

Bleuler, E. 1911. *Dementia Praecox or the Group of Schizophrenias*. Trans. J. Zinkin. New York: International Universities Press, 1952.

Bloom, M. 1993. The role of the general practitioner and other professionals in the management of Alzheimer's disease. In G. K. Wilcock, ed., *The Management of Alzheimer's Disease*, 59–76. Petersfield, Hampshire, U.K.: Wrightson Biomedical.

Blume, S. B. 1992. Compulsive gambling: Addiction without drugs. *Harvard Mental Health Letter*. Boston: Harvard Medical School Health Publications Group.

Blumenthal, S. J., and D. J. Kupfer, eds. 1990. *Suicide Over the Life Cycle*. Washington, D.C.: American Psychiatric Press.

Boll, T. J. 1981. The Halstead-Reitan Neuropsychology Battery. In S. B. Filskov and T. J. Boll, *Handbook of Clinical Neuropsychology*, 577–607. New York: Wiley.

Bolo, P. M. 1993. The biological basis of bulimia. In A. J. Giannini and A. E. Slaby, eds., *The Eating Disorders*, 44–62. New York: Springer Verlag.

Bolton, S., and J. G. Gunderson. 1996. Distinguishing borderline personality disorder from bipolar disorder: Differential diagnosis and implications. *American Journal of Psychiatry* 153 (9): 1202–7.

Bonuck, K. A. 1993. AIDS and families: Cultural, psychosocial, and functional impacts. *Social Work in Health Care* 18 (2): 75–89.

Bower, B. A. 1991. Melancholy breach. *Science News*, January 26.

Brandt, J. 1991. The Hopkins Verbal Learning Test: Development of a new memory test with six equivalent forms. *Clinical Neuropsychologist* 5: 125–42.

Brawman-Mintzer, O., and R. B. Lydiard. 1997. Generalized anxiety disorder. In A. Tasman, J. Kay, and J. A. Lieberman, eds., *Psychiatry*, 2: 1100–18. Philadelphia: Saunders.

Breitbart, W. 1988. Neuropsychiatric aspects of AIDS. *Harvard Medical School Mental Health Letter* 5 (6): 4–6. Boston: Department of Continuing Education of Harvard Medical School.

Briggs, R. 1993. What can be treated in Alzheimer's disease? In G. K. Wilcock, ed., *The Management of Alzheimer's Disease*, 45–55. Petersfield, Hampshire, U.K.: Wrightson Biomedical.

Brody, Jane. 1999. When symptoms are obvious, but cause is not. *New York Times*, March 16, F3.

Brotman, A. W. 1994. What works in the treatment of anorexia nervosa? *Harvard Mental Health Letter* 10 (1): 8.

Brower, K. J., F. C. Blow, and T. P. Beresford. 1989. Treatment implications of chemical dependency models: An integrative approach. *Journal of Substance Abuse Treatment* 6:147–57.

Brown, G. W., and M. Rutter. 1966. The measurement of family activities and relationships: A methodological study. *Human Relations* 19:241–63.

Brown, P. J. 1993. Cultural perspectives on the etiology and treatment of obesity. In A. J. Stunkard and T. A. Wadden, eds., *Obesity Theory and Therapy*, 179–93. New York: Raven.

Bruch, H. 1973. *Eating Disorders: Obesity, Anorexia Nervosa, and the Person Within*. New York: Basic Books.

Buie, D. H., and G. Adler. 1982. The definitive treatment of the borderline personality. *International Journal of Psychoanalytic Psychotherapy* 9: 51–87.

Buros, O. K., ed. 1971. *The Seventh Mental Measurements Yearbook*. Highland Park: Gryphon.

———, ed. 1978. *The Eighth Mental Measurements Yearbook*. Highland Park: Gryphon.

Bursten, B. 1989. The relationship between narcissistic and antisocial personalities. In O. F. Kernberg, ed., *The Psychiatric Clinics of North America* 12 (3): 571–84. Philadelphia: Saunders.

Buschke, H. 1973. Selective reminding for analysis of memory and learning. *Journal of Verbal Learning and Verbal Behavior* 12:543–50.

Buss, A. H., and A. Durkee. 1957. An inventory for assessing different kinds of hostility. *Journal of Consulting Psychology* 21:343–49.

Butcher, J. N. 1998. Objective study of abnormal personality in cross-cultural settings: The Minnesota Multiphasic Personality Inventory (MMPI-2). *Journal of Cross-Cultural Psychology* 29 (1): 189–211.

Butcher, J. N., W. G. Dahlstrom, J. R. Graham, A. Tellegen, and B. Kaemmen. 1989. *Manual for the Restandardized Minnesota Multiphasic Personality Inventory: MMPI-2: An Administrative and Interpretive Guide*. Minneapolis: University of Minnesota Press.

Casper, R. C. 1990. Personality features of women with good outcome from restricting anorexia nervosa. *Psychosomatic Medicine* 52:156–70.

Cattell, R. B., H. W. Eber, and M. M. Tatsuoka. 1970. *Handbook of the Sixteen Personality Factor Inventory*. Champaign, Ill.: Institute for Personality and Ability Testing.

Cayton, H. 1993. The social consequences of dementia. In G. K. Wilcock, ed., *The Management of Alzheimer's Disease*, 151–58. Petersfield, Hampshire, U.K.: Wrightson Biomedical.

Chassler, L. 1998. "Ox hunger": Psychoanalytic explorations of bulimia nervosa. *Clinical Social Work Journal* 26:397–412.

Christensen, A. L. 1975. *Luria's Neuropsychological Investigation Manual*. New York: Spectrum.

Clark, L. A. 1993. *Manual for the Schedule for Nonadaptive and Adaptive Personality (SNAP)*. Minneapolis: University of Minnesota Press.

Clarkin, J. F., G. L. Haas, and I. D. Glick. 1992. Family and marital therapy. In E. S. Paykel, ed., *Handbook of Affective Disorders*, 487–500. 2d ed. London: Churchill Livingstone.

———, eds. 1988. *Affective Disorders and the Family: Assessment and Treatment*. New York: Guilford.

Clarkin, J. F., E. Marzialli, and H. Munroe-Blum, eds. 1992. *Borderline Personality Disorder*. New York: Guilford.

Clarkin, J. F., and S. Mattis. 1991. Psychological assessment. In L. Sederer, ed., *Inpatient Psychiatry: Diagnosis and Treatment*, 360–78. 3d ed. Baltimore: Williams and Wilkins.

Clarkin, J. F., P. A. Pilkonis, and K. M. Magruder. 1996. Psychotherapy of depression. *Archives of General Psychiatry* 53:717–23.

Clarkin, J. F., and J. A. Sweeney. 1992. Psychological testing. In R. Michels and J. O. Cavenar, eds., *Psychiatry*, 1–11. Rev. ed. Philadelphia: Lippincott.

Cloninger, C. R., D. M. Svrakic, and T. R. Przybeck. 1993. A psychobiological model of temperament and character. *Archives of General Psychiatry* 50:975–90.

Closser, M. H. 1992. Cocaine epidemiology. In T. R. Kosten and H. D. Kleber, eds., *Clinician's Guide to Cocaine Addiction*, 225–40. New York: Guilford.

Coblentz, J. M., S. Mattis, H. Zingesser, S. S. Kasoff, H. M. Wisniewski, and R. Katzman. 1973. Presenile dementia: Clinical aspects and evaluation of cerebrospinal fluid dynamics. *Archives of Neurology* 29:299–308.

Cohen, C. P., and V. R. Sherwood. 1991. *Becoming a Constant Object in Psychotherapy with the Borderline Patient*. Northvale, N.J.: Jason Aronson.

Cohen, J., and S. J. Levy. 1992. *The Mentally Ill Chemical Abuser*. New York: Lexington Books.

Cooper, A. M. 1988. The narcissistic-masochistic character. In R. A. Glick and D. I. Meyers, eds., *Masochism: Current Psychological Perspectives*. Hillsdale, N.J.: Analytic.

Copeland, J. R. M. 1993. The epidemiology of Alzheimer's disease. In
G. K. Wilcock, ed., *The Management of Alzheimer's Disease*, 3–12. Petersfield, Hampshire, U.K.: Wrightson Biomedical.

Corsini, R. J., and D. Wedding. 1989. *Current Psychotherapies*. Itasca: Pea-
cock.

Coryell, W., and G. Winokur. 1991. *The Clinical Management of Anxiety
Disorders*. New York: Oxford University Press.

Costa, L. D., and R. R. McCrae. 1992. *NEO PI-R: Professional Manual*.
Odessa, Fla.: Psychological Assessment Resources.

Costa, L. D., H. G. Vaughn, E. Levita, and N. Farber. 1963. Perdue Pegboard as a predictor of the presence and laterality of cerebral lesions.
Journal of Consulting Psychology 27:133–37.

Cull, J. G., and W. S. Gill. 1986. *Suicide Probability Scale (SPS) Manual*.
Los Angeles: Western Psychological Services.

Cummings, J. L. 1992. Neuropsychiatric aspects of Alzheimer's disease and
other dementing illnesses. In S. C. Yudofsky and R. E. Hales, eds., *Textbook of Neuropsychiatry*, 605–20. 2d ed. Washington, D.C.: American
Psychiatric Press.

Dahlstrom, W. G., G. S. Welsh, and L. E. Dahlstrom. 1972. *An MMPI
Handbook*. Vols. 1 and 2. Minneapolis: University of Minnesota Press.

Dare, C. and I. Eisler. 1997. Family therapy for anorexia nervosa. In D. M.
Garner and P. E. Garfinkel, eds., *Handbook of Treatment for Eating Disorders*, 307–24. New York: Guilford.

DeFillipis, N. A., E. McCampbell, and P. Rogers. 1979. Development of a
booklet form of the Category Test: Normative and Validity Data. *Journal
of Clinical Neuropsychology* 1:339–42.

Delis, D. C., J. Kramer, E. Kaplan, and B. A. Ober. 1987. *California Verbal
Learning Test (CVLT), Research Edition Manual*. New York: Psychological Corporation.

Derby, K. 1992. The role of 12-step self-help groups in the treatment of the
chemically dependent. In B. C. Wallace, ed., *The Chemically Dependent*,
159–70. New York: Brunner/Mazel.

Derogatis, L. R. 1977. *The SCL-90R*. Baltimore: Clinical Psychometric Research.

———. 1982. Self-report measures of stress. In L. Goldberger and S. Brez-
nitz, eds., *Handbook of Stress*. New York: Free Press.

———. 1983. *SCL-90-R: Administration, Scoring, and Procedures Manual
II*. Baltimore: Clinical Psychometric Research.

———. 1992. *BSI: Administration, Scoring, and Procedures Manual II*. 2d
ed. Baltimore: Clinical Psychometric Research.

Derogatis, L. R., R. S. Lipman, K. Rickels, E. H. Uhenhuth, and L. Covi. 1974. The Hopkins Symptom Checklist (HSCL): A measure of primary symptom dimensions. In P. Pichot, ed., *The Psychological Measurements in Psychopharmacology*, 79–110. Basel: Karger.

DiNardo, P. A., K. Moros, D. H. Barlow, R. M. Rapee, and T. A. Brown. 1993. Reliability of DSM-III anxiety disorder categories. *Archives of General Psychiatry* 50 (4): 251–56.

DiNardo, P. A., G. T. O'Brien, D. H. Barlow, M. T. Waddell, and E. B. Blanchard. 1983. Reliability of DSM-III anxiety disorder categories using a new structured interview. *Archives of General Psychiatry* 40:1070–75.

Docherty, J. P. 1992. To know borderline personality disorder. In J. F. Clarkin, E. Marzialli, and H. Munroe-Blum, eds., *Borderline Personality Disorder*, 329–38. New York: Guilford.

Dowd, E. T., C. R. Milne, and S. L. Wise. 1991. The Therapeutic Reactance Scale: A measure of psychological reactance. *Journal of Consulting and Clinical Psychology* 69:541–45.

Dozois, D. A., K. S. Dobson, and J. L. Ahnberg. 1998. A psychometric evaluation of the Beck Depression Inventory-II. *Psychological Assessment* 10: 83–89.

Druck, A. 1989. *Four Therapeutic Approaches to the Borderline Patient*. Northvale, N.J.: Jason Aronson.

Dumont, M. P. 1987. A diagnostic parable (First edition — unrevised). *Readings* 2 (4): 9–12.

Dwyer, J. T., and D. Lu. 1993. Popular diets for weight loss: From nutritionally hazardous to healthful. In A. J. Stunkard and T. A. Wadden, eds., *Obesity Theory and Therapy*, 231–74. New York: Raven.

Edelstein, C. K., and B. H. King. 1992. Pregnancy and eating disorders. In J. Yager, H. E. Gwirtsman, and C. K. Edelstein, eds., *Special Problems in Managing Eating Disorders*, 163–84. Washington, D.C.: American Psychiatric Press.

Edelstein, C. K., and J. Yager. 1992. Eating disorders and affective disorders. In J. Yager, H. E. Gwirtsman, and C. K. Edelstein, eds., *Special Problems in Managing Eating Disorders*, 15–50. Washington, D.C.: American Psychiatric Press.

Ehrenkranz, J. R. L. 1993. The medical care of the patient with an eating disorder. In A. J. Giannini and A. E. Slaby, eds., *The Eating Disorders*, 147–57. New York: Springer Verlag.

Elble, R. J. 1990. Early diagnosis of Alzheimer disease. In R. E. Becker, ed., *Alzheimer Disease: Current Research in Early Diagnosis*, 19–30. New York: Taylor and Francis.

Elkin, I., T. Shea, J. T. Watkins, S. D. Imber, S. H. Sotsky, J. F. Collins, D. R. Glass. P. A. Pilkonis, W. R. Leber, J. P. Docherty, S. J. Firster, and M. B. Parloff. 1989. National Institute of Mental Health Treatment of Depression Collaborative Research Program. *Archives of General Psychiatry* 46:971–81.

Eller, B. 1993. Males with eating disorders. In A. J. Giannini and A. E. Slaby, eds., *The Eating Disorders*, 133–46. New York: Springer Verlag.

Ellison, J. M., and D. A. Adler. 1990. A strategy for the pharmacotherapy of personality disorders. In D. Adler, ed., *Treating Personality Disorders*, 43–63. San Francisco: Jossey-Bass.

Endicott, J., and R. L. Spitzer. 1978. A diagnostic interview: The Schedule of Affective Disorders and Schizophrenia. *Archives of General Psychiatry* 35:837–44.

Endicott, J., R. L. Spitzer, J. Fleiss, and J. Cohen. 1976. The Global Assessment Scale. *Archives of General Psychiatry* 33:766–71.

Endler, N. S., J. M. Hunt, and A. J. Rosenstein. 1962. An S-R Inventory of Anxiousness. *Psychological Monographs: General Applied* 76 (17, whole no. 536): 1–13.

Escobar, J. I., M. Swartz, M. Rubio-Stipec, and P. Manu. 1991. Medically unexplained symptoms distribution, risk factors, and comorbidity. In L. J. Kirmayer and J. M. Robbins, eds., *Current Concepts of Somatization and Clinical Perspectives*, 63–78. Washington, D.C.: American Psychiatric Press.

Exner, J. E. 1974, 1978. *The Rorschach: A Comprehensive System*. 2 vols. New York: Wiley.

Eysenck, H. J., and S. B. Eysenck. 1969. *The Structure and Measurement of Personality*. San Diego: Knapp.

Fabrega, H. 1991. Somatization in cultural and historical perspective. In L. J. Kirmayer and J. M. Robbins, eds., *Current Concepts of Somatization and Clinical Perspectives*, 181–99. Washington, D.C.: American Psychiatric Press.

Fairburn, C. G. 1998. Interpersonal psychotherapy for bulimia nervosa. In J. C. Markowitz, ed., *Interpersonal Psychotherapy*, 99–128. Washington, D.C.: American Psychiatric Press.

Fairburn, C. G., R. Jones, R. C. Peveler, R. A. Hope, and M. O'Conner. 1993. Psychotherapy and bulimia nervosa: Long-term effects of interpersonal psychotherapy, behavior therapy, and cognitive behavior therapy. *Archives of General Psychiatry* 50 (6): 419–28.

Fairburn, C. G., S. Welsh, H. A. Doll, B. A. Davies, and M. O'Conner. 1997. Risk factors for bulimia nervosa. *Archives of General Psychiatry* 54:509–14.

Fallon, P., and S. A. Wonderlich. 1997. Sexual abuse and other forms of trauma. In D. M. Garner and P. E. Garfinkel, eds., *Handbook of Treatment for Eating Disorders*, 394–414. New York: Guilford.

Feighner, J. P., E. Robins, S. B. Guze, R. A. Woodruff, G. Winokur, and R. Munoz. 1972. Diagnostic criteria for use in psychiatric research. *Archives of General Psychiatry* 26:57–63.

Ferguson, S. K., and M. S. Kaplan. 1994. Women and drug policy: Implications of normalization. *Affilia* 9 (2): 129–44.

Fiester, S. J., J. M. Ellison, J. P. Docherty, and Y. Shea. 1990. Comorbidity of personality disorders: Two for the price of three. In D. Adler, ed., *Treating Personality Disorders*, 103–14. San Francisco: Jossey-Bass.

Fine, C. G. 1993. A tactical integrationist perspective on the treatment of multiple personality disorder. In R. P. Kluft and C. G. Fine, eds., *Clinical Perspectives on Multiple Personality Disorder*. Washington, D.C.: American Psychiatric Press.

Finkelstein, S. N., and P. E. Greenberg. 1994. How much does depression cost society? *Harvard Mental Health Letter* 11 (4): 8. Boston: Harvard Medical School Health Publications Group.

First, M. B., M. Gibbon, R. L. Spitzer, J. B. Williams, and L. Benjamin. 1996. *User's Guide for the Structured Clinical Interview for DSM-IV Axis II Personality Disorders (SCID-II)*. New York: Biometric Research Department, New York Psychiatric Institute.

First, M. B., R. L. Spitzer, M. Gibbon, and J. B. Williams. 1995. *Structured Clinical Interview for Axis I DSM-IV Disorders—Patient Edition (SCID-I/P)*. New York: Biometric Research Department, New York Psychiatric Institute.

Foderaro, L. 1993. With reforms in treatment, shock therapy loses shock. *New York Times*, July 19, A1.

Folks, D. G., C. V. Ford, and C. A. Houck. 1998. Somatoform disorders, factitious disorders, and malingering. In A. Stoudemire, ed., *Clinical Psychiatry for Medical Students*, 343–77. Philadelphia: Lippincott-Raven.

Folstein, M. F., S. E. Folstein, and P. R. McHugh. 1975. Mini-mental State: A practical method for grading the cognitive state of patients for the clinician. *Journal of Psychiatric Research* 11:189–98.

Fonagy, P. 1999. Process and outcome in mental health care delivery: A model approach to treatment evaluation. *Bulletin of the Menninger Clinic* 63 (3): 288–304.

Forrest. D. V. 1992. Psychotherapy of patients with neuropsychiatric disorders. In S. C. Yudofsky and R. E. Hales, eds., *Textbook of Neuropsychiatry*, 703–39. 2d ed. Washington, D.C.: American Psychiatric Press.

Frances, A., J. Clarkin, and S. Perry. 1984. *Differential Therapeutics in Psychiatry*. New York: Brunner/Mazel.

Freud, S. 1917. *Mourning and Melancholia*. In *The Standard Edition of the Complete Psychological Works of Sigmund Freud*. Vol. 14. London: Hogarth.

Frierson, R. L. 1997. Dementia, delirium, and other cognitive disorders. In A. Tasman, J. Kay, and J. A. Lieberman, eds., *Psychiatry*, 1:893–926. Philadelphia: Saunders.

Gabriel, Trip. 1994. Heroin finds a new market along cutting edge of style. *New York Times*, May 8, A1, A22.

Gallo-Silver, L., V. H. Raveis, and R. T. Moynihan. 1993. Psychosocial issues in adults with transfusion-related HIV infection and their families. *Social Work in Health Care* 13 (2): 63–74.

Garner, D. M. 1992. *Eating Disorders Inventory-2: Professional Manual*. Odessa, Fla.: Psychological Assessment Resources.

Garner, D. M., and P. E. Garfinkel. 1979. The Eating Attitudes Test: An index of the symptoms of anorexia nervosa. *Psychological Medicine* 9:273–79.

———, eds. 1997. *Handbook of Treatment for Eating Disorders*. New York: Guilford.

Garner, D. M., and L. D. Needleman. 1997. Sequencing and integration of treatments. In D. M. Garner and P. E. Garfinkel, eds., *Handbook of Treatment for Eating Disorders*, 50–63. New York: Guilford.

Garner, D. M., K. M. Vitousek, and K. M. Pike. 1997. Cognitive-behavioral therapy for anorexia nervosa. In D. M. Garner and P. E. Garfinkel, eds., *Handbook of Treatment for Eating Disorders*, 94–144. New York: Guilford.

Gaw, K. F., and L. E. Beutler. 1995. Integrating treatment recommendation. In L. E. Beutler and M. R. Berren, eds., *Integrative Assessment of Adult Personality*, 280–319. New York: Guilford.

Gawin, F. H., and H. D. Kleber. 1992. Evolving conceptualizations of cocaine dependence. In T. R. Kosten and H. D. Kleber, eds., *Clinician's Guide to Cocaine Addiction*, 33–52. New York: Guilford.

Geffen, G., K. J. Moar, A. P. O'Hanlon, C. R. Clark, and L. B. Geffen. 1990. Performance measures of 16–86-year-old males and females on the Auditory Verbal Learning Test. *Clinical Neuropsychologist* 4:45–63.

Geisinger, K. F. 1994. Cross-cultural normative assessment: Translation adaptive issues influencing the normative interpretation of assessment instruments. *Psychological Assessment* 6 (4): 314–22.

Giannini, A. J. 1993. A history of bulimia. In A. J. Giannini and A. E. Slaby, eds., *The Eating Disorders*, 18–21. New York: Springer Verlag.

Giannini, A. J., and A. B. Slaby, eds. 1993. *The Eating Disorders*. New York: Springer Verlag.

Gitlin, M. J. 1990. *The Psychotherapist's Guide to Psychopharmacology*. New York: Free Press.

Golden, C. J., T. Hammeke, and A. Purisch. 1978. Diagnostic validity of the Luria Neuropsychological Battery. *Journal of Consulting and Clinical Psychology* 46:1258–65.

Goldman, R., M. Fristoe, and R. W. Woodcock. 1976. *Auditory Skills Test Battery*. Circle Pines: American Guidance Service.

Goldstein, E. G. 1984. *Ego Psychology and Social Work Practice*. New York: Free Press.

———. 1990. *Borderline Disorders*. New York: Guilford.

———. 1995. *Ego Psychology and Social Work Practice*. 2d ed. New York: Free Press.

Goldstein, E. G., and M. Noonan. 1999. *Short-Term Treatment and Social Work Practice*. New York: Free Press.

Goleman, D. 1990. Brain structure differences linked to schizophrenia in study of twins. *New York Times*, March 22, B15.

———. 1992. If hidden depression is halted, patients may get better faster. *New York Times*, August 4, C12.

Goodwin, D. W. 1989. Alcoholism. In H. I. Kaplan and B. J. Sadock, eds., *Comprehensive Textbook of Psychiatry*, 686–98. 5th ed. Baltimore: Williams and Wilkins.

Gortmaker, S. L., A. Must, J. M. Perrin, A. M. Sobel, and W. H. Dietz. 1993. Social and economic consequences of overweight in adolescence and young adulthood. *New England Journal of Medicine* 329 (14): 1008–12.

Gough, H. G. 1956. *California Psychological Inventory*. Palo Alto: Consulting Psychologist Press.

Graham, J. R. 1990. *MMPI-2: Assessing Personality and Psychopathology*. New York: Oxford University Press.

Graziano, R. 1992. Treating women incest survivors: A bridge between "cumulative trauma" and "post-traumatic stress." *Social Work in Health Care* 17 (11): 69–85.

Greaves, G. B. 1993. A history of multiple personality disorder. In R. P. Kluft and C. G. Fine, eds., *Clinical Perspectives on Multiple Personality Disorder*. Washington, D.C.: American Psychiatric Press.

Green, R. A., L. Bigelow, P. O'Brien, D. Stahl, and R. J. Wyatt. 1977. The Inpatient Behavioral Rating Scale: A 26-item scale for recording nursing observations of patients. *Psychological Reports* 40:543–49.

Greenberg, P. E., Stiglin, S. N. Finkelstein, and E. R. Berndt. 1993. Burden of depression in 1990. *Journal of Clinical Psychiatry* 54 (11): 405–18.

Greene, R. L. 1991. *The MMPI-2MMPI: An Interpretive Manual*. Needham Heights, Mass.: Allyn and Bacon.

Greenstein, R. A., P. J. Fudala, and C. P. O'Brien. 1992. Alternative pharmacotherapy for opiate addiction. In J. H. Lowinson, P. Ruiz, and R. B. Millman, eds., *Substance Abuse: A Comprehensive Textbook*, 562–73. 2d ed. Baltimore: Williams and Wilkins.

Gregg, D. 1994. *Alzheimer's Disease*. Boston: Harvard Medical School Health Publications Group.

Gregory, R. J., J. J. Paul, and M. W. Morrison. 1979. A short form of the Category Test for Adults. *Journal of Clinical Neuropsychology* 5:795–98.

Grinspoon, I., and J. B. Bakalar. 1990a. *Depression and Other Mood Disorders*. Boston: Harvard Health Publications.

——. 1990b. *Schizophrenia*. Boston: Harvard Health Publications.

Grob, P. R. 1993. Practical aspects of diagnosis and early recognition of Alzheimer's disease. In G. K. Wilcock, ed., *The Management of Alzheimer's Disease*, 21–35. Petersfield, Hampshire, U.K.: Wrightson Biomedical.

Gross, D. A. 1993. Neuropsychiatric approach to the eating disorder patient. In A. J. Giannini and A. E. Slaby, eds., *The Eating Disorders*, 93–103. New York: Springer Verlag.

Grossman, J., and R. Schottenfeld. 1992. Pregnancy and women's issues. In T. R. Kosten and H. D. Kleber, eds., *Clinician's Guide to Cocaine Addiction*, 374–89. New York: Guilford.

Gruenberg, A. M., and R. D. Goldstein. 1997. Depressive disorder. In A. Tasman, J. Kay, and J. A. Lieberman, eds., *Psychiatry*, 2:990–1019. Philadelphia: Saunders.

Grunebaum, H., and H. Friedman. 1988. Building collaborative relationships with families of the mentally ill. *Hospital and Community Psychiatry* 39:1183–87.

Gunderson, J. G. 1989. Borderline personality disorder. In H. I. Kaplan and B. Sadock, eds., *Comprehensive Textbook of Psychiatry*, 1387–95. 5th ed. Baltimore: Williams and Wilkins.

Gunderson, J. G., and E. Ronningstam. 1991. Is narcissistic personality disorder a valid diagnosis? In J. M. Oldham, ed., *Personality Disorders: New Perspectives on Diagnostic Validity*, 107–19. Washington, D.C.: American Psychiatric Press.

Guze, S. B. 1998. Psychotherapy and managed care. *Archives of General Psychiatry* 55:561–62.

Halmi, K. A., E. Eckert, P. Marchi, V. Sampugnaro, R. Apple, and J. Cohen. 1991. Comorbidity of psychiatric diagnosis in anorexia nervosa. *Archives of General Psychiatry* 48:712–18.

Hamilton, M. 1959. The assessment of anxiety states by rating. *British Journal of Medical Psychology* 32:50–55.

———. 1960. A rating scale for depression. *Journal of Neurology, Neurosurgery, and Psychiatry* 23:51–56.

———. 1967. Development of a rating scale for primary depressive illness. *British Journal of Social and Clinical Psychology* 6:278–96.

Harangody, G., and R. Peterson. 1992. A model of AIDS home care. In H. Land, ed., *A Complete Guide to Psychosocial Intervention*, 51–64. Milwaukee: Family Service of America.

Harrow, M., and D. Quinlan, eds. 1985. *Disordered Thinking and Schizophrenia*. New York: Gardner.

Harvard Mental Health Letter. 1987. *Personality and Personality Disorders. Part I and Part II*. September and October. Boston: Department of Continuing Education of Harvard Medical School.

———. 1999. *Memories Lost and Found. Parts I and II*. July and August. Boston: Harvard Medical School Health Publications Group.

Hathaway, S. R., and J. C. McKinley. 1967. *Minnesota Multiphasic Personality Inventory*. Rev. ed. New York: Psychological Corporation.

Hawkins, R. C. 1992. Substance abuse and stress-coping resources: A life-contextual clinical viewpoint. In B. C. Wallace, ed., *The Chemically Dependent*, 127–58. New York: Brunner/Mazel.

Haxby, J. V., K. Raffaele, J. Gillete, M. B. Schapiro, and S. I. Rapoport. 1992. Individual trajectories of cognitive decline in patients with dementia of the Alzheimer type. *Journal of Clinical and Experimental Neuropsychology* 14 (4): 575–92.

Hayes, R., and A. Gant. 1992. Patient psychoeducation: The therapeutic use of knowledge for the mentally ill. *Social Work in Health Care* 17 (1): 53–67.

Heaton, R. K. 1981. *Wisconsin Card Sorting Manual*. Odessa, Fla.: Psychological Assessment Resources.

Heaton, R. K., and T. J. Crowley. 1981. Effects of psychiatric disorders and their somatic treatments on neuropsychological test results. In S. B. Filskov and T. J. Boll, eds., *Handbook of Clinical Neuropsychology*, 481–525. New York: Wiley.

Heimberg, R. G., M. R. Liebowitz, D. A. Hope, F. R. Schneier, C. S. Holt, L. A. Welkowitz, H. R. Juster, R. Campease, M. A. Bruch, M. Cloitre, B. Fallon, and D. F. Klein. 1998. Cognitive behavioral group therapy vs. phenelzine therapy for social phobia. *Archives of General Psychiatry* 55:1133–41.

Heindel, W. C., D. P. Salmon, and N. Butters. 1993. Cognitive approaches to the memory disorders of demented patients. In P. B. Sutker and H. E. Adams, eds., *Comprehensive Textbook of Psychopathology*, 735–61. New York: Plenum.

Heller, N. R., and T. B. Northcut. 1996. Utilizing cognitive-behavioral techniques in psychodynamic practice with clients diagnosed as borderline. *Clinical Social Work Journal* 24:203–15.

Herman, J. L. 1992. *Trauma and Recovery*. New York: Basic Books.

Herman, J. L., J. C. Perry, and B. van der Kolk. 1989. Childhood trauma in borderline personality disorder. *American Journal of Psychiatry* 146:490–95.

Hodge, J. R., and E. A. Maseelall. 1993. The presentation of obesity. In A. J. Giannini and A. E. Slaby, eds., *The Eating Disorders*, 29–43. New York: Springer Verlag.

Hoffman, H., R. G. Loper, and M. L. Kammeier. 1974. Identifying future alcoholics with MMPI alcoholism scales. *Quarterly Studies of Studies on Alcohol* 35:490–98.

Honigfeld, G., and C. J. Klett. 1965. The Nurses' Observation Scale for Inpatient Evaluation: A new scale for measuring improvement of chronic schizophrenia. *Journal of Clinical Psychology* 21:65–71.

Horn, J. L., K. W. Wanberg, and F. M. Foster. 1986. *Alcohol Use Inventory*. Minneapolis: National Computer Systems.

Horvath, T. B., L. J. Suever, R. C. Mohs, and K. Davis. 1989. Organic mental syndromes and disorders. In H. I. Kaplan and B. J. Sadock, eds., *Comprehensive Textbook of Psychiatry*, 599–641. 5th ed. Baltimore: Williams and Wilkins.

Howard, K., R. Lueger, and M. Maling. 1993. A phase of psychotherapy outcome: Causal mediation of change. *Journal of Consulting and Clinical Psychology* 61:678–85.

Hsu, L. K. G. 1990. *Eating Disorders*. New York: Guilford.

Hudson, J. I., H. G. Pope, D. Yurgelun-Todd, J. M. Jonas, and E. R. Frankenburg. 1987. A controlled study of lifetime prevalence of affective and other psychiatric disorders in bulimic outpatients. *American Journal of Psychiatry* 144:1283–87.

Huff, F. J., C. Collins, S. Corkin, and T. J. Rosen. 1986. Equivalent forms of the Boston Naming Test. *Journal of Clinical and Experimental Neuropsychology* 8 (5): 556–62.

Hurt, S. W., J. F. Clarkin, A. Francis, R. Abrams, and H. Hurt. 1985. Discrimination validity of the MMPI for borderline personality disorder. *Journal of Personality Assessment* 49:56–61.

Hurt, S. W., P. S. Holzman, and J. M. Davis. 1983. Thought disorder: The measurement of its changes. *Archives of General Psychiatry* 40:1281–85.

Hurt, S. W., S. Hyler, A. Frances, J. F. Clarkin, and R. Brent. 1984. Assessing borderline personality disorder with self-report, clinical interview, or semi-structured interview. *American Journal of Psychiatry* 141:1228–31.

Hurt, S. W., M. Reznikoff, and J. F. Clarkin. 1991. *Psychological Assessment, Psychiatric Diagnosis, and Treatment Planning.* New York: Brunner/Mazel.

Hyler, S. E., J. K. Oldham, H. D. Kellman, and N. Doidge. 1992. Validity of the Personality Diagnostic Questionnaire—Revised: A replication in an outpatient sample. *Comprehensive Psychiatry* 33:73–77.

Hyler, S. E., R. Rieder, and R. L. Spitzer. 1978. *Personality Diagnostic Questionnaire (PDQ).* New York: New York State Psychiatric Institute, Biometrics Research Division.

Iezzi, A., and H. E. Adams. 1993. Somatoform and factitious disorders. In P. B. Sutker and H. E. Adams, eds., *Comprehensive Handbook of Psychopathology*, 167–201. 2d ed. New York: Plenum.

Jackson, D. N. 1974. *Personality Research Form Manual.* Goshen: Research Psychologists Press.

Jaffe, A. 1992. Cognitive factors associated with cocaine abuse and its treatment: An analysis of expectations of use. In T. R. Kosten and H. D. Kleber, eds., *Clinician's Guide to Cocaine Addiction*, 128–50. New York: Guilford.

Jaffe, J. H. 1989. Psychoactive substance use disorders. In H. I. Kaplan and B. J. Sadock, eds., *Comprehensive Textbook of Psychiatry*, 642–86. 5th ed. Baltimore: Williams and Wilkins.

Janowsky, D., L. Judd, L. Huey, N. Rostman, D. Parker, and D. Segal. 1978. Naloxone effects on manic symptoms and growth hormone levels. *Lancet* 2:320.

Jastak, S., and G. S. Wilkinson, 1981. *The Wide Range Achievement Test—Revised*. Wilmington, Del.: Jastak Associates.

Jenkins, C. D., R. H. Rosenman, and J. Friedman. 1967. Development of an objective psychological test for the determination of the coronary-prone behavior pattern in employed men. *Journal of Chronic Diseases* 20:371–79.

Johnson, H. C. 1991. Borderline clients: Practice implications of recent research. *Social Work* 36:166–73.

Johnson, H. C., and D. E. Goguen. 1991. Borderline personality. In A. Gitterman, ed., *Handbook of Social Work Practice with Vulnerable Populations*, 101–36. New York: Columbia University Press.

Johnson, W. G., ed. 1987. *Advances in Eating Disorders*. Vol. 1. Greenwich, Conn.: JAI.

Johnston, M. H., and P. S. Holzman. 1979. *Assessing Schizophrenic Thinking*. San Francisco: Jossey-Bass.

Kandel, E. R., J. H. Schwartz, and T. M. Jessell. 1991. *Principles of Neural Science*. 3d ed. Norwalk, Conn.: Appleton and Lange.

Kantor, M. 1992. *Diagnosis and Treatment of the Personality Disorders*. St. Louis: Ishiyaku EuroAmerica.

Kapfhammer, H. P., and H. Hippius. 1998. Pharmacotherapy in personality disorders. *Journal of Personality Disorders* 12:277–88.

Kaplan, H. I., and B. J. Sadock, eds. 1985. *Comprehensive Textbook of Psychiatry*. 4th ed. Baltimore: Williams and Wilkins.

———. 1989. *Comprehensive Textbook of Psychiatry*. 5th ed. Baltimore: Williams and Wilkins.

———. 1996. *Concise Textbook of Clinical Psychiatry*. Baltimore: Williams and Wilkins.

Kaplan, H. I., B. J. Sadock, and J. A. Grebb. 1994. *Kaplan and Sadock's Synopsis of Psychiatry: Behavioral Sciences, Clinical Psychiatry*. Baltimore: Williams and Wilkins.

Karasu, T. B. 1990. *Psychotherapy for Depression*. Northvale, N.J.: Jason Aronson.

Karch, S. B. 1993. *The Pathology of Drug Abuse*. Boca Raton, Fla.: CRC Press.

Karno, M., and G. S. Norquist. 1989. Schizophrenia: Epidemiology. In H. I. Kaplan and B. J. Sadock, eds., *Comprehensive Textbook of Psychiatry*, 699–717. 4th ed. Baltimore: Williams and Wilkins.

Karzmark, P., R. K. Heaton, I. Grant, and C. G. Matthews. 1985. Use of demographic variables to predict full scale I.Q.: A replication and extension. *Journal of Clinical and Experimental Neuropsychology* 7 (4): 412–20.

Katz, M. M., and S. B. Lyerly. 1963. Methods for measuring adjustment and social behavior in the community: I. Rationale, description, discriminative validity, and scale development. *Psychological Reports Monograph* 13:503—35.

Kaufman, E. 1992. Family therapy: A treatment approach with substance abusers. In J. H. Lowinson, P. Ruiz, and R. B. Millman, eds., *Substance Abuse: A Comprehensive Textbook*, 520–32. 2d ed. Baltimore: Williams and Wilkins.

Keel, P. M., J. E. Mitchell, K. B. Miller, T. L. Davis, and S. J. Crew. 1999. Long-term outcome of bulimia nervosa. *Archives of General Psychiatry* 56:63–69.

Keesey, R. E. 1993. Physiological regulation of body energy: Implications for obesity. In A. J. Stunkard and T. A. Wadden, eds., *Obesity Theory and Therapy*, 77–96. New York: Raven.

Keitner, G. I., ed. 1990. *Depression in Families: Impact and Treatment*. Washington, D.C.: American Psychiatric Press.

Kellner, R. 1991a. *Psychosomatic Syndromes and Somatic Symptoms*. Washington, D.C.: American Psychiatric Press.

———. 1991b. Treatment approaches to somatizing and hypochondriacal patients. In L. J. Kirmayer and J. M. Robbins, eds., *Current Concepts of Somatization and Clinical Perspectives*, 159–79. Washington, D.C.: American Psychiatric Press.

Kendler, K. S., A. C. Heath, M. C. Neale, R. C. Kessler, and L. J. Eaves. 1993. Alcoholism and major depression in women. *Archives of General Psychiatry* 50 (9): 690–98.

Kendler, K. S., M. C. Neale, R. C. Kessler, A. C. Heath, and L. J. Eaves. 1992. The genetic epidemiology of phobias in women. *Archives of General Psychiatry* 49 (4): 273–81.

Kernberg. O. F. 1989. The narcissistic personality disorder and the differential diagnosis of antisocial behavior. In O. F. Kernberg, ed., *The Psychiatric Clinics of North America* 12 (3): 553–70. Philadelphia: Saunders.

———. 1992. *Aggression in Personality Disorders and Perversions*. New Haven: Yale University Press.

Kernberg, O. F., M. A. Selzer, H. W. Koenigsberg, A. C. Carr, and A. H. Appelbaum. 1989. *Psychodynamic Psychotherapy of Borderline Patients*. New York: Basic Books.

Kessler, R. C., K. A. McGonagle, S. Zhao, C. B. Nelson, M. Hughes, S. Eshleman, H. U. Wittchen, and K. S. Kendler. 1994. Lifetime and 12-month prevalence of DSM-III-R disorders in the United States. *Archives of General Psychiatry* 51 (1): 8–19.

Kessler, R. C., A. Sonnega, E. Bromet, M. Hughes, and C. B. Nelson. 1995. Posttraumatic stress disorder in the National Comorbidity Survey. *Archives of General Psychiatry* 52:1048–60.

Kimura, D. 1967. Functional asymmetry of the brain in dichotic listening. *Cortex* 3:163–78.

Kirk, S. A., and H. Kutchins. 1988. Deliberate misdiagnosis in mental health practice. *Social Service Review* 62:225–37.

———. 1992. *The Selling of DSM*. New York: Aldine de Gruyter.

———. 1994. Is bad writing a mental disorder? *New York Times*, June 20, A17.

Kirmayer, L. J., and J. M. Robbins, eds. 1991a. *Current Concepts of Somatization and Clinical Perspectives*. Washington, D.C.: American Psychiatric Press.

Kirmayer, L. J., and J. M. Robbins. 1991b. Functional somatic syndromes. In L. J. Kirmayer and J. M. Robbins, eds., *Current Concepts of Somatization and Clinical Perspectives*, 79–106. Washington, D.C.: American Psychiatric Press.

———. 1991c. Introduction: Concepts of somatization. In L. J. Kirmayer and J. M. Robbins, eds., *Current Concepts of Somatization and Clinical Perspectives*, 1–19. Washington, D.C.: American Psychiatric Press.

Kleber, H. D., and D. Conney. 1994. Letter to the editor, *New York Times*, April 4.

Kleinman, P. H., S.-Y. Kang, G. E. Woody, R. B. Millman, T. C. Todd, and D. S. Lipton. 1992. Recovery from cocaine/crack abuse: A follow-up of applicants for treatment. In B. C. Wallace, *The Chemically Dependent*, 248–62. New York: Brunner/Mazel.

Klerman, G. L., M. M. Weissman, B. J. Rounsaville, and M. S. Chevron. 1984. *Interpersonal Psychotherapy of Depression*. New York: Basic Books.

Klove, H. 1963. Clinical neuropsychology. In F. M. Forster, ed., *Medical Clinics of North America*, 1647–58. New York: Saunders.

Kluft, R. P. 1993. Multiple personality disorders. In D. Spiegel, ed., *Dissociative Disorders: A Clinical Review*, 17–20. Lutherville, Md.: Sidran.

Kluft, R. P., and C. G. Fine, eds. 1993. *Clinical Perspectives on Multiple Personality Disorder*. Washington, D.C.: American Psychiatric Press.

Kocjan, D. K., and A. J. Giannini. 1993. The history of obesity. In A. J. Giannini and A. E. Slaby, eds., *The Eating Disorders*, 22–28. New York: Springer Verlag.

Kocsis, J. H. 1991. Is lifelong depression a personality or mood disorder? *Harvard Mental Health Letter* 8 (2): 8. Boston: Department of Continuing Education of Harvard Medical School.

Kohut, H. 1971. *The Analysis of the Self*. New York: International Universities Press.

———. 1977. *The Restoration of the Self*. New York: International Universities Press.

Kosten, T. R., and H. D. Kleber. 1992. *Clinician's Guide to Cocaine Addiction*. New York: Guilford.

Kovner, R., S. Dopkins, and E. Goldmeier. 1988. Covert recognition memory functions in two amnesic groups. *Cortex* 24:477–83.

Kroll, J. 1988. *The Challenge of the Borderline Patient*. New York: Norton.

Krueger, D. W. 1992. Eating disorders. In J. H. Lowinson, P. Ruiz, and R. B. Millman, eds., *Substance Abuse: A Comprehensive Textbook*, 371–79. 2d ed. Baltimore: Williams and Wilkins.

Kupfer, D. J., E. Frank, J. M. Perel, C. Cornes, A. G. Mallinger, M. E. Thase, A. B. McEachran, and V. J. Grochocinski. 1992. Five-year outcome for maintenance therapies in recurrent depression. *Archives of General Psychiatry* 49 (10): 769–73.

Kutchins, H., and S. A. Kirk. 1997. *Making Us Crazy*. New York: Free Press.

L'Abate, L., J. E. Farrar, and D. A. Serritella, eds. 1992. *Handbook of Differential Treatments for Addictions*. Boston: Allyn and Bacon.

Land, Helen, ed. 1992. *A Complete Guide to Psychosocial Intervention*. Milwaukee: Family Service of America.

Laporte, L., and H. Guttman. 1996. Traumatic childhood experience as risk factors for borderline and other personality disorders. *Journal of Personality Disorders* 10:247–59.

Leary, T. 1957. *Interpersonal Diagnosis of Personality*. New York: Ronald Press.

Leary, W. E. 1995. Drug for heroin addiction is being marketed for treatment of alcoholism. *New York Times*, January 18, A18.

Lenzenweger, M. F., A. W. Korfine, and C. Neff. 1997. Detecting personality disorders in a nonclinical population: Application of a two-stage procedure for case detection. *Archives of General Psychiatry* 54:345–51.

Levin, E. 1993. Care for the carers: The role of respite services. In G. K. Wilcock, ed., *The Management of Alzheimer's Disease*, 119–32. Petersfield, Hampshire, U.K.: Wrightson Biomedical.

Lewis, J. A. 1992. Treating the alcohol-affected family. In L. L'Abate, J. E. Farrar, and D. A. Serritella, eds., *Handbook of Differential Treatments for Addictions*, 61–63. Boston: Allyn and Bacon.

Lezak, M. 1969. *Neuropsychological Assessment*. New York: Oxford University Press.

Linehan, M. M. 1989. Cognitive and behavior therapy for borderline personality disorders. In A. Tassman, R. E. Hales, and A. J. Frances, eds., *Psychiatric Update: American Psychiatric Association Annual Review* 8. Washington, D.C.: American Psychiatric Press.

———. 1993a. *Cognitive-Behavioral Treatment of Personality Disorder*. New York: Guilford.

———. 1993b. *Skills Training Manual for Treating Borderline Personality Disorder*. New York: Guilford.

———. 1995a. *Treating Borderline Personality Disorder: The Dialectic Approach*. Video. New York: Guilford.

———. 1995b. *Understanding Borderline Personality Disorder* (VIDEO). New York: Guilford.

Linehan, M. M., J. L. Goldstein, S. L. Neilson, and J. A. Chiles. 1983. Reasons for staying alive when you are thinking of killing yourself. *Journal of Consulting and Clinical Psychology* 51:276–86.

Linehan, M. M., and H. L. Heard. 1992. Dialectic behavior therapy for borderline personality disorders. In J. F. Clarkin, E. Marzialli, and H. Munroe-Blum, eds., *Borderline Personality Disorder*, 248–67. New York: Guilford.

Links, P. S., ed. 1990. *Family Environment and Borderline Personality Disorder*. Washington, D.C.: American Psychiatric Press.

Lipowski, Z. J. 1988. Somatization: The concept and its clinical application. *American Journal of Psychiatry* 145:1358–68.

Livesley, W. J., and D. N. Jackson. 1991. Construct validity and classification of personality disorders. In J. M. Oldham, ed., *Personality Disorders: New Perspectives on Diagnostic Validity*, 3–22. Washington, D.C.: American Psychiatric Press.

Loewenstein, R. J. 1993. Psychogenic amnesia and psychogenic fugue: A comprehensive review. In D. Spiegel, ed., *Dissociative Disorders: A Clinical Review*. Lutherville, Md.: Sidran.

Loiselle, R. H. 1993. Sexual abuse and its relationship to eating disorders. In A. J. Giannini and A. E. Slaby, eds., *The Eating Disorders*, 128–32. New York: Springer Verlag.

Lomax, J. W. 1989. Obesity. In H. I. Kaplan and B. Sadock, eds., *Comprehensive Textbook of Psychiatry*, 1179–86. 5th ed. Baltimore: Williams and Wilkins.

Loranger, A. W. 1988. *Personality Disorder Examination (PDE) Manual*. Yonkers: DV Communications.

———. 1995. *International Personality Disorder Examination (IPDE) Manual*. New York: Cornell Medical Center

Loranger, A. W., R. M. A. Hirschfeld, N. Sartorius, and D. A. Regier. 1991. The WHO/ADAMHA International Pilot Study of Personality Disorders: Background and purpose. *Journal of Personality Disorders* 5:296–306.

Lorr, M., and D. M. McNair. 1965. Expansion of the Interpersonal Behavior Circle. *Journal of Personality and Social Psychology* 2:823–30.

Lorr, M., and R. P. Youniss. 1973. An Inventory of Interpersonal Style. *Journal of Personality Assessment* 37:165–73.

Lowinson, J. H., I. J. Marion, H. Joseph, and V. P. Dole. 1992. Methadone maintenance. In J. H. Lowinson, P. Ruiz, and R. B. Millman, eds., *Substance Abuse: A Comprehensive Textbook*. 2d ed. Baltimore: Williams and Wilkins.

Lubin, B., R. M. Larsen, and J. D. Matarazzo. 1984. Patterns of psychological test usage in the United States, 1935–1982. *American Psychologist* 39:451–53.

Lubin, B., R. M. Larsen, J. D. Matarazzo, and M. Seever. 1985. Psychological test usage patterns in five professional settings. *American Psychologist* 40:857–61.

Luria, A. R. 1966. *Higher Cortical Functions in Man*. New York: Basic Books.

———. 1973. *The Working Brain*. New York: Basic Books.

Lynch, A. A., and L. Palacios-Jimenez. 1993. Progression of an illness: The life course of AIDS. *Clinical Social Work Journal* 21 (3): 301–17.

MacAndrew, C. 1965. The differentiation of male alcohol outpatients from nonalcoholic psychiatric patients by means of the MMPI. *Quarterly Journal of Studies on Alcohol* 26:238–46.

MacKinnon. R. A., and S. C. Yudofsky. 1988. Outline of the Psychiatric History and Mental Status Examination. In J. A. Talbott, R. E. Hales, and S. C. Yudofsky, eds., *Textbook of Psychiatry*, 195–99. Washington, D.C.: American Psychiatric Press.

McGlynn, T. J., and H. L. Metcalf, eds. 1989. *Diagnosis and Treatment of Anxiety Disorders*. Washington, D.C.: American Psychiatric Press.

McKinley, J. C., S. R. Hathaway, and P. E. Meehl. 1948. The MMPI, VI: The K Scale. *Journal of Consulting Clinical Psychology* 12:20–31.

McLellan, A. T., I. O. Arndt, D. S. Metzger, G. E. Woody, and C. P. O'Brien. 1993. The effects of psychosocial services in substance abuse treatment. *JAMA* 269:1953–59.

McLellan, A. T., L. Luborsky, E. G. Woody, and C. P. O'Brien. 1980. Addiction severity. An improved diagnostic evaluation instrument for substance abuse patients: The Addiction Severity Index. *Journal of Nervous and Mental Disease* 168:26–33.

Mahler, M. 1971. A study of the separation-individuation process and its possible application to borderline phenomena in the psychoanalytic situation. *Psychoanalytic Study of the Child* 26:403–24.

Malaspina, D., H. M. Quitkin, and C. A. Kaufmann. 1992. Epidemiology and genetics of neuropsychiatric disorders. In S. C. Yudofsky and R. E. Hales, eds., *Textbook of Neuropsychiatry*, 187–226. 2d ed. Washington, D.C.: American Psychiatric Press.

March, J. S., A. Frances, D. Carpenter, and D. A. Kahn. 1997. Treatment of obsessive-compulsive disorder. *Journal of Obsessive-Compulsive Disorder* 58 (Supplement 4): 65–72.

Marengo, J., and M. Harrow. 1985. Thought disorder: A function of schizophrenia, mania, or psychosis? *Journal of Nervous and Mental Disorders* 173:35–41.

Margolin, A., and S. K. Avants. 1992. Cue-reactivity and cocaine addiction. In T. R. Kosten and H. D. Kleber, eds., *Clinician's Guide to Cocaine Addiction*, 109–27. New York: Guilford.

Markowitz, J. C. 1998a. *Interpersonal Psychotherapy for Dysthymic Disorder*. Washington, D.C.: American Psychiatric Press.

Markowitz, J. C., ed. 1998b. *Interpersonal Psychotherapy*. Washington, D.C.: American Psychiatric Press.

Markowitz, J. C., J. H. Kocsis, B. Fishman, L. A. Spielman, L. B. Jacobsberg, A. J. Frances, G. L. Klerman, and S. W. Perry. 1998c. Treatment of depressive symptoms in HIV+ patients. *Archives of General Psychiatry* 55:452–57.

Markowitz, J. C., M. E. Moran, and J. H. Kocsis. 1992. Prevalence and comorbidity of dysthymic disorder among psychiatric patients. *Journal of Affective Disorders* 24:63–71.

Markowitz, J. C., and S. W. Perry. 1992. Effects of human immunodeficiency virus on the central nervous system. In S. C. Yudofsky and R. E.

Hales, eds., *Textbook of Neuropsychiatry*, 499–518. 2d ed. Washington, D.C.: American Psychiatric Press.

Marks, I. M., and A. M. Mathews. 1979. Brief Standard Self-rating for Phobic Patients. *Behavior Research and Therapy* 17:263–67.

Marks, I. M., and W. Seeman. 1963. *The Actuarial Description of Abnormal Personality*. Baltimore: Williams and Wilkins.

Marks, I. M., W. Seeman, and D. L. Haller. 1974. *The Actuarial Use of the MMPI with Adolescents and Adults*. Baltimore: Williams and Wilkins.

Martin, R. L. 1990. The genetics of Alzheimer disease: Identification of persons at high risk. In R. E. Becker, ed., *Alzheimer Disease: Current Research in Early Diagnosis*, 31–48. New York: Taylor and Francis.

Martin, R. L., and S. H. Yutzy. 1997. Somatoform disorders. In A. Tasman, J. Kay, and J. A. Lieberman, eds., *Psychiatry*, 2:1119–55. Philadelphia: Saunders.

Marx, R. D. 1993. Depression and eating disorders. In A. J. Giannini and A. E. Slaby, eds., *The Eating Disorders*, 110–27. New York: Springer Verlag.

Marzuk, P. M., H. Tierney, K. Tardiff, E. M. Gross, E. B. Morgan, M. A. Hsu, and J. Mann. 1988. Increased risk of suicide in persons with AIDS. *JAMA* 259:1333–37.

Maser, J. D., and C. R. Cloninger. 1990. *Comorbidity of Mood and Anxiety Disorders*. Washington, D.C.: American Psychiatric Press.

Masterson, J. F., and D. Rinsley. 1975. The borderline syndrome: The role of the mother in the genesis and psychic structure of the borderline personality. *International Journal of Psychoanalysis* 56:163–77.

Mattaini, M. 1993. *More Than a Thousand Words: Graphics for Clinical Practice*. Washington, D.C.: National Association of Social Workers.

Mattaini, M., and S. Kirk. 1991. Assessing assessment in social work. *Social Work* 36:260–66.

Mattis, S. 1975. Mental Status Examination for Organic Mental Syndrome in the Elderly Patient. In L. Bellak and T. Karasu, eds., *Geriatric Psychiatry*, 77–122. New York: Grune and Stratton.

———. 1988. *Dementia Rating Scale: Professional Manual*. Odessa, Fla.: Psychological Assessment Resources.

Mattis, S., J. H. French, and I. Rapin. 1975. Dyslexia in children and young adults: Three independent neuropsychological syndromes. *Developmental Medicine and Child Neurology* 17:150–63.

Mattis, S., D. Gilliam, and R. Greenberg. 1989. The detection of brain-dysfunction in a psychiatric population: A useful instrument. *Journal of Clinical Experimental Neuropsychology* 11 (1): 33.

Mattis, S., R. Kovner, and E. Goldmeier. 1978. Different patterns of mnemonic deficits in two organic amnestic syndromes. *Brain and Language* 6:179–91.

Mechanic, D. 1962. The concept of illness behavior. *Journal of Chronic Diseases* 15:189–94.

Megargee, E. I., P. E. Cook, and A. G. Mendelsohn. 1967. Development and validation of an MMPI scale of assaultiveness in overcontrolled individuals. *Journal of Abnormal Psychology* 72:519–28.

Meissner, W. J. 1987. Psychotherapy and the paranoid personality. *Harvard Mental Health Letter* 4 (6): 4–6. Boston: Department of Continuing Education, Harvard Medical School.

Mesulam, M. M. 1985. Attention, confusional state, and neglect. In M. M. Mesulam, ed., *Principle of Behavioral Neurology*, 127–62. Philadelphia: Davis.

Meyer, C. H. 1977. *Social Work Practice*. 2d ed. New York: Free Press.

———. 1992. Social work assessment: Is there an empirical base? *Research on Social Work Practice* 2 (3): 297–305.

———. 1993. *Assessment in Social Work Practice*. New York: Columbia University Press.

———. 1995. Assessment in social work: Direct practice. *Encyclopedia of Social Work*. 19th ed. Washington, D.C.: National Association of Social Workers.

———, ed. 1983. *Clinical Social Work in the Eco-Systems Perspective*. New York: Columbia University Press.

Meyer, J. M., and A. J. Stunkard. 1993. Genetics and human obesity. In A. J. Stunkard and T. A. Wadden, eds., *Obesity Theory and Therapy*, 137–50. New York: Raven.

Michels, Robert. 1998. The role of psychotherapy: Psychiatry's resistance to managed care. *Archives of General Psychiatry* 55:564.

Miles, P. 1977. Conditions predisposing to suicide: A review. *Journal of Nervous and Mental Diseases* 164:231–46.

Miller, F. E., and W. Borden. 1992. Family caregivers of persons with neuropsychiatric illness: A stress and coping perspective. In S. C. Yudofsky and R. E. Hales, eds., *Textbook of Neuropsychiatry*, 755–72. 2d ed. Washington, D.C.: American Psychiatric Press.

Miller, N. S. 1993. Eating disorders and drug and alcohol dependency. In A. J. Giannini and A. E. Slaby, eds., *The Eating Disorders*, 213–26. New York: Springer Verlag.

Miller, R. S., and S. G. Austrian. 1980. Mental health services in primary care: The role of the social worker. Paper presented at the annual meeting of the American Public Health Association, October, Detroit.

Miller, R. S., S. Austrian, B. Morrison, and H. Rehr. 1984. Social work practice in primary health care: An assessment and outcome study. Paper presented at the National Association of Social Workers National Health Conference, June, Washington, D.C.

Millon, T. 1983. *Millon Clinical Multiaxial Inventory*. 3d ed. Minneapolis: Interpretive Scoring Systems.

———. 1992. The borderline construct: Introductory notes on its history, theory, and empirical grounding. In J. F. Clarkin, E. Marzialli, and H. Munroe-Blum, eds., *Borderline Personality Disorder*, 3–23. New York: Guilford.

———. 1994. *Manual for the MCMI-III*. Minneapolis: National Computer Systems.

———. 1996. *Disorders of Personality DSM-IV and Beyond*. New York: A Wiley–Interscience Publication.

———. 1999. Clinical syndromes and personality disorders. *Harvard Mental Health Letter* 15 (9): 4–6. Boston: Harvard Medical School Health Publications Group.

Mintz, J., L. I. Mintz, M. J. Arruda, and S. S. Hwang. 1992. Treatments of depression and the functional capacity to work. *Archives of General Psychiatry* 49 (10): 761–68.

Minuchin, S., B. L. Rosman, and L. Baker. 1978. *Psychosomatic Families*. Cambridge: Harvard University Press.

Mirsky, A. F., and C. Kornetsky. 1964. On the dissimilar effects of drugs on the Digit Symbol Substitution and Continuous Performance Tests: A review and preliminary integration of behavioral and physiological evidence. *Psychopharmacologia* 5:161–77.

Mitchell, J. E., R. L. Pyle, S. Specker, and K. Hanson. 1992. Eating disorders and chemical dependency. In J. Yager, H. E. Gwirtsman, and C. K. Edelstein, eds., *Special Problems in Managing Eating Disorders*, 1–14. Washington, D.C.: American Psychiatric Press.

Moreland, K. L., R. D. Fowler, and L. M. Honaker. 1994. Future directions in the use of psychological assessment for treatment planning and outcome assessment: Predictions and recommendations. In M. E. Maruish, ed., *The Use of Psychological Testing for Treatment Planning and Outcome Assessment*, 581–602. Hillsdale: Erlbaum.

Morey, L. C. 1991. *Personality Assessment Inventory*. Odessa, Fla.: Psychological Assessment Resources.

Mufson, M. J. 1999. What is the role of psychiatry in the management of chronic pain? *Harvard Mental Health Letter* 16 (3): 8. Boston: Harvard Medical School Health Publications Group.

Mulder, R. T., A. L. Beautrais, P. R. Joyce, and D. M. Ferguson. 1998. Relationship between dissociation, childhood sexual abuse, childhood physical abuse, and mental illness in a general population. *American Journal of Psychiatry* 155 (6): 806–11.

Munoz, R. 1987. *Depression Prevention*. New York: Hemisphere.

Murray, H. A. 1943. *Thematic Apperception Test Manual*. Cambridge: Harvard University Press.

Musto, D. F. 1992. Historical perspectives on alcohol and drug abuse. In J. H. Lowinson, P. Ruiz, and R. B. Millman, eds., *Substance Abuse: A Comprehensive Textbook*, 2–14. 2d ed. Baltimore: Williams and Wilkins.

NAMI-FACTS Staff. 1998. Celexa, a new medication for the treatment of depression. *NAMI-FACTS* 1 (1): 3.

Narrow, W. E., D. A. Regier, D. S. Rae, R. W. Manderscheid, and B. Z. Locke. 1993. Use of services by persons with mental and addictive disorders. *Archives of General Psychiatry* 50:95–108.

National Institute on Alcohol Abuse and Alcoholism. 1993. *Project Match Monograph Series*. Rockville, Md.: National Institutes of Health.

———. 1999. *Alcohol Alert* 46 (December): 1.

Nelson, H. E. 1982. *National Adult Reading Test (NART) Manual*. Berkshire: NFER-Nelson.

Nemiah, J. C. 1989. Dissociative disorders (Hysterical neuroses, dissociate type). In H. I. Kaplan and B. Sadock, eds., *Comprehensive Textbook of Psychiatry*, 1028–44. 5th ed. Baltimore: Williams and Wilkins.

———. 1993. Dissociation, conversion, and somatization. In D. Spiegel, ed., *Dissociative Disorders: A Clinical Review*, 104–15. Lutherville, Md.: Sidran.

Newman, F. L., and J. A. Ciarlo. 1994. Criteria for selecting psychological tests/instruments. In M. Maruish, ed., *Use of Psychological Testing for Treatment Planning and Outcome Assessment*, 98–110. Malvern: LEA.

Norden, K. A., D. N. Klein, S. K. Donaldson, C. M. Pepper, and L. M. Klein. 1995. Reports of the early home environment in DSM-III-R personality disorders. *Journal of Personality Disorders* 9:213–23.

North, C. S., J. M. Ryall, D. A. Ricci, and R. D. Wetzel. 1993. *Multiple Personalities, Multiple Disorders*. New York: Oxford University Press.

Noyes, R., R. G. Kathol, M. M. Fisher, B. M. Phillips, M. T. Suelzer, and C. S. Holt. 1993. The validity of DSM-III-R hypochondriasis. *Archives of General Psychiatry* 50 (11): 961–70.

Oldham, J. M., ed. 1991. *Personality Disorders: New Perspectives on Diagnostic Validity.* Washington, D.C.: American Psychiatric Press.

Olfson, M., M. Weissman, and J. F. Gottlieb. 1997. Essential roles for psychiatry in the era of managed care. *Archives of General Psychiatry* 54: 206–8.

O'Malley, S. S., T. R. Kosten, and J. A. Renner. 1990. Dual diagnosis: Substance abuse and personality disorder. In D. Adler, ed., *Treating Personality Disorders,* 115–37. San Francisco: Jossey-Bass.

Orbach, S. 1985. Accepting the symptom: A feminist psychoanalytic treatment of anorexia nervosa. In D. M. Garner and P. E. Garfinkel, eds., *Handbook of Psychotherapy for Anorexia Nervosa and Bulimia,* 83–106. New York: Guilford.

———. 1986. *Hunger Strike: The Anorectic's Struggle as a Metaphor for Our Age.* New York: Norton.

Overall, J. E., and D. R. Gorham. 1962. The Brief Psychiatric Rating Scale. *Psychological Reports* 10:799–812.

Oxman, T. E., and V. O. Emery. 1993. What is the relationship between depression and dementia in the elderly? *Harvard Mental Health Letter* 9 (10): 8. Boston: Harvard Medical School Health Publications Group.

Paradis, B. A. 1993. A self-psychology approach to the treatment of gay men with AIDS. *Clinical Social Work Journal* 21 (4): 405–16.

Paris, Joel. 1994. Borderline personality disorder: Current diagnostic and treatment perspectives. Paper presented at a symposium, June, New York Hospital—Cornell Medical Center, Westchester Division, White Plains, New York.

———. 1998. Personality disorders in sociocultural perspective. *Journal of Personality Disorders* 12:289–301.

Parsons, O. A., and S. J. Nixon. 1993. Behavioral disorders associated with central nervous system dysfunction. In P. B. Sutker and H. E. Adams, eds., *Comprehensive Textbook of Psychopathology,* 689–733. New York: Plenum.

Paulman, R. G., and W. D. MacInnes. 1991. Neuropsychological evaluation of dementia. In M. F. Weiner, ed., *The Dementias: Diagnosis and Management,* 167–84. Washington, D.C.: American Psychiatric Press.

Pear, R. 1999. Mental Disorders Common, U.S. Says; Many Not Treated. *New York Times,* December 13, A-1.

Pennebaker, J. W., and D. Watson. 1991. The psychology of somatic symptoms. In L. J. Kirmayer and J. M. Robbins, eds., *Current Concepts of Somatization and Clinical Perspectives*, 21–35. Washington, D.C.: American Psychiatric Press.

Perlick, K., P. Stastny, I. Katz, M. Mayfer, and S. Mattis. 1986. Memory deficits and anticholinergic levels in chronic schizophrenia. *American Journal of Psychiatry* 143 (2): 230–32.

Perry, J. C. 1991. Use of longitudinal data to validate personality disorders. In J. M. Oldham, ed., *Personality Disorders: New Perspectives on Diagnostic Validity*, 25–40. Washington, D.C.: American Psychiatric Press.

———. 1993. Longitudinal studies of personality disorders. *Journal of Personality Disorders* (Spring Supplement): 63–85.

Perry, J. C., and G. E. Vaillant. 1989. Personality disorders. In H. I. Kaplan and B. Sadock, eds., *Comprehensive Textbook of Psychiatry*, 1352–86. 5th ed. Baltimore: Williams and Wilkins.

Perry, S. 1994. Opening remarks. Presented at the Symposium on HIV and Depression, January, New York Hospital-Cornell Medical Center, White Plains, New York.

Perry, S., A. Frances, and J. Clarkin. 1990. *A DSM-III-R Casebook of Treatment Selection*. New York: Brunner/Mazel.

Peters, C. P. 1990. The inpatient treatment of severe personality disorders: The borderline spectrum. In D. Adler, ed., *Treating Personality Disorders*, 65–86. San Francisco: Jossey-Bass.

Pfohl, B., D. W. Black, R. Noyes, W. H. Coryell, and J. Barrach. 1991. Axis I and Axis II comorbidity findings: Implications for validity. In J. M. Oldham, ed., *Personality Disorders: New Perspectives on Diagnostic Validity*, 147–61. Washington, D.C.: American Psychiatric Press.

Pfohl, B., N. Blum, and M. Zimmerman. 1997. *Structured Interview for DSM-IV Personality (SIDP-IV)*. Washington, D.C.: American Psychiatric Press.

Pfohl, B., and D. Langbehn. 1994. *Iowa Personality Disorder Screen (Version 1.2)*. Iowa City: University of Iowa, Department of Psychiatry.

Phelan, J. C., E. J. Bromet, and B. G. Link. 1998. Psychiatric illness and family stigma. *Schizophrenia Bulletin* 24 (1): 115–26.

Phillips, K. A., J. G. Gunderson, R. M. A. Hirschfeld, and N. A. Smith. 1990. A review of the depressive personality. *American Journal of Psychiatry* 147:830–37.

Pilkonis, P. A., Y. Kim, J. M. Proietti, and M. Barkham. 1996. A screen scale for personality disorders developed from the Inventory of Interpersonal Problems. *Journal of Personality Disorders* 10:355—69.

Pinals, D. A., and A. Breier. 1997. Schizophrenia. In A. Tasman, J. Kay, and J. A. Lieberman, eds., *Psychiatry*, 2:927–65. Philadelphia: Saunders.

Pirozzolo, F. 1982. Neuropsychological assessment of dementia. *Neurology Clinics* 4 (1): 12–18.

Pope, H. G., and J. I. Hudson. 1989. Eating disorders. In H. I. Kaplan and B. Sadock, eds., *Comprehensive Textbook of Psychiatry*, 1854–64. 5th ed. Baltimore: Williams and Wilkins.

Project Match Research Group. 1997. Matching alcoholism treatments to client heterogeneity: Project MATCH posttreatment drinking outcomes. *Journal of Studies on Alcoholism* 58 (1): 7–29.

Putnam, F. W. 1989. Diagnosis and treatment of multiple personality disorder. New York: Guilford.

———. 1993. Dissociative phenomena. In D. Spiegel, ed., *Dissociative Disorders: A Clinical Review*. Lutherville, Md.: Sidran.

Putnam, F. W., J. J. Guroff, E. K. Silberman, L. Barban, and R. M. Post. 1986. The clinical phenomenology of multiple personality disorder: A review of 100 recent cases. *Journal of Clinical Psychiatry* 47:285–93.

Ranew, L. F., and D. A. Serritella. 1992. Substance abuse and addiction. In L. L'Abate, J. E. Farrar, and D. A. Serritella, eds., *Handbook of Differential Treatments for Addictions*, 84–96. Boston: Allyn and Bacon.

Raskin, A. 1982. Assessment of psychopathology by the nurse or psychiatric aide. In E. I. Burdock, A. Sudilovsky, and S. Gershon, eds., *The Behavioral Assessment of Psychiatric Patients: Quantitative Techniques for Evaluation*. New York: Marcel Dekker.

Raven, J. C. 1960. *Guide to the Standard Progressive Matrices*. London: H. K. Lewis.

Ravussin, E., and B. A. Swinburn. 1993. Energy metabolism. In A. J. Stunkard and T. A. Wadden, eds., *Obesity Theory and Therapy*, 97–124. New York: Raven.

Rea, W. S., and I. L. Extein. 1993. Biological factors in obesity. In A. J. Giannini and A. E. Slaby, eds., *The Eating Disorders*, 63–75. New York: Springer Verlag.

Regier, D. A., J. H. Boyd, J. D. Burke, D. S. Rae, J. K. Myers, M. Kroner, L. N. Robins, L. K. George, M. Karno, and B. Z. Locke. 1988. One-month prevalence of mental disorders in the U.S. *Archives of General Psychiatry* 45:977–86.

Regier, D. A., W. E. Narrow, D. S. Rae, R. W. Manderscheid, B. Z. Locke, and F. K. Goodwin. 1993. The de facto U.S. mental and addictive disorders service system. *Archives of General Psychiatry* 50:85–92.

Reitan, R. M., and L. A. Davison. 1974. *Clinical Neuropsychology: Current Status and Application*. New York: Winston/Wiley.

Rey, A. 1941. L'examen psychologique dans les cas d'encephalopathie traumatique. *Archives de psychologie* 28 (112): 286–340.

———. 1964. *L'examen clinique en psychologique*. Paris: Presses Universitaires de France.

Rhodes, R., and A. D. Johnson. 1994. Women and alcoholism: A psychosocial approach. *Affilia* 9 (2): 145–56.

Ridley, C. R., L. C. Li, and C. L. Hill. 1998. Multicultural assessment: Reexamination, reconceptualization, and practical application. *Counseling Psychologist* 26 (6): 827–910.

Rinsley, D. B. 1989. Notes of the developmental pathogenesis of narcissistic personality disorder. In O. F. Kernberg, ed., *The Psychiatric Clinics of North America* 12 (3): 695–708. Philadelphia: Saunders.

Robbins, J. M., and L. J. Kirmayer. 1991. Cognitive and social factors in somatization. In L. J. Kirmayer and J. M. Robbins, eds., *Current Concepts of Somatization and Clinical Perspectives*, 107–41. Washington, D.C.: American Psychiatric Press.

Roberts, C. S., C. Severinsen, C. Kuehn, D. Straker, and C. J. Fritz. 1992. Obstacles to effective case management with AIDS patients: The clinician's perspective. *Social Work in Health Care* 17 (2): 27–39.

Rodin, G., J. Craven, and C. Littlefield. 1991. *Depression in the Medically Ill*. New York: Brunner/Mazel.

Rogers. R. 1994. Malingering. *Harvard Mental Health Letter* 10 (9): 3–5. Boston: Harvard Medical School Health Publications Group.

Rorschach, H. 1949. *Psychodiagnostics*. New York: Grune and Stratton.

Ross, C. A. 1989. *Multiple Personality Disorder: Diagnosis, Clinical Features, and Treatment*. New York: Wiley.

———. 1997. *Multiple Personality Disorder: Diagnosis, Clinical Features, and Treatment*. 2d ed. New York: Wiley.

Rosvold, H. E., A. F. Mirsky, I. Sarason, E. B. Bransome, and L. H. Beck. 1956. A continuous performance test of brain damage. *Journal of Consulting and Clinical Psychology* 20:343–50.

Rounsaville, B. J., and S. Lithar. 1992. Family/genetic studies of cocaine abusers and opioid addicts. In T. R. Kosten and H. D. Kleber, eds., *Clinician's Guide to Cocaine Addiction*, 206–21. New York: Guilford.

Rowe, C. J. 1989. *An Outline of Psychiatry*. Dubuque: Wm. C. Brown.

Schildkraut, J., A. Gree, and J. Mooney. 1985. Affective disorders: Biochemical aspects. In H. I. Kaplan and B. J. Sadock, eds., *Comprehensive Textbook of Psychiatry*, 769–78. 4th ed. Baltimore: Williams and Wilkins.

Rush, A. J. 1998. *Mood and Anxiety Disorders*. Philadelphia: Williams and Wilkins.

Russell, G. F. M. 1997. The history of bulimia nervosa. In D. M. Garner and P. E. Garfinkel, eds., *Handbook of Treatment for Eating Disorders*, 11–24. New York: Guilford.

Sabo, A. N. 1997. Etiological significance of association between childhood trauma and borderline personality disorders: Conceptual and clinical implications. *Journal of Personality Disorders* 11:50–70.

Schroeder, L. Wormworth, J. A. and W. J. Lively. 1994. Dimensions of personality disorders and the Five-Factor Model of personality. In P. Widdeger, ed., *Personality Disorders and the Five-Factor Model of Personality*, 117–27. Washington: American Psychological Press.

Schwartz, H. J. 1990. *Psychoanalytic Treatment and Theory*. 2d ed. Madison: International Universities Press.

Sclafini, A. 1993. Dietary obesity. In A. J. Stunkard and T. A. Wadden, eds., *Obesity Theory and Therapy*, 124–36. New York: Raven.

Seashore, C. E., D. Lewis, and D. L. Saetveit. 1960. *Seashore Measures of Musical Talents*. Rev. ed. New York: Psychological Corporation.

Secunda, S. K., M. M. Katz, A. Swann, S. H. Koslow, J. W. Maas, S. Chung, and J. Croughan. 1985. Mania: Diagnosis, state measurement, and prediction of treatment response. *Journal of Affective Disorders* 8:113–21.

Seidman, I. J. 1983. Schizophrenia and brain dysfunction: An integration of recent neurodiagnostic findings. *Psychology Bulletin* 94:195–238.

Serritella, D. A. 1992. Tobacco addiction. In L. L'Abate, J. E. Farrar, and D. A. Serritella, eds., *Handbook of Differential Treatments for Addictions*, 97–112. Boston: Allyn and Bacon.

Shanks, M. F. 1993. Drug therapy in relation to current knowledge. In G. K. Wilcock, ed., *The Management of Alzheimer's Disease*, 77–86. Petersfield, Hampshire, U.K.: Wrightson Biomedical.

Shapiro, D. 1989. *Psychotherapy of Neurotic Character*. New York: Basic Books.

Shea, M. T., I. Elkin, S. D. Imber, S. M. Sotsky, J. T. Wathny, J. F. Collins, P. A. Pilkonis, E. Beckham, D. R. Glass, R. T. Dolan, and M. B. Parloff. 1992. Course of depressive symptoms over follow-up. *Archives of General Psychiatry* 49:782–87.

Shear, M. K. 1997. Panic disorder with and without agoraphobia. In A. Tasman, J. Kay, and J. A. Lieberman, eds., *Psychiatry*, 2:1021–36. Philadelphia: Saunders.

Shenton, M. E., R. Kikinis, A. J. French, S. D. Pollak, M. LeMay, C. G. Wible, H. Hokama, J. Martin, D. Metcalf, M. Coleman, and R. W.

McCarley. 1992. Abnormalities of the left temporal lobe and thought disorder in schizophrenia: A quantitative magnetic resonance imaging study. *New England Journal of Medicine* 327:604–12.

Shipley, W. C. 1946. *The Institute of Living Scale*. Los Angeles: Western Psychological Services.

Silverstone, T. 1993. The place of appetite-suppressant drugs in the treatment of obesity. In A. J. Stunkard and T. A. Wadden, eds., *Obesity Theory and Therapy*, 275—86. New York: Raven.

Simon, G. E. 1991. Somatization and psychiatric disorders. In L. J. Kirmayer and J. M. Robbins, eds., *Current Concepts of Somatization and Clinical Perspectives*, 37–62. Washington, D.C.: American Psychiatric Press.

Simon, R. I. 1992. Ethical and legal issues in neuropsychiatry. In S. C. Yudofsky and R. E. Hales, eds., *Textbook of Neuropsychiatry*, 773–806. 2d ed. Washington, D.C.: American Psychiatric Press.

Skodol, A. E., L. Rosnick, D. Kellman, J. Oldham, and S. Hyler. 1991. Development of a procedure for validating structured assessments of Axis II. In J. M. Oldham, ed., *Personality Disorders: New Perspectives on Diagnostic Validity*, 43–70. Washington, D.C.: American Psychiatric Press.

Slaby, A. E., and R. Dwenger. 1993. History of anorexia nervosa. In A. J. Giannini. and A. E. Slaby, eds., *The Eating Disorders*, 1–17. New York: Springer Verlag.

Smith, G. R. 1990. *Somatization Disorder in the Medical Setting*. Rockville, Md.: National Institute of Mental Health.

Snyder, D. K., R. M. Willis, and T. W. Keiser. 1979. Empirical validation of the marital satisfaction inventory: An actuarial approach. *Journal of Consulting and Clinical Psychology* 49:262–68.

Sobell, M. B., L. C. Sobell, F. Klajner, D. Pavan, and E. Basian. 1986. The reliability of a timeline method for assessing normal drinker college students' recent drinking history: Utility for alcohol research. *Addictive Behaviors* 11:149–61.

Soloff, P. H., A. George, J. Cornelius, S. Nathan, and P. Schulz. 1991. Pharmacotherapy and borderline subtypes. In J. M. Oldham, ed., *Personality Disorders: New Perspectives on Diagnostic Validity*, 91–103. Washington, D.C.: American Psychiatric Press.

Solomon, D. A., G. I. Keitner, I. W. Miller, M. T. Shea, and M. B. Keller. 1995. Course of illness and maintenance treatment for patients with bipolar disorder. *Journal of Clinical Psychiatry* 56 (1): 1–13.

Solovay, M. R., M. E. Shenton, C. Gasparetti, M. Coleman, E. Kestenbaum, J. T. Carpenter, and P. S. Holzman. 1986. Scoring manual for the Thought Disorder Index. *Schizophrenia Bulletin* 12:483–96.

Spanier, G. B. 1976. Measuring dyadic adjustment: New scales for assessing the quality of marriage and similar dyads. *Journal of Marriage and the Family* 38:15–28.

Sperry, L. 1995. *Handbook of Diagnosis and Treatment of DSM-IV Personality Disorders*. New York: Brunner/Mazel.

Spiegel, D. 1993a. Multiple posttraumatic personality disorder. In R. P. Kluft and C. G. Fine, eds., *Clinical Perspectives on Multiple Personality Disorder*. Washington, D.C.: American Psychiatric Press.

———, ed. 1993b. *Dissociative Disorders: A Clinical Review*. Lutherville, Md.: Sidran.

Spielberger, C. D. 1991. *State-Trait Anger Expression Inventory*. Rev. ed. Odessa, Fla.: Psychological Assessment Resources.

Spielberger, C. D., R. L. Gorsuch, and R. E. Luchene. 1976. *Manual for the State-Trait Anxiety Inventory*. Palo Alto, Calif.: Consulting Psychologists Press.

Spielberger, C. D., G. A. Jacobs, S. Russell, and R. S. Crane. 1983. Assessment of anger: The State-Trait Anger Scale. In J. N. Butcher and C. D. Spielberger, eds., *Advances in Personality Assessment* 2 (2): 1–47. Hillsdale: LEA.

Spitzer, R. L., and J. Endicott. 1977. *Schedule for Affective Disorders and Schizophrenia (SADS)*. 3d ed. New York: New York State Psychiatric Institute, Biometric Research Division.

Spreen, O., and E. Strauss. 1998. *A Compendium of Neuropsychological Tests*. 2d ed. New York: Oxford University Press.

Squire, L. R., and A. P. Shimamura. 1986. Characterizing amnestic patients for neurobehavioral study. *Behavioral Neuroscience* 100 (6): 866–77.

Staff. 1991. Post-traumatic stress: Parts I and II. *Harvard Mental Health Letter* 7 (9–10). Boston: Department of Continuing Education of Harvard Medical School.

———. 1994. Social phobia–Part II. *Harvard Mental Health Letter* 11 (5): 2–3.

———. 1995. Schizophrenia update–Part I. *Harvard Mental Health Letter* 11 (12): 1–3. Boston: Harvard Medical School Health Publications Group.

———. 1996. Personality disorders: The anxious cluster–Part I. *Harvard Mental Health Letter* 12 (8): 1–3. Boston: Harvard Medical School Health Publications Group.

———. 1998. New treatment for schizophrenia–Part I. *Harvard Mental Health Letter* 14 (10): 1–3. Boston: Harvard Medical School Health Publications Group.

————. 1999. AIDS and mental health–Part II. *Harvard Mental Health Letter* 15 (10): 1–3. Boston: Harvard Medical School Health Publications Group.

Stein, A. 1938. Psychoanalytic investigation of and therapy in a borderline group of neurosis. *Psychoanalytic Quarterly* 7:467–89.

Steinberg, M. 1993. The spectrum of depersonalization: Assessment and treatment. In D. Spiegel, ed., *Dissociative Disorders: A Clinical Review.* Lutherville, Md.: Sidran.

Stine, S. M. 1992. Cocaine abuse within methadone maintenance programs. In T. R. Kosten and H. D. Kleber, eds., *Clinician's Guide to Cocaine Addiction,* 359–73. New York: Guilford.

Stone, A. M. 1992. The role of shame in post-traumatic stress disorder. *American Journal of Orthopsychiatry* 62:131–36.

Stone, M. H. 1990. *The Fate of Borderline Patients.* New York: Guilford.

Stoudemire, A., ed. 1998. *General Psychiatry for Medical Students.* Philadelphia: Lippincott-Raven.

Stoudemire, A., J. L. Levenson, and T. M. Brown. 1998. Delirium, dementia, and other disorders associated with cognitive impairments. In A. Stoudemire, ed., *General Psychiatry for Medical Students,* 112–45. Philadelphia: Lippincott-Raven.

Stunkard, A. J., and T. A. Wadden, eds. 1993. *Obesity Theory and Therapy.* 2d ed. New York: Raven.

Sutker, P. B., and H. E. Adams, eds. 1993. *Comprehensive Handbook of Psychopathology.* New York: Plenum.

Svrakic, D. M., C. Whitehead, T. R. Przybeck, et al. 1993. Differential diagnosis of personality disorders by the Seven-Factor Model of Temperament and Character. *Archives of General Psychiatry* 50:991–99.

Swartz. H. A., and J. C. Markowitz. 1998. Interpersonal therapy for the treatment of depression in HIV-positive men and women. In J. C. Markowitz, ed., *Interpersonal Psychotherapy,* 129–55. Washington, D.C.: American Psychiatric Press.

Tasman, A., J. Kay, and J. A. Lieberman, eds. 1997. *Psychiatry.* 2 vols. Philadelphia: Saunders.

Tatarsky. A., and A. Washton. 1992. Intensive outpatient treatment: A psychological perspective. In B. C. Wallace, ed., *The Chemically Dependent,* 28–38. New York: Brunner/Mazel.

Taylor, C. B., and B. Arnow. 1988. *The Nature and Treatment of Anxiety Disorders.* New York: Free Press.

Taylor, G. J. 1989. Alexithymia. *Harvard Medical School Mental Health Letter* 5 (12): 8. Boston: Department of Continuing Education of Harvard Medical School.

Taylor, R. L. 1990. *Distinguishing Psychological from Organic Disorders.* New York: Springer.

Taylor-Spence, J. A., and K. W. Spence. 1966. The motivational components of manifest anxiety: Drive and drive stimuli. In C. D. Spielberger, ed., *Anxiety and Behavior,* 291–326. New York: Academic Press.

Tien, A. Y., and W. W. Eaton. 1992. Psychopathologic precursors and sociodemographic risk factors for the schizophrenic syndrome. *Archives of General Psychiatry* 49:37–46.

Tintner, R. J., M. F. Weiner, and F. J. Bonte. 1991. The dementia workup. In M. F. Weiner, ed., *The Dementias: Diagnosis and Management,* 47–75. Washington, D.C.: American Psychiatric Press.

Treaster, J. P. 1993a. With supply and purity up, heroin use expands. *New York Times,* August 1, A1.

———. 1993b. U.S. reports sharp increase in drug-caused emergencies. *New York Times,* October 5, B11.

True, W. E., J. Rich, S. A. Eisen, A. C. Heath, J. Goldberg, M. J. Lyons, and J. Nowak. 1993. A twin study of genetic and environmental contributions to liability for posttraumatic stress symptoms. *Archives of General Psychiatry* 50:257–64.

Tucker, G. 1998. Putting DSM-IV in perspective. *American Journal of Psychiatry* 155:159–61.

Turkat, I. D. 1990. *The Personality Disorders.* New York: Pergamon.

U.S. Department of Health and Human Services. *HHS News.* August 1993.

Tyrer, P., J. Gunderson, M. Lyons, and M. Tohen. 1997. Extent of comorbidity between mental state and personality disorder. *Journal of Personality Disorders* 11:242–59.

Vanderlinden, J., J. Norre, and W. Vandereycken. 1992. *A Practical Guide to the Treatment of Bulimia Nervosa.* New York: Brunner/Mazel.

Vitaliano, P. P., A. R. Breen, J. Russo, M. Albert, M. V. Vitiello, and P. N. Prinz. 1984. The clinical utility of the Dementia Rating Scale for Assessing Alzheimer Patients. *Journal of Chronic Diseases* 37 (9/10): 743–53.

Wadden, T. A. 1993. The treatment of obesity: An overview. In A. J. Stunkard and T. A. Wadden, eds., *Obesity Theory and Therapy,* 197–218. New York: Raven.

Wadden, T. A., and A. J. Stunkard. 1993. Psychosocial consequences of obesity and dieting: Research and clinical findings. In A. J. Stunkard and T. A. Wadden, eds., *Obesity Theory and Therapy*, 163–78. New York: Raven.

Waites, E. A. 1993. *Trauma and Survival*. New York: Norton.

Waldinger, R. J. 1987. Intensive psychodynamic therapy with borderline patients: An overview. *American Journal of Psychiatry* 144:267–75.

———. 1990. *Psychiatry for Medical Students*. 2d ed. Washington, D.C.: American Psychiatric Press.

Wallace, B. C. 1992. *The Chemically Dependent*. New York: Brunner/ Mazel.

Wechsler, D. 1997. *WAIS-III Administration and Scoring Manual*. San Antonio: Psychological Corporation.

Weiner, M. F., ed. 1991. *The Dementias: Diagnosis and Management*. Washington, D.C.: American Psychiatric Press.

Weiner, M. F., and D. Svetlik. 1991. Dealing with family caregivers. In M. F. Weiner, ed., *The Dementias: Diagnosis and Management*, 185–99. Washington, D.C.: American Psychiatric Press.

Weiner, M. F., R. J. Tintner, and K. Goodkin. 1991. Differential diagnosis. In M. F. Weiner, ed., *The Dementias: Diagnosis and Management*, 77–106. Washington, D.C.: American Psychiatric Press.

Weissman, A., and A. T. Beck. 1978. Development and validation of the Dysfunctional Attitude Scale. Paper presented at the annual meeting of the American Association of Behavior Therapists, Chicago.

Weissman, M. M., and S. Bothwell. 1976. Assessment of social adjustment by patient self-report. *Archives of General Psychiatry* 33:111–15.

Weissman, M. M., P. J. Leaf, M. L. Bruce, and L. Floris. 1988. The epidemiology of dysthymia in five communities: Rates, risks, comorbidity, and treatment. *American Journal of Psychiatry* 145:815–19.

Weissman, M. M., and J. C. Markowitz. 1994. Interpersonal psychotherapy. *Archives of General Psychiatry* 51:599–606.

———. 1998. An overview of interpersonal psychotherapy. In J. C. Markowitz, ed., *Interpersonal Psychotherapy*, 1–33. Washington, D.C.: American Psychiatric Press.

Weissman, M. M., and D. Sholomskas. 1982. The assessment of social adjustment by the clinician, the patient, and the family. In E. I. Burdock, A. Sudilovsky, and S. Gershon, eds., *The Behavior of Psychiatric Patients: Quantitative Techniques for Evaluation*, 177—209. New York: Marcel Dekker.

Welch, L. W. 1990. Organic disorders of personality. In D. Adler, ed., *Treating Personality Disorders*, 87–101. San Francisco: Jossey-Bass.

Wells, C. E. 1985. Organic mental disorders. In H. I. Kaplan and B. J. Sadock, eds., *Comprehensive Textbook of Psychiatry*, 834–82. 4th ed. Baltimore: Williams and Wilkins.

Wells, K. B., M. A. Burnam, W. Rogers, R. Hays, and P. Camp. 1992. The course of depression in adult outpatients. *Archives of General Psychiatry* 9:788–94.

Whitehouse, P. J., R. P. Friedland, and M. E. Strauss. 1992. Neuropsychiatric aspects of degenerative dementias associated with motor dysfunction. In S. C. Yudofsky and R. E. Hales, eds., *Textbook of Neuropsychiatry*, 585–604. 2d ed. Washington, D.C.: American Psychiatric Press.

Widiger, T. A., A. J. Frances, M. Harris, L. B. Jacobsberg, M. Fyer, and D. Manning. 1991. Comorbidity among Axis II disorders. In J. M. Oldham, ed., *Personality Disorders: New Perspectives on Diagnostic Validity*, 165–94. Washington, D.C.: American Psychiatric Press.

Wiggins, J. S. 1982. Circumplex models of interpersonal behavior in clinical psychology. In P. C. Kendell and J. N. Butcher, *Handbook of Research Methods in Clinical Psychology*, 183–222. New York: Wiley.

Wiggins, J. S., and A. L. Pincus. 1992. Personality: Structure and assessment. *Annual Review of Psychology* 43:473–504.

Wilcock, G. K. 1993. *The Management of Alzheimer's Disease*. Petersfield, Hampshire, U.K.: Wrightson Biomedical.

Wildman, R. W. 1992. Gambling. In L. L'Abate, J. E. Farrar, and D. A. Serritella, eds., *Handbook of Differential Treatments for Addictions*, 211–29. Boston: Allyn and Bacon.

Williamson, D. A. 1990. *Assessment of Eating Disorders*. New York: Pergamon.

Willner, A. E. 1971. Toward development of more sensitive tests of abstraction. *Proceedings of the 78th Annual Convention of the American Psychological Association* 5:553–54.

Wilson, C. P., C. C. Hogan, and I. L. Mintz, eds. 1992. *Psychodynamic Technique in the Treatment of the Eating Disorders*. Northvale, N.J.: Jason Aronson.

Wilson. G. T. C. G. Fairburn, and W. S. Agras. 1997. Cognitive-behavioral therapy for bulimia nervosa. In D. M. Garner and P. E. Garfinkel, eds., *Handbook of Treatment for Eating Disorders*, 67–93. New York: Guilford.

Winiarski, M. G. 1991. *Aids-Related Psychotherapy*. New York: Pergamon.

Winick, C. 1992. Epidemiology of alcohol and drug abuse. In J. H. Lowinson, P. Ruiz, and R. B. Millman, eds., *Substance Abuse: A Comprehensive Textbook*, 15–29. 2d ed. Baltimore: Williams and Wilkins.

Wise, M. G., and G. T. Brandt. 1992. Delirium. In S. C. Yudofsky and R. E. Hales, eds., *Textbook of Neuropsychiatry*, 291–310. 2d ed. Washington, D.C.: American Psychiatric Press.

Wonderlich, S. A., and J. E. Mitchell. 1992. Eating disorders and personality disorders. In J. Yager, H. E. Gwirtsman, and C. K. Edelstein, eds., *Special Problems in Managing Eating Disorders*, 51–86. Washington, D.C.: American Psychiatric Press.

Wurmser, L. 1992. Psychology of compulsive drug use. In B. C. Wallace, ed., *The Chemically Dependent*, 92–114. New York: Brunner/Mazel.

Yager, J. 1992. Patients with chronic, recalcitrant eating disorders. In J. Yager, H. E. Gwirtsman, and C. K. Edelstein, eds., *Special Problems in Managing Eating Disorders*, 205–32. Washington, D.C.: American Psychiatric Press.

Yager, J., H. E. Gwirtsman, and C. K. Edelstein, eds. 1992. *Special Problems in Managing Eating Disorders*. Washington, D.C.: American Psychiatric Press.

Young, J. E. Loneliness, depression, and cognitive therapy. In L. A. Peplau and D. A. Perlman, *Loneliness: A Sourcebook of Current Theory, Research, and Therapy*, 379–405. New York: Wiley.

Young, R. C., J. T. Biggs, V. E. Ziegler, and D. A. Meyer. 1978. A rating scale for mania: Reliability, validity, and sensitivity. *British Journal of Psychiatry* 133:429–35.

Yudofsky, S. C., and R. E. Hales, eds. 1992. *Textbook of Neuropsychiatry*. 2d ed. Washington, D.C.: American Psychiatric Press.

Zec, R. F. 1990. Neuropsychology: Normal aging versus early Alzheimer disease. In R. E. Becker, ed., *Alzheimer Disease: Current Research in Early Diagnosis*, 105–17. New York: Taylor and Francis.

Ziedonis, D. M. 1992. Comorbid psychopathology and cocaine addiction. In T. R. Kosten and H. D. Kleber, eds., *Clinician's Guide to Cocaine Addiction*, 335–58. New York: Guilford.

Zung, W. W. K. 1971. A rating instrument for anxiety disorders. *Psychosomatics* 12:371–79.

———. 1974. Index of Potential Suicide (IPS): A rating scale for suicide prevention. In A. T. Beck, H. L. P. Resnick, and D. J. Lettieri, *The Prediction of Suicide*. Bowie, Md.: Charles.

Zweben, J. E. 1992. Issues in the treatment of the dual-diagnosis patient. In B. C. Wallace, ed., *The Chemically Dependent*, 298–309. New York: Brunner/Mazel.

Subject Index

Abreaction, definition, 80

Acquired Immunodeficiency Syndrome (AIDS): caregivers, 232; clinical course, 224–5; and delirium, 225; and dementia, 215, 216, 222, 228–9; differential diagnosis, 48–9, 162; family involvement, 232; life-style, 229; medication, 233; and mood disorders, 36, 38 personality change, 192; and substance abuse, 116, 127, 136–7; and suicide, 43–4; support groups, 233. *See* HIV-Related Dementia

Agoraphobia: age of onset, 14; assessment, 17; cognitive therapy, 30; definition, 12, epidemiology, 14; etiology, 22; family involvement, 30–1; intervention, 30–1; medication, 287; psychological testing, 246. *See* Panic Disorder

Alcoholism: alcohol, 124–5; and amnestic disorder. 222; assessment, 137–9; dual diagnosis, 147–9; epidemiology, 122–3; etiology, 121–2; family intervention, 144–5; intervention, 139–46; medication, 145; 281–

2, psychological testing, 244–5; secondary diagnosis, 19; and suicide, 43

Alprazolam (Xanax), 288

Alzheimer Disease: assessment, 221–2, caregivers, 229–32; clinical course, 223–4; cost of care, 228, 233; definition, 216; differential diagnosis, 86, 227; epidemiology, 217; ethical issues, 231–2; etiology, 225–6; intervention, 228; psychological testing, 255; and suicide, 43; support groups, 233

Amitriptyline (Elavil or Endep): depression, 52, 278; PTSD, 26, street drug, 127

Amnestic Disorder: assessment, 222, definition, 215–6

Amoxapine (Asendin), 53

Amphetamines and Methamphetamines, 130–1; "designer drugs," 131; withdrawal, 131

Anorexia Nervosa: age of onset, 158–9; assessment, 153–58; clinical course, 159–60; definition, 152; differential diagnosis, 162–3 epidemiology, 158–9; etiology, 163–7; family 172–3,

Author Index